The New World of the Gothic Fox

The New World of the Gothic Fox

Culture and Economy
in English and Spanish America

Claudio Véliz

UNIVERSITY OF CALIFORNIA PRESS
Berkeley · *Los Angeles* · *London*

University of California Press
Berkeley and Los Angeles, California

University of California Press
London, England

Copyright © 1994 by The Regents of the University of California

Library of Congress Cataloging-in-Publication Data

Véliz, Claudio.
   The New World of the gothic fox : culture and economy in English and Spanish
America / Claudio Véliz.

    p.   cm.
   Includes bibliographical references and index.
   ISBN 0-520-08316-4
   1. Latin America—Civilization—Spanish influences. 2. North America—
Civilization—British influences. 3. Comparative civilization. 4. Latin America—
Economic conditions. 5. North America—Economic conditions. I. Title.
F1408.3.V36   1994
980—dc20   93-23709
                                                        CIP

Printed in the United States of America

1 2 3 4 5 6 7 8 9

This book is for Isaiah Berlin

Contents

Prologue

A lead article in *The Times* of November 24, 1980, complained, "Received opinions about the state of Britain . . . are perhaps as gloomy now as they have ever been in peacetime. The reasons for this are manifold, and in many respects quite real (because) by most measures of productivity and prosperity we are now among the poorer of West European nations." The editorial dejection was relieved minimally by an additional comment, possibly an afterthought, in which it was noted, "The great paradox of our condition is that Britain remains an exceptionally satisfactory country to live in. . . . Our suicide rate, that ultimate measure of how many find life in a society intolerable, is one of the lowest in the world."

This merited a reply, and in a letter to the editor, published on December 2, I noted that although a modicum of diffidence was a legitimate rhetorical device, its misuse invited misinterpretation, as in this instance, in which an excess of editorial modesty had resulted in a description that was vastly less than generous, perhaps even unfair. In my letter I argued that much more could be claimed for Britain's contribution than was suggested by *The Times*, and I proposed that our contemporaries everywhere had been born in a world "Made in England" and that it was most likely that our children and grandchildren would die of a nice old age in such a world because "Britain's brief imperial instance filled the world with symbols, forms, signs, styles and modes of behaviour that are likely to continue playing a protagonic role in shaping human conduct at least for another century, possibly longer." I went on to list "the Industrial Revolution, . . . soccer, horse racing, whisky, sherry and port wine, tennis, skiing, golf, and mountaineering (all modern sports, with very few exceptions), the Boy Scouts, the Salvation Army and the YMCA" and, most important of all, the English language, without doubt the lingua franca of our time. The circumstances of modernity, I suggested, invited cautious comparison with the Hellenistic Age, when Athens had long ceased to be the dominant power and yet the world showed itself eager to embrace the culture of the Hellenes. I ended my letter by noting that the beginning of the end of the islanders' moment in history did not arrive when Britain ceased to be a major military power but will almost certainly be with us when adequate and pleasing substitutes emerge for such durable cultural signifiers as horse racing, soccer, whiskey, bird-watching, and the English language.

Proud of having had this letter—or any letter—published in the august columns of *The Times*, I was quite swept off my feet when my good friend, Heinz Arndt, who was then editing the Australian monthly *Quadrant*, invited me to develop what I had intimated in the letter into a fully fledged article for his prestigious literary and political journal. This I did at some leisure, and "A World Made in England" appeared in the March 1983 issue of *Quadrant*, attracting more interest than I had imagined and also, most encouragingly, that year's Watson Prize.

Professor Arndt in the meantime was earnestly trying to convince me to take time off from my academic duties at La Trobe University to write a book on the same subject. Had I been free at that moment, I would have done so gladly, but I was then working on a history of Chile that had been partly sponsored by the Tinker Foundation and felt enormously disinclined to postpone its completion. As it turned out, fate intervened: our house on the Great Ocean Road, west of Melbourne, was completely destroyed in the tragic Ash Wednesday bush fires of 1983. No member of our family was hurt; that was the good news. But up in smoke, together with the house, went several chapters of the history and all the notes made during my researches in Chilean, Spanish, and British archives.

Carlyle, as we all suspect, would have rewritten the lost chapters with the greatest of ease, but for me this proved an almost insuperable task, and it was only years later that I was able to complete them. In the intervening period, I became increasingly involved with the work of the Seminar on the Sociology of Culture at La Trobe University and with the eventual establishment of the Boston, Melbourne, Oxford *Conver-*

sazioni on Culture and Society. These initiatives claimed time and energy
and diverted me from my original interest in Chile's *sui generis* insularity
with respect to the mainland of Latin America toward a general study
of the cultural aspects of the genesis of industrial modernity. These new
investigations led me to a timely and most fortunate reconsideration of
the work of Isaiah Berlin and through him, to Giambattista Vico and to
what promptly became a vigorous and continuing commitment to the
study of the cultural context and antecedents of the prowess of modern
industrial society.

Three decades earlier, while toiling on a Ph.D. at the London School
of Economics and Political Science and editing the students' journal,
Clare Market Review, for reasons that must have seemed good at the
time but appear distinctly less so today, I chose to devote a whole issue
of that hyperactive and irreverent periodical to an attack on Isaiah Berlin
that was as unfair and intemperate as it was thoughtless. Thirty-five
years later, I was back, cap in hand, eager to bestow on Sir Isaiah the
highest form of praise of which I am capable, not through slavish imitation but by adopting his splendid hedgehogs and foxes, with much
affection, in the hope that they would help me to construct what I
thought, perhaps immodestly, could be an illuminating commentary on
the differences between the two great cultural transplants of the New
World as well as a novel and plausible interpretation of modern industrial society.

It was at this juncture that Peter Berger, director of the Institute for
the Study of Economic Culture of Boston University, in a manner as
characteristically generous as it was encouraging, virtually presented me
with a sabbatical year to enable me to write a book in which would be
integrated the several strands of what I then was beginning to perceive
as a single working hypothesis about the character of the society and
the economy of the two great transplanted cultures of the New World.
This was truly an invitation that could not be refused, and it was not.
Professor Berger's selfless cooperation was not restricted to this. He took
a keen interest in the progress of the work, often discussed aspects of it
with me, and gave me many immensely helpful suggestions, most of
which I took without hesitation and for which I am in his debt; others
I did not, and I will not be surprised to discover that the flaws of this
book reflect faithfully my indefensible obduracy.

In order correctly to acknowledge my indebtedness to those whose
suggestions and comments have been helpful to me in writing this book,
I would have to list most of my students during the past three and a half

decades, here in Boston, in Santiago, and in Melbourne; many of the
participants in the *conversazioni* with which I have been associated for
several years; my colleagues in The University Professors of Boston University, in La Trobe University, in the University of Chile, especially those
in the Institute of International Studies, in the University of California
at Los Angeles, in Harvard University, and in the Royal Institute of
International Affairs. Even if this were feasible, I could not leave un-
mentioned the dinner guests that fate placed beside me during these past
few years, and who endured so patiently and with such good humor the
endless questions about this or that aspect of the working hypothesis
that was at that moment keeping me awake nights. Also, I cannot omit
mentioning the many conversations with my son, Claudio, and my
daughter, Zahira, architect and art historian, respectively, which so
gently and frequently nudged me back from the brink; nor could I possibly leave without acknowledgment the splendid bibliographical assistance of Jan McLeod, of the Borchardt Library of La Trobe University,
in Melbourne, and of Dan Lackey, here in Boston. I am profoundly grateful to Stanley Holwitz, Michelle Nordon, and Sheila Berg, of the University of California Press, for their patience, wit, and invariably valuable and encouraging editorial advice.

Most of the worthwhile insights in this book I owe to friends and
colleagues with whom I have had the honor of discussing these expla-
nations, among them, Victor Urquídi, Germánico Salgado, Helio Ja-
guaribe, George Pell, Luciano Tomassini, Brigitte Berger, Darcy Ribeiro,
Mario Vargas Llosa, Torcuato Di Tella, José Matos Mar, Robert Gaston,
Abraham Santibañez, Heraldo Muñoz, Cándido Mendes de Almeyda,
Osvaldo Sunkel, Jaime Guzmán, José Piñera, Gerald L. Gitner, Agnes
Heller, Ferenc Feher, Sergio Villalobos, Miguel Schweitzer Walters, David Martin, Michael Oshins, Ruben Rivera, Philip Ayres, Donald G.
MacRae, Eric Jones, Arturo Fontaine Talavera, Alain Touraine, Corne-
lius Castoriadis, Ann Vasaly, Rolando Stein, Alan Macfarlane, Hugh
Thomas, Carlos Forment, and above all, Sir Isaiah Berlin, on whose
seminal and splendidly illuminating work this lesser effort is so obviously founded and to whom it is gratefully dedicated.

Over the past few years I have been fortunate in working with two
exceptional colleagues whose truly selfless interest in what we have been
about made it possible for me to complete this book while continuing
to discharge academic activities that would otherwise have provided a
cast-iron excuse not to put pen to paper. Without the efficient and
devoted assistance of Mrs. June Mitchell—the now legendary "Mrs.

Mitchell," for so many years at the helm of the Melbourne *conversazioni*—this book would probably not have been born. It certainly would not have been completed without the imaginative, immensely generous and thoughtful cooperation of Mrs. Joanne Laubner, on whose inexhaustible enthusiasm depends so much of what I do at Boston University. Not suprisingly, Mrs. Laubner put a huge amount of work into what proved to be an unusually accident-prone index that was eventually completed in Australia with the help of two of my grandchildren, the fledgling lexicographers Sofía and Matías Campino.

My wife, María Isabel, presides gloriously over everything I do, most certainly over what I write. My last book before this one was dedicated to her; this was an unnecessary gesture, because everything I do is dedicated to her.

Claudio Véliz

Boston, 1994

CHAPTER I

Prefatory Metaphors

The heirs of the Iberian and the English cultural traditions in the New World have fared differently, especially with respect to their economic expectations and their political and social arrangements. This is as interesting for some as it is disquieting for others, and while a few students of economic and social history have attempted to understand the reasons for these differences, many more have tried to minimize their significance, to interpret them out of existence, to discover culprits responsible for them, or simply to reverse their import by transforming shortcomings into virtues and assets into liabilities.[1] No amount of euphemistic embellishment suffices, however, to disguise the fact that the economic prowess of the English-speaking descendants of the originators of the Industrial Revolution and its scientific and technological concomitants

---

1. There are even some authors who are convinced that industrial modernity has simply been a disaster for the region.

The imposition of modernization [is] a barrier to Latin America's development. . . . [Such trends as] the importation of technology and ideas with their accompanying values from Western Europe north of the Pyrenees and the full entrance into the world capitalistic marketplace . . . shaped those nations . . . profoundly. . . . Their promoters moved forward steadfastly within the legacy of some basic institutions bequeathed by centuries of Iberian rule. That combination of hoary institutions with newer, non-Iberian technology, values, and ideas forged contemporary Latin America with its enigma of overwhelming poverty amid potential plenty. (E. Bradford Burns, *The Poverty of Progress: Latin America in the Nineteenth Century* [Berkeley, Los Angeles, and London, 1980]: 1)

has been neither surpassed nor successfully emulated by the Portuguese-
and Spanish-speaking beneficiaries of the robust Iberian inheritance.

This is all the more interesting because these two cultural traditions,
so inextricably bound up with their respective languages and the modes
of behavior and dispositions that these nurture, are also responsible for
two of the most important transplanted societies of modern times, each
born when its progenitor was poised on the threshold of imperial greatness. Dominant in each of the hemispheres of the New World, their
geographic polarity parallels that of their European cultural inheritance;
the difference between the striking impressions they have made in the
north and in the south of the continent is as evident as the persistent
contrast between their respective economic accomplishments and not
immensely dissimilar to the distance that has separated the Iberian from
the British economy since the advent of industrialism.[2] It is not easy,
when making this comparison, to overlook the Catholicism that prevails
in the south and the Protestantism that abounds in the north. It is even
harder not to attribute whatever can be said about this dimension of
things to Max Weber or to R. H. Tawney or both,[3] which is gently unfair
to Macaulay, who advanced similar conclusions in an 1840 essay in

2. Tawney's description of Spain in the sixteenth century, when she was nearing the
zenith of her power and wealth, has yet to be challenged in court: "Spain, for centuries
an army on the march and now staggering beneath the responsibilities of her vast and
scattered empire, devout to fanaticism, and with an incapacity for economic affairs which
seemed almost inspired." R. H. Tawney, *Religion and the Rise of Capitalism, A Historical
Study* (London, [1926] 1975): 82. The contrast between the economic performance of the
Spanish- and English-speaking Americans has also lent itself to lighthearted comments.
In *The Spectator* of November 19, 1988, under the title "Spanish Chestnut," Christopher
Fildes offered the following intelligence:

> A City friend has confided to me the secret of his successful investment policy. Never,
> he says, invest in a country which has previously been governed by Spain. This principle
> has kept him out of trouble, not only in the greater part of most of South America
> (Brazil and its Portuguese rulers he had to work out for himself) but also in such
> notorious traps as the Philippines, Mexico, California (think what he could have saved
> the Midland), and Texas—where everything is the biggest, including the bank failures.
> Pleased with his policy, and anxious to apply it literally, my friend has discovered a
> catch in it—what should he do about the fashionable notion of investing in Spain? My
> advice is that he should think of Spain as a country previously governed by the
> Moors. (22)

3. Max Weber, *The Protestant Ethic and the Spirit of Capitalism*, 1904–05; Tawney,
Religion and the Rise of Capitalism (1926). This is an aspect of things that has merited
much scholarly attention in the English-speaking world. Among the more influential approaches must be counted Richard M. Morse, "The Heritage of Latin America," in Louis
Hartz, *The Founding of New Societies* (New York, 1964), in which the author proposed
that the writings of Francisco Suarez (1548–1617) "generally recognized as the thinker
who most fully recapitulated Thomist political thought in Spain's age of *Barockscholastik*
. . . are symptomatic of a postmedieval Hispano-Catholic view of man, society, and government which is by no means superseded in modern Spanish America" (153, 155).

which he invited his readers to compare England and Spain in the eighteenth century, noting that "in arms, arts, sciences, letters, commerce, agriculture, the contrast is most striking" but more important, observing that this distinction

> is not confined to this side of the Atlantic. The colonies planted by England in America have immeasurably outgrown in power those planted by Spain. Yet we have no reason to believe that, at the beginning of the sixteenth century, the Castilian was in any respect inferior to the Englishman. Our firm belief is, that the North owes its great civilization and prosperity chiefly to the moral effect of the Protestant Reformation, and that the decay of the southern countries of Europe is to be mainly ascribed to the great Catholic revival.[4]

This we now suspect to be oversimple. The experience of Catholic Bohemia and, for that matter, of Bavaria and Brabant gives us pause. For well over a century Bohemia harbored all manner of schismatic dissidence, including the millenarian expectations of Paracelsian Protestants who believed that a "chemical" golden age was at hand, until the Battle of the White Mountain, in 1620, brought the era of bizarre diversities to an abrupt end. Bohemian Protestantism, the most ancient in Europe, was virtually eliminated and Catholicism restored to a dominant position that was never to be relinquished.[5] The tenacious Protestant minority, however, was not completely eradicated; relations between the two groups remained tense and were occasionally marred by violence but never sufficiently to invalidate the weighty contrast with Catholic Castile. Also, if due account is taken of the Arab invasion and the lingering presence of Moriscos and Mozárabes in Spain, it could be argued that the credentials of Christian homogeneity and domestic har-

---

4. This comparison was also made by the Spanish philosopher Jaime Balmes, in his *El protestantismo comparado con el catolicismo en sus relaciones con la civilización europea*, published in 1842 (first English edition in 1849), but he reached exactly the opposite conclusion. Lord Macaulay, *Critical and Historical Essays Contributed to the Edinburgh Review* (London, 1874), "Von Ranke," review essay on Leopold von Ranke's *The Ecclesiastical and Political History of the Popes of Rome, During the Sixteenth and Seventeenth Centuries*, 3 vols., translated from the German by Sarah Austin (London, 1840): 559. More recently, this comparison has been the subject of an essay in which the author affirms that an essential difference between what he describes as Protestant and Catholic rationality is that "Protestant man has been primarily rational in the economic sphere and has only derivatively used the same rationality within the political world, while Catholic man has been primarily rational within the political sphere. . . . Catholic man pursues public power the way Protestant man strives for private wealth." Glen Caudill Dealy, *The Public Man, an Interpretation of Latin American and Other Catholic Countries* (Amherst, 1977): 7.

5. Hugh Trevor-Roper, "The Paracelsian Movement," in *Renaissance Essays* (London, 1985): 183–184.

mony of both kingdoms are not vastly different. Unlike Catholic Castile, however, Catholic Bohemia has shown over time a marked ability to respond to the demands of modern industrial civilization. There are complexities involved here and in the cases of Brabant and Bavaria that fall outside the boundaries of this essay, but this reference should suffice to indicate that the species of direct correlation suggested by Macaulay, between Catholicism and economic backwardness, is not necessarily self-evident.

Even when Macaulay proposed it, in the mid-nineteenth century, the comparison that led him to this conclusion was not novel, but it has rarely been so timely as today, on the threshold of the first half-millennium since the discovery, when Canada and the United States continue to prosper and most of the countries in the south are overwhelmed with debts and hounded by intractable economic difficulties. It is also as contentious a comparison as it was then, and it is further obfuscated by persistent quarrels, unwholesome enmities, and misleading metaphors. The latter are probably the most unhelpful, notably, the one first proposed almost a century ago by the Uruguayan *littérateur*, José Enrique Rodó, in an exceptionally influential essay entitled *Ariel*. Making free use of the Shakespearean dichotomy, Rodó cast Latin Americans generally in the role of the "ayrie spirit," attributing to us delicacy of feeling, spirituality, nobility of mind, and moral purpose and reserving for the Anglo-Saxon northerners the less attractive role of Caliban, the uncouth issue of the union of a devil with the witch Sycorax.[6] Rodó was convinced that the United States offers

> no insuperable obstacles to the limitless extension of the spirit of vulgarity. . . . Rich and prosperous, Americans satisfy their vanity with sumptuous

6. José Enrique Rodó, "Ariel," in *Obras Selectas* (Buenos Aires, 1964): 37–101.

Rodó depicted Ariel as the creature of intellectual and spiritual pursuits, concerned with art, beauty and moral development as ends in themselves, rather than with material progress. Ariel was used to symbolize what for Rodó was most authentic in Hispanic culture. Through the words he gave to Ariel [Rodó] chided Spanish Americans . . . for having abandoned the culture and values natural to them and having embraced the materialistic, utilitarian, mechanistic life styles associated with alien cultures, most specifically with Anglo-Saxon civilization. . . . Arielism coincided with and contributed to the growing hostility to the United States at the turn of the century[,] . . . to fear of political and economic imperialism, Arielism added a cultural dimension.   (Fredrick B. Pike, *Spanish-America, 1900–1970: Tradition and Social Innovation* [London, 1973]: 21)

Not everyone agrees. According to Gordon Brotherston, Rodó was concerned about how his book would be interpreted in Latin America and insisted that his remarks about the United States in the fifth part of Prospero's speech were meant to be merely illustrative of his main thesis, and in no sense were they intended as an indictment of that country.

magnificence, but good taste eludes them. . . . If the United States could ever give its name to a form of artistic taste, this would needs be the negation of art; characterized by the brutality of excess, . . . the cult of false *grandeur*, and the sensationalism that excludes that noble serenity that is incompatible with a feverish existence. . . . The [North American] heirs of the austere Puritans are not passionate about the ideal of beauty, nor about the ideal of truthfulness . . . [but they are] contemptuous of any thought not directed toward an immediate [practical] objective. They are not attracted to science by a disinterested love of truth. . . . They are incapable of loving science for science's sake; for them [scientific] research is merely the necessary requirement that antecedes utilitarian application.[7]

And there is much else of the same uncomplicated tenor, invariably consistent with the attribution of the qualities of Caliban to the English-speaking northerners and those of Ariel to the Latin Americans. Not hopelessly despondent, Rodó explains that it is nonetheless possible to expect that in due course, "the achievements of North America . . . will

---

Brotherston further observes that these efforts notwithstanding, "the essay became immediately famous and popular as such an indictment. As edition succeeded edition, the crude antithesis—Ariel (Latin America) *versus*, and superior to, Caliban (the U.S.A.) was ascribed more and more widely to Rodó's essay. The reasons for this lay almost entirely outside the work itself." Almost but not entirely, and to ignore the contribution that Rodó's prose made to this popular reception would appear to skirt the boundaries of disingenuousness. José Enrique Rodó, *Ariel*, ed. Gordon Brotherston (Cambridge, 1967): 9–10.

7. José Enrique Rodó, "Ariel," in *Obras selectas* (Buenos Aires, 1964): 84–85 (author's translation). The strength of feeling behind this unusual interpretation can be explained in part by noting that the war between Spain and the United States ended on December 10, 1898, with the signing of the Treaty of Paris, whereby Spain lost Cuba, Puerto Rico, and the Philippines. This resounding defeat had repercussions throughout the Spanish-speaking world, and it is most unlikely that the author of *Ariel*, published in 1900, was entirely unaffected. In his prologue to a recent English edition of this work, Carlos Fuentes castigates it mercilessly ("This is a supremely irritating book. In Spanish its rhetoric has become insufferable.") but notes the consistency between its temper and that of its time. The year 1900—"the year of Ariel"—is set almost exactly in the middle of Latin America's independent life.

Spanish America broke away from Spain between 1810 and 1821, and the break was not only political, but moral and aesthetic as well. For most liberals, independence meant renouncing the Spanish past as a reactionary, intolerant and unscientific era of darkness. It meant promptly attempting to recover lost time by achieving all that the Spanish Counter-Reformation denied us: capitalism, free inquiry, free speech, due process, parliamentarism, industry, commerce: in short, modernity. This was to be by legal *fiat*. It sufficed to copy the progressive legislation of France, England, and the United States. Democracy and prosperity would follow. It was not to be so. . . . Spain, our old empire, was defeated and dismantled by the United States, our new empire, in 1898; the Philippines and Puerto Rico became American colonies, Cuba a subject state. Our sympathies shifted to the defeated empire: the United States de-satanized Spain while satanizing itself. (Carlos Fuentes, prologue to José Enrique Rodó, *Ariel*, ed. Margaret Sayers Pedén [Austin: University of Texas Press, 1988]: 13, 15)

be useful to Ariel's cause because what that nation of Cyclops has achieved directly to enhance its material well-being with its sense of utility and its admirable aptitude for mechanical invention, other peoples, or even they themselves, in the future, will transform into . . . elements of spiritual improvement."[8]

Ariel tapped a torrent of self-justifying and oversentimental nationalistic feeling that has flowed vigorously into the Latin American cultural mainstream throughout the twentieth century. Its tenets are now part of folkloric orthodoxy, much in the fashion suggested by Lord Keynes when he affirmed that the so-called practical men of our time are frequently the slaves of defunct and long-forgotten economic theorists. In the same way it can be said that many thundering Latin American political leaders of recent decades have unknowingly derived nourishment from Rodó's slim volume of 1900, which, one suspects, few have ever heard of and fewer have read.

A knowledge of Rodó's work and its direct influence was more evident earlier in our century. José de Vasconcelos, who from his post as secretary for education in the immediate aftermath of the Mexican Revolution commissioned the well-known murals by Orozco, Rivera, and Siqueiros that so dramatically changed that country's vision of itself, embraced the spirit of Arielismo on behalf of the Mexican Revolution and in his book, *La raza cósmica*, published in 1925, bestowed on it an Indian genesis and a universal destiny. Latin America, he maintained, was the continent of the future because it had three crucial advantages over the Anglo-Saxons of North America: first, a unified society founded on the fusion of the races, *mestizaje*, instead of on the divisive domination of one race by another characteristic of the English-speaking world; second, the mastery of the tropical climate ("The great civilisations began around the tropics, and the final civilisation will return to the tropics"); and third and most important, a "cosmic race," with the spiritual resources "to direct and consummate the extraordinary enterprise . . . of discovering new zones of the spirit, now that there are no new lands left to be discovered."[9]

Vasconcelos was keenly aware of the unique opportunity offered to him, by virtue of his ministerial appointment, to implement what so many Latin Americans had spoken and written about: "Neither Rodó nor Manuel Ugarte had a chance to put into operation the things they

8. Rodó, "Ariel," 90.
9. Stephen Clissold, *Latin America, a Cultural Outline* (London, 1965): 117–119.

so excellently preached; I had had the good fortune to be able to accomplish a part of what so many had dreamed."[10] These dreams were uncomplicated, at least as they affected the comparison of English-speaking north with Iberian south, and in this respect Vasconcelos is unambiguous. Writing about his impressions of a visit to London, he notes the legend, "To the English-Speaking Peoples of the World," above the archway of the BBC's Bush House in Kingsway and comments that imperial union based on language

> ought not to be just an ideal, but a tradition and the basis of patriotism. The restoration of the unity created by the Spanish monarchy, but in the modern form of a Society of Nations, a community of people of Spanish speech, including the Philippines; how many people in our continent have the brains to grasp this simple proposal? On the other hand, let anyone examine the teaching of those who have rated as our statesmen during the lamentable nineteenth century, and he will find only lackeys of English thought, lackeys who keep repeating the ostensible doctrines of "The English-Speaking Peoples of the World." And I refuse to make an exception. . . . Juárez, Sarmiento, Alberdi. . . . What would they have said . . . if they came back and someone set them down in front of the London monument to the unity of race and language? Those who thought they were being modern by acting as detractors of that which is Spanish would tear their garments when they saw themselves reduced to what they were: mere agents of the cunning imperialism of the Anglo-Saxons.[11]

Arielismo also left its mark on Victor Raúl Haya de la Torre, the Peruvian founder of the Alianza Popular Revolucionaria Americana (APRA), as well as on his movement. Later in life, Haya de la Torre's acknowledgment of this debt was muted, but earlier he had no such reservations. In 1922 when he presided over the Peruvian Students' Federation, he went to Montevideo to help coordinate strikes in support of university reforms at the time vigorously promoted by student movements throughout Latin America. His well-publicized visit was cosponsored by the Centro Ariel, a group of intellectuals devoted to the teachings of Rodó and strongly in favor of the reforms. The *Arielistas* organized a solemn visit to the local cemetery so that Haya de la Torre

10. Manuel Ugarte (1878–1951), Argentine nationalist writer, well known for his spirited objections to what he considered the deleterious consequences of United States capitalism in Latin America. José Vasconcelos, *A Mexican Ulysses, an Autobiography*, trans. and abridged by W. Rex Crawford (Bloomington, 1963): 192.

11. Vasconcelos, *A Mexican Ulysses*, 81. Benito Juárez (Mexican president, d. 1872), Juan Bautista Alberdi (Argentine political philosopher, d. 1884), and Domingo Faustino Sarmiento (Argentine president, d. 1888) are renowned for their espousal, as writers and statesmen, of the liberal doctrines then prevalent in Europe.

could lay a wreath at the tomb of Rodó, who had died five years earlier, in 1917. According to the Montevideo newspaper, *El Día*, Haya de la Torre delivered a forceful "harangue" at the foot of the tomb, in which he informed his attentive audience that Rodó was regarded as a maestro by the youth of Peru and referred to the students' revolt in unmistakable Arielista fashion, as "a revolution of the spirit."[12] In 1924, Haya de la Torre was forced into exile by the government. On hearing this, Vasconcelos invited him to Mexico to help with his educational reforms. During this period and understandably influenced by the Mexican statesman, who was making the final revisions to his book on the "cosmic race," Haya de la Torre founded APRA, largely on doctrinal grounds readily identified as variations on the themes of Arielismo and the *raza cósmica*. It is worth noting, for example, the decidedly Arielista flavor of the Vasconcelos slogan, *Por mi raza hablará el espíritu*, which translates literally as "The spirit will speak for my race," a disconcerting affirmation of the cosmic race thesis, which to this day is the motto of the Universidad Nacional Autónoma of Mexico and which seems to have been sufficiently popular at the time to have influenced Haya de la Torre's choice of Indoamérica as the preferred *Aprista* name for the continent.[13]

Two generations later, the death in Bolivia of the Argentine revolutionary Ernesto "Che" Guevara revived the scarcely dormant metaphoric contrast between the presumably coarse, rich, powerful, and interfering northerners and the allegedly romantic, ethereal, selfless heroes of the south. At that time it was accorded suggestive expression in posters of the guerrilla chieftain's face, which young people from Buenos Aires to Barcelona regarded as a fitting comment on the martyrdom of an Ariel-like idealist at the hands of the unfeeling henchmen of the English-speaking Caliban. Yet another generation passed before the Pe-

12. *El Día*, Montevideo, March 19 and 23, 1922. It is also worth noting that Rodó heads the list of the forerunners of Aprismo that Haya de la Torre included in his *Treinta años del Aprismo*, published in Mexico in 1956.
13. The APRA flag, first displayed in Mexico in 1924 on the occasion of the foundation of the movement, was described officially as the flag of the "Indo-Hispanic" race. There can be little doubt that "Indo-América" had Vasconcelos and Rodó as godparents. This is fleetingly reflected in Haya de la Torre's justification for the new name: "The term *Indoamérica* is the most inclusive, going much further, entering more deeply into the totality of our peoples. It includes the prehistoric, the Iberian, the Latin, and the negro, the mestizo, and the 'cosmic'—we say, remembering José Vasconcelos—maintaining its validity as a term for the future." R. J. Alexander, ed. and trans., *Aprismo, The Ideas and Doctrines of Victor Raúl Haya de la Torre* (Kent, Ohio, 1973): 347–348; see also, Luis Alberto Sánchez, *Haya de la Torre y el APRA* (Lima, 1980): 125–130.

ruvian APRA finally achieved power in 1985, winning the presidential elections under the leadership of Alan García, a longtime friend and faithful disciple of Haya de la Torre. President García's forceful nationalistic rejection of economic orthodoxy in any form, including cooperative arrangements with the International Monetary Fund, was entirely consistent with an acceptance of the tenets of both Arielismo and the raza cósmica, albeit tempered, but not obliterated, by a few decades of political experience.

Arielismo was not appropriated entirely by activists and revolutionaries. Its propositions proved pervasive as well as resilient and can be discerned in the writings of authors as eminent and as different as Gabriela Mistral[14] and Octavio Paz;[15] behind the polite but deeply felt dis-

14. A sympathetic biographical study of Gabriela Mistral gives the following description of her treatment of the United States as a literary theme.

As a Hispano-American, she deeply regretted what seemed to her the errors of official North American policy in its relations with the peoples to the south; she was hurt by the economic exploitation, by the armed interventions, by the moral and material support of dictators, by the almost complete ignorance of Hispanic spirit, culture, customs, and idiosyncracies. But this critical view never caused hate or resentment on her part. She adopted, on the contrary, a free and creative attitude of love, with faith in men and nations and with firm confidence in the final triumph of reason, truth, and goodness." (Margot Arce de Vásquez, *Gabriela Mistral, the Poet and Her Work* [New York, 1964]: 140)

15. According to Paz,

The North Americans are credulous and we [the Mexicans] are believers, they love fairy tales and detective stories and we love myths and legends. The Mexican tells lies because he delights in fantasy. . . . The North American does not tell lies, but he substitutes social truth for the real truth, which is always disagreeable. We get drunk in order to confess; they get drunk in order to forget. They are optimists and we are nihilists. . . . We are suspicious and they are trusting. . . . They are activists and we are quietists; we enjoy our wounds and they enjoy their inventions. They believe in hygiene, health, work, and contentment, but perhaps they have never experienced true joy, which is an intoxication, a whirlwind. In the hubbub of a *fiesta* night our voices explode into brilliant lights, and life and death mingle together, while their vitality becomes a fixed smile that denies old age and death but that changes life to a motionless stone.

This quotation from the *Labyrinth of Solitude* is offered by the English writer John Mander to illustrate his assertion that Paz has assumed a "Rodó-like position vis-à-vis the United States" and that although Paz is certainly not "anti-American," here he finds himself speaking for Latin America and not only for Mexico. However, Mander also observes that "the potential danger, even silliness, of this line of argument is apparent from the following" and quotes Paz: "When the Mexican kills—for revenge, pleasure, or caprice—he kills a person, a human being. . . . Murder is still a relationship in Mexico, and in this sense it has the same liberating significance as the *fiesta* or the confession. Hence its drama, its poetry and—why not say it?—its grandeur. Through murder we achieve a momentary transcendence." John Mander, *Static Society: The Paradox of Latin America* (London, 1969): 57, 64.

missive anti-Americanism of the upper classes; and in some of the more
bizarre versions of the *dependencia* theories fashionable during the past
few years.

Although it has undoubtedly been alluring to some, the metaphoric
use of Ariel and Caliban has not proved useful in comparing the Iberian
half to the English half of the New World, or better, in helping to understand why the economic performance of the countries of Latin America has been so disappointing. Even if there are attitudes that can usefully be thought to correspond to types labeled "Ariel" and "Caliban,"
it is quite probable that these will be found more or less evenly distrib-
uted among the inhabitants of different countries and regions of the
world and that therefore the explanatory value of the metaphor is likely
to be limited. More important perhaps, apart from Rodó's eloquent af-
firmations and the acquiescence of his disciples, there seems to be scant
support for the belief that Latin Americans possess a spiritual disposition so pervasive and demanding that it precludes them from prospering
in the realm of material things.

A more helpful metaphor is required to analyze the intriguing differences between south and north. The discovery of such a figure of
speech is not absolutely necessary, but to find it could greatly facilitate
the comparison. The problem with such an enterprise is that metaphor
is among the most arcane, elusive, and paradoxical creatures of the human mind. Taken literally, it is almost invariably false; but it can also
be acutely sensitive, subtle, and immensely efficient in leading us toward
the truth across bridges built with lies. A comparison of metaphor and
simile illustrates this convincingly by contrasting the illuminating falsehood of metaphors with the trivial truthfulness of similes. Anything can
be *like* anything else. The vicar's niece is *like* a moon blanch'd Greek
temple by the sea or a disappointed pelican; she is *like* Caesar's wife,
the tower of Pisa, or a summer's day. However, the literal untruth of a
successful metaphor (it would be false to affirm that the vicar's niece *is*
a moon blanch'd Greek temple by the sea) appears to be intriguingly
responsible for that tension between the thing and the words used to
describe it that elicits the illuminating resemblance that we seek. The
young woman who told the poet that she *was* the rose of Sharon and
the lily of the valleys was obviously dissembling. She was neither, but
that ancient untruth led him and us and countless before us to discern
an important verity unlikely to have emerged or survived had she clad
her assertion in the austere precisions of impeccable scientific discourse.
The obvious falsity of Prufrock's affirmation that he measured out his

life in coffee spoons largely explains the clarity and immediacy of the desired effect.

Successful metaphors are often the welcome consequence of an intended encounter between something that we understand only in part (darkly? through a glass?) and wish to comprehend more fully and a more familiar entity from which we borrow not everything but only what is required for the purpose at hand. For example, we do not desist from referring to a courageous athlete as "lion-hearted" because we have been informed that he is a vegetarian, nor does the stately portliness of an accomplished coloratura prevent us from describing her as a nightingale.

These unusual qualities did not escape attention in the past; they were certainly not overlooked by Aristotle when he affirmed bluntly that "metaphor consists in giving the thing a name that belongs to something else." He thought it a charming curlicue, a clever rhetorical adornment unlikely to make a contribution to a sound and serious language of science, but such reservations notwithstanding, ours has proved a cultural tradition unerringly responsive to wine-dark seas, henpecked husbands, computer viruses, flammable tigers, postmodernisms, floating currencies, fast-breeding reactors, waves of light, electric currents, night-winged birds, and, of course, hearts cold, fiery, broken, courageous, and transplanted. Explanations are redundant. We know that the vagueness even of the most penumbral metaphoric intimation is not incompatible with precision; we also know that when we appeal to these linguistic figurations, we place ourselves beyond the comforts of didactic paraphrase and must swim or sink on the strength of a shared understanding of the particular usages that make particular words yield particular meanings.

With these risks and possible rewards firmly in mind, I believe that it is apposite and prudent to borrow and try to adapt to the task at hand one of the truly important metaphors of our time that was brilliantly proposed and applied by Sir Isaiah Berlin, but for another purpose altogether. In 1951, the great Oxford philosopher published a luminous essay on Tolstoy's philosophy of history, in which he made metaphorical use of a fragment from a text by the seventh century B.C. Greek poet Archilochus which reads, "The fox knows many things, but the hedgehog knows one big thing."[16] Isaiah Berlin noted that although scholars

16. First published in the *Oxford Slavonic Papers* 2 (1951): 17–54, under the title "Lev Tolstoy's Historical Scepticism," subsequently reprinted with additions as *The Hedgehog and the Fox* (London, 1953).

have been unable to discover what the poet originally intended to say, taken figuratively, the cryptic sentence conveys intimations about a profound difference between those thinkers and writers and human beings generally "who relate everything to a single, central vision, one system less or more coherent or articulate, in terms of which they understand, think and feel—a single, universal, organising principle in terms of which alone all that they are and say has significance," and those

> who pursue many ends, often unrelated and even contradictory, connected, if at all, only in some *de facto* way, for some psychological or physiological cause, related by no moral or aesthetic principle; these last lead lives, perform acts, and entertain ideas that are centrifugal rather than centripetal, their thought is scattered or diffused, moving on many levels, seizing upon the essence of a vast variety of experiences and objects for what they are in themselves, without, consciously or unconsciously, seeking to fit them into, or exclude them from, any one unchanging, all-embracing, sometimes self-contradictory and incomplete, at times fanatical, unitary inner vision.[17]

The former disposition corresponds to the hedgehogs; the latter, to the foxes. Without in any sense implying that this could be made into a rigorous classification, Plato, certainly, and Dante as well as Aquinas, Marx, and Proust should be counted among the hedgehogs; while Aristotle, Erasmus, Molière, Goethe, and Shakespeare definitely belong with the foxes. Like all oversimple schemes, this one, we are warned, can lapse into absurdity if pressed unduly, but also like all distinctions that embody a degree of truth, "it offers a point of view from which to look and compare, a starting-point for genuine investigation."[18]

Isaiah Berlin can affirm this with authority, because by proposing that

17. Berlin, *Hedgehog*, in *Russian Thinkers* (London, 1976): 22.
18. Berlin, *Hedgehog*, 23. This is not the first time that I find it helpful to use this seminal concept. In a book, *The Centralist Tradition of Latin America* (Princeton, 1980), I suggested that it was not unacceptable to class nations as either foxes or hedgehogs, adding that "while human beings are either one or the other throughout their brief productive lives, nations may change over time, and the Roman hedgehog evolve into an Italian fox, or the German fox into a hedgehog." I also suggested that Latin America is a hedgehog

> that since the middle of the nineteenth century has been desperately trying to become a fox, with indifferent results. The avid imitation of foxlike western Europe was not sufficient to achieve the transformation during the affluent years of the late nineteenth and early twentieth centuries; since the Great Depression of 1929 and the relative decline of the liberal democracies, the hedgehog quality of Latin American centralism has reasserted itself. . . . At times, this centralism is paradoxically established in the name of liberalism, as has happened often enough with military regimes wishing to impress foreign investors, but this should not obscure the fact that in such cases policies of economic liberalization and even what is described as political decentralization are instituted by executive decree and administered under severe central control.   (13)

Tolstoy was a sharp-eyed fox who desperately wished to be a hedgehog, he succeeded convincingly in making the most of this metaphor; he also left it, as it were, on the workbench, available for further use, an invitation all the more plausible because nothing in the dichotomy of foxes and hedgehogs renders it inappropriate as a starting point to consider the course of nations, the disposition of peoples, or the complex relation between cultural context and economic prowess nor as a vantage point from which to carry on the necessary observations and make the required comparisons. If individuals can be said to be foxes and hedgehogs, why not empires, societies, and civilizations?

Why not, indeed? Enlisting Isaiah Berlin's hedgehogs and foxes in the task of comparing the two great transplanted cultures of the New World could be helpful, perhaps even illuminating. The characteristic mode of the heirs to the Iberian and the English cultural traditions certainly provides a tenable basis for labeling them—in the guise of a working hypothesis—as foxes or hedgehogs. This is something that can legitimately be done a priori with the same confidence with which any reasonably lettered person can, without hesitation, describe Shakespeare as a fox and Plato as a hedgehog, or conclude that the authors of the *Summae* and the *Institutio* were both tenacious hedgehogs, while, say, Charles Dickens, Walt Whitman, André Malraux, Max Weber, and Lord Keynes must certainly be classed with the foxes. In the case of the New World, how can one possibly doubt that the disposition of the English-speaking northerners is far kinder to William of Ockham and Nominalism than to the Realism of the Schools and the Thomism that their southern neighbors have traditionally found so congenial? Latin Americans are bound together by an emphatically monarchical past and undisguised latter-day republican centralist inclinations, while the English-speaking northerners incline in the direction of aristocratic federalism and decentralization. The influence of the Common Law persists in the north, while the Civil Law is supreme in the south; the north succumbed early, honorably, and permanently to the romantic embrace, while the south has seldom ventured away from its attachment to unifying canonical classicism except when swept off its feet by cloying sentimentality, an experience different from the pensive, somber mood characteristic of the romanticism of the north. It is very difficult not to observe that the prevalent cultural style of the north is in harmony with the asymmetries, eccentricities, and diversities of Ruskinian Gothic, contrasting tellingly with the preference for the concentric and symmetrical Baroque modality that blossomed in the Indies of the Counter-Reformation.

This fertile metaphoric device yields an even richer harvest by directing attention to the intrinsic resistance to change of the unifying, embracing, and mutually sustaining disposition of the hedgehog, which has traditionally found it easier to lean toward an organic interpretation of things, with place and function ingeniously correlated, and in which the duty of the *res publica*, monarchical or presidential, is to intervene to ensure that from the cradle to the tomb, the man who was born to labor as "man-toe" will be as happy, prosperous, and fulfilled as the one whose origin marks him for the higher responsibilities of "man-eye." The organic society of the hedgehog can be very lively indeed, but it is also conceived, by definition, as an ordered entity exceptionally sensitive to any modification that could unleash disorder and destructive anarchy. For example, a proposal to reward the most efficient man-toe by promoting him to loftier positions (man-eye?) would find little support among true hedgehogs. It could be said, without stretching this too far, that in a world in which the primacy of change is overwhelming, the capacity of the Ibero-American peoples to resist it has been grossly underrated. Even resoundingly triumphant revolutionary initiatives that succeeded amid much tumultuous fury have failed intriguingly to bring about the profound transformations that were presumably their original and principal objective. The resilience of the hedgehog, however, does not go unrewarded, because among the traits conserved are the close family relations, old friendships, habitual landscapes, well-established social habits, and strong community feelings bound by place, blood, and status that elsewhere have almost invariably succumbed before the advances of modernity.

The sedentary preference of the Iberian hedgehogs contrasts tellingly with the unrivaled mobility of the English-speaking foxes, especially with their skill in making the most of the tidal transformations unleashed by their own Industrial Revolution. This was not achieved without cost. In order first to occupy and then to retain the vanguard of modernity for many generations, the foxes found it imperative—and possible—to divest themselves of most of those things that could encumber the agility needed successfully to outrun the flood. Allegiances sanctified by time and affection were discarded as readily as the absolute loyalties of birth, kinship, and belief celebrated by fading rites of passage; the conflictive intimacies and permanences that hold together the world of traditional community, *Gemeinschaft,* gave way to the rational arrangements of *Gesellschaft* tennis clubs, shifting neighborhoods, and corporations, not entirely without a measure of success but with enough failures to establish the fear of loneliness as a principal scourge of their prosperous modernity. That ageless witticism about the gods answering our prayers when they wish to punish us is applicable in this case. The hedgehogs have been granted the warmth of traditional community and the intimacy of the familiar for which they pray earnestly at the cost of the exacerbation of conflict brought about partly by proximity but also by the survival of traditions, regional attachments, loyalties, affections, and other amiable impediments to the mobility that factors of production require if they are to respond effectively to the economic challenge of the times. Unless all these indicators are hopelessly wrong, it seems fair to propose that the south of the New World is the realm of the hedgehog, while foxes roam at will in the north. This is tantamount to affirming that Isaiah Berlin's hedgehogs and foxes represent essential, definitive constituents of the dominant cultural traditions of the New World.

The life of metaphors is bound up inextricably with social activity. This is the reason why those that succeed best often have roots that go deep into the lore of the folk. Like good jokes or Thurber stories, they do not need and would not survive paraphrase or additional clarification. When we understand, effortlessly, what Agamemnon had in mind when he refused to be treated as "a barbarian peacocking out of Asia," we are helped along by unschooled insights of the kind that Aristotle probably wished to bring to our attention when he noted that "metaphor is not a thing whose use can be taught by one man to another." Such effortless understanding does not immediately follow when hedgehogs and foxes are pressed into service to help to explain the differences between the economy of Latin America and those of the United States and Canada. Their possible metaphoric usefulness demands much additional detailed explanation. The device is not a star but a planet; it will illuminate but only after it has been itself elucidated.

This manner of going about comparing the northern and southern settlements of the world of Columbus draws sustenance from the Vichian thesis that "there is a pervasive pattern which characterizes all the activities of any given society: a common style reflected in the thought, the arts, the social institutions, the language, the ways of life and action, of an entire society." According to Vico, "to each stage of social change there correspond its own type of law, government, religion, art, myth, language, manners." And he also explains that "fables, epic poems, legal

codes, histories, express institutional processes and structures which . . .
together form a single pattern of which each element conditions and
reflects the others. . . . This pattern is the life of a society."[19]

This approach has been echoed in our own time by other keen students of society: Merleau-Ponty, for example, observes that such patterns are perceived and comprehended by the human mind in "the form
of styles of behaviour and address that characterize things, persons, doctrines, and even historical periods." He reinforces this by explaining that
we understand artifacts and human actions by "grasping their styles,"
because even though these are never, or very seldom, fully accomplished,
they are sufficiently defined, or outlined, or intimated "to give every
act—even the seemingly fortuitous ones—a significant place. Meaning
is inevitable. . . . We are condemned to it."[20] These styles and patterns,
moreover, are shaped and reshaped over time by the changes and continuities characteristic of human society and are therefore rarely, if ever,
clear and distinct. Vico was not blind to this untidiness of historical
processes and cautioned against ignoring the slowness and unevenness
with which customs change, "not at once but by degrees and over a long
period of time," pointing out that "when men change they retain for
some time the impression of their previous customs."[21] More important
yet is that these various signs, symbols, and artifacts that are equally the
consequence of human action are not equivalent; some are vastly of
greater consequence than others. And although it may well be possible
to reconstruct our cultural moment starting from an electric toaster, a
tin of sardines, or a package of dog biscuits, this would be a marginal,
even an accidental, consequence of such insights.

The crucial Vichian argument rests on the primordial character of
language. Immensely more important than all other human artifacts,
signs, symbols, and institutions, language is the definitive element in
culture and the one that portrays most tellingly the modalities and transformations of the social ambit. Not untypically, this is also reflected in
the dominant modern metaphor for society. At various times in the past
men have found it helpful to think of society as a tree, a river, an organism, or a mechanism, but for the past century or so, the preeminent
metaphor is language—not in the form "society is *like* language," but

19. Isaiah Berlin, *Vico and Herder, Two Studies in the History of Ideas* (London,
1976): xvii, 68–69.
20. John F. Bannan, *The Philosophy of Merleau-Ponty* (New York, 1967): 13.
21. *The New Science of Giambattista Vico*, trans. T. G. Bergin and M. H. Fisch (Ithaca, 1970): 38, N.S. 249.

"society *is* language," an equivalence that suggests that the sources of meaning in one do not leave the other unaffected. This aspect of the problem was felicitously and famously addressed by Wittgenstein when he affirmed that "the meaning of a word is its use in the language,"[22] presupposing the existence of language in the social sense, that is, as a socially accessible activity, involving public objects and a body of socially accepted conventions. "To imagine a language," he added, "is to imagine a form of life,"[23] which is largely what Peter Berger and Thomas Luckmann had in mind when they observed that language not only "is the most important sign system of human society [but] . . . it is grounded in everyday life and keeps pointing back to it."[24]

Language and society derive meaning from the same source. Both depend on what human beings do, day in and day out; their meaning rests on usage. The common styles and patterns nurtured by society have no existence separate from human action; ultimately they depend on what people actually do rather than on what they think they are doing or even on what they believe they ought to do. Their meaning, if any, will rest on conduct rather than on intent, on past action rather than on mute wishes or thwarted aspirations, and therefore, by definition, it is likely to be more accessible to historical research than to the speculations of psychologists or science fiction aficionados.

This reference to the possibility of misunderstanding merits exemplification, and it would be difficult to find a better instance than that of Mausollus, the Persian satrap of Caria, famous for having inspired the huge tomb that his widow, Artemisia, built in his honor. Many years before the death of Alexander, Mausollus moved his capital from the hinterland mud-brick township of Mylasa to the port of Halicarnassus, where he built a stone and marble city that was more Greek than his models across the Aegean. Mausollus dressed like a Greek, built like a Greek, thought like a Greek, and, his enemies affirmed, fought like a Greek; but he was also a determined political and military adversary of the Athenians and went to war successfully against them in pursuit of policies that effectively ended the influence of the city-state over Chios, Cos, and Rhodes. Had Mausollus, or his scribes, his court artists, or his

22. Or the more general form, "Don't look for the meaning, look for the use." Robert Grant, *Oakeshott* (London, 1990): 11; Marcus B. Hester, *The Meaning of Poetic Metaphor, An Analysis in the Light of Wittgenstein's Claim that Meaning is Use* (The Hague, 1967): 51.

23. Hester, *Metaphor*, 52–53.

24. Peter L. Berger and Thomas Luckmann, *The Social Construction of Reality, A Treatise in the Sociology of Knowledge* (New York, 1966): 39–40, 51.

civil servants been invited to comment on the temper of their times, they probably would have shown themselves emphatically hostile to Athens (like South American revolutionaries toward Spain after defeating her in the wars of independence; or some Australian intellectuals today toward Britain, without benefit of war) and would have made much of their victorious campaigns against her. And yet, it is not military triumphs over the Athenians that explain the historical significance of Mausollus but the vastly more significant fact that he succumbed absolutely to the Hellenic cultural embrace and is justly remembered today as one of the great Hellenizing monarchs and a convincing precursor of the Hellenistic Age.

What Mausollus actually did is as important to the historian as what he believed he had done would be of interest to psychologists. What people do matters; human thought, human culture, human consciousness, all are founded on the bedrock of human activity. If human beings can be said to be, in a very real sense, what they eat, then with greater reason it can be affirmed that they are what they do; not only what they do to earn a living, presumably ordering their lives according to the melancholy slogans inspired on the "relations of production," but everything they do, with or without benefit of interpretation. This is not a problem of hermeneutics but of simple observation of everyday life. The social order—society—is not therefore part of the nature of things, nor can it be derived from the operation of "laws of nature," but it "exists *only* as a product of social activity."[25] These actions and their consequences, even if imperfectly perceived, are nonetheless susceptible of being understood by other human beings because they owe their existence to human protagonists. We always retain an additional possibility of understanding history, society, and culture better or more completely than otherwise because we are participants in the making of history, of society, and of culture; our insights are those of the fellow artisan rather than those of the disinterested onlooker. We are more likely truly to understand the actions of other human beings, even those remote from us, because we can see them from the inside, while our knowledge of the creatures and phenomena of the world of nature is, by necessity, that of outsiders.

This manner of going about the study of society can justly be described as "classic" in that it can be found, in one guise or another, in

25. Ibid., 70.

the writings of most social theorists. Tocqueville thought that this kind of undertaking was most likely to succeed when soundly based on an examination of social mores, which he meant to apply "not only to *moeurs* in the strict sense, which might be called the habits of the heart, but also to the different notions possessed by men, the various opinions current among them, and the sum of ideas that shape mental habits. So I use the word to cover the whole moral and intellectual state of a people," including, one may suppose, the daily practices of life as well as culture and consciousness.[26] More recent studies have adopted a similar approach because it affords an "insight into the state of society, its coherence, and its long-term viability . . . [and because] . . . it is in the sphere of mores, and the climates of opinion they express, that we are apt to discern incipient changes of vision—those new flights of the social imagination that may indicate where society is heading."[27]

This mode of understanding the nature of history and society is described splendidly in Vico's inspired and profoundly moving affirmation of faith in the principle of *verum et factum convertuntur*, when he tells his readers that

> in the night of thick darkness enveloping the earliest antiquity, so remote from ourselves, there shines the eternal and never failing light of a truth beyond all question: that the world of civil society has certainly been made by men, and that its principles are therefore to be found within the modifications of our own human mind. Whoever reflects on this cannot but marvel that the philosophers should have bent all their energies to the study of the world of nature, which, since God made it, He alone knows; and that they should have neglected the study of the world of nations, or civil world, which, since men made it, men could come to know.[28]

Therefore, human society is created and modified endlessly by the same processes by which institutions and artifacts are created. "Humanity is not a presupposition but a consequence, an effect, a product of institu-

26. Alexis de Tocqueville, *Democracy in America*, trans. G. Lawrence, ed. J. P. Mayer (New York, 1988): 287. An interpretation shared by Carlyle when, referring to sartorial fashions, he affirmed that "neither in tailoring nor in legislating does man proceed by mere Accident, but the hand is ever guided on by mysterious operations of the mind. In all his Modes and habilatory endeavours an Architectural Idea will be found lurking. . . . In all which, among nations as among individuals, there is an incessant, indubitable, though infinitely complex working of Cause and Effect." Thomas Carlyle, *Sartor Resartus* (London, 1888): Chap. V, "The World in Clothes," 32.

27. Robert N. Bellah, Richard Madsen, William M. Sullivan, Ann Swidler, and Steven M. Tipton, *Habits of the Heart, Individualism and Commitment in American Life* (New York, 1985): 275.

28. Bergin and Fisch, *The New Science*, 52–53.

tion building";[29] the genesis of artifacts, understood as all objects as well as all institutions and all things created or transformed by human beings acting purposefully, is definitive, because it defines the qualities that will normally determine the conditions, rigorous or tenuous, under which they will be comprehended, adopted, altered, and remembered, sometimes beyond the boundaries of ready recognition.[30]

Our present is crowded with objects and institutions that are unmistakably the consequence of human action. Michael Oakeshott has indicated, when addressing the problem of defining the limits and conditions of history as a mode of inquiry, that these objects or cultural artifacts are not

> the mere furnishings of an abode in which our doings take place; they are themselves the abode. They are themselves the language in which we compose our wants and conduct the transactions designed to satisfy them, the terms of our habits, the steps of our wanderings to and fro. Every such object noticed and attended to [or, one may ask, worn, like a pair of jeans? Or embraced, like an economic doctrine? Or consumed, like a hot dog? Or enjoyed, like a game of volleyball?] is a distinct happening, recognized in relation to ourselves as agents, responded to, valued, used, put by, ignored or rejected. Self as agent and object as concretion of qualities are counterparts of one another, distinguishable but inseparable.[31]

Genesis cannot shape artifacts permanently, but it does bequeath qualities that are, by necessity, intrinsic to subsequent modifications. Unless we are prepared to accept that cultural artifacts are absolutely and permanently interchangeable, the eloquence of origins must be granted more than a perfunctory hearing. It ought not to be a matter of indifference whether basketball originated in Massachusetts or in Tenochtitlán, or if Falstaff's progenitors were English or Bulgarian, or whether

---

29. Vico preferred to use the word *cosa*, following a relatively rare Latin usage in which *res* stands for "institution," for example, in Varro's *Antiquitates rerum humanarum et divinarum*, Antiquities of Secular and Religious Institutions. Vico translates Varro's *res humanae* as *cose umane*; *res divinae*, as *cose divine*. Bergin and Fisch explain that the reason Vico preferred *cosa* was because the term "institution" was theoretically loaded "with the very theory he was most concerned to discredit." Bergin and Fisch, *The New Science*, lii.

30. "All institutions in any culture whether they be regarded as political, economic, social or what have you are artifacts in this sense. Moreover, the members of a culture are each of them artifacts in this same sense. Each exists the way he does only as a result of his 'training.' As Vico saw clearly, what is called 'enculturation' or 'socialization' is a process which enables members of our biological species to become human persons, enables them to become participants in a culture and a history." Robert Welsh Jordan, "Vico and the Phenomenology of the Moral Sphere," in Giorgio Tagliacozzo et al., eds., *Vico and Contemporary Thought* (New York, 1976): 135.

31. Michael Oakeshott, *On History and Other Essays* (Oxford, 1983): 12.

Don Quixote grew up in La Mancha, Wessex, or Bangalore; to dismiss this intelligence as unimportant would be as bizarre as to explain the use of the Ionic and Corinthian orders in Heliopolis, Antioch, and Pergamum as an amusing coincidence or entirely to ignore the origin of the New World and of its dominant cultural transplants when endeavoring to understand why their respective economic achievements differ so markedly.

The Invention of the Indies

Amerigo Vespucci's hemisphere is the largest and most enduring creature of the Renaissance, and it is fitting that it should be named after a Tuscan navigator, friend of Ficino, Leonardo, Poliziano, and Botticelli, who began his career in the Paris embassy of Lorenzo *il magnifico*, went to Seville with the household of Lorenzo *il popolano*, and in letters to this Medici, written between 1500 and 1504, announced unhesitatingly and for the first time that a separate continent existed which he thought "we may rightly call a New World."[1] Discovered by a Genoese mariner leading an expedition of questionable legality,[2] object of claims and counterclaims by the Portuguese Crown and powerful Andalusian nobles, recognized for what it really was over a decade later by an agent of the Medici, the New World of Vespucci had a confused introduction into the European political consciousness that initially even threatened a dispersal of the political imperium over the vast, unexplored territories.

1. Roberto Levillier, *América la bien llamada* (Buenos Aires, 1948): I: xvi–xvii. Not everyone is convinced that the claims made on behalf of Vespucci are soundly based. For dissenting views, see Alberto Magnani, *Amerigo Vespucci* (Roma, 1926); for a balanced summary see J. H. Parry, *The Discovery of South America* (New York, 1979): 76–110.

2. Columbus's projected voyage could be construed as a violation of the Treaty of Alcaçovas between Spain and Portugal which thus far had been respected scrupulously by the Catholic monarchs. Queen Isabella, a pious woman, was sufficiently disturbed about this possibility that, regarding it as a moral, not a political, problem, placed it in the hands of her confessor, the priest Hernando de Talavera. Florentino Pérez Embid, *Los descubrimientos en el Atlántico y la rivalidad castellano-portuguesa hasta el Tratado de Tordesillas* (Sevilla, 1948): 229–232.

This possibility receded as the interests of Castile predominated, largely as a result of the efforts of Ferdinand, the Aragonese king, and Alexander Borgia, the Aragonese pope.[3]

Acting in concert to advance their respective and immensely practical interests, the two Spaniards, one enthroned in Spain and the other in Rome, laid the legal foundations for Castilian suzerainty over the Indies, a weightier achievement than either the nepotic advancement desired by the pontiff or the Mediterranean political maneuvers that exercised the mind of the king. Ferdinand was convinced that occurrences around the Mediterranean were vastly more important than the deeds of navigators and conquerors on the other side of the globe and devoted most of his time to the domestic affairs of the Aragonese lake, leaving the troubles and administrative problems of the distant Indies largely to Isabella and her Castilian counselors.[4] The other protagonist, Pope Alexander VI, born Rodrigo Borja, near Valencia, was greatly in need of the goodwill of Ferdinand and Isabella because he wanted to marry his favorite son, Juan de Borgia, to the king's rich and powerful cousin, doña María Enríquez. This biographical episode prompted the Spanish historian Manuel Giménez Fernández to write that

> in the games of give and take that fill the history of the Machiavellic corruptor Ferdinand V and the simoniacal Alexander VI, the concession [of the papal bulls and briefs] relating to the Indies . . . appears from the beginning intimately bound up with the delivery by the King of his cousin doña María Enríquez to marry the bastard Juan de Borgia. . . . Thus [the concession of the Indies to Castile] is nothing but the payment of the first instalment for the kinship of the King of Aragon with the sacrilegious eldest son of Alexander Borgia.[5]

The pontiff did indeed sign the necessary documents with alacrity, settling on the Castilian Crown all the lands newly discovered and those

3. The Duke of Medinaceli had not abandoned the policy pursued by his ancestors of trying to create an independent kingdom based on the Canary Islands; the Duke of Medina Sidonia was a vociferous and unrepentant defender of feudal autonomy and therefore firmly opposed to the centralizing program of the Catholic monarchs. Both knew Columbus and when they learned of his discovery, were quick to request privileges in the new lands, but their seigneurial pretensions were thwarted by the papal excommunication that barred travel to the Indies without the authorization of the Castilian monarch. Manuel Giménez Fernández, "*Las bulas alejandrinas de 1493 referentes a las Indias,*" AEA, Vol. I (1944): 243.

4. This does not mean that he was totally indifferent to matters related to the Indies, an attitude out of keeping with the monarch's personality. After all, contrary to popular belief, most of the funds to enable Columbus to go on his first voyage were found by Aragonese officials. R. B. Merriman, *The Rise of the Spanish Empire in the Old World and the New* (New York, 1918): II, "The Catholic Kings," 195.

5. Giménez Fernández, "Las bulas," 262–263.

to be discovered in the future to the west of an imaginary line, the *línea alejandrina*, running from pole to pole at a longitude of approximately one hundred leagues west of the Cape Verde islands.[6] More, the empire of the Indies was incorporated as a fief of the Castilian Crown to the exclusion of the other Spanish kingdoms—even of Aragon—from an official participation in its affairs,[7] a truly extraordinary title founded on the papal bulls and briefs of 1493, especially on *Inter caetera* of May 4, first issued in the form of a brief and subsequently modified several times to strengthen and extend the original provisions in accordance with the demands made by Ferdinand and Isabella on the advice of Columbus.[8]

These unusual transactions coincided with the aftermath of the destructive confrontation between the Crown and the Castilian nobility, which ended with a decisive and lasting reaffirmation of royal supremacy, the manner of which immediately brings to mind contemporary developments in France and England. Elsewhere in western Europe aristocratic feudal establishments were still able to obstruct, often to defy, the authority of crowned heads, but in common with Henry VII after the Wars of the Roses and Louis XI after the Hundred Years War, the Catholic monarchs, following the baronial disorders of Henry IV's ill-fated reign, pursued a policy of centralization and relentless assertion of royal preeminence that effectively neutralized the various manifestations of aristocratic military and political power and established the foundations of the modern Spanish state.[9] The administrative and political arrangements imposed in Castile extended beyond her frontiers to the rest of Spain far more effectively than, for example, those of the Tudors and Stuarts beyond England into Ireland, Wales, and Scotland, and ultimately proved as enduring as they were successful at the time of their inception. There is no doubt that a number of ancient corporations, quasi-autonomous regions, and lesser kingdoms retained some of their

6. The *línea alejandrina* alarmed the king of Portugal, Dom João II, because he thought that it could threaten his African interests. He entered therefore into direct negotiations with the Catholic monarchs that resulted in shifting the line a further 270 leagues to the west. This was formalized in the Treaty of Tordesillas of June 7, 1494. Pérez Embid, *Los descubrimientos en el Atlántico*, 229–232.

7. Antonio Domínguez Ortiz, *El antiguo régimen: Los Reyes Católicos y los Austrias* (Madrid, 1973): 65–66.

8. Parry, *The Spanish Seaborne Empire*, 46, 138, 153–154.

9. Neutralized but not obliterated; the kings did not hesitate to mete the severest punishments, including death, to the rebellious barons, but for those who supported them, or who were prepared to mend their ways, there were rewards and understanding. Ferdinand and Isabella forced the nobility to accept "the immense superiority of the throne" and in return, recognized their privileged position in the social order and invited their loyal collaboration and support. Domínguez Ortiz, *El antiguo régimen*, 13–17.

medieval privileges, albeit in residual form, throughout the reigns of Ferdinand and Isabella and their successors and well into the twentieth century and that the resulting diversity of local arrangements, often colorful and picturesque, has misled some students of Spanish history into thinking that the union forged by the Catholic monarchs was illusory and that the key to the understanding of the origins of the Iberian New World was to be found precisely in that very visible and irreducible patchwork of distinct regions, customs, and dispositions.[10]

Such an approach, however, does not accord sufficient weight to contemporary opinion about the nature and import of the union or to the dominant position of Castile within Spain during the life of Isabella and to the fact that after her death, Ferdinand established an unchallenged authority over both Castile and Aragon and passed it on to rulers as strong as himself and equally committed to absolute monarchical preeminence. About the former, it is unlikely that any explanation could improve on Elio Antonio de Nebrija's description, penned in 1492, of the *monarquía y paz* "that we are now enjoying, firstly because of divine Providence, but then because of the industry, hard work and diligence of Her Majesty, the happy consequence of which has been that the members and pieces of Spain, that were everywhere dispersed, are now brought together in the body and the unity of the realm, with such ties and ordered in such fashion that many centuries, hardships and vicissitudes will not be able to break or dissolve."[11] The passage of time proved Nebrija right, and despite an abundance of hardships and vicis-

10. According to Stanley J. Stein and Barbara Stein, for example, "perhaps the greatest myth assimilated into the European thinking of this period was the myth of 'Spain' itself. . . . The marriage of Ferdinand and Isabella, often considered the birth of the modern Spanish state, resulted not in the unification of the kingdoms of Aragon and Castile but in condominium in which the two parts of the 'Spanish Crown' coexisted as separate entities with separate laws, taxation systems, coinage and trading patterns." *The Colonial Heritage of Latin America* (New York, 1970): 14. The apparent dispersal of the many "Spains" in the face of her obvious unity has intrigued many commentators who have been tempted to propose some unusual explanations. The geography of the peninsula, according to one writer,

has always been the key to the history and even to the character of the inhabitants. Its peninsular form, and its singularly definite frontier on the one side on which it is not surrounded by the sea, give the country a superficial appearance of unity. In reality it is broken up into separate sections by a succession of transverse mountain ranges which are cut by no great river running from north to south. . . . Nature, by thus dislocating the country, seems to have suggested localism and isolation to the inhabitants, who each in their valleys and districts are walled from their neighbours.   (Alfred F. Pollard, "The 'New Monarchy' Thesis: Towards Absolutism," in A. J. Slavin, *The 'New Monarchies' and Representative Assemblies* [Boston, 1965]: 4)

11. Antonio de Nebrija, *Gramática Castellana*, ed. Pascual Galindo Romeo and Luis Ortiz Muñoz (Madrid, 1946): Prólogo, 8. The famous *Gramática*, as every Spanish-speaking schoolboy knows, first appeared in 1492.

situdes, the Spanish-speaking world did remain entirely united, without exceptions, during the imperial centuries that followed, an achievement unequaled since the days of Rome.

The diversities discovered by latter-day scholars are as real and interesting as they have been insufficient seriously to disturb the unifying disposition of the Iberians. About the latter, it is important to bear in mind that at the time of the marriage of Ferdinand and Isabella, in 1469, Castile encompassed three-fourths of the population of the Iberian peninsula and covered 65.2 percent of its territory. Taken together with the Crown of Aragon, Castile accounted for 82.4 percent of the total Iberian territory, including Portugal, and for 85.2 percent of the population. The population density in Castile was 22 inhabitants per square kilometer, while in Portugal it was only 16.7, in Aragon, 13.6, and in Navarre, 15.4. There can be no doubt that the political weight of Castile, let alone that of Castile and Aragon combined, was of overriding importance.[12] No other region or kingdom outside Castile could conceivably attain even the shadow of the centralizing power exercised by the Catholic monarchs from Valladolid, Toledo, or Madrid.[13]

That the "New Monarchies" of the sixteenth century were the precursors of the modern state is sufficiently clear, but that it was in Castile, under the Catholic monarchs, that early, successful, and lasting moves in this direction were undertaken has received less attention than it deserves, especially among Latin American historians.[14] The rest of Spain

12. J. H. Elliott, *Imperial Spain 1469–1716* (New York, 1966): 25; Merriman, *Spanish Empire* II: 84–86. The preponderance of Castile was overwhelming even before the conquest of Granada and the discovery of America, of which she was either the only or the principal beneficiary. A most telling indication of the relative importance of Castile and Aragon lies in the decision to appoint Castilian viceroys to represent the authority of the Castilian Crown in the Aragonese kingdoms; the reverse would have been unthinkable.

13. Juan Regla, "La época de los tres primeros Austrias," in J. Vicens Vives, *Historia de España y América: Social y económica*, Vol. III (Madrid, 1982): 4–12; Domínguez Ortiz, *El antiguo régimen*, 81–82. It was not until 1560 that Philip II named Madrid as the capital of Spain. Before this, the capital was simply that place where the monarch happened to be in residence. With the incessant growth of the central bureaucracy, the movement of people and documents from one city to another became increasingly difficult. Three Castilian cities were considered as possible capitals: Valladolid in the north, Toledo in the south, and Madrid, between them. For reasons not altogether distant from those that dictated the choice of Canberra and Washington, the Prudent King opted for the middle way.

14. The early development of modern absolutism in Castile, where the assertion of royal authority was virtually unrestricted by institutional obstacles, has not passed unnoticed by Spanish historians. Luis Sánchez Agesta, for example, believes that it is in sixteenth-century Spanish thought, firmly founded on contemporary political experience, that "the architecture of a theory of the State, perhaps the first theory of the State" can be discerned. According to Maravall, sixteenth-century Spanish politics are intelligible only if considered as a consequence of the early rise of the modern state in the peninsula.

outside Castile may or may not have been completely and uniformly integrated at all levels, but this did not affect the centrally devised arrangements for the New World that originated from the Castilian metropolis. The Catholic monarchs, their ministers, and their successors ruled unencumbered by doctrinal impediments or by powerful barons, whose actions could conceivably have tempered their belief in the absolute nature of regal power and in the Christian duty of crowned heads to exercise it absolutely. It was under these auspices that the administrative, legal, ecclesiastical, and political arrangements for the Iberian possessions in the New World were designed and constructed. Inadvertently, perhaps, Hernán Pérez de Oliva, author of the much-disputed sixteenth-century *History of the Invention of the Indies,*[15] directed the attention of his readers to the crucial aspect of this matter: for good or bad reasons, successfully or not, the Indies were indeed invented by Castile, and the new realm was given order, system, and hierarchy by ministers and monarchs who contemplated the world of the Renaissance not from a cultivated cosmopolitan city in a divided Italy or from a busy, pluralistic Hanseatic emporium but from the cold, windswept, and introspective Castilian capital of a Spain united under one of the strongest monarchical regimes in Europe.

Although Spain was the country least touched by the utopian fashions of the late fifteenth century and early sixteenth century,[16] a qualified

---

Sánchez Agesta, *El concepto del Estado en el pensamiento español del siglo XVI* (Madrid, 1959); also, José Antonio Maravall, *Estado moderno y mentalidad social* (Madrid, 1972).

15. Hernán Pérez de Oliva, *Historia de la invención de las Indias*, ed. José Juan Arrom (Bogotá, 1965). Used in this context, the word *invención* has a delightful ambiguity. It derives from the Latin *invenire*, to find, to come upon, to discover; for example, in the *Elegías de varones ilustres de Indias*, Juan de Castellanos writes, "The ships, inventors of regions, are sailing towards the west" (39). On the closely related concept of the "invention of the Spanish nation," see Julian Marías, *España inteligible: Razón histórica de las Españas* (Madrid, 1985): Chap. XIII, "La españolización de Castilla y la invención de la nación española," 143–156.

16. When considering a point of departure for their treatise on utopian thought, the Manuels chose the latter part of the fifteenth century and the early sixteenth century, "because of the confluence of diverse intellectual and social forces whose relation to the creation of modern utopia was provocative, if not causal." Among these they list the translation of Plato's *Republic*, "to the accompaniment of a tumultuous debate on Italian soil among Byzantine emigrés over the admissibility of Plato's communist politics into Christian society"; the appearance in print of a large part of the Greek and Latin corpus and of a stream of paradisaical, apocalyptic, and millenarian visions; and, most important, from our vantage point, "the discoveries of lands to the West, throwing open the windows of the utopian imagination to novel social and religious arrangements, as Alexander's push eastward had given rise to Hellenistic exotic novels." These seminal factors affected Europe in general, but least of all Spain. As the Manuels observe, "The absence of a sustained utopian tradition in Spain is peculiar, though free-floating utopian affect may have some-

exception should be made of the unusual motivations of Columbus, especially considering the high regard that the Catholic kings had for both his person and his achievements. In his third voyage to the Indies, the great navigator reached the mouth of the Orinoco River and was within sight of the continent but immediately sailed back to Hispaniola in great fear. This we know from his letter to Ferdinand and Isabella in which, amid frequent references to the writings of d'Ailly on the geographic position of paradise,[17] the Book of Ezra, Isidore of Seville, Bede, Ambrose, and Scotus, he explained that according to his reckoning from measurements taken by the North Star, as he approached the Orinoco he seemed to be ascending, and the turbulent current indicated that the waters of the river were running down from a high place. Knowing, as he did, that the Garden of Eden was at the highest point on earth (otherwise, how could it have survived the flood?) and that the four rivers of Eden were sweet, just like the four mouths of the Orinoco, he was not surprised to discover that the natives found in the vicinity were nude, handsome, and gentle, as would befit tho‿e who live in the neighborhood of paradise.

> The arguments from authority, the descriptions of Genesis, the astronomical measurements, the evidence of his eyes, and the taste on his lips all coincided and led him to surmise that he was . . . close by the terrestrial paradise, but he knew, as he wrote to the Spanish sovereigns, that no one might enter it except with the will of God. Frightened by the forbidden paradise and the ultimate secret it held, he fled back to Hispaniola.[18]

Were it not for the fact that Columbus insisted that his "execution of the affair of the Indies" was a fulfillment of prophecies in Isaiah and not a matter "of mere reason, mathematics and maps," this ᵔpisode could

---

how attached itself to the figure of Don Quixote. The manuscript of an Enlightenment utopia, *Descripción de la Sinapia, península en la tierra austral,* had recently been published, but it hardly modifies the generalization that Spain was relatively untouched by the utopian main current until the penetration of Marxist and anarchist thought." Frank E. Manuel and Fritzie P. Manuel, *Utopian Thought in the Western World* (Cambridge, 1979): 14–16.

17. Pierre d'Ailly, *Imago mundi,* with annotations by Christopher Columbus (Boston, 1927).

18. "There was only one difficulty: This great elevation around the equinoctial line ran counter to the view he had accepted before he embarked on his voyages that the world was a perfect sphere. Now that he had discovered the mountain of paradise, he would have to reject d'Ailly and Aristotle and conceive of a new shape for the earth. In a burst of fantasy, he concluded that it was for the most part indeed round like a *pelota muy redonda*; but on one side it had a stalk that protruded and pointed upward toward the heavens. The earth was thus more like a pear than a sphere, rather like a woman's breast with a nipple on it." Manuel and Manuel, *Utopia,* 61.

have been disregarded.[19] In the circumstances, however, and given the contemporary European intellectual climate favorable to utopian speculations, especially bearing in mind the intense piety of the queen and the extraordinary success that had attended her previous initiatives, it is legitimate to speculate that for both monarchs but especially for Isabella, the world that Columbus had placed at their feet precisely when the unification of Christian Spain had been completed must have appeared as a providential tabula rasa proffered to their Catholic Crowns, precisely so that they could put their felicitous experience to good use, designing a just and well-ordered polity that would shine forever as an exemplar of Christian perfectibility.

It is against this quasi-mystical background that we must consider the process whereby the New World of Castile was first "invented" as an exceptionally centralized, homogeneous, and stable cultural entity, almost a model of what the Catholic kings and their successors would have wished for Castile and for Spain. The Indies were born in Renaissance circumstances, but the single-minded intent with which their Castilian mentors went about their political schooling immediately brings to mind the singular assiduity of Archilochus's hedgehog. Like the Greek poet's prickly metaphorical beast, the monarchs and their ministers knew one big thing very well indeed: if their fledgling New World overseas was to be well governed, virtuous, and prosperous, they had the responsibility meticulously to exclude from it any vestige of the divisive particularisms, baronial greed, and seigneurial ambitions associated with the feudalism that was then fading throughout western Europe. The Castilian New World was therefore emphatically denied the feudal experience and its cultural and political concomitants that elsewhere played such a decisive role in the formation of institutions.[20]

From a legal vantage point, the Indies were an extension of Castile, but they were not allowed to share the administrative authorities or the institutions of the old kingdom because of the danger of aristocratic contagion that conceivably could have reached them through shared political or administrative institutions. Therefore, with the exception of the Crown itself and, briefly, the Council of Castile, soon to be superseded by the formidable Council of the Indies, Castile and the Indies had no authorities in common.

> The Castilian *Cortes*, councils and *audiencias* were not to have an atom of power in America. . . . The crown proposed to maintain exclusive control of

19. Ibid.
20. This aspect of the problem is examined in greater detail in Véliz, *Centralist Tradition,* 16–28.

the new possessions—to manage them as another hereditary domain, through a totally new set of institutions, without doubt closely similar to, and in fact modelled on, those of Castile, but entirely separate from them.[21]

Major decisions affecting the governance of the Indies were expected to be made by the monarch, advised by the Council of Castile. In practice, however, questions of policy affecting the overseas territories rarely came before the full body of the council, and after Isabella's death, Ferdinand, his hands full with Mediterranean affairs, referred these problems to individual councillors, notably, Juan Rodríguez de Fonseca and Lope de Conchillos, so that in this early, formative period "the government of the Indies was a narrow and tightly centralized bureaucracy controlled by Fonseca in the name of the king."[22] The resulting de facto concentration of executive power ensured that residual regional variations within Spain did not find their way to the New World to complicate, or in any way to attenuate, the centralist administrative and political arrangements devised for the governance of the new realm; it also eased the early introduction overseas of legislation specifically designed to thwart any seigneurial or quasi-feudal pretensions on the part of settlers and conquerors foolish enough to believe that because they were on the other side of the world they could defy with impunity the authority of the Crown.

The efficacy of these precautions cannot be doubted. After a military conquest that was as brief as it was astonishing, the skills of domesticity tended to take precedence over those of the battlefield, and the settlers wished mostly to be left in peace to consolidate and enjoy the material comforts and social status that would have been obviously beyond their reach in the peninsula and that they did not wish imprudently to put at risk. This was especially so after the sobering failure of the rebellion led by Gonzalo Pizarro in Peru, the first and only significant quasi-baronial challenge to the monarchy by Spaniards in the New World. Supported enthusiastically by every man in the viceroyalty in his opposition to the New Laws of 1542, which limited severely the privileges of landholders and *encomenderos*, the rebellious captain seemed invincible, but in the end, he was vanquished by the solitary *letrado* sent by the monarch who was armed with the formidable weapons of patronage and legitimacy.[23]

21. Merriman, *Spanish Empire* II: 222.
22. Parry, *Seaborne Empire*, 57–58.
23. Unable to send an armed force strong enough to face Pizarro on his own ground, the Emperor Charles entrusted the task of putting down the uprising to the statesmanship and experience of Pedro de la Gasca, an austere ecclesiastic and senior civil servant who

Defeated, captured, publicly executed, and, according to custom, his severed head and those of his senior officers exhibited inside an iron cage in the main square of Lima, Pizarro's melancholy fate proved exemplary, and he had no imitators during the three centuries of Spanish rule in the New World.[24]

The unqualified success of the hedgehog's approach in establishing an enduring system of central political control in the Indies was echoed in other important aspects of public life, notably, in the management of the economy, the development of the Spanish language, and the administration of the church. The Crown's interest in economic matters, for example, was meticulous, and found appropriate institutional manifestation in the monopoly vested on the much-studied Casa de Contratación from its establishment in Seville in 1503 until its dissolution in 1778. The monopolistic disposition of the Spanish monarchy was neither original nor rare; on the contrary, in those premercantilist times, as they have been described, the rarity would have been to find a New Monarchy indifferent to the conduct of economic affairs. If anything, it could be argued that compared with Portugal, where a royal monopoly directly administered by the king's household was established to exploit the country's African and Asian possessions, the Catholic monarchs and their successors erred on the side of diffidence. Such a comparison, however, misses the point, which is that neither the Portuguese nor the Spanish monarchs at that time, nor their successors in the peninsula, in the Indies, or in modern Latin America, whether republican tribunes or princes of the blood, have ever been afflicted with a horror of intervening in the management of their country's economic affairs.

Some authors have made much of the well-documented fact that the Crown did not actually finance the conquering enterprises, but left it to

---

arrived in the Indies alone and unarmed but with full powers from the Crown to deal with the situation as he thought best. Cajoling, threatening, compromising, and distributing rewards, in a brief period he raised an army, routed Pizarro in the battle of Xaquixaguana, and ended the revolt. Modern scholarship has not bettered Prescott's magnificent account of the crushing of Pizarro's rebellion by La Gasca. It will probably remain unsurpassed for a very long time. William H. Prescott, *History of the Conquest of Peru* (London, 1847): Bk. 5.

24. The head was placed on a gibbet, with a label bearing the inscription, "This is the head of the traitor Gonzalo Pizarro, who rebelled in Peru against his sovereign, and battled in the cause of tyranny and treason against the royal standard in the valley of Xaquixaguana." His estates, including his mines in Potosí, were confiscated; his mansion in Lima was razed to the ground, the place strewn with salt, and a stone pillar set up, with an inscription interdicting anyone from building on a spot that had been profaned by the residence of a traitor. Prescott, *Conquest of Peru*, Bk. V, Chap. IV.

each private adventurer to raise the required capital. This is true. What has not also been pointed out is that in these arrangements, the monarch risked nothing and legitimately stood to win all. If the conquering expedition failed, the leaders could lose limb, life, and property; but if it succeeded and great civilizations sprinkled with cities of gold were discovered and conquered, the victorious adventurers were entirely at the mercy of the Crown; there were no guaranteed rewards or recognition. If the senior bureaucrats in power at that moment, or their successors, had reason to believe that the conquering hero's behavior was immoral, or worse, that it could be construed to have been consistent with dangerous seigneurial aspirations, the rewards would be very slow in coming and could even be postponed indefinitely.[25]

Their momentous victory over what they would have regarded as the de facto separatism of Granada and the resolution of the problems caused by an unruly nobility very much in their minds, the Catholic kings were understandably inclined to believe that the decisive factor in the construction of a worthy Christian polity and economy in the Indies was precisely the unity of purpose that they had espoused so zealously within Spain, with such rewarding results. In its absence, no economic enterprise could, indeed, should, be allowed to proceed, and such a unified and unifying intent could not be sustained except by a homogeneous people, honoring the same ancestry, worshiping the same God, and awed by the same monarch. Diversity, heterogeneity, adulteration, and discontinuity in any form were considered to be inimical to the flawless unity demanded for this elevated purpose; purity alone would sustain the unwavering loyalty that spans oceans and wastelands and would ensure the rejection of novelty, heresy, and corruption.

When looking back at these events from our vantage point in the closing years of the twentieth century, it is virtually impossible to avoid doing so through the glass of classical sociological concepts that have

25. Pedro de Valdivia, the conqueror of Chile, waited eight years for his de facto governorship to be formally confirmed by the Crown. Among the reasons for the delay were various charges of misconduct that eventually led to a trial that acquitted him of some, but not all, of the charges. He was found guilty as charged that "throughout the time that he has been in Chile, and since he left Cuzco, more than eight years now, he keeps this woman [Inés Suárez] as his mistress, and they sleep in one bed and eat off one plate, and they invite each other publicly to toast in the Flemish fashion by saying; I drink to you." One of the formal conditions for his appointment as governor to be confirmed was precisely that he should cease cohabiting with Inés Suárez, which instruction he obeyed by having her marry Rodrigo de Quiroga, a loyal friend and subordinate who subsequently, after Valdivia's death at the hands of the Araucanians, was himself appointed governor. Diego Barros Arana, *Proceso de Pedro de Valdivia* (Santiago, 1873): 126, 184.

been the object of much popularization and have consequently become part of the baggage of modernity. With this in mind, it would be difficult, for example, to overlook the parallelism between the moral and political expectations of Ferdinand and Isabella and the conditions that Émile Durkheim proposed in his description of "mechanical solidarity." Thus, the society preferred by the Catholic monarchs would have been one in which the values of the traditional community predominated, in which the system of justice was principally directed toward ensuring the subordination of every member to what today, without hesitation, would be described as the "collective consciousness," and in which homogeneity would be the condition sine qua non of its continued existence. Even if in every respect the resulting society turned out to be a mere approximation, a shadow of this description, it could still be used as a serviceable example of Durkheim's "organic solidarity."[26]

It is in this very basic understanding of the nature of unity, politics, piety, the dangers of diversity, and the rewards of conformity that much of the explanation can be found for the policies designed by the Catholic kings and their ministers to ensure that only fit persons were permitted to settle in the Indies. Anyone wishing to sail was required to obtain a license from the Crown, which had to be authenticated at the time of departure from Seville. Contrasting dramatically with what occurred a century later with the English emigration to the North American colonies, no infidels, heretics, or dissidents of any description, or their descendants down to the fourth generation, were to be permitted to sail to the New World. This crucial task of supervision and control of passenger traffic was also placed in the hands of the bureaucracy of the Casa de Contratación. As J. H. Parry has observed, the Catholic kings, busily converting their Muslim subjects and deporting the Jews, were anxious to prevent members of either group from finding refuge in the Indies, where it was feared they would pollute the incipient society with the same practices and ideas that, in their estimation, had so grievously

26. There is no need to classify Queen Isabella as a proto-Durkheimian. She was simply observing that among the most expeditious forms of unity must be counted those based on similarity. For entirely different reasons, she probably would have agreed with Durkheim in thinking that the one incontestable rule of conduct in society is the one that orders us "to realize in ourselves the essential traits of the collective type." The French sociologist went further, of course, and explained, "Among lower peoples, this reaches its greatest rigour. There, one's first duty is to resemble everybody else, not to have anything personal about one's beliefs or actions. In more advanced societies, required likenesses are less numerous." Émile Durkheim, *The Division of Labour in Society* (New York, 1964): 396.

threatened the purity of religion and the political tranquillity of the realm.[27]

Kingly rapacity, a disruptive factor during the worst years of financial distress later in the century, did not weigh in the decision of 1503, or its confirmation in 1529, to retain the Crown's exceptionally strong trade monopoly through the Casa de Contratación.[28] This all-embracing responsibility for the economic life of the New World was assumed centrally, because from the vantage point of the Catholic throne, in this as in other matters of public importance, there was only one overriding and transcendental truth, and this was bound up inextricably with the requirements of a good Christian life, defined by the monarch; everything else, most certainly the activities associated with material gain, was secondary, instrumental, or, worse, erroneous. Economic motivations, in particular, were the object of suspicion because they were seen to be borne on the shoulders of powerful appetites, and therefore, as is the case with other strong passions, what they called for was not encouragement but repression, to ensure that they did not disturb the harmony, the balance, and the health of the Christian realm. Like the proverbial hedgehog, the Catholic monarchs saw one shining truth surrounded by the shadows of many errors, pitfalls, and temptations that could, if ignored and allowed to persist, threaten the well-being of the larger community; they did not feel free to abdicate the responsibility of directing things economic because they were convinced that this was the only way effectively to frustrate the egoistic appetites nourished by greed and ambition and thus to prevent them from disrupting the efficient functioning of the incipient but well-ordered Christian society in the Indies or from usurping precedence over the legitimate interests of the Crown. It would be another century before foreign foxes settled in the New World, and there was no actual occurrence or portent that could remotely be con-

27. Parry, *Seaborne Empire*, 56. The Casa was founded in 1503; Isabella died a year later, and Ferdinand, in 1516. A year later still, Luther nailed his theses in Wittenberg. In due course, Protestants and other *heterodojos* were added to Jews and Muslims in the list of those who were not to be allowed to settle in the Indies.

28. The Casa de Contratación was the first of the many administrative institutions created by the Crown for the governance of the Indies. Originally it was established in Seville and charged with the responsibility of registering and issuing licenses for all the vessels, crews, and merchandise sent to the Indies, to supervise the activities of merchants and authorize the passage of prospective settlers, to collect taxes, and generally to enforce the laws and regulations affecting the economic life of the Indies. Partly because of the silting of the Guadalquivir and the administrative reforms introduced under the Bourbons, in 1717, the Casa was removed to Cadiz, the loud protests of the powerful Seville commercial interest notwithstanding. Geoffrey J. Walker, *Spanish Politics and Imperial Trade, 1700–1789* (London, 1979): 102–103.

strued as an intimation that worthy consequences could come about from a multitude of things believed, known, or (why not?) possessed. In the absence of alternatives, the Castilian hedgehog remained in full and serene enjoyment of the knowledge of that one big thing, clear, simple, and satisfying, that would shape and color its world for centuries to come.

The certainties that sustained the Crown's intervention in economic and political affairs were also mirrored most convincingly in the manner of going about the use and development of the vernacular. The Spanish language, that is, *castellano*, or the language of Castile, and English[29] differ in all the ways in which most modern European languages are expected to differ, but in addition they have generated strikingly different institutional and regulatory arrangements to address the inescapable challenges of growth and change. Although as early as 1664 it was reported that members of the Royal Society had "voted that there should be a committee for improving the English language," the idea of establishing an English Academy modeled on the one that Richelieu had founded in 1635 never managed to get off the ground.[30] The users of English do as they please today, and they have been doing this for several centuries, but the Spanish language has the Royal Academy to preside over its destiny. Founded in 1714 by the first Spanish Bourbon, Philip V,

29. One wonders why English never became "British" in the same way that *castellano* became Spanish and the Tuscan dialect, Italian.

30. In 1697, during one of the periodic discussions about the subject, Daniel Defoe pointed out that if an academy were created, "it would be as criminal to coin words as money." Voltaire disagreed and thought it a pity that there was no English Academy. The next best thing, the Royal Society of London, did not impress him because it lacked "the two things most necessary to men: rewards and rules." Even more irritating was that in the closing years of Queen Anne, "the famous Dr. Swift had a plan to set up an academy for the English language, following the example of the Académie Française. The members who were to have composed it were men whose works will endure as long as the English language: Dr. Swift, Mr. Prior, . . . Mr. Pope, the English Boileau, Mr. Congreve, who might be called their Molière. . . . But the Queen died suddenly, the Whigs took it into their heads to hang all the patrons of the Academy, which, as you may well imagine, was fatal to literature." Voltaire, *Letters on England*, trans. L. Tancock (London, 1980): 116. Dr. Johnson disapproved strongly: "If an academy should be established for the cultivation of our style, I . . . hope the spirit of English liberty will hinder or destroy [it]." Samuel Johnson, *Dictionary of the English Language* (1755), Preface. Robert McCrum, William Cran, Robert MacNeil, *The Story of English* (London, 1986): 129–131. The first academy, founded by Richelieu and Louis XIII precisely to safeguard the purity of the language, is still hard at work. Recently, it achieved some notoriety by approving unanimously a very unusual attempt to reform spelling; *oignon* and *croque-monsieur*, the learned academicians decided, should henceforth be spelled *ognon* and *croquemonsieur*, and words of foreign origin such as kidnapper and leader, would add a *u* to reflect their French pronunciation, thus *leadeur* and *kidnappeur*, but the public outcry has been such that the Academy prudently reconsidered the matter and early in 1991 abandoned its bizarre initiative.

it is the oldest such institution in the Spanish-speaking world and has traditionally been known simply as the Academia Española. Its principal responsibility is to watch after "the purity and propriety of the Castilian language," and among its many important publications must be mentioned the first dictionary of the language, in 1726–1739, completed almost simultaneously with Nathan Bailey's pioneering albeit less ambitious dictionary of English words "in good usage," and a good twenty years before Dr. Johnson's monumental work, unquestionably the first standard English dictionary.[31] The English language is asymmetrical and diverse, its growth a reflection of the life, the virtues, and the shortcomings of those who use it; *castellano* also responds to these influences but under the severe guidance of the Academia. The Spanish language is centrally controlled, wisely, no doubt, but centrally controlled nonetheless. In English, there is no such thing as officially correct orthography; in Spanish, there is only officially correct orthography. There are many acceptable English usages; there is only one correct Spanish usage.[32] The English language is a decentralized diversity; the Spanish language, a self-assured centrality. English is the language of the fox; Castilian, the language of the hedgehog.

The obvious correlation between the ascent of the grandson of Louis XIV to the Spanish throne, the establishment of the Academia Española, and the mood that greeted the dawn of the Enlightenment tends to obscure the immensely important appearance, more than two centuries earlier, under the Catholic kings, of the first fully fledged grammar compiled for any modern European language, a work that in its contents,

31. Bailey's *Universal Etymological English Dictionary* was first published in 1721, but even its revised edition in 1736 cannot be considered a standard dictionary. Dr. Samuel Jonhson set out in 1746 to produce such a dictionary and succeeded most memorably. "When it appeared in 1755, in two large folio volumes, each the size of a lectern Bible, it swept the field, and maintained its position in England for nearly a century." E. L. McAdam and George Milne, eds., *Johnson's Dictionary* (London, 1982): vii–viii.

32. There have been some interesting attempts officially to depart from the path signposted by the Academia Española. One of the better known is that promoted by Andrés Bello, in 1843, as rector of the newly founded University of Chile. In one of the first sessions of the University Council, Domingo Faustino Sarmiento, who later became president of Argentina but was then living in exile in Chile, submitted a program of orthographic reform similar in spirit to the one proposed almost a century later by George Bernard Shaw for the English language. The principal feature of the reform was the proposal to spell words exactly as they are pronounced, thus instead of *hacendado* and *que*, it should be *acendado* and *qe*, because the *h* and the *u* are mute and therefore, according to Sarmiento, superfluous. Bello espoused the reform with enthusiasm and, throwing his great prestige behind it, convinced the government to legislate accordingly. For a few years academic and official government publications provided amusement throughout the Spanish-speaking world until the practice was quietly abandoned and Chile returned to the fold. Eugenio Orrego Vicuña, *Don Andrés Bello* (Santiago, 1940): 220–221.

intent, and certainly its timing, provides a cogent demonstration of the style and disposition of the cultural moment that flourished and faded under the auspices of those unhesitant Castilian hedgehogs. The humanist, lexicographer, and grammarian Nebrija presented his *Gramática Castellana*, fresh off the press, to Queen Isabella in August of the *annus mirabilis* of 1492, eight months after the surrender of Granada and fifteen days after Columbus had departed on his first voyage of discovery. It is worth noting that within the span of that incredible year, the Catholic kings consolidated their hold over a united Spain; gave their blessing and financial support to a foreign navigator who would repay them with a New World; and received from the hands of Nebrija the grammar of the language that was to become one of the most powerful instruments for holding together an empire judged by contemporaries to have been the greatest that the world had ever seen.[33] More, the brilliant grammarian was not innocent of the significance of his seminal work. In the opening lines of the Prologue, he noted succinctly, "My certain conclusion is that language is the companion of empire," and further on, describing a previous interview with the queen, who had inquired about the practical use of such a treatise, he relates that Isabella's confessor, Hernando de Talavera, who was also present, "answered for me, saying . . . Your Majesty will bring under her yoke many barbarian peoples and nations with strange languages, who, having been defeated, will have to receive the laws that the victor imposes on the vanquished, and with them, our language; it is then that they will use this art to learn it."[34] This was penned ten months or more before Columbus returned from his first voyage and has therefore given rise to much speculation about its quasi-prophetic tenor, intended or not. It is uncertain whether Talavera or Nebrija—or Isabella, for that matter— had in mind a policy of African conquests, but a few paragraphs later, Nebrija's meaning cannot be misunderstood when he writes that "not only the enemies of our faith will feel the need to learn the language of

33. It appears that the bishop of Avila, Hernando de Talavera, was partly responsible for the idea of compiling the *Gramática*. The writing and printing of the book took several years; it is known that some of it was already in existence by 1486, when Nebrija, accompanied by Talavera, showed a "sample" to the Queen. The printing of the book was completed in the Salamanca presses on August 18, 1492. It was thus the first grammar of a modern European language, soon followed by Pietro Bembo's *Prose della volgar lingua* (Venice, 1525); Barclay's first French grammar, written in English and published in London, in 1521; and the first Portuguese grammar of Fernão de Oliveira, which appeared in 1536. Nebrija, *Gramática*, xiv–xv, xxxix–xl; see also, Fernando Díaz Plaja, *Otra historia de España* (Madrid, 1987): 94–98.
34. Nebrija, *Gramática*, 5, 10–11.

Castile but also the Basques and the Navarres"—an affirmation consistent with the grammarian's unifying nationalism cited above.[35] Equally important is his anticipation of the adoption of fixed rules of orthography and of the future rise of academies. The modern editors of the *Gramática* point out that no one before Nebrija had ever attempted to regulate the anarchy of contemporary spelling, and, even at that early date, "he was already thinking of the need to have official rules supported by the State, thus proposing for the first time the establishment of the Academies." His is undoubtedly the earliest modern reference to the monarch as an arbiter of linguistic usage, when he writes that a rule of orthography will stand unless "Your Majesty's authority intervenes" and when he brings his Prologue to a close by reiterating the opening dedication to "The Very High and Enlightened Princess Doña Isabel the Third of This Name Queen and Natural Ruler of Spain . . . in whose hand and power the things of the language are as much as everything else about us."[36]

If we are still prepared to agree with Wittgenstein that "to imagine a language, is to imagine a form of life," then we must accord the immortal grammarian the attention that his pioneering effort so justly deserves and note that the young language to which he gave lasting order and discipline proved a worthy companion of the imperial enterprise, and, as is the case with old married couples or friends of many years, it mirrored the society that used it and was mirrored by it. Its orthodoxy was that of the single-minded hedgehog: ill at ease with confusing diversities and content to have the royal hand at the helm; more than happy to welcome the Academia under whose learned, often somnolent, but always well-meaning, central authority it would thrive and prosper. Canadians, Californians, Australians, and G. B. S. may or may not accept being ruled by *Webster's* or the *OED*; they may wish to spell *thru*, *nite*, *labour*, or *honour* in any way that strikes them as acceptable, but

35. See above; also, Nebrija, *Gramática*, 11.

36. Formal references to Isabella as Queen of Spain, rather than of Castile alone, are not frequent before this date, and the manner and reiteration of the title in Nebrija's work have not passed unnoticed by modern scholars who credit him with one of the very early literary expressions of the emerging Spanish nationalism. Julian Marías, for example, proposes that since the Catholic kings, "there is no power other than royal power, that is to say, the power of the State; there is no army other than the royal, that is, the national army." Further on, under the title, "The Invention of the Spanish Nation," he adds that with Nebrija "emerges a new sense of being, a new society, a new dimension of the use of 'we'; not anymore 'we, the Castilians,' or 'we, the ones from Aragon,' still less 'we, the old Castilians' or 'we, the Catalans'; from then on it is 'we, the Spaniards.'" Julian Marías, *España inteligible: Razón histórica de las Españas* (Madrid, 1985): 155–156; Nebrija, *Gramática*, 5, 12.

after half a millennium, Nebrija's passionate scholarship can still claim at least part of the credit for the grammatical discipline and the orthographic predictability of the language of Castile.

The centralist disposition responsible for the tenor of Nebrija's grammar, the Crown monopoly of commerce and the discouragement of baronial pretensions in the Indies, was also reflected in the sui generis Castilian regalism that presided over the ecclesiastical affairs of the realm. By the time that Pope Alexander VI assigned to Castile dominion de jure over the New World, the political life of the kingdom was already strongly centralized, and the ecclesiastical control that was still lacking Ferdinand wrested from Pope Julius II fourteen years later, when the warrior-pontiff was threatened by an imminent French invasion and felt obliged to negotiate for Spanish support. The justly famous bull, *Universalis ecclesiae regimini*, of 1508, in which the pope conceded to the Crown of Castile in perpetuity "the privilege of founding and organizing all churches, and presenting to all sees and livings in all overseas territories which they possessed then or might acquire in future," legitimized this most remarkable and unprecedented regalist victory.[37] Joaquín García Icazbalceta, the Mexican historian, commented that Julius II had ceded to the Spanish monarchs "a power in the ecclesiastical government of the Indies which, except in purely spiritual matters, was almost pontifical."[38] After 1508, the authorization of the monarch was required before any hospital, church, or bishopric could be founded; neither priests nor bishops could cross to the Indies without a specific royal permit, but the king could appoint bishops and send them overseas to their duties without awaiting papal confirmation. This was probably the single most important concession ever wrested by any government from the bishop of Rome and the basis for the *Patronato de Indias*, a source of much disputation after 1810 between the new republican regimes and the Vatican, as the former endeavored to retain it as heirs of the ousted colonial administrations, while the pontiff saw in the dissolution of the empire an opportunity to recover the ground lost to regalism three centuries before.[39] With the exception of decisions affecting doctrinal mat-

---

37. Parry, *Seaborne Empire*, 154. According to Domínguez Ortíz, "The authority of the institution of the monarchy reached unprecedented levels; its control over the Spanish church established the foundations of its ecclesiastical policy with such vigor that vestiges of it survive even today." *El antiguo régimen*, 10.

38. Joaquín García Icazbalceta, *Don Fray Juan de Zumárraga* (México, 1881): 128–129.

39. W. Eugene Shiels, S. J., *King and Church: The Rise and Fall of the Patronato Real* (Chicago, 1961).

ters of the faith, the head of the Church in the Indies was not the pontiff in Rome but the king in Madrid; no monarchy in Christendom had ever legitimately exercised such unfettered ecclesiastical power; none would ever do so again.

When Isabella was proclaimed Queen in 1474, Spain was an untidy diversity of Christians, Jews, and Muslims who after centuries of proximity had grown more or less accustomed to each other's presence; by 1516, when the widowed Ferdinand died, the country had accepted a common Catholic orthodoxy as an efficient substitute for the kind of national spirit that could otherwise have generated the seamless political unity desired by the monarchs. Indeed, Castilians, Basques, Murcians, Catalans, and Andalusians were bound together "in the single purpose of ensuring the ultimate triumph of the Holy Church" to the exclusion of Muslims, Jews, Albingenses, Illuminists, Erasmians, and other dissenting groups, who were either extirpated or presented with a dismal choice between ruinous exile or the abandonment of their ancestral beliefs.[40] To ensure that the forbidden religions were not kept secretly alive by *conversos* who had embraced Christianity, often under duress, solely to avoid expulsion, and who, here and there, may have shown signs of reverting to the faith of their fathers, Ferdinand and Isabella formally applied to the pope for authorization to introduce the Holy Office of the Inquisition into Castile. The climate of the Renaissance had transformed the old Italian Inquisition into a languishing, powerless, almost moribund institution, potentially a formidable instrument for the perfectability of faith and morals, if only placed in the hands of prelates and officials determined to put it to good use.[41] The papal authorization was promptly forthcoming, and in November 1478, five years before the birth of Martin Luther, Pope Sixtus IV authorized the Crown of Castile to appoint ecclesiastics as inquisitors for the detection and suppression of heresy.

Observed from the Castilian hinterland, life under the Catholic kings need not have seemed unattractive; loyal subjects of the Crown appeared to be united indissolubly by a common religion and to live reasonably prosperous lives under powerful and truly sovereign monarchs whose austerity and piety were unquestioned. The integrity of their homeland

40. Elliott, *Imperial Spain*, 108; William H. Prescott, *History of the Reign of Ferdinand and Isabella the Catholic* (London, 1885): 161–173.
41. After their ratification in the Councils of Narbonne, in 1227, and Toulouse, in 1229, the early inquisitorial courts that had been operating intermittently since the twelfth century spread everywhere in Christendom, except England. B. J. Kidd, *The Counter-Reformation, 1550–1600* (London, 1963): 40–41.

was as well-protected by their victorious armies as their redeeming faith was efficiently defended from dangerous thoughts and practices by the vigilance of the Tribunal of the Holy Office.[42] In little more than four decades, Ferdinand and Isabella had transformed Castile—and Spain— from an obscure and impoverished frontier territory racked by internecine warfare into an incipient New Monarchy, strong, respected, competently administered, and occupying a principal position among the European powers, but when the young Charles was proclaimed King in 1518 and Holy Roman Emperor a year later, Spain's imperial summer was just beginning; Pavia, Mühlberg, St. Quentin, Breda, Nördlingen, and the countless other memorable feats of the *tercios* in the battlefields of Europe were as much in the future as the conquest of Mexico and Peru and the flood of precious metals from Zacatecas, Popayán, Carabaya, and Potosí. Also in the future was the uprising of the *comuneros* in Castile and the *Germania* rebellion in Aragon; the ruinous, inglorious war in Flanders; the struggle with England and the disaster of the *Invencible armada*; the pitiless Araucanian War, the "Flanders of the Indies"; recurring bankruptcy and military defeat; the massacre of the tercios at Rocroi; the pervasive deterioration of public life; and, of course, the "Golden Age," when, dismissing the somber intimations of decline, Spain brought poets, painters, playwrights, architects, and novelists to the center of the stage and astonished all with the undimmed glory of a blossoming of the arts that enriched the world forever with the creations of Zurbarán, Murillo, Churriguera, Alonso Cano, Cervantes, Lope de Vega, Quevedo, Calderón de la Barca, Velázquez, Góngora, and Gracián.

The young Castilian hedgehog growing up robustly in the New World was spared the formative immediacy of some of these experiences; the news of military victories, to be sure, was loudly proclaimed and celebrated, but the Crown censors did not go out of their way to allow the dissemination of detailed accounts of setbacks and defeats, and when information about these eventually reached the shores of the Indies, it did so muffled by time and distance. The contrast between the clarity

42. This central role of Catholicism is undoubtedly a lasting and definitive characteristic of Spanish life. In a famous essay on what he describes as the "inferiority complex" of his fellow countrymen, López Ibor described the religiosity of the Spanish people as a principal and defining characteristic and proposed that while a Frenchman can be a good patriot without being a Catholic, this is not possible in the case of a Spaniard. He cited Morente approvingly, affirming that there cannot be true *Hispanidad* in the absence of a profound Catholic faith. Juan José López Ibor, *El español y su complejo de inferioridad* (Madrid, 1958): 187; Manuel García Morente, *Ideas para una filosofía de la historia de España* (Madrid, 1957).

and brilliance of victories and good news, especially during the decades of the Spanish ascendancy, and the grayish ambiguity and imprecision of the rest helped importantly to create and sustain in the Indies an impression of imperial greatness that would prove extraordinarily durable, even after it became impossible to overlook the overwhelming evidence of decline. These distortions were also exacerbated because the nature of Spain's woes was such that it was not until very late in the day that the malaise was reflected in military setbacks. The disaster at Rocroi in 1643, for example, is frequently taken to mark the beginning of the end of Spanish preeminence in the battlefields of Europe, but the financial troubles of the Crown, the bankruptcies, and the pilfering by the penurious emperor of the property of his defenseless subjects preceded Rocroi by almost a century. All the good news from Europe sailed swiftly across the ocean, but only the bad news that could not possibly be suppressed—like the failure of the armada—reached the shores of the Indies, and even then, it was mostly doctored by official interpretations. An eminent historian of nineteenth-century Australia justly affirms that the antipodean continent suffered then from a "tyranny of distance";[43] how vastly more justified it is to apply this verdict to the Indies of Castile; but while in Australia distance was universally regarded as an obstacle to be overcome, from the vantage point of the Castilian Crown, the immense distance that separated her from her exotic fief was regarded as a stout defense, a welcome hindrance to the dissemination of dangerous thoughts, a bulwark against heresy; and for many settlers, it was an amiable oceanic waste indeed that mitigated the rigor of ordinances as frequently as it tempered the clarity of arrogance and clouded over the distinctiveness of error.

More important, the very great distance insulated the crucial measures of political and economic centralization, and those affecting religious and linguistic orthodoxy, from the continuing and abrasive proximity of the circumstances that had originally breathed life into them; distance preserved them, as it were, in amber, beyond the reach of those undesirable factors and adverse conditions that helped to bring them about in the first place. Each of those carefully designed policies represented a Spanish response to a challenge rooted in Spanish conditions that continued there to exert an influence and to temper, perhaps even to modify substantially, the original response. This, however, did not

43. Geoffrey Blainey, *The Tyranny of Distance: How Distance Shaped Australia's History* (Melbourne, 1966).

occur in the Indies, where the responses invariably arrived unaccompanied by the challengers that had helped to engender them and remained largely unchallenged—and therefore, unchanged—throughout the imperial centuries. For example, the antiaristocratic political resolve of the Catholic kings was importantly the consequence of the disorderly and divisive behavior of the Castilian barons; it was an unambiguous response to a challenge that though successfully neutralized, did not vanish but continued in various ways to influence Spanish political life for many centuries. Not so in the Indies, where the early response of the Crown, embodied in legislation, arrived promptly but on its own, without the original challengers, the *grandes* of Spain, the violent barons, and their armed retainers. The legislation was imposed by the metropolis in its original form, and it remained virtually unquestioned and unchanged in spirit until the dissolution of the empire and beyond. It was never successfully challenged in the Indies because, apart from Pizarro and his friends, there were no challengers; nor was it ever tempered by the need to compromise with regional quasi-seigneurial holders of effective power because these were never tolerated by the Crown.

The establishment of the *Patronato de Indias* had comparable consequences. This extraordinary institution was justified in the eyes of the monarch because it resolved the recurring problems of ecclesiastical jurisdiction between the Crown, the Holy See, and a few weighty nobles and because it brought to an end the illegitimate interference of the pontiff in the sovereign affairs of Spain. Once established, however, it became, unavoidably, an untidy avenue for dispensing patronage and a perennial source of litigation, controversy, and political intrigue. Its subsequent history in Spain is certainly not uneventful, but when it was transplanted to the Indies, it went on its own, leaving behind the interfering insolence of the nobility and the nepotism of the princes of the church, and found itself in novel circumstances that included an emphatically regalist clergy and a very distant pope. Once again, the challengers never reached the Indies, but the *Patronato*, the monarchical response to their actions, certainly did and functioned smoothly and efficiently during the ensuing three centuries of Spanish rule, unhindered by barons and unquestioned by pontiffs.

The effortless imposition of linguistic orthodoxy in the Castilian Indies was also not an exception. There is no evidence that before the publication of Nebrija's pioneering *Gramática*, the use of many and very different Iberian languages caused significant friction or confrontation. However, the difficulties that later accompanied the adoption throughout Spain of the language of Castile appear to be consistent with the implied challenge and resistance offered by the other languages and dialects. These difficulties, one may add, never quite disappeared and continue to merit attention in the closing years of the twentieth century. Although there was no Crown policy of encouragement of the use of the language of Castile in the Indies, or discouragement of the rest, *castellano* went with the large number of Castilian, Andalusian, and Murcian settlers authorized to sail, while its potential challengers stayed behind in Catalonia, the Basque country, Galicia and Asturias. The relatively few emigrants permitted to settle overseas who did not master the language of Castile were dispersed throughout the continent, their vernacular eventually succumbing before the overwhelming popularity of *castellano*.

A generation after the discovery and a century before the beginnings of English colonization, the New World of Castile lived under one religion, one language, and one ruler. Even if nothing else had occurred, the prospect for lasting stability appeared on the surface to be reasonably good, but closer scrutiny would have revealed that the centralizing policies and unifying orthodoxies imposed from Castile were either immediately instrumental, like the trade monopoly, or directly the consequence of the exercise of absolute power, like the Patronato de Indias, or founded on an oversimple understanding of the conditions for social cohesion, like the criteria for authorizing prospective settlers to sail to the Indies. The arrangements for the structuring of the incipient society of the New World had accumulated one on top of the other, like bricks without mortar; each of them was an expedient device for achieving a very concrete and practical objective. Leaving aside the unquestioned acceptance of the divine provenance of regal responsibility and the will of the Catholic monarchs, there was no coherent philosophy, no body of political principles, nothing, other than bureaucratic expediency or inertia, to hold together these diverse policies and decisions or to ensure their continuity. With the death of Isabella and Ferdinand, much of this, if not all, could presumably have been erased or changed beyond recognition by a handful of determined ministers and a compliant monarch, but the fledgling empire was spared this particular outcome: as the young Charles sailed from Flanders to take possession of his Spanish kingdom, Luther's hammering at Wittenberg heralded a religious cataclysm that by thrusting on Spain the protagonic role of defender of orthodoxy, rampart of Catholicism, and champion of the Counter-Reformation, helped to bring about the firm and lasting unity that otherwise could have evaded the better efforts of the Catholic monarchs.

The Spanish Counter-Reformation

We know about the Protestant Reformation. The Catholic kings did not. With hindsight, obviously, but most legitimately, the Castilian decades of Ferdinand and Isabella can now be regarded as an apprenticeship, a preparation for the struggles that followed. It can even be proposed that had there not been a Protestant challenge, much of the obsessive centralism and the demands for purity, homogeneity, and conformity enforced with such exorbitant zeal both by the Crown and by the Holy Office would have been judged either unnecessary or, worse, cruel and harmful. Whether the totally unrelated rise of Protestantism vindicates those severities is not at issue. What can be stated with confidence is that if Spain and her Indies had not been under the control of the Crown of Castile as they were at the time, it is conceivable that the open or latent divisions that plagued the country before the advent of the Catholic monarchs would have surfaced, rendering it vulnerable to the onslaught of the Reformation. As it turned out, when the challenge did come, Spain was found to be holding generous reserves of the spiritual energy and political steadfastness that were so notoriously lacking in Renaissance Rome and was prepared to place them at the service of the defense and renewal of her Catholic faith.

The victorious crusade of the Counter-Reformation completed the protracted and demanding process of forging a unified Spanish-speaking world. Bringing together the Spain and the Indies of Ferdinand and Isabella had depended on the strength of will and the astuteness of the monarchs and the relative weakness of pontiffs and barons. In the absence of such an equation, the de facto Castilian empire would have vanished overnight; worse, people and institutions would have succumbed under the flood of gold and silver from the Indies as readily and impressively as they proved capable of deriving spiritual strength from centuries of adversity. The imperial Spain that survived for three hundred years athwart two worlds necessitated a convincing architecture as well as good bureaucratic carpentry, plumbing, and stonemasonry.

Ferdinand and Isabella were both consummate politicians, but neither presumed of philosophy, which is tantamount to saying that they were superb carpenters but had no head for architecture. It is fair to add that it was not because of Ferdinand's piety or philosophical skills that Machiavelli chose him as his princely model,[1] and it does not diminish the stature of the monarch one bit to observe that not even his most enthusiastic biographers have been tempted to describe him as a Thomist scholar. Neither Ferdinand nor Isabella would have understood how or why Thomism could have been called on to resolve the problems of national integration that they bequeathed to Charles V, but this is more or less what did occur. Not only the ordering and unifying political thought of Aquinas but also the stern repression instituted by the Holy Office, the inspired teaching of the Jesuits, and the extraordinarily popular, bureaucratic, and classless Castilianism of Philip II[2] all contributed significantly to the forging of a feeling akin to nationalism that by the closing decades of the century, many problems notwithstanding, appeared to explain, perhaps even to justify, the aplomb with which the Iberians occupied the center of the world. Vicens Vives observed that when the Hispanic monarchy took upon its shoulders the burden of defending Catholicism,

> it perfected the rudimentary attempts at centralization initiated by the Catholic Monarchs and by Charles I. The instrument used in this process was a system of Councils, meeting in permanent session, in a fixed capital—in Ma-

1. Machiavelli was fulsome in his praise. "Nothing," he observed, "gains estimation for a prince like great enterprises. Our own age has furnished a splendid example of this in Ferdinand of Aragon. We may call him a new king, since from a feeble one he has made himself the most renowned and glorious monarch of Christendom; and, if we ponder well his manifold achievements, we must acknowledge all of them very great, and some truly extraordinary." Niccolò Machiavelli, *Il Principe*, chap. 21 (Geneva, 1798), cited in Prescott, *Ferdinand and Isabella*, 701.
2. "The fundamental characteristic of Philip II's empire was its Spanishness—or rather Castilianism—a fact which did not escape the contemporaries of the Prudent King, whether friend or foe." Fernand Braudel, *The Mediterranean and the Mediterranean World in the Age of Philip II*, Vol. II (London, 1973): 676.

drid, which at the end of the sixteenth century achieved its rank as the historic capital. . . . The important thing was the system: the network of Councils—a concert of aristocrats and lawyers, bureaucrats and employees of all levels—which Philip II pressed into the service of his Crown. A tide of paper spread and engulfed the entire land, inundating the Councils themselves and exhausting their administrative resources, bewildering even the highest ranking bureaucrat of the state—the scrupulous reigning monarch. Yet Philip kept a tight hold over the Councils, and so his political directives were only delayed, not distorted, by administrators.[3]

This unintended and distant consequence of the Counter-Reformation proved extraordinarily resilient, and it can be argued that not a few emphatically republican regimes of the New World are still living today under the centralist shadow of Philip II's extraordinary decades.

Descriptive names such as Counter-Reformation, belle époque, Hellenistic Age, Middle Ages, Renaissance, and Industrial Revolution invariably irritate purists and invite pedantic dismissal, but they are not as unhelpful as their critics would have us believe, for they frequently allow us to address complex and tenuously defined series of related events with the succinctness and immediacy that are normally the first victims of prolixity. These names are rarely associated with clear and distinct beginnings and ends, but they are nonetheless useful because they refer to readily identifiable historical occurrences that share distinct features about which it is possible to make general statements. For example, it can be affirmed that in every one of its definitive characteristics, certainly in its hierarchical understanding of social order, in its doctrinal and liturgical arrangements, in its political support for monarchical institutions, and in the stylistic canon of its artistic manifestations, the Counter-Reformation exhibited the kind of satisfying symmetry, predictability, and unifying disposition that would have pleased Archilochus's hedgehog immensely. The difficulty is that although general statements of this kind can be illuminating in other ways, they cannot readily be enlisted as supporting evidence for even a cautious attempt to discover, or precisely to describe, or define, the distinguishing characteristics of a phenomenon as complex as the Counter-Reformation. This, however, is a challenging and important task and justifies a measure of insistence. Bearing these difficulties very much in mind, it is possible that a more attentive examination of the Thomist zeal of the Dominican scholar Tomás de Vío, better known as Cardinal Cajetan, and its prob-

3. Jaime Vicens Vives, *Approaches to the History of Spain*, trans. and ed. Joan Connelly Ullman (Berkeley and Los Angeles, 1970): 100.

able consequences could open up a promising alternative path for this inquiry.

Cajetan went to Germany in 1518, as legate of the pope, to confront Luther at the diet of Augsburg and two years later helped to draft the bull to excommunicate the reformer. The influential Dominican was the author of several works on the thought of Aquinas, including important commentaries on the *Summa Theologiae* and *De Ente et Essentia*, and although his overenthusiastic Thomism has been described as "brittle and formal," it played a crucial role, as the Counter-Reformation gained momentum, in the transformation of the incipient Thomist revival into "a vital force in the theological definitions of the Council of Trent in the mid-century and in the thought of Dominican apologists and philosophers such as Francisco Suárez."[4]

The fervent advocacy of Cajetan was important in placing Thomism at the heart of the Counter-Reformation, and it would be very strange indeed to discover that it had no influence whatsoever on its adoption by another Dominican scholar, Francisco de Vitoria, who was appointed *Prima* Professor of Theology at the University of Salamanca a decade after the momentous nailing of the Lutheran theses at Wittenberg.[5] From this principal chair in one of the most prestigious universities of the world, he made an unparalleled contribution to what can fairly be described as the "theology-led" Spanish intellectual Renaissance. According to Vitoria, the duties and functions of theology properly understood, in the widest sense possible, "extend over a field so vast, that no argument, no discussion, no text, seems alien to [its] practice and purpose."[6] He therefore found it understandably more congenial to associate his teaching with the broad and confident sweep of Thomist thought than

4. Lewis W. Spitz, *The Protestant Reformation, 1517–1559* (New York, 1985): 285. Given the direction of the argument presented above, it is not out of place to stress that Tomás de Vío was born in Naples, lived much of his adult life under the Spanish Crown, and two of his most distinguished neo-Thomist followers, Vitoria and Suárez, were also Spanish.

5. It was named *Prima* by opposition, because the lectures had to be delivered *prima luce*, with the sunrise, in contrast to its counterpart, delivered at vespers. The prima chairs were accorded a superior status to the evening ones. It was also a chair by opposition, that is, the candidates had to lecture in public and submit to questions—and heckling—during a period of up to five weeks. The appointment was decided by a majority of student votes weighted in accordance with the number of courses successfully completed, that is, two hundred second-year students, for example, had as many weighted votes as one hundred fourth-year students. Francisco de Vitoria, *Relecciones del estado, de los indios, y del derecho de la guerra*, ed. and intro. Antonio Gómez Robledo (México, 1974): xii–xiii.

6. James Brown Scott, *The Spanish Origin of International Law: Francisco de Vitoria and His Law of Nations* (Oxford, 1934): 253.

with the traditional method of detailed and ingenious exegesis of Peter Lombard's *Libri Quattuor Sententiarum*, which for three centuries had dominated European universities, and consequently, without hesitation, he substituted the *Summae* for the *Sentences* as the foundation of his lectures.[7] With this departure from tradition, assisted by his legendary eloquence, wit, and intellectual courage, Vitoria gave a vigorous impulse to the process whereby Thomist thought, after the waning of its influence during the latter part of the Middle Ages, was once again thrust to the forefront of Spanish affairs, on this occasion precisely at the time when its tenets could most usefully assist the political purposes of the Crown and the defense of religious orthodoxy—more so in a united Spain, under an imperial monarch, than in a hopelessly weak and disunited Italy torn by internecine warfare and used moreover as the cockpit for the European powers.[8]

This may appear to be an excessive claim for a series of academic lectures, but in the circumstances of Salamanca, and Spain, it is almost unnecessarily modest. The University of Salamanca was without question one of the most prestigious centers of learning in Europe and one of the largest. When Vitoria won his chair, Salamanca boasted well over five thousand students destined, on completing their courses of study, to make up a sizable proportion of the contemporary intelligentsia.[9] Certainly of those who managed to complete successfully the law course, a perennial favorite, the majority went directly into lesser or greater posts in the judiciary and the bureaucracy. The lectures of an eminent scholar such as Vitoria would certainly have been attended by large numbers of students; it would be difficult to imagine that any student at Salamanca at the time did not exert every effort to listen to the Dominican.

There can be no doubt about Vitoria's share of the responsibility for the resurgence of Thomism in sixteenth-century Spain, especially among the senior levels of administration, the judiciary, and the church, a matter of consequence, given the consistency between the philosophy of Aquinas and the direction that the emperor endeavored to impress on

7. Guenter Lewy, *Constitutionalism and Statecraft During the Golden Age of Spain: A Study of the Political Philosophy of Juan de Mariana, S. J.* (Geneva, 1960): 14–15.

8. It is more than a coincidence that the subject of one of Francisco de Zurbarán's finest works, painted in 1625, was the reception of Saint Thomas Aquinas into the Society of the Blessed, as a fifth doctor of the church. James Stothert, *French and Spanish Painters* (London, 1877): 35.

9. The University of Salamanca has kept detailed records of student registrations from the first half of the sixteenth century onward. According to these records, the highest number of enrollments under the Hapsburgs was achieved in 1584–85 when 6,778 students were registered. Domínguez Ortíz, *El antiguo régimen*, 320–321.

public affairs. How could Charles V have objected to the Thomist proposition that among the forms of government known to man, monarchy was the most conducive to unity and the most "natural" and this being so, that it possessed "analogies with God's rule over creation"? More, that the state had positive functions and responsibilities that precede and are distinct from those of the church; that the state therefore exists as a "natural" institution before the church, in other words, that kings precede popes in the natural order of things. The state and the church must coexist but each shouldering its own responsibilities, which in the case of the state, include ensuring the unity, peace, and good order of the community; directing its energies to good actions; and administering it so that there is always a sufficiency of the supplies necessary for a good life.[10] More still, that the individual, being only a part of the community, is naturally subordinated to the larger community in the same way and for the same reasons that we expect our limbs to respond loyally to the needs and welfare of the whole body. Four centuries later, Tawney wrote disapprovingly about these holistic political and social conceptions of the scholastic era, commenting that they made it impossible to argue against "class privilege, class oppression, exploitation and serfdom," because these social imperfections had been rationalized and given ethical meaning by considering that society, like the human body,

> is an organism composed of different members. Each member has its own function, prayer, or defence, or merchandise, or tilling the soil. Each must receive the means suited to its station, and must claim no more. Within classes there must be equality; if one takes into his hand the living of two, his neighbour will go short. Between classes there must be inequality; for otherwise a class cannot perform its function, or—a strange thought to us— enjoy its rights. Peasants must not encroach on those above them. Lords must not despoil peasants. Craftsmen and merchants must receive what will maintain them in their calling, and no more.[11]

Unlike Tawney, Vitoria made these propositions his own and in his famous *Relecciones* affirmed that "no society can continue to exist without some force and power to govern and provide for it . . . just as the human body cannot be preserved in its integrity, without some directing force to regulate the various members, making them of mutual use and of service to the whole man; even so the State would necessarily lose its integrity, if every individual were solicitous for his own welfare and

10. F. C. Copplestone, *Aquinas* (London, 1975): 238–241.
11. Tawney, *Religion and the Rise of Capitalism*, 35–36.

heedless of the public good." Who is to wield this awesome power to do good and discourage evil? asks Vitoria, and his answer is unequivocal: kings, and this is as it should be for the institution of monarchy is not only just and legitimate but its power "is derived from divine and natural law."[12]

The earnest Dominican's espousal of Thomism was not an isolated eccentricity but a portent of what would follow throughout the years of the Counter-Reformation and later, when the schism in Christendom assumed the character of a confrontation between the centrifugal tendencies released by Protestantism and the centripetal convictions normally associated with papal orthodoxy. It would have been strange, given such a contest, for the stern integrating energy of Thomism to have been overlooked as a suitable weapon for the arsenal of the Catholic renewal. Scholars like Cajetan and Vitoria must have reconsidered the path that led to Wittenberg and realized that with Aquinas, scholasticism reached a summit as an integrating and harmonious philosophical system and that after the departure of the *doctor angelicus*, the path descended aimlessly until, seen from their vantage point, it became bogged in the *via moderna* ushered in by the skeptical criticism of William of Ockham. They evidently concluded that it was principally in the writings of Saint Thomas that scholastic thought came closest to consolidation into a system permeated with confidence in the synthetic power of reason—not reason as the Greeks understood it, or as we understand it in the twentieth century, but reason subordinated to the needs of the Church, reason as the handmaid of faith.

The definitive intellectual task of the time had been the reconciliation of Aristotle with the requirements of Christian theology. To achieve this, the Schoolmen tried to encompass, describe, and classify all there is and all there is to be known in huge inclusive systems—*summae*—that is, summations and summaries of all knowledge that allowed nothing to remain outside their field of vision; theirs was a species of conceptual taxonomy that attempted to impose hierarchy, order, and moral purpose on the chaotic diversity of nature and the human condition.[13] "On the

---

12. Brown Scott, *Spanish Origin*, 258–259.

13. It is not inopportune here to note that the modern English version of Aquinas's *Summa Theologiae* fills sixty volumes that, even making generous allowances for the duplication of parallel texts, editorial notes, and explanatory appendixes, remains, in addition to its qualitative excellence, a very considerable literary production. Approaching the subject from another direction, Emile Mâle regarded that splendid thirteenth century as "the century of Encyclopedias. In no other period were so many Surveys, Mirrors, or

surface," explains the editor of the modern English version of Saint Thomas's *Summa Theologiae*, this treatise

> may seem a mixture, of passages, sometimes long sustained, of pure ratio-
> nalism and of Scriptural exegesis, of severe demonstration from the necessity
> in things and of recommendation from a vivid sense, quaint sometimes to
> modern tastes, of the analogies running through the whole universe and king-
> dom of God; topics of no direct religious interest appear to engross large
> sections. Penetrate more deeply, however, and all parts are seen to be com-
> bined and charged with one common purpose, namely to show God's own
> truth, not in its proper terms, for that is not possible even were it called for,
> not even in poetic terms to evoke its secret glance, but more plainly in the
> terms of sacred history and of a universal and communicable human philos-
> ophy.[14]

Once more, we have an eminently plausible description that would have charmed Archilochus's helpful hedgehog, one with intimations of similar orderings of disparate elements later on. Perhaps it is not amiss to observe here that what we are being invited to consider is the possibility of an immense diversity that when examined superficially may suggest capriciousness, chaos, and possibly disorder, but properly considered, all its parts "are seen to be combined and charged with one common purpose."

Unconvinced and disapproving though he was, Tawney nevertheless believed that in their *Summae*, the Schoolmen had succeeded in working out the "architectonics" of a world in which the ultimate standard of human institutions and activities was religion and was impressed with the contrast that this offered with modernity's characteristic obsession with the discovery of appropriate means to achieve a multiplicity of ends, or, as he put it, with a modern temper that "takes destination for granted, and is thrilled by the hum of the engine." However, medieval scholasticism, especially Thomism,

> strains every interest and activity, by however arbitrary a compression, into
> the service of a single idea. The lines of its scheme run up and down, and,
> since its purpose is universal and all-embracing, there is, at least in theory,
> no room for eccentric bodies which move in their own private orbit. That

Pictures of the World published." Emile Mâle, *L'Art religieux du XIIIe siecle en France* (Paris, 1902): chap. 2, trans. by Dora Hussey as *The Gothic Image: Religious Art in France in the Thirteenth Century* (New York, 1958), cited in Denis Hollier, *Against Architecture: The Writings of Georges Bataille* (Cambridge, 1989): 38.

14. St. Thomas Aquinas, *Summa Theologiae*, ed.Thomas Gilby O.P. (Cambridge, 1964): Vol. I, App. I, 43–44.

purpose is set by the divine plan of the universe. . . . Hence all activities fall within a single system, because all, though with different degrees of immediateness, are related to a single end, and derive their significance from it. The Church in its wider sense is the Christian Commonwealth, within which that end is to be realized; in its narrower sense it is the hierarchy divinely commissioned for its interpretation; in both it embraces the whole of life, and its authority is final.[15]

Only one generation separated the Spain of Charles V from the victorious conclusion of seven centuries of war against the Moorish invaders; the emperor's Iberian realm was the creature of that longest of all Christian crusades, fought with fire and sword and without benefit of much philosophy other than that required to satisfy the elemental claims of loyalty and survival. When the rise of Protestantism in the north of Europe again threatened with heresy and dissolution, it was obvious to many of those who meditated on the nature of the crisis that although well-drilled pikemen would be invaluable, they would not suffice to turn back the Protestant tide.

Piety and philosophy were needed as much as swords, and Spain pressed the integrating vigor of Thomism to the task of marshaling those spiritual and political resources that she had in abundance but that were so critically lacking in the capital of Christendom. That she succeeded in this enterprise is demonstrated abundantly by a Counter-Reformation that became the greatest and most enduring achievement of her impressive imperial moment. The conceptual edifice of the crusade against heresy was so strongly put together, in a style so well and essentially suited to the disposition of her people and the circumstance of the challenge, that it has survived virtually unscathed both the passage of time and the frequent visitations of passionate wreckers. The stability of its uncompromising symmetries largely dominates, even to this day, the lives of the Spanish-speaking peoples almost as convincingly and pervasively as the dynamic asymmetries of the Industrial Revolution preside over the English-speaking world. Just as the Reformation was emphatically a European rather than a German phenomenon, the Counter-Reformation was Spanish rather than Italian or European.[16] Certainly

15. Tawney, *Religion and the Rise of Capitalism*, 32–33.
16. The opinions of eminent English-speaking historians notwithstanding. Hugh Trevor-Roper, for example, disagrees with those who affirm that "the Escorial is the expression of the spirit of the Counter-Reformation of which Philip himself was the secular champion." Not so, states Trevor-Roper, "for I do not believe that the Counter-Reformation . . . really corresponded with the ideals of Philip or was willingly forwarded by him. The Counter-Reformation, in its original inspiration, was an Italian movement."

no account of this chef d'oeuvre of Spain's imperial moment can omit reference to the principal importance of the Inquisition and the Compañía de Jesús, the Society of Jesus, in the determination of its character and direction, or to the decisive intervention of the Spanish monarch and of the Jesuits in the making of policy and the definition of doctrine at the Council of Trent; nor is it possible to overlook the creative intimacy that existed between the protagonists of the Counter-Reformation and the blossoming of the Baroque in Naples and Rome as well as in the Castilian heartland and throughout the Indies.

The Inquisition of the Counter-Reformation originated not in the Roman but in the Castilian institution that impressed Cardinal Caraffa, who later became Pope Paul IV, as "a terrible but effective engine of uniformity" when he served as nuncio in Spain. An uncle of the duke of Alba suggested to Caraffa that the best way to save the church in Italy, at that time living through very troubled times indeed, including the open advocacy of Lutheran ideas in Venice and Lucca and a disturbingly enthusiastic and quasi-evangelical armed uprising in Perugia, was to reintroduce the Spanish Inquisition. This opinion was supported by "another Spaniard . . . of great note in history," later known as Saint Ignatius Loyola.[17] Caraffa then conceived the idea of "setting up a centralised, permanent and universal tribunal on the Spanish model,

---

And further, "If Philip, late in his reign, used the forces of the Counter-Reformation in politics, it was always hesitantly, reluctantly, suspiciously. Rather, he was a man of the Anti-Reformation. He looked not forward, but back: back to the serene mental world of the high Renaissance, as yet undisturbed by heresy." While disagreeing with Trevor-Roper, I believe that in the last sentence quoted above lies the clue to what may only be an apparent paradox, for neither Philip nor the Society of Jesus nor the Holy Office, or their successors for the next two centuries and more, ever showed the slightest disposition to compromise, nor did they have any doubts about their preference; given the choice, they would have opted without hesitation for a world both serene and without heresy. Hugh Trevor-Roper, *Princes and Artists: Patronage and Ideology at Four Habsburg Courts, 1517–1633* (New York, 1976): 71–72.

17. The first inquisitors were sent to Aragon by Gregory IX who authorized their activities by the bull *Declinante* of May 26, 1232, but their activities were of marginal importance. The institution languished, and by the fifteenth century it was virtually inoperative. In Castile, the Holy Office was created in 1480 by Ferdinand and Isabella without assistance from the papacy, the result of an unusual combination of national pride, religious zeal, and racial enmity. The Inquisition of the Counter-Reformation was the direct descendant of this Castilian initiative. In 1540, Perugia rebelled "in the name of the Saviour," to whom were offered the keys of the city; coins were minted with the inscription "Perugia, the city of Christ"; the treasures of the churches were seized, and order was only restored when troops stormed the city after a siege. In 1542, Bernardino Ochino, the greatest preacher of his time, vicar-general of the Capuchins since 1536, and almost a cardinal two years later, escaped to join Calvin in Geneva, accompanied by the Augustinian sage, Pietro Martyr Vermigli. The times were indeed troubled for the defenders of Roman orthodoxy. Pierre Janelle, *The Catholic Reformation* (Milwaukee, 1963): 55.

which should operate without exemption of any from its jurisdiction. . . . Heresy was now to be exterminated, not copied or conciliated by reforms." So the Roman Inquisition was established by the bull *Licit ab initio* of July 21, 1542, along the lines suggested by Caraffa, whose advice to the pontiff was decisively supported by two Spaniards, Juan Alvarez de Toledo, Cardinal Archbishop of Burgos, and Ignatius Loyola.[18]

The new inquisitorial office had only tenuous links with the medieval Roman institution or with the one established in Aragon by Pope Gregory IX, both of which had languished and become largely ineffective after an initial period of repression and notoriety. In the Spanish case, the ancient Inquisition of Aragon had been as circumscribed by the reservations of monarchs suspicious of Roman interference as by adverse popular feeling, but the new Inquisition was altogether different, reflecting the regalist zeal of a Castile fired with religious fervor and intent on the elimination of heretical deviations.[19] Two inquisitors general in matters of faith were appointed with a formidable authority "over all sorts and conditions of men . . . to appoint officials, . . . to degrade clerics, . . . to visit opponents with censure, and to call in the aid of the secular arm." And Paul III added that whatever these two very powerful men, or their deputies, did, "we decree to be completely valid and to be observed in perpetuity." The two cardinals entrusted to guide the Holy Office through this decisive period were Alvarez de Toledo and his good friend, the former papal nuncio in Spain, Cardinal Caraffa.[20]

The Inquisition impresses mainly as a repressive and negative instrument of policy, cowing and destroying heretics and dissenters but not necessarily affirming wisdom and piety; its true importance as a structural element in the architecture of the Counter-Reformation can be exaggerated as easily and fruitlessly as it can be unnecessarily diminished. Taken in isolation, it merits attention as a cautionary experience,

18. Kidd, *Counter-Reformation*, 42–43.
19. The resurrection of the Holy Office in Castile was principally directed against the defeated Moslems; it was in a sense, a "national Inquisition," established without direct papal support, save for a perfunctory enabling bull from Sixtus IV, and mainly directed against local dissidence. Domínguez Ortiz, *El antiguo régimen*, 23–31.
20. There was an intriguing touch of populism in the procedures of the Holy Office. Caraffa issued four basic rules for the conduct of the investigations: first, the Inquisitors must punish even on suspicion; second, they must have no regard for the great; third, they must use greater severity against those who shelter behind the powerful; fourth, they must show no mildness, least of all against Calvinists. The former nuncio and future pope believed that the highest duty was to strike at those in high places "for on their punishment the salvation of the classes beneath them depends." Kidd, *Counter-Reformation*, 43–44.

replete with horrifying anecdotes not altogether untypical of the Europe of that period. What is important is that it did not occur in isolation but was bound up intimately with other decisive Spanish contributions to the Catholic Reformation, including the foundation of the Compañía de Jesús, the most influential and characteristic order of the many founded at that time to address the crisis of belief and renewal.[21]

Macaulay was attuned to the consensus when he affirmed last century that in the Society of Jesus was concentrated "the quintessence of the Catholic spirit" and that its history could be taken to be the history of the Counter-Reformation.[22] So much has been written about the Jesuits and their nefarious or beneficent actions that it should be unnecessary to rehearse here the details of their origins, their rapid early develop-ment, their identification with the crusade of the Counter-Reformation, their subsequent expulsion from most of the principal Christian king-doms, and the reputation earned by their members for worldliness, learning, and political adroitness.[23] What must be said, that bears rep-etition, is that the Compañía was conceived by a Spaniard and founded by Spaniards, at a time when Spain was gaining the upper hand in her struggles with France over Italy and Spaniards were becoming masters of much of the country;[24] that its internal organization mirrored the

21. After some interesting opposition from the conservative papal bureaucracy, Pope Paul III issued the bull *Regimini militantis ecclesiae*, which gave formal birth to the *So-cietas Jesu* in September 1540.

22. Macaulay, *Historical Essays*, "Von Ranke," 550–551. Nearer our time, a histo-rian of the period concurs, describing the Society of Jesus as the greatest and the most typical of the Counter-Reformation orders. Henry Kamen, *The Iron Century: Social Change in Europe, 1550–1660* (London, 1971): 234.

23. Macaulay thought that the latitude of the Society merited attention. "The gay cavalier who had run his rival through the body, the frail beauty who had forgotten her marriage-vow, found in the Jesuit an easy well-bred man of the world, who knew how to make allowance for the little irregularities of people of fashion. The confessor was strict or lax, according to the temper of the penitent. The first object was to drive no person out of the pale of the Church. Since there were bad people, it was better that they should be bad Catholics than bad Protestants." Macaulay, *Historical Essays*, "Von Ranke," 551.

24. This did not invariably endear them to the Italians. The sack of Rome had not vanished from people's memories, and in Rome all Spaniards, "even priests, and those Romans who consorted with them, were regarded with suspicion and dislike. . . . The Popes with whom Ignatius had to deal were generally anti-Spanish, even if they sometimes found it prudent to conceal the fact. Paul IV died of apoplexy brought on by a violent outburst of rage at Spanish arrogance. . . . Ignatius's friendship with some Italians and recruitment of a good many more into his Society did not, in the eyes of most Romans, offset his Spanish nationality, pride and lifelong inability to master the Italian language." Of the original ten founders of the Society, including Ignatius, five were Spaniards. When Loyola died, the Spanish Jesuit superiors refused to travel to Rome for the election of the new general, demanding that the election take place in Spain and that the headquarters of the Society be placed there permanently. Philip II was at the time at war with the Papal

centralist political arrangements associated with the genesis and early decades of the Spanish imperial moment, with a key role assigned to compulsory dependence and a rigid hierarchy as bulwarks against unwanted individualism and the consequential risk of disorder; that they brought to the education of the young systematic skills and zeal without precedent, making the foundation and efficient running of schools one of the principal instruments of their apostolate; and that what distinguished the Compañía most tellingly during those critical decades was the importance it assigned to its novel vow of obedience. "Other religious associations," wrote Loyola, "may exceed us in fastings, in vigils, and the like rigorous observances; it behoves our brethren to be pre-eminent in true and absolute obedience, in abnegation of all individual will and judgment,"[25] and to make his meaning absolutely clear, he added that "obedience must be cultivated . . . first to the Pope, then to superiors . . . to keep ourselves right in all things we ought to hold this point: what I see as white I would believe black if the hierarchical Church determined it so."[26]

The extraordinary effectiveness of the Compañía during the demanding vicissitudes of the Counter-Reformation was not a consequence solely of the aptness of articles and regulations contained in a less or more exacting constitution, or of skillful spiritual exercises, or binding vows of obedience and rigorous discipline, but principally of the passionate and exemplary leadership of Loyola, whose "activity and zeal bore down all opposition." Loyola interpreted correctly the temper of the times and placed in the hands of his followers the intellectual and moral weaponry required by the very special circumstances of the challenge to the Catholic faith. To dismiss the methods and the intentions of the Jesuits simply as clever casuistry or disingenuous probabilism is entirely to misunderstand their contribution to the prowess of the Counter-Reformation. Quite the opposite approach is required to begin to comprehend the zeal and the commitment that Ignatius's *Exercises* and regulations inspired when interpreted, during and after his life, by his Jesuit brethren.

States and obliged by forbidding all Spanish Jesuits permission to go to Rome. J. C. H. Aveling, *The Jesuits* (London, 1981): 96, 124.

25. W. C. Cartwright, *The Jesuits: Their Constitution and Teaching* (London, 1876): 15.

26. Aveling, *Jesuits*, 120.

It has been suggested that rhetoric lies at the very heart of the Baroque disposition. If this is so, then it is fitting to appeal to Macaulay's sedate Victorian rhetoric to attempt to recapture the well-ordered enthusiasm with which the Jesuits led the Catholic renewal and helped to bring about the triumphant moment of the Baroque. Under Loyola's leadership, affirmed the historian, the Society of Jesus

> grew rapidly to the full measure of his gigantic powers. With what vehemence, with what policy, with what exact discipline, with what dauntless courage, with what self-denial, with what forgetfulness of the dearest private ties, with what intense and stubborn devotion to a single end, with what unscrupulous laxity and versatility in the choice of means, the Jesuits fought the battle of their church, is written in every page of the annals of Europe during several generations. . . . That [Jesuit] order possessed itself at once of all the strongholds which command the public mind, of the pulpit, of the press, of the confessional, of the academies. Wherever the Jesuit preached, the church was too small for the audience. The name of Jesuit on a title-page secured the circulation of a book. It was in the ears of the Jesuit that the powerful, the noble, and the beautiful, breathed the secret history of their lives. It was at the feet of the Jesuit that the youth of the higher and middle classes were brought up from childhood to manhood, from the first rudiments to the courses of rhetoric and philosophy. Literature and science, lately associated with infidelity or with heresy, now became the allies of orthodoxy. . . . Nor was it less their office to plot against the thrones and lives of apostate kings, to spread evil rumours, to raise tumults, to inflame civil wars, to arm the hand of the assassin. Inflexible in nothing but in their fidelity to the church.[27]

Except as a label of convenience, there has never been a single historical occurrence, or a series of occurrences, with a distinct beginning and an end called "the Counter-Reformation," but there can be no doubt that there was a Council of Trent. The use of the term "Counter-Reformation" has even given rise to some controversy,[28] and there are those who would prefer to see it discarded in favor of "Catholic Reformation," or "Catholic Renewal"; no such reservations affect the Council of Trent, which began its deliberations in 1545, largely under the auspices of Charles V and with the reluctant acquiescence of the Papacy, and met intermittently during the following eighteen years, until its final adjournment in 1563. The council provided the efficient channel into which converged the various responses of the Catholic church to

27. Macaulay, *Historical Essays*, "Von Ranke," 550–551.
28. Among the weightier objections, that of none other than Maravall, who considered "untenable" the use of the term "Counter-Reformation." José Antonio Maravall, *La cultura del barroco: Análisis de una estructura histórica* (Barcelona, 1983): 47.

the challenge of the Reformation and flowed on like a majestic torrent in a direction that was as consistent with the wishes of the Spanish monarch and the Society of Jesus as it was respectful and deferential toward the Holy Father. Those who toiled in the Tridentine harvest brought in the fruits of years of work by the neo-Thomists, the Holy Office, the Jesuits, and the Spanish Crown and placed them in the hands of the bishop of Rome.

It would clearly be untenable to assign solely to Spain the responsibility for the convocation, the tenor of the discussions, and the ultimate consequences of the council; phenomena such as these are not susceptible of simplistic causal attributions. And yet, it is impossible to ignore the Spanish imprint on an initiative that obviously would not have occurred in the absence of the emperor's insistence, nor would it have found political support and doctrinal commitment elsewhere in Europe remotely comparable to the one it received from Philip II and the Society of Jesus. It was only later, especially toward the latter sessions of the council it had done so much to postpone, that Rome found a sufficiency of that necessary courage and zeal, the dearth of which had largely precipitated the crisis, to support the uncompromising positions defended by the Spaniards.

Although it is very clear that the desire substantially to reform the Church was widespread and that it had many and distinguished precursors in regions other than those that rallied to Luther immediately before and after his "Here I stand" at Worms,[29] Marcelino Menéndez Pelayo cannot be faulted for asserting that the Council of Trent "was as Spanish as it was ecumenical," nor can Spanish historians be dismissed as overly nationalistic for directing the attention of their readers to the crucial role that their compatriots played during the three stages of the council or for naming the most conspicuous among them.[30] Other historians believe that the Spanish participation at Trent is fundamental to a proper understanding of why it was in Spain and the Indies that the Tridentine postulates were embraced most faithfully.[31] The problem, however, is

29. No account of the antecedents of the Reformation and the Counter-Reformation can leave out, for example, the extraordinary work of Francisco Jiménez de Cisneros (1436–1517), Archbishop of Toledo, who succeeded in reforming the Spanish monastic orders and died in peace without ever having heard of Luther.

30. Regla went to the trouble of noting that 163 Spaniards took part in the deliberations of the council. Juan Regla, "La época de los tres primeros Austrias," in J. Vicens Vives, ed., Historia de España y América, 71.

31. Among the earliest responses to the decisions of the Tridentine fathers must be counted the one from the Synod of Quito in 1570, which singled out the use of imagery for emphatic support through a decree ordering priests to explain to the Indians that "the

not simply one of listing Spanish ecclesiastics distinguished at Trent but of understanding that the ones whose voices and votes truly decided the crucial issues discussed in that council never even intended to travel to the banks of the Adige. Of course, no one can fairly ignore the weighty contribution to the proceedings of the Jesuits Laínez and Salmerón, of Cardinal Pacheco, of the archbishop of Braga, of the Dominicans Melchor Cano and Pedro and Domingo de Soto, the Franciscans Francisco de Orantes and Francisco de Zamora, and the canonists Antonio Agustín and Diego Covarrubias, and many others, but their impressive work at Trent was only a distant reflection of the passionate faith that animated the Spain of Saint Teresa of Avila, Saint John of the Cross, Saint Peter of Alcántara, Saint John of God, and so many others whose intellectual stature, literary genius, selflessness, and piety adorn the great century of the Spanish ascendancy. It was their devotion to others, their austerity, their scarcely disguised contempt for the worldliness of the capital of Christendom that inspired the tenacious and intransigent defense of orthodoxy characteristic of the Spanish position at Trent. It was not just a handful of eager clerics and overenthusiastic bureaucrats acting on their own behalf but the spiritual ambassadors of a nation fired with a victorious faith that gave the architecture of Trent a shape that was decisive, lasting, and in accordance with the Spanish conception of things.

When the weighty matters of sin and justification were discussed at Trent, it was the vigorous insistence of the Spanish bishops and especially of the Jesuits on the necessity of good works for justification and salvation that proved decisive. What was at issue was whether salvation could be attained by faith alone; whether faith without good works is worth anything; whether it is possible to attain a private certainty of salvation without the assistance and participation of the mystical body of the Church. There were delegates who represented a liberal Catholic tradition, keenly interested in preventing an irreversible schism, and consequently committed to a latitudinarian definition that would keep open the door of compromise, but their efforts were frustrated by the Spaniards under the unwavering leadership of Laínez, who rejected any for-

---

crucifixes and images of Our Lady and the Saints . . . are a manner of writing to represent and help them to comprehend that which they represent, and that they should have them in great veneration, and that when they prayed to those images, that they should do it in the knowledge of God, Saint Mary and the Saints, as the Sacred Council at Trent has ordered." Isabel Cruz de Amenábar, *Arte y sociedad en Chile, 1550–1650* (Santiago, 1986): 34–35.

mula that could conceivably be construed as a subordination of good works to faith. Their intransigence brought about a spirited argument that was only resolved when, by 32 votes to 5, the council formally adopted a definition in strict accordance with the position of Saint Thomas Aquinas.[32] The breach with Protestantism was made absolute. The Jesuits had succeeded in impressing on the council a definition that was active, participatory, and communitarian rather than passive; salvation could not be attained simply by accepting a gift of divine grace privately discerned and defined but had to be earned actively, conquered by good works and a good life lived within the Christian community. This truly momentous decision set the style of the Counter-Reformation, away from the private quest for personal salvation and toward the spiritual healing and the salvation of all men. In short, it turned "from prayer to activity, from contemplation to apostolate";[33] from the introspective diversities of the Gothic to the public symmetries of the Baroque.

The secular militancy implicit in this decision influenced all the subsequent arrangements decreed by the council, especially those affecting the liturgy, the conduct of the Mass, the modes of public participation, and the place of the arts in worship. Against the Protestant stance, the council stressed the importance of the Sacrifice of the Mass and insisted that the faithful should be able to follow and understand the actions of the officiant. Consequently, the Jesuits designed the interior of their churches so that the sanctuary should be visible from every part of the building and every member of the congregation could observe the priest at the altar. Preaching was singled out by the council as a duty of bishops and clergy, and this led to the placing of the pulpit in a central position in the nave. Acoustics became a matter of concern, and the new churches were designed as a species of lecture hall, without obstructing pillars, aisles, and other interfering features that could render the voice of the preacher inaudible in parts of the building. That these matters of design were not of marginal importance is shown by the requirement that the plans of all projected Jesuit churches be sent to the father general of the Society for approval before construction could begin.[34] The effectiveness of this central control is evidenced by the similarity of the Jesuit churches built during the first century after the Council of Trent. Making allowances for slight changes here and there dictated by local conditions, they can be described collectively as a series of inspired variations on the

32. Spitz, *Protestant Reformation*, 313.
33. Kamen, *Iron Century*, 232.
34. Janelle, *Catholic Reformation*, 172–175.

single theme of Giacomo da Vignola's Gesù, in Rome, which was started in the immediate aftermath of Trent and has rightly been considered ever since as the quintessentially Tridentine church.

The fathers at Trent were as clear in their intention to assign a centrally defined religious purpose to painting and sculpture as they had been in the case of architecture. Their approach to the problem can be described very simply: the arts must be functionally subordinated to the requirements of religion, and it is the responsibility of the Church to determine their mode and direction. These views were incorporated in that now famous decree on the arts in which the bishops are instructed to teach

> that the story of the mysteries of our Redemption, expressed by paintings or other representations, instructs and confirms the people in remembering and assiduously rehearsing the articles of the faith; that sacred images are the source of great spiritual profit, not only because the people are thus reminded of the blessings and help which Christ has granted them but also because the marvels and wholesome examples of God are through his saints placed before the eyes of the faithful, so that they may thank God for them, and rule their life and manners after those of the saints, and may be incited to worship and love God, and cultivate piety.[35]

This was not merely an expression of hope but a firm directive and justification based on the most convincing argument possible—that the manner of life of the faithful could be influenced by what they saw with their eyes. Additionally, there can be no doubt that in thus defending the value of imagery, the Tridentine fathers had found a brilliant and attractive argument to use against the iconoclasm of the Protestants, and the opportunity that this offered was not wasted.

> Against the Protestantism that forever divides Christendom, post-Tridentine Catholicism opposed a formidable repertoire of images as an effective, far-reaching weaponry for the conquest by the true faith of the vast and mostly illiterate masses of Europe and America. . . . More than aesthetically appropriate, the art of the Counter-Reformation is ethically correct; more than a technique for the creation of beauty, it is directed to the glorification of God. . . . Ecclesiastical art acquires an official character in the Catholic countries, that is also transplanted to America. The Church is not interested in art being "creative" or "imaginative," but in it being fundamentally instructive, seductive and emotive, and that it should reflect orthodoxy in an unequivocal way, free from capricious interpretations. . . . Compared with the

35. Ibid., 160.

dangers of artistic freedom, the production of stereotypes is regarded very much as the lesser evil.[36]

Among the great achievements of the Baroque must be counted the revival of images and of the visual arts generally—and of the skills required to produce them—and their inspired enlistment in one of the greatest attempts of persuasion ever undertaken, a fact consistent with the scholarly consensus that has for so long assigned an Aristotelian origin to the poetics and the rhetoric that preside over this whole epoch.[37] Rhetoric is the art of persuasion, and the Tridentine fathers decided that to discharge successfully the principal task of convincing large numbers of people to reject Protestantism and return to their traditional faith, they could make legitimate and very practical use of the immediacy of visual demonstration, thus opening the door to the encouragement of the more spectacular and dramatic forms of imagery and representation, whether in religious ritual, the theater, popular processions, or the proliferation of emblematic and allegorical themes in architecture, and the magnificent preponderance of painting over all the arts of the period.[38]

This should not require reiteration, but if proof were needed of its wide and lasting influence, the manner in which Peter Paul Rubens responded to the Tridentine appeal should suffice to make the point. A devout Catholic, the artist worked closely with the Jesuits in the design, construction, and decoration of the great Antwerp church dedicated to the founder of the Order. Rubens had already executed, in Rome in 1609, some illustrations for the life of Saint Ignatius, but his most important collaborative enterprise with the Society of Jesus was in this vast marble temple, "the most magnificent of its kind in the country,"[39] for which he agreed to provide thirty-nine paintings and to design a pair of imposing altarpieces representing the miracles of Saint Ignatius and Saint Francis Xavier, foremost among the Spanish champions of the Counter-Reformation, mounted and arranged with pulleys and counterweights so that they could be either exhibited in accordance with the requirements of the church calendar or stored in the crypt below the

36. Cruz de Amenábar, Arte y sociedad, 35.
37. Santiago Sebastian, Contrarreforma y barroco: Lecturas iconográficas e iconológicas (Madrid, 1985): 14.
38. Maravall has examined convincingly and in detail this important aspect of the Baroque in an Appendix that is virtually an essay in its own right. See "Objetivos sociopolíticos del empleo de medios visuales," Apéndice, in Maravall, Barroco, 499–524.
39. Helen Braham, Rubens, Paintings, Drawings, Prints, in the Princes Gate Collection (Courtauld Institute Galleries, University of London, 1988): 2.

high altar.[40] Neither unintended nor capricious, the theatricality of these displays and the emphatic and skillful use of art as propaganda were not restricted to the ecclesiastical realm; Rubens was also responsible for the design and construction of "the most spectacular of all ceremonial structures," the grand Porticus Caesareo-Austriaca, erected in Antwerp in 1635 to welcome the Cardenal-Infante Ferdinand, brother of King Philip VI (who with his Queen was the subject of Velázquez's *Meninas*), when he arrived to assume his duties as governor of the Netherlands. The portico had massive proportions and its plan, based on a deep curve, brings to mind Bernini's curved colonnade at Saint Peter's, executed twenty years later. Flanked by life-size statues of the twelve Hapsburg emperors and decorated profusely with appropriately symbolic inscriptions and allusive designs, including a series of "pillars of Hercules" wrapped in scrolls bearing Charles V's motto *Plus ultra*, it made the most forceful political statement imaginable in a country torn by war.[41] This intention was equally evident in the elaborate displays designed by Rubens on the occasion of the Joyeuse Entrée of the Cardenal-Infante into the principal cities of the Netherlands, culminating at Antwerp with an abundance and magnificence worthy of Rubens's ability to cloak "political statements in splendid visual imagery."[42]

There remained the poetics of the problem, of harnessing the requirements of mimesis to the principle *ut pictura poesis*, essential when approaching nature, discerning its ethical condition, or aspiring to similitude. A number of theologians came to the rescue, the most influential of which was the Jesuit Antonio Posevino, who explained that to be useful, painting had to be truthful. "I assert," he wrote, "that the highest pitch of art consists in imitating reality, the martyrdoms of martyrs, the tears of those who weep, the pain of those who suffer, the glory and joy of those who come to life again." To attain this necessary truthfulness, the artist should endeavor to feel what he wants to represent. "In order that the most fatal death of Christ our Redeemer . . . should breed ad-

---

40. Two other paintings by followers of Rubens were later added to the repertoire: Segher's *Raising of the Cross* and Schut's *Coronation of the Virgin*. The new church of the Jesuit College of Antwerp was first dedicated in 1621 to the Blessed Virgin and the Blessed Ignatius Loyola, but a year later, when Loyola was canonized, it was rededicated to Saint Ignatius alone. Destroyed by a fire in 1718, the church was rebuilt along its original design, though in a less grandiose fashion, and once again rededicated, on this occasion to Saint Charles Borromeo. Braham, *Rubens*, 2.

41. Braham, *Rubens*, 14–15.

42. "The propaganda of the displays was . . . unusually pointed, adulation of the ruler and the House of Hapsburg being followed by pleas for peace and prosperity for the city stricken by the results of hostilities." Braham, *Rubens*, 14.

miration and a sharp grief in others, it is needful that something in the soul of the painter should rouse the greatness of admiration and draw forth the rushing of grief."[43]

The forceful religious renewal became art and architecture, and the measured gesture, the witty worldliness, the elegant restraint of the Renaissance Spring of the Italians gave way, overwhelmed by the triumphant flowering of the Baroque Counter-Reformation in that High Summer of imperial Spain. The art that crossed the Atlantic to the Indies was imbued with this Baroque pragmatism of the Counter-Reformation; its object was not to interpret nature or please the senses but to propagate and glorify the true faith. Without this essential dimension very clearly in mind, the risk of misunderstanding is not negligible because, as a distinguished student of this period has asserted, "from the romantic vantage point of 'art for art's sake,' free, unhindered and original, neither the buildings, nor the paintings or the sculptures of Viceregal America will ever reveal their true meaning."[44]

43. Posevino also objected strongly to the painting or sculpting of pagan and lascivious images. The devil, he explained, incensed at being thrown out of the Indies where his sanctuaries were being obliterated, was counterattacking in Europe with two formidable weapons: unchaste books and "outrageous images of nude women, of fauns and satyrs, infamous statues, and even fragments of idols dug out of the bowels of the earth." Janelle, *Catholic Reformation*, 161–162. An observer need not be a cynic to note the resemblance between the well-intentioned Tridentine policy toward the visual arts and that espoused, many centuries later, by authoritarian regimes in Germany, Russia, and China. Certainly the Maoist "Cultural Revolution" and Zhdanov's "socialist realism" were not immensely dissimilar, albeit with very different objectives in mind, to what Father Posevino had in mind.
44. Cruz de Amenábar, *Arte y sociedad*, 36.

Baroque Hedgehogs

The Baroque offers a magnificently appropriate metaphor for the golden summit of the Spaniards, replete with richly suggestive modes and manifestations, including the sobering awareness that in its aftermath, there has been little else but a steady and melancholy descent. Since Jacob Burckhardt and Wilhelm Lübcke gave international currency to the otherwise obscure word "Baroque," a number of scholars have adopted it as an apposite descriptive term for one of the more interesting periods in the history of the Christian Mediterranean in general and, more controversially, for Counter-Reformation Spain in particular.[1] This latter usage is in part the paradoxical and obviously fortuitous consequence of equivocal statements by Burckhardt's disciple and eventual successor

---

1. The term "Baroque" was first proposed in 1855 simultaneously by Jacob Burckhardt in his seminal *Der Cicerone* and by Wilhelm Lübcke in his *Geschichte der Architektur*. Among those authors who noted the affinity between the Baroque and the epoch of the Counter-Reformation can be mentioned Alois Riegl, *Die Entstehung der Barockkunst in Rom* (Vienna, 1908); Werner Weisbach, *Der Barock als Kunst der Gegenreformation* (Munich, 1921); and Sacheverell Sitwell, *Southern Baroque Art* (London, 1924). In his University of London lectures of 1939, Weisbach summarized the orthodox position by stating simply that "Baroque art has for Spain an especial importance in so far as there is reflected in it something intrinsically national and Spanish" and that "Counter-Reformation and Absolutism found their expressive symbols in the creations of the baroque style." Werner Weisbach, *Spanish Baroque Art* (Cambridge, 1941): 6–7. Any short list of recent scholarly contributions to the subject must include Santiago Sebastián's *Contrarreforma y barroco: Lecturas iconográficas e iconológicas*, the title of which is itself a statement about the characteristically Baroque importance accorded to imagery by the Council of Trent.

in the chair of art history at Basle; in his seminal essay, *Renaissance und Barock*, published in 1888, Heinrich Wölfflin went out of his way to disassociate himself from what he described disparagingly as the *kulturhistorisch* approach to the understanding of style. "What has Gothic to do with the feudal system or with scholasticism? What bridge connects Jesuitism with the baroque? Is there aesthetic significance in the fact that the Jesuits forced their spiritual system on the individual and made him sacrifice his rights to the idea of the whole?"[2] Wölfflin dismissed these rhetorical questions loftily, adding that "little is gained by enumerating such general cultural forces" and inviting his readers, rather disconcertingly, to examine the possibility of resolving the problem by making analogous comparisons between architecture and the human body.[3] The questions, however, would not vanish. Nor did his "corporeal" arguments prove satisfying, even to himself, and in an essay published late in life, in 1940, he reversed dramatically his original stance by affirming that "the Baroque is incomprehensible without the spirit of the Counter-Reformation."[4]

This volte-face clarified one issue but obscured another, because considered in this context, the term "Counter-Reformation" leaves out too much, and what is retained within its boundaries has an unnecessarily negative and derivative emphasis that does not disappear—it may even

2. Heinrich Wölfflin, *Renaissance and Baroque*, trans. Kathrin Simon (London, 1966): 76–77. The problem of where Mannerism ends and Baroque begins remains. Wölfflin, for example, has been criticized for assuming an uninterrupted transition between the Renaissance and the Baroque, thus ignoring the Mannerist interlude. Pevsner was unimpressed by Mannerism but did not ignore it. "If balance and harmony are the chief characteristics of the High Renaissance, Mannerism is the very reverse; for it is unbalanced, discordant art—now emotional to distortion, . . . now disciplined to self-effacement. . . . The High Renaissance is full, Mannerism is meagre." Nikolaus Pevsner, *An Outline of European Architecture* (London, 1951): 136. It could be argued that Mannerism was predominantly a Roman pause, almost a diversion, in a European progression that led to a Baroque rooted in Naples, Spain, and Germany as well as in the Holy City and that this would explain the dearth of Mannerist work in the Spanish cradle of the Counter-Reformation.

3. He had evidently read Vico, for his explanation is almost a paraphrase of the Neapolitan's observations on the origins of metaphor: "We interpret the whole outside world according to the expressive system with which we have become familiar from our own bodies," but then he moves in a novel direction by suggesting that "it is clear that architecture, an art of corporeal masses, can relate only to man as a corporeal being. It is an expression of its time in so far as it reflects the corporeal essence of man and his particular habits of deportment and movement. . . . In a word, architecture expresses the *Lebensgefühl* of an epoch." And even more boldly, he asserted that "the significance of reducing stylistic forms into terms of the human body is that it provides us with an immediate expression of the spiritual." Wölfflin, *Baroque*, 77–78, 80.

4. This important statement is found in a 1940 Appendix added to a short essay entitled *Das Erklären von Kunstwerken*, published originally in 1921. Peter Murray, Introduction, in Wölfflin, *Baroque*, 3–4.

be exacerbated—when substituted by "Catholic Reformation" or "Catholic Renewal." It is undeniable that the cultural antecedents associated with the Counter-Reformation originated many generations before Luther and had an influence that went beyond the ecclesiastical enterprise, but it is nonetheless true that many developments associated with the Baroque were the direct consequence of activities by entities that owed their existence to the Catholic resurgence, especially those associated with the Society of Jesus. Fernand Braudel has even suggested that the adjective "Jesuit" should be preferred to "Baroque" as a fitting descriptive term for the artistic and religious expansion characteristic of the period.[5] It appears that in this instance, as is the case in so many other controversial issues in cultural interpretation, a generous approach facilitates understanding, which here would require noting that these two sets of facts are complementary rather than contradictory and that neither clashes with a Baroque style and disposition more readily associated with extravagance than with parsimony.

By the time Wölfflin changed his mind, the bridge between Counter-Reformation and Baroque had been in use for many decades, and those who thronged across it, backward and forward, could not ignore the crucial Spanish involvement in the great religious enterprise and, even if only by implication, its influence on the literature, the architecture, the political arrangements, and the visual arts of the period.[6] The Baroque is a creature of the Counter-Reformation but transcends it and per-

5. Braudel, *The Mediterranean*, II: 831. About the multiplicity of factors associated with both the Baroque and the Counter-Reformation and trascending both, see Maravall, *Barroco*, 47; also Philip Butler, *Classicisme et Baroque dans l'oeuvre de Racine* (Paris, Nizet, 1959): 50.

6. Wölfflin established a link between the Baroque in literature and the visual arts, pointing out that the essential differences between the Renaissance and the Baroque were as tellingly reflected in the distance between *Orlando furioso*, published in 1516, and *Gerusalemne liberata*, which appeared in 1575, as in any work of sculpture, painting, or architecture. As Segel explains, Wölfflin understood Ariosto's epic to be "in mood and language, simple, cheerful, and lively; Tasso's, on the other hand, has a world-weary hero, is 'heavier' in rhythm and sentence structure, and grander in lexicon and imagery." Harold B. Segel, *The Baroque Poem: A Comparative Survey* (New York, 1974): 16–17. Further, Wölfflin saw the atmosphere of that post-Renaissance period as "fundamentally solemn. This solemnity was brought to bear in all spheres of life: religious conscience, a renewed distinction between the worldly and the ecclesiastical, the ceasing of the uninhibited enjoyment of life. . . . In social intercourse the general tone became formal and solemn; the light and easy grace of the Renaissance gave way to seriousness and dignity, the gay playfulness to pompous, rustling splendour." Wölfflin, *Baroque*, 83–84.

Finally, Segel also notes that the great Spanish religious writers of the period reflected "the fervor of post-Tridentine Catholicism" and explains that he mentions their influence, especially that of the Spanish mystics, because of their importance not only within Spain but outside as well. Segel, *Baroque Poem*, 72–73.

meates the social and political life of the whole epoch in ways that are convincingly and especially consonant with the mood, the strengths, the weaknesses, the brilliance, and the miseries of Spain's great moment in history. Undoubtedly, the Baroque flourished in many other European countries, but nowhere else did it find such a vast and fitting stage, such a satisfying partnership with imperial power, such an effortless accord with the mood of a nation, as it did in Spain and her Indies. To the modern mind, the Golden Age of Spain appears intriguing, at times almost incomprehensible, because it was neither uniquely nor principally the consequence of economic prosperity or unhindered imperial preponderance. The explanation, however, must be sought in the religious well-being of a country largely cleansed of heresy and with its spiritual ramparts well and truly manned.

Rodó's oversimple explanations notwithstanding, it is evidently true that supreme confidence can be founded on the tangible material affluence that comes from economic buoyancy; it can also be the outcome of the very real spiritual well-being achieved by participating in a victorious crusade to ensure the survival of the true faith. We know best, because we have been well served by the assiduous researches of statisticians and economic historians, and can affirm with confidence that during the latter years under the Emperor Charles V, the Spanish treasury was technically insolvent, that this situation did not improve during the whole reign of Philip II, and that the fiscal penury endured under both reigns was such that from time to time the Crown was not above using dishonorable means to ease its financial difficulties.[7] The monarch knew this, and so did his ministers, his agents, and his victims. The rest of the Spanish world did not and basked in the glory of centuries of crusading victories, first against the Moors of the south and now against the Protestants of the north. Contemporaries did not think the Spain of the aftermath of Trent exceptionally vulnerable. Quite the opposite, the overriding impression conveyed by the "Prudent King" was one of quiet, understated strength sustaining a vocation for victory befitting the champion of the Catholic religion. Financial matters were at worst an irritant; at best, properly subordinate to the moral purposes for which they were expected to supply the necessary means. Spain was a glorious

---

7. "In order to meet the deficit the Emperor was compelled to resort to a number of expedients, such as appropriating the remittances of American silver to private individuals—as happened on no less than nine occasions during his reign—and 'compensating' the victims with *juros*, or Government bonds." Elliott, *Imperial Spain*, 206.

realm not because of her efficient bookkeeping but because in a world
racked by doubt and confusion, she was steadfast in her faith, and her
armies were invincible in battle.

Braudel asserted in 1949 that the Baroque "drew its strength both
from the huge spiritual force of the Holy Roman Empire and from the
huge temporal force of the Spanish Empire," but it can be argued that
his attribution to the Holy Roman Empire of a "huge spiritual force"
was excessively generous, and his reference to Spain's participation, astonishingly austere.[8] This kind of evenhanded interpretation has gained
currency, and in the process, nuances have vanished and the oversimple
contrast has prevailed. A few years after Braudel, Paul Johnson felt able
to assert that "the essence of the Counter-Reformation . . . was Spanish
power. It was not a religious movement. It had no specific programme,
other than the negative one of stamping out Protestant 'error.'"[9] Apart
from the questionable—and anachronistic—attribution of religious significance to the possession of a "specific programme," this is unfairly
dismissive of what proved to be the decisive and specifically religious
contribution of the Spanish mystics, the Spanish orders, certainly including the Compañía de Jesús, and the Spanish theologians. Spain's
spiritual participation in the Counter-Reformation was certainly as significant as that of her well-trained tercios, perhaps even more so, and
although both Counter-Reformation and Baroque owed much to Rome,
neither found in the fragile *imperium* of the pontiff or the corrupt and
vulnerable Roman polity a sufficiency of support and inspiration for its
universal venture. It is impossible to apportion precise responsibilities
in complex matters of this kind, but the circumstances and the eventual
outcome of the great religious crusade suggest most forcibly that without
the stiffening of Spanish power and religious intransigence, the importance of the Counter-Reformation and its Baroque inheritance would
have been extraordinarily circumscribed.

All metaphors are open to the charge of falsehood, and architectural
metaphors are not an exception. Societies are neither buildings nor built
like houses, palaces, or cathedrals; domes are not designed by hedgehogs, and foxes do not feel particularly at home in parish churches with
flat roofs. One distinct pattern of human action, or institution, or habitual profession, or academic discipline should not be confused with
another, even metaphorically, and this is so true that there has never

8. Braudel, *The Mediterranean*, II: 827.
9. Paul Johnson, *A History of Christianity* (London, 1976): 298.

been a dearth of scholars prepared to point out, for example, that Ruskin erred when he confused theology with architecture and that we are well advised to clarify this confusion so that architecture can "confine itself to the construction of good buildings; and religion . . . to spiritual truth."[10] Objections such as these are invariably plausible, often learned, and mostly founded on common sense, and yet, it is impossible to ignore the fact that after many centuries of severe scholarship and an abundance of earthy common sense, untruthful metaphors in general and untruthful architectural metaphors in particular have not been dislodged from the arsenal of devices that prove helpful when trying to understand human society. Antique buildings are not societies, but the Parthenon is fifth-century Athens and Harlech Castle is not; societies are not designed like palaces, but Versailles is the France of Louis XIV and El Escorial is not; cathedrals are not mirrors of society, but no one could doubt the Spanishness of Santiago de Compostela or Murcia, or the Englishness of Salisbury, Wells, and Lincoln. Architectural metaphors may be dismissed as facile but only by accepting their validity; to note that a metaphor is obvious is not to refute it, especially if what we expect from it is to help make explicit, to illuminate, to elicit essential features that otherwise would remain less visible, or even invisible.

The Baroque is much more than a stylistic intermezzo between Mannerism and Neo-Classicism; certainly more than a serviceable name for the art of the Counter-Reformation. The Baroque is a metaphor for Spain and her Indies at their triumphant best. It is a reminder of imperial greatness, an obstacle to dissolution, a technique for the preservation of unity, an alibi for the central control of diversity, a justification for the pursuit of glory, a noble excuse for the recurrence of defeat. More important still, especially in the context of this work, the Baroque is an assertion of stability, a refusal to give way, a glorification of obstinacy, an affirmation of belief, an indictment of change as an illusion, a reiteration of faith in things as they are, a rejection of the lure of things as they could be; the Baroque is the mode of the hedgehog.

Maravall preferred the usage "culture of the Baroque" and described it as *un concepto de época*, an epochal concept, corresponding to the hundred years that separate the time of Philip the Prudent from the time of Charles the Bewitched.[11] He also wrote a couple of perfunctory paragraphs to explain, unconvincingly, that he was addressing his subject in

10. Quinlan Terry, "Classical Architecture and the Christian Faith," unpublished paper read at the Department of Philosophy, Kings College London, February 22, 1990.
11. Maravall, *Barroco*, 48.

general terms and that the references to Spain were there only to illustrate the nuances of the general phenomenon when considered from a special vantage point. Uncomfortable with this qualification, he added, "To say Spanish Baroque is the equivalent of saying European Baroque, as seen from Spain. It is possible, and it is perhaps convenient as well, to write about the Baroque in a single country, but only if one remembers to keep the [national] theme within its general context." He indicated nonetheless that because of the principal importance of events in Spain during this Baroque period, Spanish influence and participation in European affairs had been altogether exceptional and decisive.[12] This disclaimer is either overcautious or unnecessary. The Baroque, like the Gothic before it and the classic and Gothic revivals that followed, reached many different countries where they were shaped and reshaped by regional factors and conditions until they acquired a character that not infrequently was effortlessly associated with that particular locality.

To observe that occurrences within Spain weighed decisively elsewhere in Europe would seem to be at least as important as to note that their influence in the Indies was very great and that among them the culture of the Baroque requires special attention. While in the rest of Europe the Baroque was only one stage in a continuing series, in Spain and the Indies it presided virtually unchallenged over the centuries of imperial suzerainty. A significant aspect of this predominance is that in spite of the variations imposed by the availability of building materials, the distance from the European sources, the passage of time and the imperfect recollection, there is no doubt that most of the buildings erected in the Indies were designed, built, and used by people attuned to the epochal culture of the Baroque. Céspedes del Castillo does not indulge in eccentricity when he affirms that the most beautiful and important works of art of the Indies were Baroque in inspiration and expression and goes on to explain, "Much more than in the (Iberian) peninsula, the centre of gravity of Hispanic Baroque is to be found in America where it can truly be described as the essential *arte criollo.*"[13] That these churches and works of art are not exactly like Baroque churches and buildings in Bohemia, England, and Italy is also very clear, but the differences are not greater than those between, for example, the Cartuja of Granada and Salzburg Cathedral, or Blenheim and the Palazzo Massimi alle Colonne. More important than to belabor distinguishing features that, real though they are, do not affect the kinship with the

12. Ibid., 48–49.
13. Guillermo Céspedes del Castillo, *América Hispana, 1492–1898* (Barcelona, 1983): 407.

European source is to stress that the Baroque moment of the Spanish-speaking world was not the creature of a lesser principality, tiny and splendid, nor the outcome of vagaries of fashion or the caprice of princes, but the dominant organizing concept of an epoch centered on the Spain of the Golden Age, which expanded lustily within the empire, providing the most immediately apparent nexus between the metropolis and her overseas dominions.[14]

There are alternative interpretations to this one. Anthony Blunt, for example, perhaps overly impressed with the Italian and Central European variations on this theme, concluded, "From the point of view of planning or spatial invention, there are hardly any churches in the Spanish Colonies which deserve to be called Baroque." And further, he lists Mexico's Sagrario, the Santísima Trinidad, and the churches of Tepotzotlán, Taxco, and Ocotlán and affirms that "these churches have even less claim than the sacristy of the Cartuja of Granada to be called Baroque . . . Every decorative element is taken from the Late Mannerist vocabulary."[15] This opinion is based on an exceptionally narrow understanding of the Baroque, and it is very distant from José Antonio Maravall's concept of *una cultura de época*. These things are never decided by ballot, but it is fair to note that Blunt's views are not widely shared. It is overwhelmingly clear that the culture of the Baroque spilled over generously from Spain to the Indies and that its imprint can be readily perceived in all the arts during the seventeenth and eighteenth centuries, especially in architecture; the fact cannot possibly be ignored that between 1650 and 1800, the Spaniards built fifteen thousand churches in the Indies in styles that, different though they often are from Borromini's Collegio di Propaganda Fide, are undeniably Baroque in inspiration and execution.[16] A far more helpful explanation of the Mannerist survivals mentioned by Blunt is that when the Baroque reached the Indies in the

14. In architecture as well as in literature and the other visual arts. For a defense of this approach, see Alvaro Uribe Rueda, "Sor Juana Inés de la Cruz o la culminación del siglo barroco en las Indias," in *Thesaurus, Boletín del Instituto Caro y Cuervo, Bogotá,* Tomo XLIV (enero–abril de 1989): 112–148.

15. Blunt is not the most reliable source. The few paragraphs he produced on the architecture of the Indies contain a generous share of errors and misprints. Quito, for example, is neither in "Columbia," nor in Colombia; Cholula was not originally designed "like a mosque," but its seven aisles are so many additions to what was originally an ingenious arrangement for holding open-air masses. Anthony Blunt, ed., *Baroque and Rococo, Architecture and Decoration* (New York, 1978): 314–316.

16. A few churches, not many, were built on elliptical or round plans presumably patterned after the Roman models. Among these can be mentioned the chapel of Pocitos in Guadalupe, Los Huérfanos in Lima, and the unfinished church of St. Teresa in Cochabamba. Antonio San Cristóbal, *Arquitectura Virreynal Religiosa de Lima* (Lima, 1988): 69.

late seventeenth century, the earlier stylistic influences did not vanish, especially from the smaller townships of the Andean hinterland where they persisted robustly, which also explains their prompt resurgence during the years of the late Baroque in the eighteenth century, when fashion switched to a more intimate, graceful, and refined reading of the style, as opposed to the monumental, solemn, and transcendental themes of its earliest manifestations.[17] Possibly the uncontroversial acceptance of the presence of the Baroque in the Indies can be best, and briefly, illustrated by reproducing the relevant section of the contents of Leopoldo Castedo's text on the art and architecture of Latin America. In Part II of the book, under the subtitle "The Encounter with Europe," he has the following entries: "The Baroque in Mexico," "The Baroque in Central America and the Caribbean," "The Baroque in Quito and the Viceroyalty of New Granada," "Peruvian Baroque and the Colonial Period in Argentina and Chile," "Brazilian Baroque."[18]

Maravall based his thesis of the concepto de época on the attribution to the Baroque of four definitive characteristics: that it is a centrally directed cultural moment, una cultura dirigida; that it is una cultura de masas, a mass culture; that it is an urban culture; and that it is essentially a conservative culture. None of these is incompatible with the stylistic features stressed by Wölfflin many decades earlier which are as clearly consonant with the unifying, integrating disposition of Archilochus's hedgehog as are the four attributes enumerated by Maravall. Wölfflin noted, for example, that "the baroque firmly repudiated [the] principle of articulation. Absolute unity became the rule, and subordinate parts were sacrificed." He compared this with the Renaissance, which "took delight in a system of greater and lesser parts, in which the small prepared one for the large by prefiguring the form of the whole. It is for this reason that even colossal buildings like the St. Peter's of Bramante have a less than overwhelming effect. The baroque has large forms only. . . . The baroque is a search for the intimidating and overwhelming."[19] Wölfflin had no doubts about the significance of this trend, noting that "increasing size is a common symptom of art in decline."

17. Jorge Bernales Ballesteros, "La pintura en Lima durante el Virreinato," in Pintura en el Virreinato del Perú (Lima, 1989): 44; see also Alfredo Benavides Rodríguez, La arquitectura en el Virreinato del Perú y en la Capitanía General de Chile (Santiago, 1941), especially Chap. V, "Fusión del arte hispano-aborígen de la región de la costa del Perú con el barroco del Reino de Baviera. Also Pal Kelemen, Baroque and Rococo in Latin America (New York, 1967): 15–17.
18. Leopoldo Castedo, A History of Latin American Art and Architecture (New York, 1969): 8.
19. Wölfflin, Baroque, 42–43.

Given the Baroque disdain for articulation, the ability to respond to the character of individual parts is lost; the Renaissance façade consisting of series of equal stories became unacceptable; the dynamic alternation of elements had to be abandoned in favor of façades that revealed themselves only as a unified body. If there was movement, it affected the whole structure, and it was illusory; reality was bound up with a solid, immovable structure in which nothing could be changed without loss; nothing could be added or subtracted because it mirrored and was constructed to serve a well-ordered world in which any change was for the worse and in which *sosiego*, the aloof calmness exemplified by the monarch, was a virtue. The same process of unification presided over the spatial organization of the interior of these Baroque buildings, and "self-contained, subordinate spaces made way for one single overwhelming central space," in accordance with the requirements brought about by the resurgence of preaching as a principal post-Tridentine responsibility of the church militant.

The need to reach large numbers of people was a principal component of the characteristically post-Tridentine perception of a "public opinion" worth the while of preachers, pontiffs, and kings to instruct, to influence, or to guide. This same perception helped to bring about the essentially modern transformation of art, especially the visual arts, into didactic devices or, more interestingly, into propaganda and, in a different direction but with the same general intent, the creation of a vast network of efficient and accessible educational institutions devoted to the intelligent and systematic propagation of religious orthodoxy.[20] The consequent recruitment of the arts, literature, and learning into the service of the faith was founded precisely on this awareness of the existence of a public opinion formed by a far greater number of people than was previously the case who were susceptible of being influenced by persuasion and propaganda.

These developments emphasized the paradoxical "populist" temper of the Baroque epoch and contributed importantly to its becoming what Maravall described as *una cultura masiva*, "a mass culture," almost a

20. "The Council of Trent had brought educational questions to the fore by prescribing the creation of seminaries for the training of priests. The facilities thus provided for the clergy were soon to be extended to the laity as well, in response to the universal demand for Christian schools." None succeeded better than the Jesuits in providing schools for the post-Tridentine period. Their educational methods were embodied in the famous *Ratio studiorum*, constructed on Erasmian, humanistic foundations but designed to serve the purposes of the faith. "Pedagogy as such . . . is only an instrument in the Jesuit scheme, the main purpose being always to build up in each student a strong religious personality." Janelle, *Catholic Reformation*, 115, 124.

precursor of what centuries later was to accompany the advent of mass communications. It could be argued that the role played by the printing press in helping to bring about this *cultura de masas* is comparable to the one so aptly fulfilled by mass circulation newspapers, radio, and television in the industrial world, but such a comparison should not be allowed to diminish the importance of the antiaristocratic New Monarchies in nurturing the incipient populism of the Baroque epoch. Stripped of secondary complexities and depending solely on the allocation of voices and votes, all systems of governance known to man can be reduced to three elemental caricatures: they are monarchical when there is effectively one vote and one voice; aristocratic, when there are only a few votes and voices; and democratic, when there are many. Considered in this summary manner, there can be no doubt that Baroque political arrangements were monarchical and therefore antiaristocratic and populist, because, suspicious of their immediate entourage, monarchs sought support among their subjects at large who generally shared their distrust of barons and welcomed the protection of the Crown. Kings had to reach to the people, to public opinion, over the heads of the barons; times were changing, and although democratic practices were still very far over the horizon, competing claims and loyalties presented problems, and policy could not proceed entirely in the absence of a popular support that required cultivation. Contemporary opinion affirmed that "the greatness and power of the king is not his own, but resides in the will of his people."[21] This elusive will, moreover, could be secured "by touching the springs that move popular feeling" or by coaxing the people in the right direction, making judicious use of pomp and splendor.[22]

This antiaristocratic character can be perceived elsewhere; good taste ceased to be associated exclusively with an elite but became a matter of opinion, that is, of public opinion, and this vast mass of opinion was susceptible of being wooed, lured, or manipulated. Quality gave way to quantity; elegance was displaced by magnificence; the subtle stroke, the fine detail, the understated witticisms were overwhelmed by monumental size, vivid dramatic effects, and vulgar appeals to the emotions.[23]

21. D. Saavedra Fajardo, cited by Maravall, *Barroco*, 204. These sentiments were not unusual, and the trend was well summarized by J. A. de Lancina, also cited by Maravall, when he observed that "the prince must endeavour that his governance be such that it will merit the applause of his subjects." See also, José Luis Comellas, *Historia de España moderna y contemporánea* (Madrid, 1983): 135–139.

22. F. Chueca and V. L. Tapié, cited by Maravall, *Barroco*, 203.

23. Maravall attributes decisive importance to the emergence of kitsch under the auspices of the Baroque epoch and observes that while it is evident that great art is produced during this period, there is also a surfeit of mediocrity; more than ever before. There is

Vulgarity became a ubiquitous ingredient of everything produced during the Baroque epoch for the simple reason that those productions were meant to be understood by the many, not the few. In politics, in learning, religion, and the arts, the Baroque was una cultura de masas, an epochal concept of that moment when the mass culture of modernity made its first, tentative, and decidedly undemocratic appearance.

The Spanish Baroque epoch was also a centrally conceived cultural ambit, and it was therefore, by definition, pervaded with intentionality. Not particularly tolerant, never random or haphazard, not unusually diverse; in the Baroque there was little that could be considered fortuitous.[24] It was an epoch distant from spontaneity, bold flights of fancy, and Quixotic impetuosity and inclined rather to purposive deliberation, a feature singularly and appropriately reflected in the suggestion that it is possible to define it as the name for the art of the Counter-Reformation, or even that "Jesuit Art" would have been preferable. Both these well-founded and scholarly suggestions are based on the attribution to the Baroque of a distinct Tridentine parentage; in other words, it was the felicitous issue of one of the lengthiest and most earnest deliberations in Western history. This should not be understood to mean that the object of the discussions at Trent was to engender the Baroque but only that four centuries later it is possible for the style itself to be regarded by scholars as eminent as Braudel or Werner Weisbach as the consequence, obviously unintended, of prolonged and prolix premeditation.

In the Spain of the Golden Age, the consideration of public issues tended effortlessly to generate a flood of rules, ordinances, and laws. The fear of dispersal and disorder, or of the unexpected, made for a climate of pragmatic bureaucratic prudence that found comfort in carefully filed official documents. Taking its cue from the Prudent King himself, Spanish Baroque society sought the legitimacy of legal sanction for

---

hardly a great work of art of this period, he asserts, that is not tainted by kitsch, and as examples he mentions Bernini's *St. Teresa*, Poussin's *Pastoral*, and Calderón's *La vida es sueño*. Maravall, *Barroco*, 200.

24. This intentionality, prudent and pragmatic, was a ubiquitous trait. Consider, for example, this description of Velázquez's self-portrait: "It is unlikely that there was anything haphazard in Velázquez's choosing to depict himself in the act of painting, the tools of his art forming an essential, though not dominant, element in the iconography of *Las Meninas*. By showing painting as a dignified activity worthy of being exercised in the presence of a royal personage, Velázquez gives sophisticated and elegant expression to an idea that seems pervasive throughout the Spanish treatises on painting—that the technical means for achieving a creative statement are not only of practical concern, but, as the tools necessary to one of the liberal arts, can themselves attain a kind of dignity." Zahira Véliz, ed. and trans., *Artists' Techniques in Golden Age Spain* (Cambridge, 1986): xi.

everything it did, ensuring moreover that this would not go unrecognized by securing an abundance of well-authenticated and appropriately certified documentation. The fledgling bureaucracy of Hapsburg absolutism must have discovered early the sheltering comforts of an obedient disposition and, not surprisingly, when confronted with the perplexing problem of administrative responsibility, adopted with ease what can perhaps be described as a Jesuitic stance, in complete agreement with the members of the Compañía who declared that their great consolation was "the assurance we have that in obeying we can commit no fault . . . if you can give a clear account in [this] respect, you are absolved entirely. . . . God wipes it out of your account and charges it to the superior."[25]

Zeal, dedication, and obedience were indeed important virtues but not as important as their correct certification and documentation. The notary public, the escribano, and the letrado acquired unprecedented importance and were kept busy directing an immense flow of testimonials, petitions, and well-intentioned regulations of every aspect of human activity into their appropriate channels. According to Castilian folklore, a good king will provide "an abundance of law." Measured with this yardstick, Philip II and his Baroque successors were indeed very good kings, whose reigns bequeathed to the Spanish-speaking world one of the most bureaucratic, legalistic, and well-documented political traditions of the modern world; they also left behind a polity accustomed to absolute monarchical governance, invariably centralist, occasionally efficient, sometimes authoritarian, but always representing the dominance of that "way of life" which Trevor-Roper has so aptly described as the "triumph of princely bureaucracy, of an official class in a monarchical society, constantly growing both in numbers and in appetite, and living to a large extent on taxes, which also grow as it grows."[26]

25. Johnson offers an example of the effectiveness of Jesuit discipline, citing Juan Polanco's relation about a mortally ill novice who asked the Master for permission to die, "something which caused great edification." Johnson, *Christianity*, 301.

26. By the turn of the sixteenth century, this vast class of bureaucratic courtiers had embraced the official ideology of "the court." This ideology was shared even by the merchants who benefited from the great monopolies or collected taxes and felt themselves half-courtiers. "It was consecrated by the Church, which was a court-church, and particularly by the religious orders: most of all by the courtliest of all orders, the Jesuits, who at this time were the invariable allies of Spain. Such a system had its outward charm, of course. The bureaucracy patronized official art and architecture; it advertised itself and its solidity through magnificent buildings which we admire today and magnificent shows and pageants which dissolved overnight. But it also had its weakness. Though it created a form of 'state capitalism,' it discouraged private trade and industry." Hugh Trevor-Roper, "The Outbreak of the Thirty Years War," in *Renaissance Essays*, 289.

The Spanish Baroque was indeed a symbol of the triumph of monarchical absolutism, and it is fitting that the one building that faithfully embodies the spirit of the age inaugurated by the Prudent King should also be the one that best exemplifies the beginning of the Baroque epoch in Spain. Philip II wanted a convent, a church, a palace, and a royal tomb combined. The building material chosen was the somber granite hewn from the Guadarrama mountains and the site, a barren, windswept plain at the foot of those mountains. There rose El Escorial, "something of an extraordinary size, unrivalled in Europe. In the immense proportions, in the unified grouping of the various functional parts of the building round several courts, in the distribution of accents and the elevation of the church to the status of a central dominating feature, we can trace the germs of the baroque style."[27] When Philip built his palace, the feudal aristocracy had already been obliterated as an alternative source of power, while the commercial patriciate of Barcelona or Seville was either in its infancy or quite incapable of thwarting the royal will. The transition from feudal dispersion to unifying absolutism substituted the wishes of one prince for those of many barons and ushered in a Baroque political mode well attuned to the stern maxim of the Romans, *quod principem placuit habet legis vigorem* (What pleases the prince, has the force of law), that for centuries has reminded those who need reminding about the abiding certainties of kingly power.

The role accorded to central governance was so comprehensive that it extended even to the realm of disorder. This was noted by Maravall, who commented that herein the explanation can probably be found for why it is that the Baroque, exaggerations and excesses notwithstanding, was a cultural moment in which "even disorder [was] centrally governed and regulated,"[28] a comment that fittingly describes a frequently overlooked but essential feature of the most representative architecture of the period. The inimitable profusion of decorative devices that crowds the eye in the Sacristy of the Cartuja in Granada, for example, or in the *transparente* of Narciso Tomé in Toledo, or in the façade of the Mexican Sagrario Metropolitano delights and overwhelms, but it also blinds the onlooker to the equilibrium and meticulous order that preside over the apparent disorder, as Sacheverell Sitwell was obviously blinded when he dismissed the transparente as "a maelstrom of limbs, volutes, winged cherubs' heads, and rays of light"[29] without noticing that the confusion

27. Weisbach, *Baroque*, 8–9.
28. Maravall, *Barroco*, 141.
29. Sacheverell Sitwell, *Spanish Baroque Art* (London, 1931): 21.

and the disorder were an illusion and that every volute, every capricious curlicue and whirling angel on one side, was deftly balanced by a comparable detail on the other, resulting overall in a subtle predominance of symmetry over what at first sight seems to be chaotic and haphazard.

This crucial dimension of the Baroque escapes the attention of those who, persuaded by the incomparable rhetoric of sculpture and architecture, succumb to the theatrical illusion of walls that move, marble angels that fly, and bronze apostles who catch their breath between sentences.[30] To discipline diversity into order requires strict and meticulous central direction and premeditation; the façade of the cathedral in Murcia could not possibly have been the result of a cumulative process during which earlier designs and methods of construction were progressively discarded, altered, perfected, or superseded. Nor is it conceivable that the Salamanca Clerecía of the Jesuits could have been started before Trent, modified and continued in its aftermath, and completed, say, under the Bourbons. The Baroque buildings were conceived and designed as unified wholes; every part depending on every other, so that the addition of anything that does not respect absolutely the spirit and the form of the whole will necessarily be discordant and inadmissible. It is not difficult to understand, for example, why attempts to lengthen the nave of Borromini's San Carlo alle Quattro Fontane, in Rome, or to add a transept to San Luis, in Seville, would be dismissed immediately as absurd, while the addition of a new tower to Rheims, a Lady Chapel to León, or a new transept to Hereford is perfectly possible and acceptable. The Gothic disposition, like the style, can live with diversity and eccentricity and is responsive to exotica, while the Baroque intent is essentially unifying, symmetric, and concentric, almost invariably centrally directed and singularly impervious to external influences, particularly those of exotic provenance.

In our own time, L. P. Hartley has memorably proposed that the past is a foreign country. If this is so, then it can be affirmed that from the vantage point of the Spanish Baroque mind, the past of a foreign country must needs be doubly foreign, and the challenge posed by this emphatic

---

30. Philippe Minguet lists among the principal features of the Baroque "the lack of balance, . . . the breakdown of unity." Yves Bottineau, *Iberian-American Baroque* (London, 1971): 83. But not everyone agrees. The Baroque has also been described as "an art which is spatially complex and full and which is informed by sweeping movements and gestures, by balanced dissonances and disharmonies." John Golding, "The Expansive Imagination," a review of Frank Stella's *Working Space*, in *TLS* (March 27, 1987): 311.

foreignness to be made intelligible was not accepted with enthusiasm. It is a matter of wonder, for instance, that the Spain that basked in the creative brilliance and refinement of the *siglo de oro*, when her arts and letters attained unsurpassed heights, was so indifferent to the exotic forms discovered in her distant colonial possessions. With the exception of some minor literary allusions and witticisms at the expense of the *indianos* who returned to Castile with their newly acquired riches, two or three lesser plays, and Alonso de Ercilla y Zúñiga's *La Araucana*, Castilian Spain remained intriguingly untouched by the unusual landscapes and novel cultural productions of the New World.[31] The most perspicacious seventeenth- or eighteenth-century traveler roaming at leisure throughout Spain could not possibly have suspected, from the visible evidence, that the domains of the Aztecs and of Tahuantinsuyo were fiefs de jure of the Castilian Crown. There is nothing in the architecture or the visual arts of that splendidly creative period susceptible of being interpreted as a reflection of the existence of the great pre-Columbian civilizations of the Indies, and the few exceptions that come readily to mind only add force to this general statement;[32] for example, the large battle paintings commissioned by Gaspar de Guzmán, count-duke of Olivares, to decorate the walls of the Buen retiro with celebrations of victories for which he wanted somehow to claim responsibility. Most of the encounters depicted in these canvases took place in Europe, including the surrender of Breda, immortalized by Velázquez, but there were four that occurred in the Indies: the expulsion of the Dutch from Bahia, by Juan Bautista Maino (now in the Prado); the recapture of St. Christopher (St. Kitts), by Felix Castelo (also in the Prado); the expulsion of the Dutch from Puerto Rico and the capture of the island of St. Martin, both by Eugenio Cajes.[33] We now know, of course, that it is not in the minimal importance of these four military encounters that we will find the justification of these commissions but in the dire need of good news by a minister alarmed by his falling popularity and a surfeit of reverses

31. Not ignoring that the great epic poem on the Chilean war tells us more about Ercilla's debt to Homer, Tasso, and Ariosto than about the novel landscapes and the architecture that he must have observed during the seven years he spent in the Viceroyalty of Peru.

32. An apposite example from a later century and a different dynasty can be found in the Royal Palace of Aranjuez, where one of the upper corners of the main dining room is decorated with a few Indians accompanied by a crocodile, to symbolize the imperial presence in the New World. Paulina Junquera y María Teresa Ruiz Alcón, *Real Sitio de Aranjuez* (Madrid, 1985): 60.

33. Jonathan Brown and J. H. Elliott, *A Palace for a King: The Buen Retiro and the Court of Philip IV* (New Haven, 1980): 164–166.

nearer to home.[34] Knowing that in the absence of great victories, little ones will do, if suitably augmented, the count-duke put the court painters to work in the creation of a pantheon of contemporary Spanish triumphs. The inclusion of the four skirmishes in the Indies was not, therefore, a consequence of their importance or of a new and more sensitive political or cultural appreciation of events overseas but simply of the propagandistic ingenuity of a troubled *favorito*.[35]

This contrasts strikingly with the English experience, so characteristically associated with the invention of tourism to foreign parts, the introduction of exotic motifs in domestic architecture, the less or more systematic collection of curious objects from elsewhere, and the deliberate attempt to domesticate the wilderness through the creation of the aptly named *jardin anglo-chinois*. Only an exceptionally uncultivated traveler visiting England in the early nineteenth century, for example, could have failed to notice the Oriental influence in the design of artifacts and buildings as unmistakably English as Mr. Chippendale's furniture, Sezincote in Gloucestershire, or the Royal Pavilion at Brighton or remained oblivious to the gallant attempts to landscape the wilderness into picturesque prospects and sublime perspectives.

The Spanish Baroque epoch was also emphatically urban, deriving neither inspiration nor any significant form of expression from rural life or from nature.[36] Unimpressed by the ferocity of tempests, the sublimity of craggy mountains, raging seas, or penumbral forests, it showed itself profoundly disinclined to enter into communion with nature in any of

34. The victories in the Indies were remarkably unimportant. The Dutch, whose expulsion Maino celebrated in his canvas, were back in possession by 1630, five years before the unveiling of the painting. The capture of St. Kitts by don Fadrique de Toledo, whose martial portrait dominates the canvas, did indeed occur, but he left no garrison when he sailed away, and the island was promptly reoccupied by many of the same pirates and adventurers that he had expelled a few weeks earlier. Responding to a report that a party of thirty Dutch had occupied the tiny island of St. Martin, Olivares added 10 galleons and 1,600 soldiers to the Indies fleet under the command of the marquis of Cadereita and ordered him to expel the intruders, which he did, following their formal surrender after withstanding an eight-day siege. Brown and Elliott, *Palace*, 164, 166.

35. As Brown and Elliott indicate in their definitive study, Olivares "lost no opportunity to enlist . . . painters . . . to defend his record against his detractors." "It may not be entirely fortuitous that the commissioning of the battle paintings appears to date from about the same moment as the circulation at court of a new opposition pamphlet which alleged that the count-duke's disastrous policies were to blame for the decline of Spain's military prestige." Brown and Elliott, *Palace*, 162, 168.

36. In a manner remarkably consistent with Thomist antecedents. As Morse has noted, St. Thomas displays an urban bias. "It is solely the city that St. Thomas takes into account. In his view man is naturally a town-dweller, and he regards rural life only as the result of misfortune or of want." Ernst Troeltsch, *The Social Teachings of the Christian Churches*, 2 vols. (New York, 1960): I, 76, cited by Richard M. Morse, "The *Heritage* of Latin America," in *The Founding of New Societies*, edited by Louis Hartz (New York, 1964): 156–157.

its manifestations. The boundaries of the Baroque city were those of civilization. Without there was a wilderness teeming with dangerous beasts and useless vegetation where, other than suitably choreographed royal hunting parties, only peasants, penitent pilgrims, fugitives from justice, and transient foreigners were to be found; within was the civic ambit, populous, bustling, well and truly paved, filled with good and pleasant objects, its horizon gloriously crowned by the noble façades of great buildings, full of artifice, beauty, and contrivance, symbolizing the civilizing mastery of man over the barbarism of nature.[37]

Among the more telling and intriguing manifestations of this urban disposition is the absence of landscape painting from what is without doubt one of the most distinguished creative traditions in the visual arts.[38] With the revealing exception of El Greco's "portrait" of Toledo, which could be classed—incorrectly—as a landscape, and a couple of hunting scenes by Velázquez, there are simply no landscapes worth mentioning in centuries of richly productive work. Until well into the nineteenth century, then mainly in response to external influences, the Iberian world showed itself decidedly disinclined to place nature in the center of the canvas. Even during the Golden Age, neither Spain nor her Indies showed an interest in natural scenery. The conquerors of the New World were confronted with immense mountain ranges, huge forests, wild shorelines, and peaceful estuaries that impressed them not at all. The Indies produced no landscapes save the few painted by the Dutch during their decades in Pernambuco or by European, mainly English and German, naturalists, traders, or travelers early in the nineteenth century.[39] The viceregal courts and the ecclesiastical establishments patron-

37. Possibly this could be explained more succinctly by suggesting that a proposal to plant trees in the Plaza Mayor of Salamanca, or in the Signoria in Florence, or in front of St. Peter's in Rome, or in the Plaza Mayor in Madrid is unlikely to win overwhelming local approval.

38. This is not a novel observation. A nineteenth-century treatise on Spanish painting notes that in the Spanish tradition, "landscape, except as an auxiliary to sacred history and portraiture, is comparatively rare, and hardly deserving of serious mention." Stothert, *French and Spanish Painters*, 3.

39. It is possible that the first and for a long time the only landscape paintings of the Iberian half of the New World were those by Frans Post (1612–1680) and Gillis Peeters (1612–1653) who visited Brazil during the Dutch occupation of Pernambuco between 1630 and 1654. Even in this case, when even a remote possibility existed that the Dutch could have left imitators and followers after their departure, it is difficult to quarrel with Brazilian art historians who affirm that landscape painting was introduced into the country by the German artist Georg Grimm who arrived in 1868 and spent the next two decades teaching Brazilians how to paint trees and mountains from nature. See Quirino Campofiorito, *A Proteção do Imperador e os Pintores do Segundo Reinado 1850–1890* (Rio de Janeiro, 1983): 70–71; also Evaldo Cabral de Mello, *Imagens do Brasil Holandês 1630–1654* (Rio de Janeiro, 1987): 53–69. This unusual feature is reflected in the studies devoted to the visual arts of the period. A reasonably detailed and profusely illustrated

ized a large number of skillful artists, Indian as well as Spanish, who produced an abundance of portraiture and important paintings devoted to sacred themes—but no landscapes. Elsewhere, writing about a related subject, I devoted a whole chapter to an analysis of what I described as the preindustrial urban culture of Latin America.[40] It seems to me beyond doubt that the Indies, and the Spanish-speaking world generally, are now and have been for a very long time of an urban disposition that originated centuries before the advent of modern industrialism. I do not find it difficult, therefore, to agree with Maravall when he describes the epochal concept of the Baroque as *una cultura urbana* and suggests that this is one of its defining characteristics. No one who has visited Spain or Latin America can be in any doubt about this persistent and most visible difference between the cultural traditions that prevail in the south and north of the New World. The urban disposition of the Baroque is even mirrored in the geographic distribution of its most characteristic buildings. None of the great Spanish churches of the Baroque epoch were erected outside the great cities, unlike some of the principal Romanesque and Gothic constructions; there are no Baroque counterparts of Chartres, Ely, or Durham, or of Cluny, Monte Cassino, or Hildesheim.[41] Some authors, notably V. L. Tapié, have erred interestingly, attributing rural and feudal sources to the Baroque. The reference to feudalism is hardly worth a rebuttal, considering the close relationship between the emergence of the Baroque and monarchical absolutism.[42] As for the rural sources, this error has probably been caused at least in part by a willingness to assign too much importance to the prevalent mode of production in the countries and regions that cradled the Baroque.[43] It is

---

account by Kelemen, for example, does not even bother to list the word "landscape" in the index and, naturally, does not include any landscapes among the paintings cataloged or illustrated in the book. Kelemen, *Baroque* (New York, 1967).

40. Véliz, *Centralist Tradition*, chap. 10, "A Pre-Industrial Urban Culture."

41. The English aristocratic preference for rural settings was exceptional and largely accounts for Blenheim, Castle Howard, Seaton Delaval, Swynnerton Hall, Crowcombe Court, and other important Baroque country houses, but even in England there are very few Baroque churches of any consequence built outside London or the major cities. One of the first to be built outside London, if not the first, was All Saints, in Oxford, 1707–1710, hardly a rural setting. The rebuilding of the London churches after the Great Fire, especially St. Paul's, was, of course, of decisive importance, and the history of church architecture during the period between the Civil War and the Hanoverians is clearly dominated by the figure of Sir Christopher Wren.

42. Maravall calls it "the art of the grand monarchies . . . because it emerges from the same social circumstances of monarchical absolutism." Maravall, *Barroco*, 298.

43. V. L. Tapié, *Baroque et Classicisme* (Paris, 1957): 60, 134 et seq., cited in Maravall, *Barroco*, 96, 226–231.

undeniable that the economies of Italy, Spain, and Central Europe generally were predominantly agrarian during the seventeenth century, but this was a generic condition shared with most human societies for the past two or three millennia. What is worth notice is that the regions where the Baroque flourished were the least affected by that agrarian predominance, either because they showed an emphatic urban disposition, as in Castile, the Papal States, or the Two Sicilies, or because an incipient bourgeoisie was taking shape under the protection of city walls, as occurred in Bohemia, Tuscany, and Bavaria.

Neither the location of El Escorial nor the location of the many churches in the rural hinterland of the Indies contradict the emphatic urban bent of the Baroque. The palace of the Prudent King was certainly sited away from Madrid, but no one who has ever visited it can doubt its uncompromising urban character. El Escorial is a city built for a king; nothing in it suggests rusticity, and in spirit it is as distant from a hunting lodge, or an English country house, as the Palazzo Farnese is from a thatched cottage in the West Country. As for the churches of the Indies, most of them built after the Council of Trent, they reflect the pragmatism and the expansionist determination of the age. In Spain and Italy, the number of important post-Tridentine churches built outside the major cities is insignificant, but in the tabula rasa of the Indies, the missionaries and their churches had to go where the people lived. Tenochtitlán was an exception. The pre-Columbian civilizations did not have many urban centers of consequence; the population was dispersed throughout the fertile rural areas; and given their agrarian economy and mode of production and the interest of the conquerors in encouraging the mining of precious metals, a sudden rise in the population of cities was not very likely. The decision, therefore, to build the churches in the demographic center of the hinterland regions was consistent entirely with the object of building churches in the Indies at all, which was to address the spiritual needs of the indigenous inhabitants, an object best served by placing churches in the interior, in addition to monumental cathedrals in the capital cities of the viceroyalty. Almost as if to stress the persistence of this sui generis preindustrial urban disposition, the Mexicans of the twentieth century have regaled us with the visible evidence of the Zócalo in Mexico City, possibly the largest public square in the New World without a single tree, devoid absolutely of vegetation, completely and serenely paved; a place of civilization and civility suitably distant from the wilderness without, as well as a gentle reference to the cultural moment that created the meticulously paved Plazas Mayores in Madrid and Salamanca.

The culture of the Baroque also showed a clear inclination toward conserving things as they were. It was suspicious of novelty; it sided with Sancho Panza rather than with his master; it placed an understandably high value on the pleasures and permanence of traditional community (Gemeinschaft) and felt threatened by the mobility and impersonality of modern association (Gesellschaft). Although the more intimate social aspects of this species of conservatism were comfortably consistent with the Thomist resurgence that accompanied the Counter-Reformation, its prevalence and strength owed less to doctrine than to the pervasive prudence of the epoch. Once it became generally accepted that Baroque society was firmly established, pious, well ordered, legitimately governed, and victorious, steadfastness in resisting change merited applause, and obduracy achieved the status of a cardinal virtue. "The worst enemy of what is good," affirms the old wisdom, "is what is better."

This quiet, almost inarticulate disinclination to change anything has proved unusually persistent and ought not to be ignored when considering the culture and society of the Latin American beneficiaries of the Baroque inheritance. Since the nineteenth century, the rest of the world has grown accustomed to thinking of Latin American countries as singularly prone to rapid and unexpected changes; "volatility" became a favorite epithet, and instability was invariably paraded as a main obstacle to progress. This perception has resulted in a fundamental misunderstanding, because in spite of its reputation for frequent and violent political upheaval, the principal feature of modern Latin America is its overwhelming stability. There exists in the region a resilient traditional structure of institutions, hierarchical arrangements, and attitudes that qualifies every aspect of behavior and that has survived centuries of colonial government, movements for independence, foreign wars and invasions, domestic revolutions, and a confusingly large number of lesser palace revolts. In our time, it has not only successfully resisted the initial impact of technological innovation and industrialization but appears to have been strengthened by it.[44]

This conservatism is decidedly of Iberian provenance and is also mirrored in the architecture of the Baroque epoch. As noted above, the Baroque edifice does not readily admit modifications; each component part can only be where it is and nowhere else; the whole structure is

---

44. This aspect of the problem was examined at a conference convened in London in 1965 by the Royal Institute of International Affairs, which resulted in a volume of essays published by the institute. C. Véliz, ed., *Obstacles to Change in Latin America* (London, 1965).

originally designed and constructed as a seamless, integrated whole, in a manner that accords with the Thomist organic view of society, and is not enormously distant from the crucial Renaissance antecedent requirement that there should be "a harmony of all the parts . . . fitted together with such proportion and connection, that nothing could be added, diminished or altered, but for the worse."[45] In such a world it was as difficult for "man-toe" to become "man-eye" as it would have been to promote the lower story to the upper level of Vignola's Gesù, or to add a neo-Gothic tower to Guerrero y Torres's Pocito Chapel in Guadalupe, or substitute clean Doric orders for the Salomonic columns in the Cartuja of Granada. To guard the social ambit against comparable desecrations, Philip IV, the most Baroque of all monarchs, took measures.

At the time, the third decade of the seventeenth century, it had become generally and loudly accepted that the essential function of prudence was to conserve things as they were, that the "main office of the prince is to conserve his estates,"[46] and that the most important policy to frustrate the decay of the social order on which rested the institutions of the monarchy was to ensure that things remained the way they were— that people did not change status, that children embraced the profession of their parents, that the passage from one social condition to another was made as difficult as possible. "We must endeavour for everyone to remain in the [social] position that the traditional order and his inheritance have assigned to him."[47] On February 10, 1623, the king decreed that no schools should be authorized to function in small townships, because the level of instruction would be unavoidably poor and students would be unfairly encouraged to waste their time learning Latin, instead of working at more useful trades, when their chances of gaining access to institutions of higher learning were virtually nonexistent.[48] Many social evils were said to result from the frustrated ambitions of those who had been given to understand that they could ascend to a level higher than that warranted by their proper condition.

Spanish Baroque society was not sufficiently removed from Renaissance influences to be able to discard entirely the belief that "it was in the nature of compound bodies to disintegrate; and [that] human societies and institutions were compound bodies in this sense; . . . [therefore] decline was in the ordinary processes of time, only to be checked

---

45. Leone Battista Alberti, *Ten Books on Architecture*, ed. J. Rykwert (New York, 1966): Bk. VI, Chap. II, 113.
46. Maravall, *Barroco*, 274–275.
47. Ibid., 278.
48. Ibid., 277.

by unsleeping vigilance and extraordinary endeavour. A great law-giver, a mighty act of volition, a stroke of fine fortune, might bring a state to a condition of greatness and power [but] corruption soon set in, if vigilance was relaxed for a moment and extraordinary energy was not continuously displayed." More important, it was also generally accepted that "the ascent of states, the rise to prosperity and virtue, [were] something of a miracle, a wonderful over-riding of the normal working of things in nature."[49] Early in the sixteenth century, when the shadow of the Sack of Rome still lay across the land and the momentous victories at St. Quentin and Lepanto were still very much in the future, and when even a muted expression of hope in a robust Catholic resurgence would have seemed astonishingly optimistic, popular wisdom inclined largely toward a somber, rather embittered view of things, agreeing with Machiavelli that although there had been some exceptional novelties and discoveries, civilization could not be expected endlessly to produce rewarding innovations and continue to expand indefinitely. Equally weighty was the residual Renaissance conviction that the boundaries of human achievement had been found and staked forever by Greeks and Romans and that since those brilliant classical times, men roamed in darkness, and the best they could bring themselves to hope for in the lingering aftermath of the Renaissance of classicism was to equal the prowess of the ancients.

Two generations later, Baroque triumphalism had seized the center of the stage. Heresy was retreating everywhere, and a flood of gold and silver from the Indies was pouring into the royal coffers. The Prudent King had championed gloriously the cause of Christendom, and the edifice of arts, letters, and the imperium of good laws had been crowned with the great dome of the true faith that had been denied to pagan antiquity. The prowess of the ancients had not only been equaled but surpassed; Spain had perfected her world and rendered further innovation superfluous. There was only one fixed, unifying truth but very many errors. Writing three centuries later, the Catholic philosopher Jaime Balmes compared Catholicism with Protestantism and attributed the virtues of the former to what he described as fixedness of idea, unanimity of will, wisdom and constancy of plan, and definite objectives, in short, an admirable unity, a summation of wisdom, that differed dramatically from what he described as the "whirlwind" of Protestant sectarianism.[50]

---

49. Herbert Butterfield, *The Statecraft of Machiavelli* (London, 1955): 48–49.
50. Jaime Balmes, *Protestantism and Catholicity Compared in Their Effects on the Civilisation of Europe*, trans. C. J. Hanford and R. Kershaw (London, 1849): 16, 18.

The resulting conception of things was quintessentially Baroque: concentric, symmetrical, and intolerant of impediments and formal imperfections. Like its architectural expression, it was a complete design impressing on every wall an upward movement that proceeded without interruption until it resolved itself in the unifying statement of the dome. The striking contrast between this cultural mode and and the one presiding over the English-speaking half of the New World can justly be described as a reassertion of the immensely plausible and persistent cultural polarity first adumbrated as such in the often-quoted 1519 letter to Pope Leo X on the protection of the ancient buildings of Rome. The author of that document described the classical antiquity that fathered the Baroque and the *maniera tedesca* (German manner) that we now know as Gothic as *due extremi direttamente oppositi* (two extremes, directly opposed). According to Paul Frankl, in making this assertion, the anonymous author of the memorandum stood "on most modern ground . . . inasmuch as we today regard antiquity, as it is represented in the Parthenon, and Gothic, for example, in Cologne Cathedral, as polar, stylistic opposites."[51] This is indisputable, but if precision was required, which it is not, then the comparison and the resulting confirmation of polarity ought properly to be as nearly contemporaneous as possible and should therefore be made between the Baroque and the High Gothic. This, however, is pedantic and misses the point, which is not to describe styles of architecture but to find a metaphor that fits. It is in this context that the dichotomy perceived by the author of the memorandum of 1519 becomes relevant, because if Spain and her Indies, and their republican heirs, can be said to constitute the ambit of the Baroque hedgehog, then we cannot overlook the appropriateness of considering the contrasting mode, dominant among the English-speaking inhabitants of the New World, as the one favored by the Gothic fox.

51. Paul Frankl, *The Gothic: Literary Sources and Interpretations Through Eight Centuries* (Princeton, 1960): 273–274. For over two centuries the authorship and the date of this famous letter has been the subject of disputation, its presumed authors ranging from Frankl's "pseudo-Raphael" to Germann's Bramante, but it is now reasonably well established that it was conceived by the real Raphael and drafted for him by Baldassare Castiglione in 1519. Vincenzo Fontana and Paolo Morachiello, eds., *Vitruvio e Rafaello, Il "De Architectura" di Vitruvio nella traduzione inedita di Fabio Calvo Ravennate* (Rome, 1975): 26–27. See also, George Germann, *Gothic Revival in Europe and Britain: Sources, Influences and Ideas* (London, 1972): 28.

CHAPTER V

Gothic Foxes

Searching diligently after the Englishness of the art of the English, Nikolaus Pevsner concluded, among much else, that there was little "in every respect so completely and so profoundly English as . . . the big English parish churches of the late Middle Ages." And among the definitive and easily recognizable features of these very special Gothic buildings, he listed their tall proportions, their thin, sinewy, very emphatically perpendicular piers, their low-pitched timber roofs, the almost total absence of vaults, and their long, angular, and square-ended chancels and transepts so visibly paralleled by the flat-topped towers of most English country churches.[1]

These features he considered to be efficiently summarized in the perpendicular angularity that presides over every aspect and dimension of

---

1. Sir Nikolaus also noted that "the Perpendicular style has in its details not even a remote parallel abroad, and so much so that it lasted unchanged for nearly two hundred years. This has been adduced as a sign of conservatism, but it is really also a sign of Englishness." Nikolaus Pevsner, *The Englishness of English Art* (London, 1956): 81, 83, an expanded and annotated version of the Reith Lectures broadcast in October and November 1955. Pevsner is not the only one to regard Perpendicular Gothic as a uniquely English variant. According to John Harvey,

> Perpendicular . . . is a pragmatic architecture [that] developed and flourished mightily, first because it pleased King Edward III, and later because it became a national second nature. The sum total of the many individual expressions of artistic creativity in the style constituted a national idiom and the natural flowering of the period. Nothing really comparable appeared elsewhere during the Middle Ages. In no European country is there an architectural countenance of equivalent and recognizable individuality."
> (*The Perpendicular Style 1330–1484* [London, 1978]: 238)

the buildings and that he described as an "unrelieved rectangularity [that] comes out equally convincingly in the plans of churches," not just parish churches but all churches, because "England's preference for walls meeting at right angles and remaining separate from each other and for the enclosed space being like a box, or cube, or block is [also] eminently characteristic of the cathedrals of the classic Gothic century, the thirteenth, of cathedrals such as Lincoln and Salisbury."[2] This "unrelieved rectangularity" found striking expression in square chancels and what are, in effect, flat roofs that are "a triumph of the joiner . . . [and] while they prove the English faith in oak, they also prove negatively a peculiarly English neglect of space-moulding, one might even say of pulling a building together." Vaults and domes are unifying devices; when they exist, the character of the walls continues upward without interruption, until it resolves itself clearly and convincingly in the crown of the vault above, or better, in the coalescing, centralizing statement of the dome. Like the vault, the dome embraces and connects all parts under it, and it is significant that very few English churches of the late Middle Ages have stone vaults; most have timber roofs, so that what one experiences is "one wall, another wall, and beams across. Parts are left as parts, separated from each other." Even the very occasional spires that seen from a distance could suggest a unifying intent are in fact placed over the building without visual or spatial connection with the interior; they are yet another compartment in an architectural universe made up of discrete, well-mannered, and emphatically separate components, the privacy of each convincingly protected by the decisive restrictions on their capacity to intrude into the neighboring space.[3]

The Gothic did not originate in England, nor the Baroque in Spain, but just as the world of Spain in the Indies is the largest and most enduring creature of that crepuscular phase of the Italian Renaissance, the English-speaking peoples overseas are in their separate ways credible heirs of the islanders' singular variant of the Gothic cultural mode, and among them, none has thrived on the diversity intrinsic to that inheritance as convincingly and effectively as the English-speaking Americans. A precise description of what this Gothic mode entailed in the past and

2. Pevsner, *Englishness*, 81, 83.
3. Having established the pragmatic character of Perpendicular Gothic, Harvey suggests that the most significant change wrought by the availability of building materials was possibly "the lowering of the pitch of roofs during the fourteenth century. Associated as this is with the saving of timber and lead, we may suspect that economy had something to do with the elimination of the spire and the new aesthetic of horizontals complementing, though subordinate, to verticals." Harvey, *Perpendicular*, 239.

what it represents today is neither easy to produce nor absolutely necessary to justify its use; what is required and should prove sufficient for the purpose is an outline of its principal features, for it is not intended that its function should be that of a mirror but of a metaphor; it is not meant to be a detailed portrait but a well-founded intimation, a glimpse that one hopes will be revealing and will help to discern what would otherwise remain obscure.

The use of historical parallels as explanatory devices, metaphorical or otherwise, or of straightforward correlations that may imply causality has been decried often and frequently, not least in introductory disclaimers by authors attempting to establish historical parallels or correlations heavily laden with causal implications. Among the most respected and influential incursions in this perilous direction must be counted Erwin Panofsky's important essay on the relationship between Scholasticism and Gothic architecture in which, having asked his readers to set aside "all intrinsic analogies," he jumps in *medias res* by noting that "there exists between Gothic architecture and Scholasticism a palpable and hardly accidental concurrence in the purely factual domain of time and place."[4] Early Scholasticism, he proposes, was born at the same time and in the same environment that witnessed the birth of Suger's Saint-Denis; both the new style of building and the new mode of thought arose within a couple of days' walk from Paris and continued to be centered there for the next century and a half.[5] Thus, the High Gothic of Chartres and Soissons, he affirms, was mirrored in the *Summae* of Aquinas and Alexander of Hales, but after the death of Aquinas, the disintegration set in of the centrally arranged system of understanding erected during the centuries of the Schoolmen. In music and architecture as well as in philosophy and politics, there was a discernible trend toward decentralization, with even the thrusts of creativity tending to occur farther and farther away from the ancient Parisian center, in the Germanic countries, in Italy, South France, and England. The *Summa* approach was gradually displaced in favor of an Augustinianism that asserted the independence of the will from the intellect, and Aquinas's anti-Augustinian commentaries merited formal condemnation scarcely three years after his

4. Erwin Panofsky, *Gothic Architecture and Scholasticism* (New York, 1957): 2.
5. The Gothic style of architecture was cradled in the Ile de France, and its earliest manifesto was Abbot Suger's choir at Saint-Denis, completed in 1144. However, the earliest combination of diagonal ribs with groin vaults, crucial in defining the style, is found in Durham Cathedral (commenced in 1093), but this, not surprisingly, was the work of a Norman architect. See, Frankl, *Gothic*, 3–24; W. Swaan, *The Gothic Cathedral* (London, 1981): 56; Louis Grodecky, *Gothic Architecture* (New York, 1976): 36–37.

death. In architecture, the well-integrated, "classic" cathedral design was abandoned in favor of "less perfectly systematized . . . solutions."[6] But it was not until the middle of the fourteenth century that the qualitative change finally came about; the conventional date for the transition from High to Late Scholasticism is 1340, three years after William of Ockham's *Contra Benedictum*, when he first tried to define the limits of papal power and when his ideas had already become sufficiently influential to attract the accolade of pontifical condemnation. Ockham understood all created things to be contingent, untouched therefore by regulatory preconceptions in the mind of God; it is thus not possible "to conceive of a stable order in the universe . . . in Ockham's world, there is no 'chain binding bodies together.' . . . Bodies are absolutes, numerically distinct."[7] They can be in order, in that their place with respect to each other modifies and determines their relationship, but this should not be construed as implying an essential unifying order.

This takes us some considerable distance from Aquinas, for whom form was a rational, organizing principle that reflected the essence of things as objects of knowledge and enabled us to understand particulars only after we had grasped their unifying essence. The beginning of this very great change, never quite completed, from the Thomist world of universals to the Ockhamist ambit of particulars, was also marked by the flowering of that formidable intellectual effort so rightly called "modern" by the Schoolmen, when Ockham's critical nominalism was used as a battering ram with which to demolish the unifying structures built earlier by the "ancients" and when, for the first time, the human mind grappled with the daunting problem of reconciling general statements with a proliferation of particular instances. Peter Aureolus put it succinctly in a sentence that became a battle cry: *omnis res est se ipsa singularis et per nihil aliud*, everything is individual by virtue of itself and by nothing else.[8] The great confrontation between the moderns and the ancients paralleled the controversy of the Universals, between Realists and Nominalists, which truly ushered in the modern world of science, industrial technology, and incessant change. According to the Nominalists, there is no such thing as whiteness; there are only white hands, white wine, white lies, and white knights but no whiteness; and there is no such thing as a human being in general but only particular men, women, and children. "Whiteness" and "human beings" are only

6. Panofsky, *Scholasticism*, 9–10.
7. Umberto Eco, *The Aesthetics of Thomas Aquinas* (Cambridge, 1988): 207–208.
8. Panofsky, *Scholasticism*, 12.

convenient labels, names, *nomen*—hence, Nominalists. Their opponents, in contrast, firmly believed that "whiteness" was a *res vera*, a real
thing, hence Realists. Without in any way diminishing the importance
of the many weighty complexities of this problem, it can be affirmed
with confidence that given the choice, the hedgehog of Archilochus
would without hesitation side with the Realists, while the fox would
swiftly count himself a Nominalist. The Realists were, and are, conversant with a unity that transcends empirical evidence; theirs is in effect a
form of mysticism sustained by revelation, or by a species of subjective
understanding not infrequently supported by profound belief. The Nominalist fox, however, tends to be unerringly aware of the multiplicity of
particular things and psychological processes as well as aware that it is
virtually impossible to reduce the enormous diversity to any manageable
system, organic or otherwise, amenable of being understood or centrally
controlled and directed. The change from High Gothic to Late Gothic,
therefore, can be additionally interpreted as one from unity to diversity,
from the ambit of the hedgehog to that of the fox, from a well-integrated
and unchallenged Realist world to one assailed by the uncertainties of
Nominalism, from the vaulted, universal orthodoxies of "classical"
Gothic to the flat-roofed regional compartmentalization of the English
variant. It also coincided with the generalized acceptance of Giotto's
perspective interpretation of space, with the early development of the
"portrait," depicting the sitter as a distinct individual "by virtue of himself and nothing else," and, most important, with the blossoming of
English Perpendicular architecture.

Panofsky proposes that during the crucial phase of what he rightly
describes as the "astonishingly synchronous development" of Gothic art
and Scholasticism, the nexus between them was vastly more complex
and interesting than a simple parallelism. The relationship he perceived
differs in that it is "a genuine cause-and-effect relation; but in contrast
to an individual influence [it] comes about by diffusion rather than by
direct impact."[9] Its effectiveness is not the consequence of an uncomplicated causal link but of the widespread acceptance of what he calls "a
mental habit" or, as the Schoolmen would have described it, "a principle
that regulates the act," adding that such habits of the mind (styles? dispositions? modes of conduct?) are at work in all and every civilization.

Ockham was not the sole progenitor of Panofsky's "mental habit,"
nor was he an architect or a patron of the arts, but his thoughts and

9. Ibid., 20–21.

actions were consistent, if not conterminous, with the "mental habits" of those of his contemporaries and predecessors responsible, directly or otherwise, for the blossoming of the Perpendicular. To observe, therefore, that he spent the last twenty years of his life in southern Germany does not invalidate the linkage between his works and the Perpendicular Gothic of the English. He was certainly not alone in thinking in the way he did, although he was evidently among the very few of his contemporaries able to articulate those thoughts and feelings. While he was engaged in ecclesiastical controversy and penning his seminal works in Munich, back in his native England, many thousands of his fellow Englishmen conducted their lives, made arrangements for the administration of affairs, and designed and constructed buildings in ways that accorded with writings that they would never read, written by a man whom they would never meet and whose name meant nothing to them. Very few southern Germans would have done the same had they read attentively what Ockham had to say. Then as now, it is unlikely that great numbers of people will alter the way they think and live solely in response to literary strictures. As Oakeshott once wrote, a knowledge of cooking must precede writing, reading, and using cookery books. The existence of a cookery book is formidable evidence that cooking of that kind already occurs. Italians do not cook the way they do because they mastered books on Italian cooking; rather, Italian cookery books can exist because Italians already cook like Italians.

Ockhamism and the Perpendicular were rooted in the same soil; they were conversant with the same manner of life; they referred to the same cultural tradition and subsequently both proved to be impressively consistent with what the island people had to offer in the centuries that followed. Why or how exactly Ockham did what he did is not a matter to be considered here.[10] What can be affirmed without hesitation is that while pursuing his spiritual, ecclesiastic, and political objectives, he es-

10. The English philosopher William of Ockham (1300–1349), also known as *Doctor invincibilis* and *Venerabilis inceptor*, was born in Ockham, Surrey, joined the Franciscans early in life, and went on to study at Merton College, Oxford, where he remained as a teacher until 1324 when he was ordered to Avignon to defend some of his doctrinal statements before the papal theologians. Two years later, he and Michael of Cesena, the Franciscan general, joined the Emperor Louis of Bavaria, who was then engaged in controversy with the papacy. He appears to have died at Munich, a victim of the Black Death. Ockham was a principal figure in the confrontation between the pope and the emperor, which together with the disintegration of scholasticism laid the foundations for the rise of theological skepticism and modern political thought. Among his most influential works, the *Super potestate summi pontificis octo quaestionum decisiones* (1339–1342) attacks the temporal supremacy of the pope. See Arthur Stephen McGrade, *The Political Thought of William of Ockham, Personal and Institutional Principles* (Cambridge, 1974).

poused a radical narrowing of the functions of the secular government
and stressed the specifically spiritual responsibilities of ecclesiastical authorities. This was not an accidental result. He believed firmly in the
value of individual freedom, not simply the inner tranquillity that could
flow from a sincere subordination to higher principles but the power of
individuals to be masters of their own actions and, therefore, through
those actions, less or more flawed, ill-advised, wise or stupid, able responsibly to produce varying kinds of decentralized disorder. Ockham's
works and teaching can fairly be regarded as marking the beginning of
"the end of . . . the hierocratically inspired descending thesis of government with its resulting program of moulding society from above."[11] They
also helped to usher in a disposition, perhaps even a capacity, to come
to terms with the uncertainties and risks of eccentric diversities; a rejection of polite regularities; a Gothic ease with improvisation and disorder; a disinclination blindly to accept the comforts of order that can
now be seen as a portent of the inauspicious way in which, two centuries
later, the style of the Goths was accorded a place at the wrong end of
the polarity of civilization and barbarism. Also interesting is that such
traits and habits are consistent with the romantic disposition that so
decisively accompanied the early decades of English industrialism and
that has been so notably absent from the cultural tradition of the
Spanish-speaking peoples, but more about this later.

Giorgio Vasari reflected best the dismissive attitude of his contemporaries toward the northern style that he considered to be marred ir-
remediably by its unacceptable departures from the classical canon.
Writing in 1550, he described it as "lacking everything that can be called
order. Nay, it should rather be called confusion and disorder. . . . Their
buildings . . . are ornamented with columns which . . . cannot have the
strength to sustain a weight, however light it may be . . . so that it appears impossible that the parts should not topple over at any moment.
Indeed, they have more the appearance of being made of paper than of
stone or marble."[12] A century later, at the height of the Baroque moment
in Rome, Filippo Baldinucci named the *maniera tedesca* an *ordine got-
tico* and defined it as "the working method in vogue under the
Goths, . . . a kind of proportion which has nothing in common with the
five orders of good architecture; on the contrary, it is a completely bar-

11. McGrade, *William of Ockham*, 221.
12. T. S. R. Boase, *Giorgio Vasari: The Man and the Book* (Princeton, 1971): 94–95.

baric fashion . . . with no order, no rule, no proportion and no taste."
Without doubt, a maniera fitting for those who stormed the walls of
Rome in 410 and returned to sack her again one thousand years later;
an ordine unrestrained by conventional rules, without discipline and as
coarse and inelegant as the wild northerners who devised it in their dark
forests and cold, inhospitable flatlands; an order but without order.[13]

The same apparent disorder was perceived by Horace Walpole, but
his interpretation was radically different. Attuned to the mood that was
beginning to overtake mid-eighteenth-century England, he compared the
style of the Goths with that of "Grecian antiquity" and found the latter
wanting because "the variety is little, and admits of no charming irregularities," an attitude consistent with the vigorous reawakening of interest in nature, especially with the vogue for "English gardens" that so
efficiently prepared the ground for the romantic blossoming of a generation later. Asymmetry and variety were principal themes of the new
style of landscape design that Walpole labeled with the pseudo-Chinese
name of "Sharawaggi," declaring himself to be "almost as fond of Sharawaggi, or Chinese want of symmetry, in buildings as in grounds or
gardens."[14]

Romanticism dominated the cultural horizon and the Gothic revival
was well under way when the need arose to rebuild the Palace of Westminster after the disastrous fire of 1834, ten years after Byron's death
and thirty-six years since the publication of the *Lyrical Ballads*. The
reconstruction of the Houses of Parliament in the perfected Gothic style
of the revival is without doubt one of the signal feats of that extraordinary intellectual and artistic movement. Revivalists are invariably more
papist than the pontiff, and the essential nature of the thing revived is
often found expressed more clearly in the imitation than in the original.
The Westminster episode was certainly not an exception to this generalization, and by the middle of the century of the English Industrial
Revolution, the largest, most imposing, and most visible neo-Gothic
building on earth was flaunting its decisive asymmetry and eccentricity
on the banks of the Thames. The Gothic had by then overflowed the
boundaries of art and architecture, and in the eyes of some of its most
distinguished and enthusiastic upholders, notably, A. Welby Pugin, the
Catholic architect, William Morris, the socialist poet, and John Ruskin,

13. Germann, *Gothic Revival*, 15.
14. Ibid., 54.

the Protestant critic, it became a way of life, a prescription for moral regeneration, a liturgical mode and a profession of faith.

Pugin was undoubtedly the leading figure of the crucial phase of the Gothic revival, especially through his best-known book, *Contrasts; or, a Parallel Between the Noble Edifices of the Fourteenth and Fifteenth Centuries, and Similar Buildings in the Present Day; Shewing the Present Decay of Taste, Accompanied by Appropriate Text*, published in 1836, and through his involvement, with Sir Charles Barry, in the reconstruction of the Palace of Westminster. Pugin's *Contrasts* was the single most influential tract of the Gothic revival, and although it was unashamedly polemical and had as much to do with religion, history, and politics as it did with architecture, it established him as one of the precursors of modern functionalism with his thesis that "the great test of Architectural beauty is the fitness of the design to the purpose for which it was intended, and that the style of a building should so correspond with its use that the spectator may at once perceive the purpose for which it was erected."[15]

With such antecedents, one cannot ignore the significance of the checkered reception that the revived style was accorded in different parts of the modern world and, ultimately, the geographic distribution of the completed buildings. The eagerness with which different countries accepted the tenets of industrialism and modern technology—and many other cultural signifiers of English provenance—was not paralleled by their approval of the Gothic revival. Japan, for example, after the Meiji Restoration, tried gamely to incorporate as much as it could of Western ways but was unmoved by the Gothic revival; nor was the eagerness with which the "Young Turks" and their successors endeavored to bring modernity to Turkey reflected in an acceptance of industrial Gothic. The former Spanish Indies, intent as they were in imitating the attractive ways of their modern industrial mentors, were nonetheless singularly unimpressed by the new fashion, and throughout Latin America today it would be difficult to find more than a handful of neo-Gothic structures of any quality or importance. The fate of the revival in the English-speaking world was quite different, not only in the imperial domain but most important in the United States where neo-Gothic was embraced with unparalleled enthusiasm, acquiring an almost official status as the correct style for uses academic and ecclesiastical and quickly making its

15. A. Welby Pugin, *Contrasts: or, A Parallel Between the Noble Edifices of the Middle Ages and Corresponding Buildings of the Present Day: Shewing the Present Decay of Taste, Accompanied by Appropriate Text* (London, 1836): 1.

way into a vernacular that was about to find an overwhelming and distinct expression in the modern skyscraper.[16] It is not difficult to imagine that the time may come when Manhattan and Chicago, with their uncompromising diversity and enabling architectural latitudinarianism, will be regarded as the ultimate Gothic statements of our modern industrial moment.

There is no dearth of definitions and meticulous descriptions both of Gothic architecture and of the Gothic mode that moralists, theologians, and social critics considered worth resurrecting in the nineteenth century, but possibly the most popular and influential is that offered by Ruskin in the second volume of *The Stones of Venice*. Here, much in accordance with Panofsky's "mental habits," he distanced himself from the strictly architectural and assigned to the Gothic a vastly wider social and cultural connotation that he believed was sustained and justified by "moral and imaginative elements," which he listed in the order of their importance as savageness, changefulness, naturalism, grotesqueness, rigidity, and redundance.[17] Ruskin contrasted savageness in the building, or "rudeness" in the builder, with sophistication, polish, the quest for predictability and perfection, formal correctness, and the consequent obliteration of individuality. "It is true, greatly and deeply true, that the architecture of the North is rude and wild; but it is not true, that, for this reason, we are to condemn it, or despise. Far otherwise . . . we should err grievously in refusing to recognise as an essential character . . . this wildness of thought, and roughness of work; this look of mountain brotherhood between the cathedral and the Alp; this magnificence of sturdy power."[18]

General perfection and regularity in design and execution he thought could only be secured by eliminating particular imperfections; the precise rendering of a line or a curve many times over can only be purchased at the unacceptably high price of the loss of freedom to make mistakes and the enslavement of the imagination. Ruskin firmly believed that the best in man "cannot manifest itself, but in company with much error." He entreated his readers to gaze attentively at the front of the old Gothic

---

16. Phoebe B. Stanton, *The Gothic Revival and American Church Architecture, 1840–1856* (Baltimore, 1968).

17. "These characters," Ruskin explains, "are here expressed as belonging to the building; as belonging to the builder, they would be expressed thus: 1. Savageness or Rudeness. 2. Love of Change. 3. Love of Nature. 4. Disturbed Imagination. 5. Obstinacy. 6. Generosity." John Ruskin, *The Stones of Venice* (London, 1874): II, 154.

18. Ruskin, *Stones of Venice*, 155, 157.

cathedrals and "examine once more those ugly goblins, and formless monsters, and stern statues, anatomiless [sic] and rigid; but do not mock at them, for they are signs of the life and liberty of every workman who struck the stone; a freedom of thought, and rank in scale of being, such as no laws, no charters, no charities can secure. . . . To banish imperfection is to destroy expression, to check exertion, to paralyse vitality."[19] From Ruskin's description there emerges the outline of a world with many truths and many errors that is as compatible with the tenets of his Protestantism as it is antagonistic to the "one truth, many errors" of the Counter-Reformation Baroque. Christianity, he explains, not only recognizes the individual value of every soul but also

> confesses its imperfection, in only bestowing dignity upon the acknowledgement of unworthiness. . . . That admission of lost power and fallen nature, which the Greek . . . altogether refused, the Christian makes daily and hourly, contemplating the fact of it without fear. . . . And it is, perhaps, the principal admirableness [sic] of the Gothic schools of architecture, that . . . out of fragments full of imperfection, and betraying that imperfection in every touch, indulgently raise up a stately and unaccusable whole.[20]

Changefulness, or variety, and all the other "moral and imaginative elements" are virtual corollaries of that first condition of stylistic savageness and rudeness of execution, but none are more important than this one, to which Ruskin assigns the status of vital principle: "not the love of Knowledge, but the love of Change. It is that strange disquietude of the Gothic spirit that is its greatness; that restlessness of the dreaming mind, that wanders hither and thither among the niches, and flickers feverishly around the pinnacles, and frets and fades in labyrinthine knots and shadows among wall and roof, and yet is not satisfied, nor shall be satisfied."[21] This perpetual change is neither chaotic nor haphazard but the reward for allowing each individual workman as much freedom as possible, because only workmen who are "utterly enslaved" will produce a building the parts of which are absolutely the one like the other. Ruskin rejects such uniformity because he considers that change and variety are "necessities of the human heart. . . . We must no more expect to derive either pleasure or profit from an architecture whose ornaments are of one pattern, and whose pillars are of one proportion, than we should

19. Ibid., 163.
20. Ibid., 159–160.
21. Ibid., 181.

out of a universe in which the clouds were all of one shape, and the trees of one size." The changefulness of the Gothic, however, is not capricious, but functional and rational, because it is untrammeled by preordained rules, symmetries, or proportions. "Nothing is a great work of art," affirms Ruskin, "for the production of which either rules or models can be given. Exactly so far as architecture works on known rules, and from given models, it is not an art, but a manufacture." The Gothic at its best is free from any such encumbrance. "Undefined in its slope of roof, height of shaft, breadth of arch, or disposition of ground plan, it can shrink into a turret, expand into a hall, coil into a staircase, or spring into a spire, with undegraded grace and unexhausted energy; and whenever it finds occasion for change in its form or purpose, it submits to it without the slightest sense of loss." All this is readily achieved because among the principal and definitive virtues of the great Gothic builders was that "they never suffered ideas of outside symmetries and consistencies to interfere with the real use and value of what they did. If they wanted a window, they opened one; a room, they added one; a buttress, they built one; utterly regardless of any established conventionalities of external appearance, knowing that such daring interruptions of the formal plan would rather give additional interest to its symmetry than injure it." This explains why in some of the greatest Gothic constructions, built over long periods of time, each successive architect "built the pieces he added in his own way, utterly regardless of the style adopted by his predecessors; and if two towers were raised in nominal correspondence at the sides of a cathedral front, one was nearly sure to be different from the other, and in each the style at the top to be different from the style at the bottom."[22]

There is in Ruskin's conception of the Gothic a persistent rejection of the constraints imposed by artifice and contrivance and an unmistakable moral propensity to discover beauty in truthfulness, in integrity, and in function fulfilled responsibly. Such traits are seldom far removed from a keen appreciation of nature, and this instance is not an exception. "Naturalism," Ruskin's third moral characteristic, is defined as "the love of natural objects for their own sake, and the effort to represent them frankly, unconstrained by artistical laws." Ruskin married the detailed study of natural forms implicit in much Gothic design to an oversenti-

22. Ibid., 179. As is the case, for example, in Amiens, Canterbury, Ely, Chartres, León, and Bourges.

mental but otherwise perceptive understanding of the special importance of the rural ambit in the genesis of English Romanticism and the
subsequent vogue for nature studies. He was evidently convinced that

> the affectionate observation of the grace and outward character of vegetation
> is the sure sign of a more tranquil and gentle existence, sustained by the gifts,
> and gladdened by the splendour, of the earth. In that careful distinction of
> species, and richness of delicate and undisturbed organization, which char-
> acterize the Gothic design, there is the history of rural and thoughtful life,
> influenced by habitual tenderness, and devoted to subtle inquiry; and every
> discriminating and delicate touch of the chisel, as it rounds the petal or guides
> the branch, is a prophecy of the development of the entire body of the natural
> sciences.[23]

Extravagant, perhaps, but none the less helpful as a reminder of how
distant this is from the urban culture of the Baroque and how near to
the English-speaking peoples' quasi-idolatrous cult of nature.

A good Gothic structure, according to Ruskin, should have "the sort
of roughness, and largeness, and nonchalance . . . of the broad vision,
and the massy power of men who can see past the work they are doing,
and betray here and there something like disdain for it and find delight
in the fantastic, the ludicrous and the grotesque."[24] This fourth characteristic listed by Ruskin—grotesqueness—also depends on savageness,
diversity, and an earthy capacity to enjoy uninhibited mirth, rough wit,
feeling, and good humor. Here again one is reminded of the very considerable distance that separates the polish and refinement of the Baroque from the rustic frolickings of the Gothic.

It is possible to argue that the names chosen by Ruskin to describe
the moral and imaginative elements of the Gothic are not exceptionally
felicitous, and rigidity, the fifth element, is not the least unhelpful. What
he had in mind in this instance he describes as "not merely stable, but
active rigidity; the peculiar energy that gives tension to movement, and
stiffness to resistance, which makes the fiercest lightning forked rather
than curved, and the stoutest oak-branch angular rather than bending,
and is as much seen in the quivering of the lance as in the glittering of
the icicle." Writ large, this is another manifestation of that "unrelieved
rectangularity" of English Gothic that impressed Pevsner so much and
provides such a striking contrast with the propensity to round chancels,
corners, and transepts that predominates across the English Channel.
Setting side by side the ground plans of Lincoln, Salisbury, Ely, Peter-

23. Ibid., 201.
24. Ibid., 203, 229–230.

borough, York, and Canterbury and those, say, of Bourges, Freiburg, Cologne, Albi, Chartres, and Rheims illustrates most convincingly the dramatic difference perceived by Ruskin between the rigid rectangularity of the former and the plasticity and sense of molded, encompassing space of the latter. This unusual rigidity can also be seen in Gothic ornamentation, which compared with that of the Greeks and the Egyptians, mostly surface engravings or paintings with lithe and luxuriant lines, "stands out in prickly independence, and frosty fortitude, jutting into crockets, and freezing into pinnacles; here starting up into a monster, there germinating into a blossom, anon knitting itself into a branch, . . . thorny, bossy, and bristly, . . . but, even when most graceful . . . never for an instant languid, always quickset; erring, if at all, on the side of brusquerie." Ruskin attributes the responsibility for such designs and execution principally to the "independence of character, resoluteness of purpose, impatience of undue control, and that general tendency to set the individual reason against authority, and the individual deed against destiny" of the peoples of the Gothic tradition.[25]

Even less apt than rigidity is redundance, the last "moral and imaginative element" in Ruskin's listing, but his explanation compensates for the inadequacy of the label. "No architecture is so haughty," he affirms, "as that which is simple; which refuses to address the eye, except in a few clear and forceful lines; which implies, in offering so little to our regards, that all it has offered is perfect; and disdains, either by the complexity or the attractiveness of its features, to embarrass our investigation, or betray us into delight. That humility, which is the very life of the Gothic school, is shown not only in the imperfection, but in the accumulation, of ornament." We must be content, he enjoins his readers, "to allow the redundance which disguises the failure of the feeble, and wins the regard of the inattentive" and also welcome this generosity because it is caused by "a magnificent enthusiasm, . . . an unselfishness of sacrifice, which would rather cast fruitless labour before the altar than stand idle in the market; and, finally . . . rising out of Naturalism . . . a profound sympathy with the fulness and wealth of the material universe."[26]

Against this background, it should be pointed out again that the metaphoric usage proposed here is unashamedly cultural, and although it recruits architectural imagery into its service, it does so with diffidence

25. Ibid., 204.
26. Ibid., 207.

and, it is to be hoped, prudence. The assertion that the prevalent cultural mode of the English-speaking Americans corresponds to that of the Gothic fox is certainly not strictly or even mainly architectural but cultural. It refers to a manner of conceiving the world, a mode of thought and conduct that originated during the protracted aftermath of the imperial dissolution in the West and that acquired a distinct and separate character in England during the medieval centuries; achieved a quasi-nationalistic flavor under the Tudors; was briefly diverted by the ill-fated centralizing efforts of Stuarts and Puritans and having been fleetingly disconcerted by the pseudo-Cartesian precisions exemplified by the Enlightened despotisms of the day, turned away, preferring instead the pleasantly insular understanding—an amiable entente?—between Puritanical steadfastness and aristocratic compromise that matured together with the Industrial Revolution and flowered in the New World into unprecedented creativity, prosperity, and universal acceptance, while the early blooms of the French Revolution wilted and decayed into dark intolerances and elegant introspections.

A reasonable condition that should be satisfied to establish the usefulness of a metaphoric concept such as the one proposed here is that it should have greater explanatory scope than alternative proposals applicable to the same problem, in this instance, to the comparison of the predominant cultural modes and dispositions in the northern and southern regions of the New World. It is virtually impossible to ascertain precisely and exhaustively what the key characteristics are that shape the continuously evolving national disposition of a people as diverse as those of the United States and Canada, taken separately or together, but if such a hypothetical ranking could be drawn up, it is unlikely that the listed traits would fail to find an ancestry or a secure shelter under the conceptual canopy of the Gothic cultural mode described by Ruskin. Even a succinct description of his moral and imaginative elements will include many unmistakable intimations of everyday life in the realm of the English-speaking foxes of the New World, as well as additional reminders of the considerable distance that separates them from the polite symmetries and urbanities favored by the heirs of the Baroque imperial moment. Ruskin's splendid prose can also be read as an eloquent adornment, a fitting rhetorical accompaniment for what would otherwise be a very simple list of characteristics familiar to all but very few English-speaking Americans.

"Love of change," for example, is almost a summary description of the attitude of a people who not only have come to terms successfully with the challenge of ceaseless change, but also have for long exhibited an enabling familiarity with the demands generated by the mobility of the factors of production and a seasoned ability to respond without unnecessary stress to the multiple requirements of modernity. Their earliest responses to these challenges can now be seen to have been portents of what was to follow. For instance, as the ordinary unpredictability of modern life became pedestrian and commonplace, they countered by inventing the modern concept of "adventure," transforming what human beings had feared and avoided for millennia into the heart of a thriving industry. Tourism is a monumental achievement of the English-speaking peoples' love of change which, combined effortlessly with their entrenched "love of nature," has brought forth a numerous and vigorous progeny of mountaineering clubs, geographic societies, yachting associations, hang gliding federations, botanical gardens, zoological societies, societies royal for the prevention of cruelty to animals, wilderness societies, gardening subcommittees, conservation societies, green parties, angling clubs, landscape painting societies, animal liberation zealots, bird-watching clubs, bush-tucker clubs, four-wheel-drive associations, Antarctic societies, and international associations for the protection of the kangaroo. As for the Ruskinian "grotesqueness," it can without violence be rendered as "sense of humor" and is found as much in evidence in the work of Charles Chaplin, the Marx Brothers, and Monty Python as it is in the utterances of W. C. Fields, the pages of the *New Yorker*, or the adventures of Tom and Jerry.

"Redundance" Ruskin translates simply and fittingly into "generosity," and who could question this interpretation who has ever visited the homes of English-speaking Americans and seen and enjoyed that profusion of things, that abundance of adornment, that disorder of objects strewn about without premeditation or intent which these amiable people dismiss so elegantly with the explanation that the house is "lived in." So it is, and Ruskin would have concurred. Because he knew very well that disorder of that ilk was in some sort essential to life: "It is a sign of life in a mortal body, that is to say, of a state of progress and change. Nothing that lives is, or can be, rigidly perfect; part of it is decaying, part nascent. . . . in all things that live there are certain irregularities and deficiencies which are not only signs of life, but sources of beauty . . ."; but life is extravagant and full of redundancies and exaggerations; are there too many buttercups in a meadow? How many leaves are enough? How much rain is a sufficiency? How can we have too much if we select only the best? How can the frugality of perfection ever adequately take the place of a living and disorderly imperfection? How indeed, and Ruskin makes certain that we are not allowed to overlook the fact that humility, "which is the very life of the Gothic school, is shown not only in the imperfection, but in the accumulation, of ornament. The inferior rank of the workman is often shown as much in the richness, as the roughness, of his work; and if the cooperation of every hand, and the sympathy of every heart, are to be received, we must be content to allow the redundance which disguises the failure of the feeble, and wins the regard of the inattentive."[27] Does not this mean that we ought not to complain if confronted by two dozen distinct models of electric toasters? Should we translate this into a plea for a great diversity of automobile designs, a redundance of brands of toothpaste, many conflicting versions of the occurrences of the day printed on a large number of autonomous newspapers, and a veritable surfeit of different productions of *The Ring*, *Rigoletto*, and *Madama Butterfly*, some less vulgar and objectionable than others?

Finally to "savageness" and "rigidity," which are but rich and elaborate euphemisms for the kind of soaring individuality of mind and deed that is presumed responsible for almost everything that the English-speaking Americans have done that is modern, novel, and successful. Ruskin's argument does not allow his modern readers to stray easily from such an interpretation, and when he paraphrases and supports and reiterates, he does it with phrases such as "prickly independence" and "frosty fortitude" and "independence of character" and "impatience of undue control," and he does not hesitate to praise the "tendency to set individual reason against authority," or to encourage the defiant stand of the "individual deed against destiny." These flights of inspired prose convey views and perceptions that are tellingly concordant with Panofsky's references to the "unrelieved rectangularity" of the Perpendicular and also with the enhanced appreciation of privacy characteristic of the English-speaking Americans, with their secular encouragement of individuality, personal initiative, and self-reliance, which is in turn mirrored in an abundance of colloquialisms and lively bits of folkloric parlance about standing up for oneself, working one's way up on one's own, digging in, having the courage of one's convictions, facing the music, biting bullets, and generally putting mouth and money in the same place and, if asked, owning up to having chopped down cherry trees here and there.

The Gothic cultural mode is also a morality, reliant for its lasting

27. Ibid.

vigor on the disposition of individuals freely to accept and discharge responsibility for their actions. This first and crucial "moral element" that Ruskin labeled, almost mischievously, "savageness" is a forthright endorsement of the definitive moral role of the "aristocratic" freedom to err when setting the boundaries of individuality; conversely, it is a loud warning about the consequences of succumbing to the inducements offered by an excessively solicitous and comforting "monarchical" centralism. The least attractive and most profound change that could affect the cultural mode of the English-speaking peoples anywhere could well be this one, bringing in its wake the threat of dissolution as the price for the abdication of individual responsibility, whether that of climbing dangerous mountains, smoking cigars, investing abroad, or eating large quantities of food.

The reiteration of this moral dimension is also helpful to explain some of the similarities between the American heirs of the English cultural tradition and those in other former British colonies. At first sight, it would appear that the origins, say, of the United States, New Zealand, Canada, and Australia are sufficiently different to impress on each of these countries distinct and possibly diverging characters and dispositions. The 1788 settlement of Australia occurred precisely as Britain marked her first century of unimpeded aristocratic predominance, while the establishment of New Zealand came about a few generations later, at a time when the North American settlements had already been in existence for well over two hundred years. The English-speaking colonies in North America were established under religious, social, and political auspices quite different from those of Australia and New Zealand and went on to secure their independence in a way that was unprecedented and that inspired no imitators in the English-speaking world. These differences notwithstanding, there can be no doubt that from a cultural vantage point, all these English-speaking countries are islands off the coast of Kent; the cliffs of Dover can be seen as clearly from Cincinnati as from Edmonton, Wellington, and Ballarat. They certainly have more in common with each other than with any other cultural tradition, and although every day that passes they move away from each other and from their common English ancestry, many centuries will elapse before they cease to have more in common than separates them. They all share, for example, a profound and irreverent distrust of bureaucrats, bureaucracy, and regulations that would be out of place in France, Turkey, or Mexico, while they exhibit a propensity to volunteer (prompted possibly by the wish to keep offers of time and energy constantly under review) that Greeks, Paraguayans, and Hungarians would find decidedly disconcerting. They are almost identical in their eager intellectual receptivity to exotica, while the imprint of rural life and their passionate appreciation of nature are pervasive in every aspect of their existence, from landscape painting and the unquenchable hunger for periodic and detailed weather reports to their lusty familiarity with outdoor sports, the disapproval of loquacity, the ability to "make do," with little fuss, rustic sartorial preferences, and the development of extensive pseudo-rural suburbs, as evident in Los Angeles or Boston as they are in Winnipeg and Auckland.[28] Such suburbs are characteristically inhabited by proportionally greater numbers of enthusiastic and well-organized amateur astronomers, cat fanciers, train spotters, country-style dancers, pigeon fanciers, bush trekkers, cake decorators, bird-watchers, gardeners, and vintage car enthusiasts than have ever gathered anywhere and at any time to devote so much time and attention to what are, by definition, characteristically nonprofitable "hobbies."

What is adumbrated here is the same polarity between *due extremi direttamente oppositi* that during five centuries echoed loudly through every quarter of the Western cultural tradition, losing none of its force with the passage of time. When first proposed by Raphael and Castiglione in their 1519 letter to Pope Leo X, it was perceived solely in stylistic, architectural form, but this narrowed it unnecessarily; it is now evident that it shapes and qualifies virtually every principal aspect of life, transcending generously the boundaries of style and architecture. It is a polarity much in evidence, for example, when the laws that England and Castile bequeathed to their distant imperial possessions are placed side by side. The Common Law of the English and the Civil Law of Spain and of most of the peoples of the European mainland have for many centuries stood as symbols of the two principal juridical traditions of the Western world, reflecting quite distinct social attitudes and different

---

28. It is worth noting that two generations before Constable's *White Horse*, livestock had already become a popular subject of portraiture in Britain, with large canvases being commissioned by proud farmers to immortalize their prize sheep, bulls, and pigs. "Portraits of animals in the eighteenth century came out of a venerable tradition. By and large it was connected with sport, and the great animal painters of the period—Wootton, Seymour and Stubbs—all had work in this area as their basis. But a significant feature of the growing strength of farming at this time is the development of new breeds and the wish to celebrate these by portraiture. Stubbs becomes involved in this as part of his wider practice of animal painting. . . . Even more than the 'working landscape,' this kind of painting was for strictly rural clientele—being of more interest to the producers rather than the consumers of livestock." Nothing even remotely comparable occurred elsewhere in the world, certainly not in the Spanish Indies; there was never a George Stubbs in Spain, Mexico, or Venezuela. Demelza Spargo, ed., *This Land Is Our Land: Aspects of Agriculture in English Art* (Royal Agricultural Society of England, London, 1989): 11.

styles of life and thought. This notable dichotomy cannot be mentioned without inviting detailed additional comment, but in the context of this explanation, it suffices to remark that the Common Law derives sustenance and authority from a multiplicity of responsible sources whose proceedings are recorded and reported, and it is this empirical corpus of case law, continuously modified by the changes that affect the society that gives it life, that provides the precedents for subsequent decisions.[29] In the Civil Law tradition, however, including both its Roman ancestry and its Napoleonic progeny, the law is determined centrally and the peripheral judiciary applies it. This refers solely to the sources and manner of application of the laws, not to their quality, fairness, or appropriateness; to confuse these two quite separate aspects would be as bizarre as to believe that the Gothic style is better than the Baroque for keeping out the rain. The persistence of the Common Law tradition in the English-speaking countries, albeit variously modified, is paralleled by the resilience of Civil Law in the former Indies of Castile, which after three hundred years under Spanish laws, overwhelmingly, though not exclusively, influenced by Roman Law, immediately they donned their republican garb gave themselves Civil Codes patterned after the Napoleonic Code of 1804, itself based principally on the Roman model, and with various less or more interesting changes have remained steadfast and unlikely to do otherwise for a very long time indeed.[30]

The definitive importance of the Common Law tradition has not been

29. In the early sixteenth century, mainly as a consequence of the revival of interest in juridical studies and the availability of translations of the classical texts, most European countries underwent what has become known as the "Reception," referring to the reception of Roman Law, which gradually replaced customary, or folk, law. The most notable exception was that of England where the Inns of Court successfully defended the traditional practice of basing jurisprudence on the "Year Books," that is, the medieval law reports. The political consequences of this victory were very great, for the absolutist doctrines enshrined in Roman Law never gained a convincing foothold in English Common Law. It is not surprising that among the greatest champions of the liberties of the subject against the centralist claims of the Stuart kings were the common lawyers, most ably represented by the redoubtable Sir Edward Coke, who believed that Magna Carta, for example, being a simple declaration of the Common Law granted many years before the advent of Parliament, was nonetheless "such a sovereign that he hath no fellow," meaning that it partook of a character so fundamental, being of the Common Law, that not even Parliament could touch it. Subsequently this gave way to the doctrine of parliamentary supremacy but not before the unique value of the sources of the Common Law had become firmly established.

30. There were three great codifications after the secession from Spain: the Andrés Bello Code in Chile, completed between 1846 and 1855; the code of Dalmacio Vélez Sarsfield in Argentina in 1863–1869; and the code of Teixeira de Freitas in Brazil in 1856–1865. These three served as models for the civil codes of the rest of the continent with the sole exception of Cuba, which adopted the Spanish Civil Code of 1889, itself closely modeled after the Napoleonic model. See K. L. Karst and K. S. Rosen, *Law and Development in Latin America* (Berkeley, Los Angeles, and London, 1975): 45–47.

overlooked or underrated by English legal scholars. J. H. Morgan, K.C., who held the chair of constitutional law in the University of London at the time when he was appointed editor of the Law Section of the 14th edition of the *Encyclopaedia Britannica*, believed that

> in its freedom from the infection of foreign influences, the common law is as much a national possession as the English language itself. It is instinct with the English genius for practice as opposed to theory and of no other system of law can it be said so truly, in the language of Mr. Justice Oliver Wendell Holmes that "the life of the law is not logic but experience." The Pilgrim Fathers took it with them to America, even as they took the English speech, with the result that it is the foundation of the law of the United States.[31]

Fulsome but not unacceptably off the mark, and if the character and the diversity of the sources of the Common Law are borne in mind, it is not difficult to equate the spirit of the English juridical edifice constructed in this way with Ruskin's vivid assertion that "the principal admirableness of the Gothic schools of architecture, that they thus receive the results of the labour of inferior minds; and out of fragments full of imperfection, and betraying that imperfection in every touch, indulgently raise up a stately and unaccusable whole."[32] This striking assertion is equally apposite when applied to the construction of the edifice of the English language, devoid of master plan or regal academies, at the mercy of the robust everyday usage of countless scarcely lettered speakers, each freely producing "fragments full of imperfection." And yet, the language continues to wax healthy and endlessly creative on a diet of Californian spelling eccentricities, pidgin syntaxis, and pedestrian mercantile and technological accretions.

That the Common Law and the Civil Law preside over the legal arrangements of the two great cultural transplants of the New World cannot simply be dismissed as a curious but unimportant coincidence. Neither can it be regarded as conclusive evidence of the persistence of the polarity suggested by the Gothic and Baroque cultural modes, but the plausibility of this polarity is strengthened significantly if these differing legal traditions are considered together with the language, the religion, and, most important, the politics of the English and Castilian progenitors. In the countries of the former Spanish Indies, the dominant tradition is monarchical and therefore centralist. It originated with the policy of the Catholic monarchs of bringing the Castilian baronial periphery firmly under the control of the Crown and was subsequently consoli-

31. J. H. Morgan, entry under "Common Law," *Encyclopedia Britannica*, 14th ed.
32. Ruskin, *Stones of Venice*, II: 159–160.

dated by Philip II, the arch-bureaucratic Prudent King, and the reformist Charles III. After the wars of independence, it was embraced by the nascent republics in its most emphatic centralist form and has survived virtually undiminished into our time, largely in association with populism and the rise of modern industry. It has no political color and is as evident in the single-party systems of Mexico and Cuba as it was in the former authoritarian regimes of Chile and Argentina, or the social democratic regimes of Peru, Colombia, and Brazil.

The democratic and federal political arrangements of the United States and Canada bear the imprint of their aristocratic origin as clearly as Latin America her monarchical antecedents. Even during the relatively brief periods when Tudors, Stuarts, and Lord Protectors endeavored to secure an absolute and lasting preponderance, the administration of the realm was characteristically and almost uniquely based on the widespread involvement of the aristocracy in the ordinary business of government. Under the Tudors, when the gradual transformation of royal household into bureaucratic structures was only just beginning, the major entities of rule, including Parliament, the elaborate panoply of shire governance and the apparatus of justice, all rested on what Marc Bloch described as "that collaboration of the well-to-do classes in power, so characteristic of the English polity as long ago as the middle ages."[33]

Almost to the day one century before the United States proclaimed her constitution, the "Glorious Revolution" of 1688 turned the page forever on the more recent centralizing efforts of Puritans and Stuarts and inaugurated the longest-lasting and most influential period of aristocratic dominance in modern history.[34] During the centuries that fol-

---

33. Marc Bloch, *Feudal Society* (London, 1967), 2 vols., continuously paginated, 371. This argument is advanced by Philip Corrigan and Derek Sayer in *The Great Arch: English State Formation as Cultural Revolution* (London, 1985): 16.

34. The aristocratic preponderance in the House of Commons was quite overwhelming. As John Cannon, a recent historian of the period observes,

> The cohesiveness of the eighteenth-century House of Commons, from which sprang a sense of common values and a sense of confidence, made it one of the most exclusive ruling elites in human history. In 1715, out of 558 members, no fewer than 234 had fathers who had also served in the House: by 1754, the number had grown to 294, well over 50%. . . . In addition to the 294 referred to, another twenty-nine members of the House had grand-fathers who had served. A further forty-two had brothers serving with them or who had already served. . . . Another twenty-two members had uncles or great uncles who had served, and ten more had cousins who were or had been members. The grand total of additions is therefore 103 which, added to the previous 294, gives 397 members who had or had had close relatives in the House— well over 70%. Nor should it be presumed that the remaining 25–30% of the House were men of humble antecedents or lacking in good connections. Thomas Potter, not included in any of the above categories, was the son of the Archbishop of Canterbury; . . . John Fitzpatrick was son of an Irish baron, married to the daughter of an

lowed, a relatively weak Hanoverian monarchical establishment surrounded by a relatively strong baronial periphery provided the setting for the development of the habits, attitudes, and institutions that were so distinctively to influence the shape and institutions of transplanted English societies overseas, including Australia and New Zealand as well as the American colonies, both before and after gaining their independence from Britain. The English baronial periphery prospered under a monarch without an army, who depended on the generosity of Parliament for his annual allowance and who was effectively deprived of the means of maintaining a credible court. After 1688, an English Versailles is inconceivable. Queen Anne and the early Hanoverians had to make do with a frugal civil list (Walpole regained favor at the time of the accession of George II by promising an increase of 130,000 pounds), at the same time that Philip V was building the vast and sumptuous Palacio de Oriente in the heart of Madrid because he thought El Escorial unsuitable for his court. In the absence of a preponderant regal entity and a convincing court, the aristocratic holders of effective social and political power remained, by default or by choice, *in situ*, in their own manorial courts, meeting each other at neighboring hunts or at Westminster, where the center of their attention was not the royal court, as it would have been, say, under Louis XV or Philip V, or even Charles III, but the sessions of a Parliament that they largely controlled and the intentions of ministers they did not fear.[35] Geographically distant one from the other, they were responsive to a diversity of regional and other particular circumstances and consequently were far from constituting anything even remotely resembling an aristocratic Fronde.

The memory of the sanguinary troubles of the seventeenth century did not vanish quickly, and its persistence explains in part the preoccu-

---

earl and brother-in-law to a duchess; Robert Lee was son of an earl and another illegitimate grandson of Charles II; William Ponsonby was son of a British baron and Irish earl and married to a daughter of the 3rd Duke of Devonshire. (*Aristocratic Century: The Peerage of Eighteenth-Century England* [Cambridge, 1984]: 114–115)

35. There were some who did not think this an ideal state of affairs, among them, John Hampden, who argued in 1846 that 1688 had indeed brought in a "reign of aristocratic humbug" that had lasted until his own time, when "a mighty and wealthy and luxurious aristocracy . . . are, in truth, the possessors of all and everything in England. They possess the crown. . . . They possess the House of Commons, by their sons, their purses, and their influence. They possess the church and the state, the army and the navy. They possess all offices at home and abroad. They possess the land at home, and the colonies to the end of the earth." J. V. Beckett, *The Aristocracy in England, 1660–1914* (London, 1988): 404.

pation with ensuring the stability of an aristocratic arrangement largely dependent on the conviction that the well-being of each patrician should not be secured at the expense of the others. This helped to enshrine reasonable compromise among equals and a keen distrust of excessive power or influence in any hands, especially in those of one's peers, as twin civic virtues necessary for survival and tranquillity, confirmed by practice and common sense. It also nurtured a robust disdain for paid officials and bureaucrats and a correspondingly strong approval of voluntary work. A recent history of the period lists as their characteristic traits "parsimony, isolationism, xenophobia and instinctive hostility to the executive."[36]

Rural England in the eighteenth century, according to G. M. Trevelyan, the preferred ambit of the baronial aristocracy, was governed "by the Patriarchal sway of the Justices of the Peace," who, though nominally officials of the Crown, were in reality appointed by the lord lieutenant following the opinion of the local gentry. "The Revolution of 1688," explains Trevelyan, "had been a revolt of these unpaid Magistrates against the Central Government which had overstrained their loyalty in religion and politics." These magistrates had many responsibilities that were discharged without an effective administrative bureaucracy because this would have resulted in unacceptable increases in local taxation, and "they preferred inefficient local government provided only it was cheap."[37] Against all imaginable odds, the exertions of those unlikely amateur administrators proved successful and helped to accord lasting social prestige to those prepared to do unpaid work for the public good. The volunteer as well as the unpaid public servant and the amateur sportsman are all creatures of the aristocratic century of England, and it should suffice to note what the French, Spanish, or Italian counterparts of the English landed gentry and aristocracy were doing at the time to appreciate the uniqueness and significance of this social phenomenon.

Things change, and our understanding of the nature of change must be among the truly paradoxical feats of the human intellect, because when we affirm, as we do in this case, that something has changed, we are simultaneously affirming that something has not changed. Our understanding of change combines an awareness of alteration with an equally keen awareness of permanence. Unless the thing remains itself,

36. J. R. Jones, *The Revolution of 1688 in England* (London, 1988): 330.
37. G. M. Trevelyan, *English Social History* (London, 1947): 352–353.

to some degree unchanged, we cannot state that it has changed. As Oakeshott explains,

> If there were no alteration, there would be an unbroken sameness; if there were no remaining the same there would be the recollection of that which had unaccountably gone and the observation of that which had unaccountably appeared. . . . The idea of change is a holding together of two apparently opposed but in fact complementary ideas; that of alteration and that of sameness; that of difference and that of identity.[38]

The world has undergone enormous changes during the past five centuries, but these have not affected all societies equally; some have sustained greater transformations than would have been thought possible only a few generations ago, while others have scarcely moved away from the most primitive modes of subsistence agriculture. The advanced industrial countries of the English cultural tradition must be numbered without hesitation among those that have experienced the most profound alterations of all, and it should not be difficult to list some of the more important among these changes—easier by far than to list those cultural traits that have remained sufficiently unaltered to enable us to speak of change at all. In the light of this explanation, however, it should be possible to propose, even if in the form of a working hypothesis, that those traits, or "moral and imaginative elements" or "mental habits," of the cultural tradition inherited by the English-speaking Americans have changed less that most faithfully accord with the acknowledgment of privacy and the matter-of-factness that Pevsner perceived in the Englishness of the Perpendicular style, with the robust, unhindered, and creative individualism that dominates Ruskin's interpretation of the Gothic, and with Ockham's portentous aperture toward a modernity beset by the challenge of diversity. Each of these is consistent with each other and with the definitive religious, legal, political, and linguistic arrangements of the English-speaking Americans. Every one of them is at ease with a diversity and pluralism that elsewhere would be dismissed as disorderly if not chaotic. All are conversant with the disposition of a Gothic fox who knows many things, thrives on diversity, responds to eccentric particularisms, is familiar with the asymmetries of privacy and individuality, and believes, with Ruskin, that the best in man cannot manifest itself but in company with much error.

38. Oakeshott, *On History and Other Essays*, 98.

CHAPTER VI

Hellenistic Aftermath

Nothing in the Spanish cultural tradition can compare with the prowess of the Catholic Reformation, and nothing that the English people have done can compare with their Industrial Revolution. The Counter-Reformation is to the cultural tradition of Spain and her Indies what the Industrial Revolution is to that of the English-speaking peoples everywhere, especially in Britain and North America; the principal difference between them is that the English feat engendered an immense number of cultural traits and artifacts that proved effortlessly and universally attractive not only to those in the neighborhood but to millions obviously beyond the reach of any form of direct influence or compulsion. Certainly, England never forced the French to play rugby, Uruguayans to join the Boy Scouts, or Bulgarians to watch television. The massive diffusion of these and countless other traits and artifacts proceeded unhindered by the declining fortunes of the empire. It could even be argued that the acceptance of the creatures of English provenance became more general, even enthusiastic, precisely when the islanders were visibly relinquishing their military and political primacy.

This is a rare occurrence, without precedent other than that suggested by the Hellenistic Age, when the culture of an Athens that had long ceased to lead an empire or dominate the Aegean world expanded and flourished into the splendid centuries that spanned classical Greece and Augustan Rome. When Aristotle was born in 383 B.C. in Stagira, a colonial settlement as distant from the Athens and Thebes of the day as

Melbourne, New York, and Toronto are today removed from Gatwick and Heathrow, two generations had already elapsed since the close of the great period of Athenian political and military domination, and when he died, in 322 B.C., one year after his pupil Alexander, he left behind him a Hellenistic world that saw the culture of Athens retain the center of the stage for another three remarkable centuries. It is now over one hundred years since British industrial might was overtaken by the United States and Germany, and the beginning of the dissolution of the empire immediately following the Second World War has already receded into the mists of history. And yet, it is possible to affirm that regardless of country of origin or place of residence, ourselves and our contemporaries were all born and live today in a world made in England, and the world in which our great-grandchildren will mellow into venerable old age will be as English as the Hellenistic world was Greek, or better, Athenian.

In untroubled circumstances, the influence of the English in shaping the modern world would be clear and indisputable, but in our time, it has been clouded over by a surfeit of warnings and lamentations, some very dire, about Britain's plunge to the lower depths of international postimperial anonymity not immensely dissimilar to the ones that accompanied the decline of Athens after the collapse of the Delian Confederacy. A few of these are somber and sobering descriptions of the obvious (Britain has ceased, for example, to rule the waves, or to be a principal exporter of motorcycles), but many are shrill and implausible, and others barely conceal obscure animosities.[1] Their abundance is nonetheless intriguing, especially because it stems largely from the assumption that solely because the islanders' military and political power diminished in important ways in recent decades, what they achieved in the past at home or overseas or are endeavoring to do today is necessarily quaint or defunct, or is doomed to rapid obsolescence.

This is wrong not because of the likelihood that Britain will suddenly astonish all by regaining Phoenix-like her industrial vitality and imperial

---

1. Jay Carr, a film reviewer for *The Boston Globe*, commenting on the revival of Sir Laurence Olivier's 1960 film *The Entertainer*, pointed out that it was not every day "an actor gets the chance to portray England itself, as Olivier did in the person of Archie Rice—the seedy, lecherous music-hall second-rater with nothing going for him but endurance. Archie personifies England in the wake of Suez, going down the tubes—cheating, lying, wheedling, betraying the only people who care about him." More politely, Derek Bok, president of Harvard University, expressed comparable misgivings when he said that the United States is now "in the early stages of a long decline like that of Britain in the early part of the 19th century which continues to the present day." *The Boston Sunday Globe* (August 6, 1989): 34.

preeminence but because the facile correlation between the end of empires and the decline and disappearance of the cultures they engendered, conquered, or embraced, is not inevitable. It may have the semblance of a general explanation, but it misleads by ignoring the fact that the survival of culture is bound up inextricably with that of the forms, signs, symbols, and, generally, traits and artifacts to which it gave birth, and these, like lingering echoes, can persist for a long time after the dissolution of the military and political enterprises that presided over their inception. Cultural forms and their imperial begetters can prosper separately as well as sink together into oblivion, and while survival in any guise is normally beyond the reach of earthly guarantees (remember Ozymandias?), the haste with which many have rushed to class the British moment with that of Mayans and Assyrians is unjustified.

It is also infelicitous because it coaxes us into accepting the deception that the Industrial Revolution has disappeared from view and that we are now entering an enfeebled, barren, rather precious and ineffectual postindustrial epoch, presumably different from the noisy, congested, brash, and feverishly creative mode that we have learned to associate with successful industrialism. This malaise is presumably responsible for a parallel crisis in the arts that would appear to justify Daniel Bell's assertion that today "modernism is exhausted. There is no tension. The creative impulses have gone slack. It has become an empty vessel." The principal cause of this undoing is presumably the substitution of consumption for production as the driving force of the modern economy. Earlier in the process, Puritan restraint limited consumption and created the savings that sustained capitalist accumulation and investment; but today, we are told, with the disappearance of moral and cultural restraints, "the justification of capitalism has become hedonism, the idea of pleasure as a way of life. . . . What defines bourgeois society is not needs, but wants. Wants are psychological, not biological, and are by nature unlimited."[2] Presented against such a discouraging background, the restful suggestion is very welcome indeed that with industrial modernity vanishing behind us, only a modicum of effort is required to move away from the anxieties that bedeviled our yesterdays and into a gentler, greener world of stately trees, weekend painting, frolicking dolphins, neoclassic architecture, cuddly koalas, and chamber music in the barn.

This, of course, is not so. We are not elsewhere but very much in the

2. Daniel Bell, *The Cultural Contradictions of Capitalism* (New York, 1976): 20–22.

middle of an English Industrial Revolution that is scarcely more than two centuries old and shows no symptoms of weakness or decline. On the contrary, vigorous, relentless change remains the characteristic sine qua non of the modern industrial ambit, and the resulting immense flow of major and lesser innovations ceaselessly adds complexity and diversity to the leading countries of a world that is certainly not tottering on the brink of dissolution. The vitality of the center is echoed on the periphery by countless millions of fellow human beings who wish enthusiastically to embrace industrial modernity in any of its many guises, some of which are as vulgar as their immense popularity suggests, with a readiness that owes nothing to duress but reflects the persistent attraction felt almost everywhere for its symbols, artifacts, modes of conduct, and styles of living. To describe, therefore, the closing decades of the twentieth century as "postindustrial" is incorrect and misleading as well as inelegant, and in such circumstances it is helpful seriously to reconsider the analogy between the cultural disposition of our time and that of the Hellenistic Age.

At some time or another during this century, the world crossed a barely perceptible but real threshold into a quasi-Hellenistic period (neo-Hellenistic?) during which the cultural traits and artifacts generated by the English-speaking peoples, especially during their Industrial Revolution, have been consolidated as principal strands in the fabric of knowledge, affectations, beliefs, and Tocquevillian "habits of the heart," on which rest the quality and the survival of our civilization. The similarity between this process and the sequel to the dissolution of Athenian imperial power suggests explanations and complexities vastly more plausible than the ones associated with the presumed inception of an epoch that will turn the page on the culture of industrial modernity.

An early problem in suggesting this analogy arises from the misleading precision of the conventional dates for the Hellenistic Age, from the death of Alexander the Great in 323 B.C. to the Battle of Actium in 31 B.C., which confirmed Roman supremacy over the Mediterranean. Exactitude of this kind implies that complex cultural processes such as the diffusion of Hellenic culture can have clear-cut ends and beginnings, a nonsense in our time as well as in antiquity. (When did the Reformation end? When did Romanticism begin? When did the Industrial Revolution get under way?) Used here, these crisply precise dates force us to ignore that Alexander's father, Philip, and his uncle, Perdiccas, and his grandfather, Amyntas III, and Archelaus, his distant predecessor on the throne, had all been thoroughly Hellenized many years before 323 B.C.

Three generations before Alexander's death in Babylon, Archelaus had befriended Socrates and Plato and invited Euripides to the Macedonian court at Pella.[3] Philip's adolescent years were spent as a hostage in Thebes, but the inauspicious circumstance did not cool an admiration for the culture of the Hellenes that could not have diminished when on his return to Pella, he learned that Perdiccas III, his elder brother and predecessor on the throne, kept a correspondence with Plato and that it was on the philosopher's advice that he gave him a portion of Macedonian territory and his first military command.[4] The Hellenistic inclination of the great Macedonian king was clearly reflected in his choice of Aristotle as tutor to young Alexander, but its most unexpected and lasting consequence was his decision to make Attic Greek, instead of his own Macedonian, the official language at court and chancery, a choice that Arnold Toynbee thought had done more than the literary genius of Euripides and all the other Athenian men of letters to establish the lingua franca of the post-Alexandrine world.

Overprecise conventional dates are also unhelpful because they emphasize the demise of the conquering Macedonian protagonist while entirely overlooking the departure of the Athenian progenitors. The problem of determining when the Athenian ascendancy came to an end has exercised historians for a long time and is unlikely to be resolved here.[5] Probably the most plausible interpretation is that it came about as a direct consequence of the catastrophic failure of the Syracusan expedition in 413 B.C., an event that preceded the death of Alexander by almost a century.[6] Indeed, the uniqueness of the Hellenistic period as a phenom-

3. George Grote, *A History of Greece: From the Earliest Period to the Close of the Generation Contemporary with Alexander the Great* (New York, 1971): IX, Chap. LXXXVI, 203–204; Arnold Toynbee, *Hellenism: The History of a Civilization* (London, 1959): 121; J. R. Ellis, *Philip II and Macedonian Imperialism* (London, 1976): 41–42.

4. Grote, *History*, IX, Chap. LXXXVI, 204. When Philip assumed the throne, Speusippos, Plato's disciple in the Academy, reminded him "that he owed the origin of his rule to Plato." Earlier, Perdiccas asked Plato for a counselor, and the philosopher sent his pupil Euphraios to Pella where, according to a contemporary account, "he regulated court society in such bad taste that only those who knew geometry or philosophy were admitted to the king's table." Paul Friedlander, *Plato* (Princeton, 1969): 92, 102.

5. Plutarch, moved by his aversion for the post-Alexandrine monarchies, believed that Athens had died with Demosthenes, in 322 B.C. A more orthodox view is that the final chapter was written by Philip's Macedonian pikemen, in 338 B.C., on the plains of Chaeronea. "The great lion, which today rises from the lonely sweep of Boetia [marking the battleground] does more than honour the fallen; it marks the end of the (Athenian) city-state." G. W. Botsford and C. A. Robinson, *Hellenic History* (New York, 1948): 295.

6. Thucydides, a contemporary and a combatant, described the Athenian expedition to Syracuse in 413 B.C. as "the greatest action that we know of in Hellenic history—to the victors the most brilliant of successes, to the vanquished, the most calamitous of defeats; for they were utterly and entirely defeated." *History of the Peloponnesian War*, trans.

enon of persistent cultural diffusion owes less to the brief and rather thin
Alexandrine imperial presence than to the early disappearance of its
Athenian source. Athenian rather than Greek, as it should be Castilian
rather than Spanish and English rather than British, although this may
appear as dismissive of Thebes, Corinth, and Sparta or, across the sea,
Samos, Chios, and Miletos; as today the use of the "English" label could
be construed to be dismissive of Scotland and Canada or the "Castilian"
one, of Catalonia and Andalusia. It is precisely the preeminence of Athens that lies at the heart of the rise and decline of Hellenism during the
sixth and fifth centuries B.C., and this emphatic centrality does not dissipate when attention is directed away from military and political affairs
to philosophy, literature, and the visual arts. "The eye of Greece," Mil-
ton's apposite description of the Athenian city-state, was not intended
to dismiss the distinction attained by the other centers of Hellas but to
note that Athens encompassed them splendidly, which feat has justified
for millennia the now respectable habit of looking at Hellenism through
the prism of the Athenian achievement.

  Once the narrow chronology of the Hellenistic Age is discarded in
favor of a broader view, more compatible with the cultural antecedents
of the period, conventional uses based on the faulty chronology also go
by the board. The use of the descriptive phrase "fourth century" for the
period 400 B.C. to 323 B.C., for example, becomes untenable, being the
kind of oversimple precision that would have us agree that art became
Hellenistic when Alexander expired and remained such until the Roman
victory at Actium. This distortion is probably tolerated simply because
323 B.C. is a difficult date to overlook when searching for a chronolog-
ical boundary in the latter decades of the fourth century, but the dis-
crepancy between the contrivance and what was actually happening at

---

Rex Warner (London, 1982): 536–537. Modern scholarship has not attenuated the severity of this verdict. Grote believed that the downfall of Athens had "one great cause—
we may say one single cause—the Sicilian expedition. The empire of Athens both was,
and appeared to be, in exhuberant strength when that expedition was sent forth—strength
more than sufficient to bear up against all moderate faults or moderate misfortunes . . .
but . . . after the Syracusan catastrophe, the empire . . . was irretrievably broken up."
Grote, *History*, VI, Chap. LXV, 505–506. Almost a century after Grote, the author of a
recent work on the Syracusan expedition also declined to accept that it was the Macedonian phalanx at Chaeronea that brought Athens to her knees, explaining that "the
Athenians who went down at Chaeronea . . . were fighting for a chimera: the Athenian
polis had run its course three quarters of a century before. . . . All it stood for lay bleached
and dry among the white-picked bones of Athens's dead soldiers in Sicily. The spring had
gone out of the Periclean year, and the high summer too." Peter Green, *Armada from
Athens* (New York, 1970): 355–356.

the time has not escaped attention, and the aesthetic argument has been put forward that the art of the fourth century, from beginning to end, has more in common with that of the Hellenistic Age than with its classical antecedents. The period should be viewed "as a continuum, with the major break between 'classical' and whatever one chose to call the succeeding era occurring around the end of the Peloponnesian War."[7] This is a much more convincing argument and when extended beyond the visual arts to the sciences, philosophy, and politics, serves as a helpful reminder that the emphatically proto-Hellenistic fourth century was, after all, the age of Plato, Aristotle of Stagira, Zeno, and Epicurus, of Demosthenes, Lysias, Isocrates, and Xenophon, of Zeuxis, Timanthes, Praxiteles, Skopas, Lysippos, Diogenes, Theophrastus, and Menander, and that the earliest universities and libraries originated not from the classical severities of the Periclean Age but from the lush soil of that first Hellenistic century. Plato's Academy and Aristotle's Lyceum and their Alexandrian offspring, the Library and the Museum, have as valid a claim as the ubiquitous *Gymnasium*, Xenophon's *Anabasis*, or Zeno's Stoicism to be numbered among the Hellenistic cultural forms that did not require duress or zealous proselytism to transcend the boundaries of their time and place.

The emergent paradox is that of sumptuously textured Hellenistic centuries shaped by the arts, language, ideas, institutions, daily practices of life, and cultural artifacts of an Attic metropolis the military and political preeminence of which had vanished three, perhaps four, generations before the Macedonian onslaught. Alexander crossed the Hellespont in 334 B.C. leading an army of scarcely sixteen thousand of his countrymen and about an equal number of Greek allies and tribal levies from the Balkans. For a dozen years he campaigned triumphantly from Libya to the Punjab without stopping long anywhere, and after his death the short-lived empire fell apart swiftly in the struggle over his succession. It is partly because it was completed by a small force and in such a very short time that the Alexandrine prowess impresses the more, but humbled Asian monarchs and a string of victories are insufficient to resolve the inconsistency between an unquestionably exiguous imperial presence and the remarkably unforced extension of a Hellenism that blossomed into the enduring richness of the age. The Macedonian invasion may have been necessary to bring this about, but it was certainly not sufficient.

7. J. J. Pollitt, *Art and Experience in Classical Greece* (Cambridge, 1972): 136–137.

The Hellenistic Age cannot be properly understood except as a consequence of the attraction felt for the culture of the Hellenes by the
people with whom it came into contact and who, with minor exceptions,
were satisfied to embrace its symbols and cultural traits without compulsion. It owed as much to the appeal that the culture of Hellas had
for the conquerors who, after all, included only a very small number of
Athenians, as for the conquered and even for those who never saw an
armed Macedonian in their lives. This is equally true of Egypt, Persia,
and Judaea, where deeply rooted religious and indigenous monarchical
traditions could have raised impregnable barriers against the Hellenizing
tide.[8] In these regions there was some tenacious resistance, but it was
still insufficient to find means other than the Greek language to reach
the faithful when the ancestral languages had fallen into desuetude,
swept aside by the Hellenizing tide. The Greek translation of the Bible
known as the *Septuagint*, or "Translation of the Seventy," came into
being in early third-century Egypt precisely because the Egyptian Jews
"had lost both their Hebrew and their Aramaic," and they were not the
only ones who made good use of this Greek version of the Scriptures;
the *Septuagint* achieved wide circulation throughout the Mediterranean
world and eventually became, most tellingly, the Bible of Paul of Tarsus.[9]

8. The Maccabean uprising against the Seleucid king, Antiochus IV Epiphanes, cannot
be understood except against the background of pervasive Hellenization that preceded
and outlived the troubles. When Antiochus assumed the throne, the Jews had been living
for many generations in the Hellenistic kingdom, peacefully and prosperously. Under the
Ptolemies, especially, the Jewish population "was so much Hellenized that it could hardly
speak anything but Greek. . . . The aristocracy of Jerusalem, even the priestly aristocracy,
had become Hellenized." The high priest of the Temple, who had earlier Hellenized his
name from Jesus to Jason, thought it fitting proudly to sponsor the conferral on Jerusalem
of the privilege to constitute itself into a polis. Following Greek tradition, the Council of
Elders became a municipal senate, and both a *gymnasium* and the institution of the *ephe-
beia*, essential features of the Hellenistic cultural landscape, made their appearance in the
heart of the city. According to II Maccabees, the popularity of the gymnasium was such
that "the aping of Greek manners reached a peak and the adoption of gentile ways a height
such that the priests were no longer eager to perform their duties at the altar but made
light of the temple and neglected the sacrifices . . . [and put] the highest value on Greek
honours." Pierre Jouguet, *Macedonian Imperialism and the Hellenization of the East* (London, 1928): 377–378; II Maccabees, trans. A. Goldstein (New York, 1983): Chap. IV,
12–15; Robin Lane Fox, "Hellenistic Culture and Literature," in John Boardman, Jasper
Griffin, and Oswyn Murray, eds., *Greece and the Hellenistic World*, Oxford History of
the Classical World (Oxford, 1988): 340–341.
    9. The legendary explanation of the origin of this translation, which may have been
produced as propaganda, is that Ptolemy Philadelphus (285 B.C.–246 B.C.) summoned
seventy-two Jewish scholars who, ordered to make individual translations of the Scriptures
into Greek, produced seventy-two identical versions of the sacred text. The ostensible
object of the legend was to accord divine validation to the Greek version of the Jewish
Bible then circulating in Egypt. F. E. Peters, *The Harvest of Hellenism* (New York, 1970):
299.

The expansion of Hellenism was not the one-dimensional consequence of a successful military venture but an exceptionally complex and long-lasting process of unforced cultural diffusion. The problem is that Alexander's feat of arms towered so impressively over the horizon of antiquity that it has been understandably easy for historians to assign to the great chieftain the principal responsibility for the vast process of Hellenistic acculturation, helped somewhat by the prosaic incentive of the vanquished to embrace the culture of the victors and the predictable inclination of the conquerors to derive as much comfort as possible from their triumphs. This oversimple attribution, however, fails to explain the earlier Hellenization of Alexander himself, of his ancestors, and of Macedonia, a country never conquered by the Greek-speaking southerners, or the spread of Hellenism far beyond the boundaries of the regions over which Alexander and his successors retained control.[10]

Addressing this aspect of the matter, M. Rostovtzeff agrees emphatically with Toynbee, although with some exaggeration, when he affirms that "the Greeks did not force their civilization upon any man. To make proselytes by force never occurred [to them]."[11] The truly remarkable feature of the period was "the peaceful penetration of the Hellenic culture into regions never trodden by Hellenic conquerors even at the high tide of Hellenic expansion," brought about, as Toynbee points out, by the adoption of the culture of the Athenians by peoples who "were under no external compulsion to open their hearts and minds to it" and resulting in post-Alexandrine Hellenism making "peaceful conquests of ground which had not been won for it by Macedonian soldiers."[12] Nor

10. Jouguet observed that among the most significant results of the Hellenization of Asia was "the influence of Greek civilization on kings who were neither Greek nor Macedonian. The ruling houses of Bithynia, Cappadocia and Pontus . . . adopted the manners and the language of the Greeks, they protected and founded Greek cities, and Hellenism rested there, as elsewhere, on the traditional institutions of the *polis*." Jouguet, *Macedonian Imperialism*, 390.

11. "Upon any man"? Not even, one may ask, the Jews? Lane Fox may be leaning too far in the opposite direction when he affirms that "Greek culture was not always imposed," but he then qualifies this with the observation that "it could exert its own fascination. Among the Jews we know of voluntary Hellenizers who wished to go over to Greek ways and religion. They were only stopped after a bitter war, and Jewish culture emerged into the Maccabean age [175–63 B.C.], essentially resistant to the hard core of Hellenism." Further on, he adds, "Greek culture was so lively and such fun. It had theatres and athletics, some fascinating books, and a refined style of dining, the symposium. . . . In their trading and art, their warfare and intellectuality, their literature and culture, the Greeks towered over their Asian subjects." Lane Fox, "Hellenistic Culture," 340–341; M. Rostovtzeff, *Greece* (New York, 1970): 281.

12. "A Philadelphia and an Adrianople, whose names commemorate their foundation by some Macedonian or Roman potentate, are less eloquent monuments of the Hellenic's intrinsic attractiveness than a Nicomedia and a Nicaea, whose names commemorate their

had it been won by Athenian, Theban, Corinthian, or Spartan soldiers, because the definitive characteristic of the period is that the Hellenic cultural inheritance flourished, expanded, and acquired its universalist mode long after Athens had vanished from the front rank of the powers.[13]

Two centuries after the destruction of the Athenian empire, the lingua franca of the known world was Greek, and Hellenism—a term derived from a Greek word meaning "to speak Greek"—reigned supreme.[14] Had this occurred during the dominance of Athens' Delian Confederacy, it would hardly merit a footnote. Conquering armies frequently try to force their language and customs on defeated adversaries who tend mostly to come to terms with the new situation by adopting the cultural traits of the victor as a means of ensuring survival and well-being. This readiness seldom outlasts the power of the victors, as the modern post-imperial experience of Portugal, the Netherlands, Spain, Germany, and, more recently, Russia clearly indicate; the Dutch left their East Indies scarcely two generations ago after three and a half centuries of uninter-rupted commercial, political, and cultural presence, and it is already evident that apart from quaint vestiges here and there, their language is disappearing from the Indonesian archipelago as rapidly as the cultural traits with which it is associated. The German experience has not been remarkably dissimilar, and it is not easy to find many German words still in common use in Papua New Guinea or East Africa. As for Russia's

---

foundation by the Philhellene descendants of a barbarian prince of Bythinia who had thrown off the yoke of the Achaemenidae, had escaped being conquered by Alexander, and had successfully resisted the imperialism of the Seleucidae." Arnold Toynbee, *A Study of History* (London, 1954): III, 408, 416.

13. Among the more bizarre latter-day consequences of the dissolution of the Euro-pean empires during the postwar decades must be counted the tendency to abuse ancient history so as to attack modern imperialisms. A recent historian of antiquity, for example, apparently moved deeply by anti-imperialist zeal, prefaces a massive volume with the as-sertion that he "must state plainly at the outset that I regard the whole notion of a con-scious, idealistic, missionary propagation in conquered territories of Greek culture, mores, literature, art, and religion . . . as a pernicious myth, compounded of anachronistic Chris-tian evangelicism and Plutarch-inspired wishful thinking, and designed (whether con-sciously or not) to provide moral justification for what was, in essence, despite its romantic popularity, large-scale economic and imperial exploitation." This author rather disarm-ingly rounds out this particular complaint by pointing out, "Despite the widespread adop-tion of Attic *koine* as a Hellenistic *lingua franca*, it is notable—and symptomatic—how resistant it remained to foreign loan words." This assertion alone confirms every "exag-geration" ever made about the ubiquity of the culture of the Hellenes. Peter Green, *Alex-ander to Actium: The Historical Evolution of the Hellenistic Age* (Berkeley, Los Angeles, and Oxford, 1990): XV, 312.

14. F. W. Walbank, *The Hellenistic World* (London, 1981): 14.

more recent discomforts, it is hardly necessary to enlarge on the melancholy fate of the many thousands of teachers of the Russian language who have been left unemployed in the former German Democratic Republic as well as throughout much of Eastern Europe. French has fared better, especially in Quebec and Lebanon and in the former colonies in Africa and Asia where its use remains widespread. Elsewhere things have not gone so well, and there has been a perceptible decline in popularity during the past half century, from its heyday in the period between the wars when it appeared to have successfully consolidated an elegant claim to be the language of diplomacy and the beau monde. Since then, and in spite of the persistent efforts of the Alliance Française, it has lost ground visibly, and only the unusually zealous would maintain today that it has even a remote chance of displacing English from its dominant position.

Spain and Portugal ruled for three hundred years over the greatest empire since that of the Romans, and the Spanish and Portuguese languages are still in current and vigorous use in almost every region of the New World that was once under their suzerainty—but not in all and certainly not an inch beyond them. The well-publicized use of the Spanish language in certain regions of English-speaking North America is an entirely different phenomenon; a consequence of the movement across frontiers—not invariably legal—of large numbers of people pushed by penury and attracted by the prosperity of the United States and Canada, it can hardly rank as an instance of the unforced adoption of the Spanish language by the inhabitants of the host country. Moreover, the special social circumstances of the majority of these immigrants and the inevitable process of acculturation have resulted in linguistic practices that are increasingly distant from the Spanish language and are probably best described by the revealing name of "Spanglish."[15] It is unlikely that Spanglish will prevail over English; the probable outcome will simply be the eventual adoption by the newcomers, especially the first generation of

15. There is irony in the choice of this ghastly but accurate descriptive name for what passes for Spanish in many of these regions. "Spanglish" is, pseudonationalistic protestations notwithstanding, an unseemly, scarcely literate linguistic hodgepodge that would not be tolerated in any country within hearing distance of the Real Academia. The irony is that the admixture of extraneous bits of flotsam, the adulteration of spelling and syntaxis, and the virtual abandonment of all grammatical decorum are only possible because this patois found shelter in the ambit of the Gothic fox. Every time they open their mouths, the users of "Spanglish" proclaim *urbi et orbi* that they have embraced the "mental habits," the cultural dispositions, and the customs of the English-speaking host nation with enthusiasm, and to prove it, they present their listeners with the tattered, pitiful remains of the language they inherited from Nebrija.

those born in the English-speaking world, of the language preferred by the host country, not the other way around. Such a result would mirror the fact that the dramatic retreat of the Iberian languages from places where it had been well established, such as the Philippines, Texas, California, Florida, and Goa, has not been compensated by the widespread use of Spanish or Portuguese in countries that were never part of the empire.

It would have required rare prophetic gifts in the immediate aftermath of the Roman defeat at Cannae, in 216 B.C., to have predicted that the language of the Hellenes would in time be displaced by the language of the Latini; gifts as rare would be needed today to predict the language that will eventually take the place of English as the lingua franca of the modern world. This very difficulty, perhaps impossibility, of imagining a successor can be regarded as the most telling measure of the vitality of the sustaining culture.[16] This is not being overlooked elsewhere, and today the most popular specific pursuit in educational institutions outside the English-speaking world is unquestionably the acquisition of a working knowledge of the language of Shakespeare, the Beatles, and the Teenage Mutant Ninja Turtles. According to estimates by The Economist Intelligence Unit, the study of English is compulsory for over fifty million pupils in nineteen countries, ranging from China to Gabon, and an optional subject for another twenty million in seventeen other countries. Regardless of semantic and statistical niceties, it is evident that this has a significance that transcends instrumental efficiencies or the improvement of skills in technological and administrative manipulation, although this aspect of the matter should not be overlooked, as these same recent researches indicate that "over sixty percent of the world's scientists are able to read English, seventy percent of the world's mail is written in English, and eighty percent of all the information in the

16. This aspect of the matter may not have been accorded sufficient importance in otherwise weighty studies of the presumed economic and military decline of the United States. According to Paul Kennedy, for example, "the two great tests which challenge the *longevity* of every major power that occupies the 'number one' position in world affairs [are] whether, in the military/strategical realm, it can preserve a reasonable balance between the nation's perceived defense requirements and the means it possesses to maintain those commitments; and whether, as an intimately related point, it can preserve the technological and economic bases of its power from relative erosion in the face of the ever-shifting patterns of global production." In fact, as the centuries of the Hellenistic aftermath clearly showed in antiquity and the comparable experience of the quasi-Hellenistic decline of the British Empire appears to confirm in our time, it is at least arguable whether failure in both the Kennedy tests will of itself lead either rapidly or necessarily to the rubbish heap of history. *The Rise and Fall of the Great Powers: Economic Change and Military Conflict from 1500 to 2000* (New York, 1989): 514–515.

world's electronic retrieval systems is stored in English."[17] The achievement of the status of universal lingua franca entails much more than widespread acceptability, for language is the foremost carrier of cultural significance, and a strong case could be made for the Hellenistic analogy based solely on the extent of English usage. However, this is overaustere and ignores the large number and the importance of other cultural artifacts and traits created and bequeathed by England during her amazing innings.

Modernity, civilization, and diversity thrive together. This has not always been true, but it is certainly so in the latter decades of the twentieth century. A modern world such as ours, shaped by industry, political pluralism, and social mobility, intriguingly modified by a period of peace and prosperity that by any reckoning must be one of the longest in history, cannot but draw its cultural sustenance from many sources. How can China be ignored when considering noodles, paper, or fireworks? Or France disregarded when metrication reigns supreme and champagne is the universal beverage for making whoopee? Or the contributions of Comte, Weber, and Marx ignored when discussing the Industrial Revolution? Or Italy overlooked when opera prospers everywhere and the vocabulary of music is embraced by millions? Or Persia be forgotten by chess aficionados? A very long time will almost certainly elapse before commissar, cadres, Stakhanovite, Molotov cocktail, and kulak disappear entirely from the lexicon of earnest revolutionaries, or before lovers of symphonic music can be found who are completely ignorant of the German contribution to the form, or before menus in good restaurants cease to be written in French.

The processes of civilization continuing more or less without interruption for some thousands of years has ensured that save for a few notable exceptions largely the result of extraordinary geographic inaccessibility, the diversities of human culture have become increasingly and intricately interdependent, thus far neither erased nor homogenized by the passage of time but endlessly modified, recombined, reformed, occasionally destroyed and recreated, and producing in consequence a splendidly rich and complicated pattern. To claim purity of cultural lineage or absolute originality in these circumstances is a naive enterprise.

17. According to the same report, the teaching of English has become one of the world's important professional and commercial activities, generating an annual turnover of more than $10 billion and still growing strongly, and it adds, "Any country wishing to modernise, industrialise, or become technologically competitive must develop the capacity to assess and use information written in the English language." *English: A World Commodity* (The Economist Intelligence Unit, London, 1988).

There are those who believe that given sufficient time, even the most sharply defined cultural frontiers will become blurred, but we also know that more than awesome courage is required to determine the number of years, decades, centuries, or millennia that will make up that sufficiency. As Lord Keynes reminded us, in the long run we will all be dead. In the meantime, however, we are here and must make do with what is at hand, in this case, an infinity of forms and symbols, emblems and signifiers, traits and artifacts of diverse antiquity and provenance strewn over a vast and untidy landscape, almost without exception bearing the recognizable marks of their origin or of their latest transformation. This is the stuff of human culture, simultaneously shaping and being shaped by our actions and omissions and containing within itself that complex of "habits of the heart," usages, and, generally, socially inherited factors that the better definitions of the concept of culture convincingly make virtually conterminous with man himself.

There are many definitions of culture, and none satisfies all the demands made on this superbly elusive and useful concept, but there are also some crucial convergences. For example, most definitions, if not all, hinge on culture being a social attribute; it is also regarded as an order of sorts, a system rather than a species of chaos, and as significant rather than meaningless.[18] It is not difficult, following the implications of these convergences, to nod approvingly toward those inspired fragments of sociological jargon that, echoing Ferdinand de Saussure, invite us to consider culture as a "signifying system" (Raymond Williams), or better, "a system of significances" (Philip Rieff). If this is so, then the significances are of the essence, and so is the specific manner in which they are to signify. A good indication of what these significances are was given by T. S. Eliot when to the question of what should be included under such a decisive category as "culture," he replied by listing "Derby Day, Henley Regatta, Cowes, the twelfth of August, a cup final, the dog races, the pin table, the dart boards, Wensleydale cheeses, boiled cabbage cut into sections, beetroot in vinegar, nineteenth-century Gothic churches and the music of Elgar."[19] If cheeses signify, so do languages, and at the most decisive level this is realized when words are proffered,

18. This social condition of culture has attracted attention beyond the frontiers of anthropology and sociology. Possibly one of the clearest statements on it comes from the pen of T. S. Eliot. "The culture of the individual is dependent upon the culture of a group or class, and . . . the culture of the group or class is dependent upon the culture of the whole society to which that group or class belongs. Therefore it is the culture of the society that is fundamental." *Notes Towards the Definition of Cultures* (London, 1948): 21.
19. Eliot, *Notes*, 31.

recognized, and accepted, each such transaction an act of intellectual intimacy, a meeting on common ground, an agreement, mistaken or not, about meaning and significance, and also a cluster of actions constitutive of culture. It is in this fashion that "every word, . . . every gesture, every work of art and every historical deed is intelligible because the people who express themselves through them and those who understand them have something in common; the individual always experiences, thinks and acts in a common sphere and only there does he understand."[20] To understand the signs, artifacts, and symbols devised by others requires movement beyond the halfway mark; to understand is to undergo a change, and neither this change nor the act of understanding can be realized without those "modifications of our human mind" that Vico so perceptibly placed at the very center of the process whereby culture is constituted.

Irrespective of uniqueness, relative importance, or eccentricity, traits, artifacts, and significances are neither random occurrences nor permanent features of the cultural landscape; the idea of an internal combustion engine could not have blossomed spontaneously in the mind even of the most accomplished Periclean functionary, nor could *Madame Bovary* have been penned by a committee of Cherokee warriors. As for permanence, there is no plausible reason why these artifacts and traits, including varieties of cheese, metaphysical speculations, hobbies, and sartorial fashions, that flourished under the imperial governance of Carthage or Rome, the Spanish Hapsburgs, or the Ottoman sultans—or of England—should endure forever. Whether the process whereby tribes, families, nations, civilizations, and commonwealths take turns to shoulder the responsibilities of cultural genesis is, or should be, rational, just, anarchic, orderly, or divine is difficult to ascertain, but it is impossible to overlook the fact that the vanguard changes frequently and that the ascription of exceptional virtue to its tenure at any given time may prove to be either unnecessary or unwarranted.

To say that a human group is capable of begetting cultural forms, signs, symbols, and artifacts is tautological, for if it were unable to do so, it would not be human. The very existence of human society, even at its most elemental levels, is intimately bound to this creative capacity. It is an achievement of an entirely different kind, however, to generate

20. Rudolf A. Makkreel, *Dilthey, Philosopher of the Human Studies* (Princeton: Princeton University Press, 1975): 308–309, cited from Wilhelm Dilthey, *Gesammelte Schriften*. Vol. VII. *Der Aufbau der geschichtlichen Welt in den Geisteswissenschaften*, 2d ed., ed. B. Groethoysen (Stuttgart, 1958): 146.

"exportable" artifacts and traits that can travel without compulsion beyond the cultural and political boundaries of their homeland. This is
infrequent to the point of rarity, and it should not be confused with the
none-too-subtle cultural replications that may follow the exercise of imperial duress. To attribute the widespread acceptance of cultural traits
simply to the fact of empire is altogether to miss the point, as the Hellenistic aftermath clearly illustrates and the experience of Castile and of
modern Russia so forcibly confirms.

The Spanish empire was the richest, largest, and most formidable
since the Romans; it was ruled by monarchs not renowned for diffidence
who, in common with their subjects, seldom entertained doubts about
the worth of their religion, manners, language, morals, or domestic habits. It was also an empire remarkably well served by the creative talents
of a people who from the sixteenth century onward, almost without
pause, even in the darkest periods of decline, astonished with the originality and excellence of their literary and artistic productions. There
was an abundance, in that extended Castilian ambit, of will and of ability. And yet, how difficult it is to discover cultural traits and artifacts of
Spanish origin that succeeded in gaining universal acceptance. There are
a few, some of them truly distinguished, like the Catholic Reformation
and all its institutional and doctrinal concomitants, but after the inclusion of a couple of glorious archetypes (Don Juan and Don Quixote),
the Society of Jesus, the common canary, the word *liberalismo*,[21] Merino
sheep, and the modern design of the Persian guitar, the list thins rapidly;
bullfighting and castanets traveled badly, and Fígaro, Carmen, and Es-
camillo cannot be included as they, and much else popularly associated
with Spain, are the creatures of enthusiastic foreigners some of whom
never set foot on Spanish soil. More, while the considerable influence of
the culture of the Counter-Reformation was mainly a function of inspired proselytism or military success, there is a striking contrast with
an English Industrial Revolution that from its very beginnings exhibited
a notable capacity to generate cultural forms that proved effortlessly
acceptable virtually everywhere, even in places where no one had ever
seen an English missionary or heard of the British Empire. The cultural
boundaries of the realm of Charles V and Philip II were staked by the

---

21. It is fair to add that its international career was actually launched by the poet
Robert Southey who, in 1816, used the Spanish form as a scornful epithet addressed to
the British Whigs whom he described as "British *liberales*" in an obvious reference to the
Spanish political faction responsible for the disorderly and ultimately unsuccessful reforms
initiated by the Cortes of Cádiz in 1812.

pikes of the tercios; those of the culture of the English are nowhere to be seen.

The prowess of the language of the English as an exportable significance accords with the extraordinary ubiquity and longevity of vast numbers of the islanders' other symbols, signs, and forms that have traveled well and thrown roots far beyond the frontiers of their homeland. It is at this characteristically practical level that the English imprint acquires its decisive, formative importance in our quasi-Hellenistic moment in history, for its evident acceptability and staying power appear convincingly to mirror a robust capacity to respond to wishes, aspirations, and ambitions that are obviously spread very widely and cannot possibly all be of English origin. Cultural significances have myriad other attributes less obvious than ubiquity and longevity—but few, if any, more telling. This need not be taken to mean that these qualities are the cause of anything being valuable, attractive, or good; if the Book of Genesis is to be believed, then the innings that greed, murder, and deception have enjoyed since their debut is very extended indeed, but this has not made them more palatable. Widespread and persistent usage is nonetheless important when considered against the convergent suggestions of Vico and Wittgenstein that meaning and use are related; that what human beings do, matters; that the processes of culture and society do have a bearing on those intriguing "modifications of the human mind" or, less emphatically, that we are not absolutely impervious to our own acts, even though we may presume—often wrongly—to be unaffected by those of others.

If it were possible precisely to arrange cultural significances horizontally from "high" to "low," and also spatially, following regional affiliations, it would become evident that the prospect of our time is crowded at every level and in every quarter with signs, symbols, and forms of English ancestry that range generously from rarefied "high" culture preciosities to the less demanding but overwhelmingly popular instances of the islanders' inventiveness, of which sports and tourism are undoubtedly among the more noticeable. They are certainly associated in a direct and plausible fashion with many of the social transformations brought about by the Industrial Revolution; so much so, that it is possible, with few and heavily qualified exceptions, to assert that modern sports are a by-product of an English Industrial Revolution that created a need for new community arrangements, a substitute for the proximity, the intimacy, and the *Gemeinschaft* displaced by advancing industrialism.

Sports provide a colorful and reassuring source of intense emotional arousal for large numbers of people living under those routinized restraints of urban civilization that Wordsworth almost certainly had in mind when, in the Preface to the *Lyrical Ballads*, he referred to "the increasing accumulation of men in cities, where the uniformity of their occupations produces a craving for extraordinary incident." Regardless of other contributions, good or bad, memorable or inane, the sports of the English, enjoyed and practiced by millions of people everywhere on earth, have obviously provided a very considerable sufficiency of "extraordinary incidents" to satisfy the craving so perceptively noted by the poet. Perhaps herein lies the most interesting explanation of why it is that the sports invented, transformed, codified, or otherwise revived and institutionalized by the English have proved so universally acceptable. This is so much the case that it can be affirmed without hesitation that with the understandable exception of the significances associated with the rites of passage or with the immediate satisfaction of biological needs, these sporting activities of English origin engage the attention of more people, at more frequent intervals, and in more different places than any other cluster of comparable activities.[22] Moreover, their importance and acceptance are everywhere increasing; they can now claim the status of national sport in an astonishingly large number of countries, and it is becoming difficult to think of any in which the more popular games are not of English origin. When future social historians learn that in our time the most popular sporting activities in Japan were baseball, golf, and tennis, they will probably find it easier to see in this a significance that today may well elude us.

The foremost among these exportable sporting significances is, of course, the game of football and its modern variants, all of which trace their proximate origin to the legendary meeting of old boys from Winchester, Eton, Harrow, Rugby, and Shrewsbury at which was drafted the first "Cambridge Rules" in 1846 which laid the foundation for the future

22. The influence exercised by sports on many aspects of modern life offers a very wide field of inquiry that merits separate consideration; it can certainly not be dealt with in a note. It would be remiss, however, not to mention, even if only in passing, that sporting activities are probably the single most important influence in the determination of everyday contemporary sartorial usage. Before the Second World War, whether in the fabled Little Lord Fauntleroy attire or the ubiquitous sailor suit, little children were dressed like adults; today, we live in a world in which very large numbers of adults are happy to go about dressed like little children, and the explanatory linkage is invariably the popularity of a sporting activity. Even a cursory observation of a large assemblage of people in any Western country will show that many of the articles of clothing worn by most of those present owe their shape, color, and occasionally their very existence to one or another sport invented, modified, or popularized by the English-speaking peoples.

development of the game.[23] Half a century later, very few, if any, Poles, Brazilians, Algerians, Italians, Spaniards, Bulgarians, Peruvians, Rumanians, or Uruguayans played soccer, but today this English schoolboys' game is without question the most popular sport in each of these countries, none of which was ever colored pink by the imperial cartographers.[24]

Kicking a ball around a field has been a pastime of man from earliest antiquity, but present-day football is firmly rooted in the England of the nineteenth century and owes its form and original character to the social climate generated by triumphant Victorian industrialism in all its manifestations, most certainly including that earnest "muscular Christianity" of the rising middle sectors so perceptively interpreted by Thomas Hughes when he was pleased to think of the Nazarene as "a virile, sim-

23. According to a commemorative plaque on a boundary wall at Rugby School, the game of rugby originated when a boy named William Webb Ellis "with a fine disregard for the rules of the game of football . . . took the ball in his arms and ran with it, thus originating the distinctive feature of the rugby game." During the first half of the nineteenth century, football was played in a variety of ways, two of which were loosely related to what we now call soccer and rugby. Following the drafting of the second Cambridge Rules in 1863 and the formation of the Football Association whose preferred game was promptly nicknamed soccer, the Blackheath Football Club, which favored the rugby variant, seceded and helped to found the Rugby Union in 1871. The variant practiced in the United States and mainly identified with interuniversity competition is a direct descendant from the rugby game introduced from England by D. S. Schaft, a former Rugby schoolboy who in 1873 was a student at Yale University. The legalized forward pass, which ensured the distinctiveness of the United States variant, was not introduced until after 1906. The Australian variant, like the American one, was essentially a local modification of the English game. "It arose in the late 1850's when the various kinds of English football were still in flux and, at the beginning, it borrowed extensively from these games and especially from Rugby." The legendary first game of Australian football is commemorated by a dark marble plaque on the outer wall of the Melbourne Cricket Ground which reads, "On this site the first game of Australian football was played on August 7th, 1858, between Scotch College and Melbourne Grammar School." David Riesman and Reuel Denney, "Football in America: A Study in Culture Diffusion," in Eric Dunning, ed., *The Sociology of Sport* (London, 1971): 153, 155, 162; Geoffrey Blainey, *A Game of Our Own: The Origins of Australian Football* (Melbourne, 1990): 7, 17.

24. As this is being written, the whole of Germany, now united once again, is wildly celebrating the victory of its national team in a world competition for primacy in a sport invented by the headmaster of a tranquil English public school scarcely 150 years ago. The coverage in the German press and television invites the casual observer to accept that soccer is that country's national sport. This may or may not be so, but it is absurd to explain the current and growing popularity of soccer in Germany as the consequence of two military defeats sustained at the hands of the footballing islanders and their allies. Soccer was first introduced into Brazil by British sailors in the decade of the 1860s, and for many years it was played only by employees of British and German firms who later were joined by a few young men from the country's upper class. Toward the closing years of the century, *futebol* started to acquire a growing working-class following, and by 1914, it had become the country's most popular sport. Janet Lever, "Soccer in Brazil," in J. T. Talamini and C. H. Page, eds., *Sport and Society* (Boston, 1973): 141–142.

ple, and courageous fellow, a sort of working-class gentleman and regular old boy" who would without doubt have played the straight game had the opportunity offered.[25]

Football is the best known but not the only game invented or transformed by the makers of Victorian England and their emulators overseas. The ancient regal game of tennis was also rejuvenated with new rules, strict ritual, and a system of competition, initially under the sponsorship of Maj. Walter Clopton Wingfield, who devised an hourglass-shaped court and the improbable name of "Sphairistike" for the new sport that he introduced to a gathering of friends at Nantclwyd Hall in Wales.[26] The game quickly gained a vast following of enthusiastic but by no means uncritical players. The reservations about Wingfield's version of the sport were sufficiently important to warrant a decision by the All-England Croquet Club to form a subcommittee to reexamine the rules of the game. After two years of deliberations, the subcommittee dropped Wingfield's bizarre name in favor of "lawn tennis"; it adopted the now familiar rectangular court and the scoring system of *real* tennis (15–30–40); it lowered the net and put the server back on the baseline; it allowed an extra serve if the first one was unsuccessful; and it improved control of the ball by having it covered with white flannel. By 1877, the hardworking subcommittee had fixed the regulations and form of the game in a way that has remained almost intact to the present, its labors fittingly reflected in the change of the name of the club to the All England Lawn Tennis and Croquet Club of Wimbledon, where the first of the now famous tournaments was held in that same year.[27] Croquet, not cricket: the first croquet championship tournament was not

25. Thomas Hughes was the author of *Tom Brown's Schooldays*, a book that contributed greatly to the creation and popularization of the legendary figure of Dr. Thomas Arnold, the headmaster of Rugby, as a zealous advocate of the role of sports in the formation of moral character. John MacAloon, *This Great Symbol: Pierre de Coubertin and the Origins of the Modern Olympic Games* (Chicago, 1981): 64.

26. The game resembling modern tennis, which was enjoyed by practically every monarch during the three centuries that followed the Renaissance, virtually disappeared by the end of the seventeenth century. In its time, it was a favorite pastime of Henry VIII (the "*real* tennis" court at Hampton Court is the oldest in existence and is still in use), who in 1523 partnered Charles V, the Holy Roman Emperor, in a doubles game with the princes of Orange and Brandenburg, and was considered by Castiglione to be the pastime most "befitting a man at court." It had indeed been the sport of kings, and only kings or very rich courtiers could enjoy it. Modern lawn tennis is of course distantly related, but its very basis, a grass court in the open air, reflects its less exalted character, not yet democratic but certainly accessible to the numerous members of a rising bourgeoisie and a farming interest able to hang a net between a couple of poles and compete trying to keep a ball within bounds. William J. Baker, *Sports in the Western World* (Champaign-Urbana, 1988): 65–67.

27. Ibid., 180–183.

held in France, where a rudimentary form of the game known as *le jeu de maille* was known of old, but in Evesham, Worcestershire, in 1867, and three years later it moved to Wimbledon, where rules and specifications were drawn up that survive to this day.[28]

Baseball, notwithstanding efforts to prove otherwise by Messrs. A. G. Spalding & Bros. in 1907, certainly originates from the medieval stool-ball, originally played by milkmaids who used their familiar milking stool as a wicket and tried to hit it with a ball.[29] By the eighteenth century, the game had evolved into the popular children's game (described by Jane Austen in *Northanger Abbey*) known as "rounders" in the West Country, "feeder" in London, and "baseball" in the southern counties.[30] Swimming is probably as old as walking, but the sport of swimming, formally organized for competition, dates from 1869, when the first Amateur Swimming Association was founded in England. It is worth noting that the fastest stroke, generally known as crawl or, in effect, free-style, was introduced into international competition in 1900 by the Australian Richard Cavill, who used it to break the world record for the one hundred yards. Before the arrival of the Spaniards, the Araucanian Indians of Chile used to play *chueca*, a violent team game that consisted in using a crooked stick to push a wooden ball around an open field; so did Persians, Greeks, Romans, Algonquians, and Powhatans; but modern field hockey and all its variants date from 1886, when the Hockey Association was founded in England and rules were adopted, including that of the striking circle, which remains unaltered to this day. As for badminton, it was given its name by British officers who were staying at the country estate of the duke of Beaufort, in Badminton, Gloucestershire, in 1873, while on leave from India, who amused themselves playing a game invented a few years earlier in India by fellow officers the name of which—Poona—displeased them.

Athletics (track and field sports) declined after the fall of Rome and

28. Ibid., 180.
29. To settle the disputed question of the origin of a game in which he had excelled as a youth and on which he had based a very successful business career as a manufacturer of sporting goods, Albert G. Spalding instituted a well-publicized investigation that concluded, perhaps not surprisingly, that it was unrelated to any English game but had been invented by Col. Abner Doubleday in 1839. This conclusion has not been confirmed by later researches. It is now quite clear that, as William Baker indicates, "although modern baseball is primarily American, urban, and male, its roots are medieval, English, rural and female." Baker, *Sports*, 48.
30. Rupert Brooke visited the United States in 1913 and was invited to watch the Harvard-Yale baseball match played during the commencement celebrations. He found it "a good game to watch, and in outline easy to understand, as it is merely glorified rounders." Rupert Brooke, *Letters from America* (New York, 1916): 83.

did not revive convincingly until the early decades of the nineteenth century when the first regularly organized athletic meeting of modern times was promoted by the Royal Military Academy, Woolwich, in 1849. This occurred half a century after the genesis of the gymnastic movement elsewhere in northern Europe, but it was still visibly associated with military preparedness; virtually all the pioneers of systematic gymnastics had emphasized the contribution their activities made to the martial readiness of their respective countries. The founder of Swedish gymnastics, Per Henrik Ling, promoted disciplined group exercises under the orders of an instructor because "the execution of gymnastics at the word of command reinforces the effect of strictly military drill." His Danish neighbors agreed, and in 1804, the government created the Military Gymnastic Institute for the training of army officers, under the direction of Franz Nachtegall, the pioneer who founded the first private gymnasium in Copenhagen. These developments were paralleled in Germany, where Friedrich Ludwig Jahn, "the father of German gymnastics," harnessed a passionate nationalism to the task of rescuing young Germans from what he regarded as the stultifying passivity induced by classical education.[31]

The revival of athletics in England departed visibly from these diverse manifestations of earnest patriotism, and one of the early casualties of the new trend was precisely the Woolwich initiative, which proved distinctly unpopular and was soon abandoned. A year later, in 1850, Exeter College, Oxford, inaugurated an emphatically amateur and civilian athletic tournament that has continued without interruption until our time. A few years later, in 1866, the Amateur Athletic Club was founded in London, not to train army officers or harden the military resolve of the young but "to supply the want of an established ground upon which competitions in amateur athletic sports might take place between gentlemen amateurs." It is not unimportant to note that twenty-two years elapsed before the foundation of the United States Amateur Athletic Union, in 1888.

31. Gymnastics in Denmark, Sweden, and Germany, and Europe generally, retained a military character for most of the century. When Russia invaded Sweden in 1808, taking over more than a third of her territory, Ling offered his program of gymnastic exercises to the government as a means of strengthening the moral and physical condition of Swedish youth to prepare them for war. Jahn established a public playground, Turnplatz, on the outskirts of Berlin with parallel bars, jumping ditches, running tracks, and other such facilities. The Turnplatz was a great success, mostly impelled by nationalistic motives, and Turner (gymnastic) societies proliferated all over Prussia. The *Turnvereine* had an emphatically egalitarian and patriotic character, which Jahn encouraged through the use of uniforms to lessen class distinctions. Baker, *Sports*, 100–102.

Even sports as unlikely as mountaineering and alpine skiing bear the marks left by those keen Victorian amateurs.[32] It is obvious that people who live in the vicinity of great mountain ranges have been reluctant climbers from the dawn of time. It is also a commonplace that Petrarch was the first man to climb a mountain for enjoyment and that he had no immediate imitators. Less well known is that the birth of the modern sport of mountaineering can be dated confidently from the 1854 ascent of the Wetterhorn by Sir Alfred Wills and the foundation in London of the first Alpine Club, in 1857.[33] As for skiing, there can be no doubt that the Scandinavian people used skis as a means of transportation for a very long time prior to the nineteenth century, and this pioneering role is properly commemorated in the classic nordic competitions of *langlauf* and ski jumping; it is equally appropriate that the premier alpine competition, the Arlberg-Kandahar, which includes downhill and slalom races, should have been named after Lord Roberts, first Earl of Kandahar, for it was the British who first developed a set of rules and then secured international recognition for these races. Fittingly, the first international rules for slalom racing appeared in the *Public Schools Alpine Sports Yearbook* of 1923.[34]

The antecedents of boxing, horse racing, fox hunting, and golf are decidedly closer to the rough and ready tastes of Georgian landowners and dandies than to the earnest exhortations of Victorian social improvers. For all that, they are nonetheless English, or, in the case of golf, Scots, versions of antique activities. Pugilism remained disturbingly

32. And angling as well. Human beings have been eating fish for millennia, but the sport of fishing, including its subtle eccentricities, the meticulous observance of proper sporting conduct, and the shape and function of its paraphernalia, can be dated with confidence from 1496, when Dame Juliana Berners's *Treatyse of Fysshinge With an Angle* first saw the light of day, included in the second edition of *The Boke of St. Albans*. The stout tradition was further reinforced with the publication in 1653 of Izaak Walton's immortal *The Compleat Angler*, which laid, once and for all, in English, the foundations of the modern sport.

33. The "heroic" period of alpine climbing opened with the ascent of the Wetterhorn and closed with the conquest of the Matterhorn by Edward Whymper in 1865. Mont Blanc was first climbed in the late eighteenth century, but this ascent was performed as a feat for prize money, a motivation very distant from those of English climbers of the age of Wills and Whymper. George D. Abraham, *The Complete Mountaineer* (London, 1907): 18.

34. *Slalom* is, after all, a Norwegian term, and so are *Telemark* and *Christiania*, but the pioneering stage of Scandinavian skiing was strictly of local importance and in the absence of English intervention would almost certainly have remained confined to the nordic countries for a very long time. The Norwegian Ski Association was founded in 1883, and the first nordic games were organized in 1902, retaining throughout their emphatically local character. It is interesting, additionally, to note that the oldest surviving ski club in the world is the Kiandra Ski Club, in New South Wales, Australia, founded in 1873 by Norwegian immigrants attracted by the gold rush. Baker, *Sports*, 156.

faithful to its brutal classical origins until the English prizefighter Jack Brougham invented the padded glove in the mid-eighteenth century and one hundred years later, in 1867, John Graham Chambers devised the rules that, sponsored by the eighth Marquess of Queensberry, transformed the ferocious brawls into a sport worthy of the attention of gentlemen and pedagogues. As for the golf of the Scots, it was sufficiently popular by the fifteenth century to attract prohibition because it kept the king's subjects away from the more important practice of archery. It later traveled south with James I, who played a few holes on Blackheath Common, east of London, where the Royal Blackheath Golf Club, the world's oldest, was founded early in the seventeenth century (the Royal and Ancient Club of St. Andrews was established later, in 1754). Games reminiscent of golf were played elsewhere in earlier times, especially in the Netherlands, but there is no doubt that the modern version of the game is of robust Scottish ancestry. Much the same can be said of the English origins of modern horse racing, which must be counted among the most popular usages of leisure in modern societies. In the United States, well over sixty million people attend about eight thousand racing dates every year, placing bets of well over $9 billion, while another $3.5 billion is bet at off-track casinos and legal facilities, and there is no reason to suppose that this pastime enjoys considerably less popularity in Argentina, France, Singapore, or Australia. Probably as ancient as the domestication of horses, horse racing in its present form is unmistakably an English creation, from the apparel and accoutrements of the riders and the conditions governing the classic races[35] to the standards imposed effortlessly throughout the world since the appearance in London of the first Racing Calendar in 1727,[36] the foundation in Newmarket of the Jockey Club in 1750, and the publication in 1781 of the first volume of

35. The five classic races are now to be found, under one name or another, occupying principal positions in the racing calendar of virtually every country on earth. Of the five, the Oaks and the Thousand Guineas are restricted to fillies; the other three, the Derby, the Two Thousand Guineas, and the St. Leger, are for all comers. It is in England, moreover, that we find the earliest known act of Parliament referring to horse racing arrangements. In 1740, under the reign of George II, Parliament passed an act establishing the earliest scale of weight for age; thus five-year-olds had to carry 10 stone; six-year-olds, 11 stone; and seven-year-olds, 12 stone.

36. The compiler of that first Racing Calendar was John Cheny, of Arundel, in Sussex, and in the title page of the novel publication he described it as "an hystorical list on account of all the horse-matches run, and of all the plates and prizes run for in England [of the value of ten pounds or upward] in 1727, containing the names of the owners of the horses, etc. that have run, as above and the names and colours of the horses also, with the winner distinguished of every match, plate, prize, or stakes" (London, 1727).

the General Stud Book. It is of course well known that all the thorough-bred horses in the world trace back in direct male line to three horses—the Byerly Turk, the Darley Arabian, and the Godolphin—imported into England early in the eighteenth century, whose progeny has been system-atically listed and certified in the pages of the General Stud Book.[37] Even in France, and already under Louis XVIII, horse racing and betting were given system and organization in keeping with the English models, and the institutionalization of the sport was completed with the foundation in 1833 of the appropriately named French Jockey Club.

The cultural significance of this shared English provenance of modern sports is not so much a consequence of the survival or popularity of this or that activity but of the universal acceptance of the concept of sport itself, so much an English invention that the word has proved untranslat-able in practice and is therefore incorporated in its original form into practically every modern language.[38] Even the intrusions of profession-alism into sport (not an absolute departure from nineteenth-century prizefighting and cricket contests between "gentlemen and players") are almost without exception the creatures of the English-speaking world, most certainly including the travesty of Olympic competitions in which the principal motivation for athletes to excel is the wish to secure lucra-tive commercial contracts and advertising sponsorships.

This general acceptance of the concept of sport, especially when mod-

37. The Byerly Turk was imported into England by Captain Byerly, who used him as his charger throughout King William's wars in Ireland; the Darley Arabian was imported by Mr. Darley, of Aldby Park, between York and Malton; the legendary Godolphin was discovered in Paris around 1728 by none other than the famous agriculturist Mr. Coke, of Norfolk, who first saw the horse pulling a water cart. The horse, a brown bay, was eventually presented to the Earl of Godolphin. He stood about 15 hands and died in 1753.

38. "Modern sport, a ubiquitous and unique form of non-utilitarian physical contests, took shape over a period of approximately 150 years, from the early eighteenth to the late nineteenth centuries. Speaking historically, we can be reasonably precise about place as well as time. Modern sports were born in England and spread from their birthplace to the United States, to Western Europe, and to the world beyond." Allen Guttman, *From Ritual to Record: The Nature of Modern Sports* (New York, 1978): 57. In 1810, Prince Puechler-Muskau, who knew England well, wrote confidently that "'sport' is as untranslatable as 'gentleman,'" and thirty years later, another German author, J. G. Kohl, could explain about sport that "we have no word for this and are almost forced to introduce it into our language." Norbert Elias, "The Genesis of Sport as a Sociological Problem," in Dunning, ed., *The Sociology of Sport*, 88–89, 115. Later still, in 1936, the year of the German Olympic Games, yet another German author affirmed that "as is well known, England was the cradle and the loving 'mother' of sport. . . . It appears that English technical terms referring to this field might become the common possession of all nations in the same way as Italian technical terms in the field of music. It is probably rare that a piece of culture has migrated with so few changes from one country to another." Agnes Bain Stiven, *En-glands Einfluss auf den deutschen Wortschatz* (Marburg, 1936): 72.

ified by these latter-day trends, is reflected tellingly in the preferential treatment meted to sports information in newspapers and radio and television news programs all over the world. Sporting activities are allotted the largest continuing proportion of newspaper space in almost every country (the exceptions usually reflect the influence of various forms of religious fundamentalism) and are the only human activities, as distinct from regular reports on meteorological conditions, accorded separate and special treatment in radio and television news programs. Broadcasting time is also occasionally set aside for financial information, but this is not a universal practice, while sporting reports are an integral part of virtually every news program on earth. At the time of Waterloo, this elusive concept of sport was either unknown outside the English-speaking world or regarded as a bizarre eccentricity; by the time Queen Victoria celebrated her Diamond Jubilee, it was so universally acceptable that it became possible to institutionalize it in a most unexpected, visible, popular, and ultimately significant manner through the successful initiative of Pierre de Coubertin to resurrect the Olympic Games in 1896 after an interruption of one and a half millennia.

Baron de Coubertin was an enthusiastic Anglophile and an admirer of what he understood to be the educational methods of Dr. Thomas Arnold, the headmaster of Rugby School. An early reading, when he was twelve years old, of *Tom Brown's Schooldays*, Thomas Hughes's famous book on student life at Rugby, made a deep and most favorable impression on him that the fashionable Anglophilism of the times did nothing to attenuate.[39] Subsequent visits across the channel to study the educational system only confirmed these first impressions until "he developed a profound identification with the English" that reached almost mystical levels in 1886 when, aged twenty-three, he experienced a vision during a visit to the Rugby School chapel which years later he recalled with a candor as convincing as it was revealing: "In the twilight, alone in the great gothic chapel of Rugby, my eyes fixed on the funeral slab on which,

39. In one of his autobiographical essays, Coubertin wrote that he carried his English-language copy of *Tom Brown's Schooldays* in "all my peregrinations through the public schools of England, the better to help me bring to life again, in order to understand it, the powerful figure of Thomas Arnold and the glorious contour of his incomparable work." Pierre de Coubertin, *Une campagne de 21 ans* (Paris, 1908): 3, trans. and cited by MacAloon, *Olympic Games*, 53. The Anglophilia of French intellectual circles of the time was pervasive, as Zeldin has indicated. "Charles de Remusat declared in 1865, 'I confess willingly that the dream of my life has been the English system of government in French society.' The 'republic of dukes,' of 1871–79 was deeply impregnated by Anglophilism, as were also liberal Catholics of the school of Montalembert, Orleanists like Leroy-Beaulieu and Michel Chevalier." Theodore Zeldin, *France 1848–1945*. Vol. II. *Intellect, Taste, Anxiety* (Oxford, 1977): 101–102.

without epitaph, the great name of Thomas Arnold was inscribed, I dreamed that I saw before me the cornerstone of the British Empire."[40]

The suspicion that Coubertin's researches into English education amounted to little more than a patient confirmation of what he had read in *Tom Brown's Schooldays* is well founded. This confirmation progressed unimpeded and convinced Coubertin that the prosperity and the power of Britain were neither accidental nor due to race or heredity but were the consequence of the methodical application in Victorian schools of what he understood to be the Arnoldian system of *la pedagogie sportive*, which, though allocating an important place in its program to moral development and social education, relied mainly on the beneficial and exemplary effects of regular sporting activity.[41] As one of his French biographers put it, "Pierre [de Coubertin] avait laisse le feu s'eteindre. . . . Il était devenu Tom Brown, it devenait Thomas Arnold. Se degageait du livre et frappait l'esprit du jeune homme comme un tamtam la clé de voue de l'oeuvre de Thomas Arnold: le sport . . . le sport . . . le sport . . . le sport."[42] Coubertin hoped that the general adoption of this sui generis version of the Arnoldian system would, as he graphically expressed it, *rebronzer la France* after the disasters of 1871. More important, he was convinced that the widespread practice of sports and the adoption of the English concept of sportsmanship would improve the conduct of international affairs as efficiently as it had earlier perfected the character of the builders of the British Empire. From such a spacious conception to the Olympic Games, the distance was minimal, and although the idea of reviving the ancient athletic tournament did not originate with Coubertin, his were the initiative and the entrepre-

---

40. Coubertin, *Une campagne*, 5, in MacAloon, *Olympic Games*, 59. The belief in the Arnoldian genesis of the greatness of Britain was explicitly and loyally held. In a 1910 article, Coubertin reiterated it, explaining that "Arnold draws up . . . the fundamental rules of the *pedagogie* of sport. From Rugby, he affects the other public schools by the contagion of his example, without resounding phrases or indiscreet interference; and so the keystone of the British Empire is laid. I know that this point of view is yet that of . . . the British themselves, but I am content to have had it approved by one of the greatest survivors of the Arnoldian period—Gladstone. When I put the question to him . . . he asked me for time to think the matter over, and having thought it over he said: 'You are right, that is how it happened.'" Coubertin, "Olympia," cited by MacAloon, *Olympic Games*, 51, 80.

41. A view shared by Dr. Arnold's most famous biographer, who observed, "The earnest enthusiast who strove to make his pupils Christian gentlemen and who governed his school according to the principles of the Old Testament has proved to be the founder of the worship of athletics and the worship of good form." Lytton Strachey, *Eminent Victorians* (London, 1948): 221.

42. Marie-Thérese Eyquem, *Pierre de Coubertin: L'Epopée Olympique* (Paris, 1966): 31.

neurial genius of combining the moral intent of an Arnoldian system centered on sports with an international festivity echoing the immensely successful Crystal Palace Exhibition of 1851, variously described by awed contemporaries as "this Olympic game of Industry, this tournament of commerce," and "the first grand cosmopolitan Olympiad of Industry."

During the eighteenth and nineteenth centuries, there were a number of unsuccessful attempts to resurrect the Olympic Games in Germany, Sweden, Greece, Britain, France, and the United States, but with the notable exception of the "Olympic Games of Much Wenlock," in Shropshire, there is no evidence that Coubertin was particularly interested in them or that he was informed about them at all. In 1889, when he had already made a name for himself as an international apostle of sports, he received an invitation from Dr. W. P. Brookes, the founder and self-styled *archon* of the games of Much Wenlock, which had been taking place there at regular intervals since 1849. And in October 1890, he traveled to the Border Country to observe the improbable Olympiad. The experience was memorable and decisive. In the words of his biographer, the French aristocrat was "utterly bemused and delighted with what he saw," so much so that when he recounted the visit a few years later in an article in which he referred to the origins of the Athens Games of 1896, he singled out the people of Much Wenlock as the only ones who "have preserved and followed the true Olympian tradition."[43]

It is not possible to question the inspiration and encouragement that Coubertin derived from what was in effect a fundamental misunderstanding of the character of these resurrected contests. The games of Much Wenlock, or any modern athletic contest, for that matter, could not possibly have preserved the Olympian tradition because there is an essential discontinuity between the ancient and the modern games, partly caused by the intrusion of the Industrial Revolution and partly caused by the unacceptably high level of violence permitted in the Greek games and the strikingly low "threshold of revulsion against people wounding or even killing each other in the contests, to the delight of the spectators." The modern concept of sport that presumably presided over the rebirth of the Olympic Games in 1896, and over all modern sporting activities, did not originate in ancient Greece but in the heart of Victorian England.[44]

    43. Pierre de Coubertin, "A Typical Englishman: Dr. W. P. Brookes of Wenlock," *American Monthly Review of Reviews* 15 (1897): 63; see also, by the same author, "Les Jeux Olympiques de Much Wenlock," *Sports Athlétiques* 1 (25 December 1890).
    44. Elias, "Genesis of Sport," 88–89.

Endeavors such as Coubertin's are the outcome of a multiplicity of factors, and it would be absurd to explain them as the result merely of one or two discrete causes. Nevertheless, if the noble Frenchman's own appraisal of his life's work, its inspiration and its guidelines, are to be taken seriously, then the search for the genesis of the modern Olympic Games and the accompanying systematization and institutionalization of sport and of the concepts that define its various manifestations (amateurism, professionalism, performance, record, sporting and unsporting behavior, and the like) must necessarily lead to his peregrination to Rugby and to Much Wenlock and to his quaint Arnoldian crusade so disarmingly founded on what *Tom Brown's Schooldays* purports to teach about the education of the English.

Like sports, modern tourism is also a child of the English Industrial Revolution. Human beings have traveled to and fro since antiquity, but very few did it for pleasure. Pilgrims, conquerors, ambassadors, and fugitives moved under duress, for unavoidable professional reasons, for the health of their bodies or the well-being of their immortal souls, but the idea that things elsewhere are worth an expensive tour away from home is very much a marginal and totally unintended consequence of the self-confidence, prosperity, and latitudinarianism of the English aristocracy during the early years of our modern industrial era. Tourism is a distant relation of the mobility of the factors of production that sustains the industrial effort. Everything moves; stability and passivity are negative values; they lead either to boredom or to stagnation. The English anointed mobility as an essential component of production and a preferred means of consumption. Simply to mention the Grand Tour, or the "invention" of the French Riviera by Lord Brougham, establishes the English parentage of an eminently social and cultural activity that was subsequently given lasting popular form under the sponsorship of Thomas Cook, the architect of modern tourism.[45] Cook devised and arranged the first ever advertised "tourist" excursion, from Leicester to Loughborough. The return fare was one shilling, and the unprecedented offer attracted 570 paying customers. By 1855, he was marketing the first foreign excursions to attend the Paris Exhibition; by 1864, more

45. The term "Grand Tour" first appeared in printed form in Richard Lassel's *Voyage of Italy*, in 1760, although the word "tourist" did not appear until 1800. Christopher Hibbert, *The Grand Tour* (London, 1987): 18. Lord Brougham, former Lord Chancellor, traveled to Italy in 1834. When on his way, a cholera epidemic broke out in Provence, and travelers were not allowed to cross the Var, at Antibes. Brougham was forced to remain in the tiny village of Cannes and liked it so much that he returned to it every winter for the rest of his life, dragging his titled and fashionable friends with him, including Queen Victoria and the Prince of Wales. He died and is buried in Cannes, and the grateful municipal authorities have looked after his grave ever since.

than a million passengers had used the services of his now legendary firm.[46]

The imprint of its English progenitor is also perceived in the swift expansion of modern tourism, which would not have been possible in the absence of railways, steamships, reliable plumbing, postal services, washable fabrics, electricity, and the widespread social mobility and paid vacations that followed in the wake of the economic prosperity of the Industrial Revolution. However, of the many crucial English contributions to the development of tourism, one of the more lasting, influential, and least expected is that of the modern luxury hotel, which brought together under one roof many of the diverse improvements in the comfort of travelers made possible by contemporary technological innovations.

The advances in the iron, steel, and engineering industries responsible for the first network of railways in the world were also behind the technology that permitted the construction of unusually spacious buildings, suitably equipped to offer comfortable and safe hospitality to the unprecedented numbers of travelers who could alight simultaneously from a passenger train. The construction of railways generated a great demand for hotel accommodation that the old coaching inns could not satisfy. The now legendary British railway terminus hotels were the progenitors of the modern tourist establishments to which we have by now become accustomed. A few Swiss, French, and German hotels had achieved a high standard of service during the latter decades of the nineteenth century, but their material facilities were distressingly primitive, occasionally squalid.

The Savoy Hotel, inaugurated off the Strand in London in 1889, was the first truly modern luxury hotel; certainly, it was the first with electric illumination throughout, six lifts, and seventy fully equipped bathrooms—the largest number in any single building in Europe.[47] Most important, the owner, Richard D'Oyly Carte, of Gilbert and Sullivan fame, invited Cesar Ritz and Georges Auguste Escoffier to preside over the management and cuisine of the new establishment. Jokes about English cooking notwithstanding, it was from the Savoy that Ritz and Escoffier revolutionized the social life of late Victorian London. They suc-

---

46. George Young, *Tourism, Blessing or Blight?* (London, 1973): 20–21.

47. D'Oyly Carte's Savoy Theatre was built in 1881 and succeeded so well that in seven years, he was able to fund the construction of the Savoy Hotel next door. Elsewhere, the 13-story New York Waldorf was completed in 1893 and the adjoining 17-story Astoria in 1897.

ceeded so well that a group of London financiers approached Ritz with the suggestion that he should consider founding his own hotel in Paris. At first he was hesitant; he was not French and had never worked in Paris above the rank of restaurant manager. Eventually, although not overenthusiastic about the project, he agreed to become a founding member of the Ritz Hotel Syndicate Ltd., formed in London in 1896 under the chairmanship of Henry Higgins, a respected lawyer and *bon viveur*. The Paris Ritz opened in 1898, nine years after the Savoy; the London Ritz, seventeen years later, in 1906.[48] If it is true that imitation is the most convincing form of flattery, then these two aristocrats of the tourist industry can justly be regarded as thriving monuments to the imaginative entrepreneurship of D'Oyly Carte and his associates on whom ultimately should rest the laurels for the creation of the first modern luxury hotel in the world.

Approximately two miles due northwest from the Savoy Hotel, in a modest house in the heart of London's Soho, in 1923, the first television apparatus was invented, constructed, and successfully operated by J. L. Baird.[49] In November 1936, Britain inaugurated the first public television service using a system developed by the Marconi E.M.I. Television Company and making use of the Emitron, an electron tube device incorporating a photosensitive mosaic screen. Half a century later, although many advanced industrial nations have become principal producers of television programs and equipment, Britain has not relinquished her vanguard position as the world's foremost producer of quality television. The BBC and ITV have between them won the Prix Italia, the highest accolade for quality television, more often than any other group of national competitors. In common with the rest of the progeny of the English Industrial Revolution, the invention of television

48. When instructing his architect in Paris, Cesar Ritz said, "My hotel must be the last word in modernity. Mine will be the first modern hotel in Paris: and it must be hygienic, efficient, and beautiful." The lessons of the Savoy had been well learned. Marie Louise Ritz, *Cesar Ritz, Host to the World* (London, 1938): 208; see also Christopher Matthew, *A Different World* (London, 1976): 173–174.

49. In 1928, Baird made the first long distance television broadcast, from London to the Cunard liner *Berengaria*, in mid-Atlantic. In that same year he successfully made the first color transmission. By 1930, Baird television sets were on sale in England. On September 7, 1928, a 21-year-old American inventor, Philo T. Farnsworth, working quite independently in San Francisco, produced the first television picture in the United States. Vladimir Zworykin, a Russian immigrant living in New York, built the first practical television camera and succeeded in broadcasting pictures with 240 scanning lines, compared with the 525 lines in current use in the United States. Present-day television is the result of many technological and scientific advances, but there can be no doubt that the first successful apparatus for the transmission of images was constructed by Baird.

marks the apex of a very broadly based pyramid of technological innovations, scientific inventions, and improved production methods span-
ning many generations and many countries, but television is without
doubt as English a cultural artifact as the modern computer, also a social
invention, in that it is the current result—because it is still being modified and perfected—of many advances pointing roughly in the same direction, the first of which may have been the abacus. The computer owes
its modern form mostly to the remarkable partnership of the mathe-
matician Charles Babbage and Lord Byron's daughter Ada, Countess of
Lovelace; Babbage invented and constructed the analytical engines,
unique precursors of the modern computer, and Ada was the world's
first "computer programmer."[50]

We now know that watching television is by far the single most popular leisure activity in the advanced industrial countries, engaging the
attention of the average person for well over twenty hours every week.
We also know that with global annual sales of goods and services in
excess of $2,600 billion, tourism is by far the world's biggest industry.
It employs over one hundred million people, which is the equivalent of
one in every sixteen gainfully employed workers on earth; it represents
11 percent of all consumer spending, exceeded only by expenditure in
food and housing, and accounts for over 5 percent of the world's gross
national product (GNP). If travel and tourism were a country, its GNP
would place it fourth in the world after the United States, Japan, and
Germany.[51] The people who use computers, watch television, practice
or follow sporting activities, and travel for pleasure make up a very
considerable plurality of mankind, which proportion increases impressively if it is added to the users of the many other exportable signifiers
of English origin. This exercise will inevitably bring to mind amusing
attempts by patriotic officials elsewhere to prove that their fellow-
countrymen invented most things under the sun a few decades earlier,
but this is obviously not the object of this somewhat haphazard enu-

50. By 1836, after the introduction of the punched card input system, "Babbage had
developed methods by which computation could influence the program, both by advancing
and backing the string of cards, and hence the sequence of instructions to the Engine, and
also by controlling the number of times a given operation was repeated." As Babbage also
thought of storing instructions and then operating on them, he had mastered the basic
principles of the modern computer with the sole and understandable exception of the use
of binary logic. However, he did develop what he called "the principle of the chain," which
though not the binary operation realized in mechanical form, clearly pointed in that direction. "One of the great intellectual achievements in the history of mankind," is how a
recent biography describes Babbage's work. Anthony Hyman, *Charles Babbage: Pioneer
of the Computer* (Princeton, 1982): 1, 245.
51. *The Economist*, April 15, 1989, 73.

meration; rather, it is to note the very large number of cultural traits and artifacts of English provenance that are now an integral part of the common culture of modernity.

For example, it is clear that only very few countries have never been reached by the YMCA or the YWCA, the Salvation Army, the Boy Scouts, or the Girl Guides, but there are none where the use of postage stamps to expedite letters on their way has not become part of the fabric of social habits following Rowland Hill's ingenious "penny post" reforms of 1836, or where the helpful pillar box invented by Anthony Trollope has never made an appearance in any color or shape. It would be even more difficult in these nationalistic times to discover a country that has not followed the example set by the loyal Britons who first sang "God Save the King" in 1745 and has refused to have a national anthem to be sung reverently on special occasions. The International Red Cross has firm roots in Geneva, but how could its existence be disassociated from the nursing profession and the pioneering activities of Miss Nightingale at Scutari?

Insurance arrangements of various kinds were ancient lore by the time the Hanoverians ascended the throne of England, but the authority accorded to Lloyd's during the ensuing two hundred fifty years was unprecedented, and even now, when the ancient firm is experiencing some very unusual tribulations, it remains unsurpassed. Today the trade and the merchant marine of Britain are not flourishing, and rival listings have been put forward to challenge the once-hallowed Register of Shipping, but the heirs of Edward Lloyd's coffeehouse clientele continue to bear a considerable portion of the responsibility for making London the insurance capital of our world.

The elegantly aging metropolis is also the center from whence the Kennel Club and Crufts exercise their good-natured ascendancy over the definition and classification of canine breeds and where daily newspapers, from racy tabloids to respected leaders of opinion, first acquired their present format and stylistic conventions, including that keen awareness of the difference between news and opinions that may well have been the most important contribution of *The Times* to the development of civilized journalism.[52] Even an enumeration as unsystematic as this one would be inexcusably incomplete if it did not mention clubs and clubmanship, at least in passing; or the ubiquitous safety match; or

---

52. With respect to format, there are very few exceptions, among which probably the most conspicuous are the Madrid *ABC* and the Paris *Le Monde*.

the foundation in 1840 of the very first Society, Royal, of course, for the Prevention of Cruelty to Animals; or the crucial invention and early development of the now commonplace radar system for aircraft detection; or Whittle's jet engine; or the increasingly popular institution of the weekend; or Sherlock Holmes and the detective novel;[53] or the influence exercised by Sotheby's and Christie's in guiding and shaping the fine art market;[54] or the decisive role of Covent Garden in modern opera; or the ease with which the rhetoric of English parliamentary practices (the spirit has proved less adaptable) has become assimilated into practically every corner of the globe deemed worthy of separate representation before the General Assembly of the United Nations.

A comparable feat of assimilation has resulted in the generalized acceptance of the basic tenets of English classical economics, even by those who until recently were vociferously opposed to them. Forty years ago Lionel Robbins thought that it was impossible "to understand the evolution and the meaning of Western liberal civilization without some understanding of Classical Political Economy."[55] This was true then, and it is doubly so today, when the Iron Curtain has disappeared and millions of disillusioned Communists are desperately endeavoring to discover

53. According to Vico, "The reason why the Greek peoples so vied with each other for the honour of being [Homer's] fatherland, and why almost all claimed him as citizen, is that the Greek peoples were themselves Homer." This seminal suggestion notwithstanding, in our own modern time archetypes are normally the children of one mind, although not infrequently they tend to outshine their progenitors; Candide will probably outlive his creator, and perhaps the same will occur with Don Quixote; how many otherwise well-read people know the name of the creator of Don Juan? Lope de Vega was described as a *monstruo de la naturaleza* by his admiring contemporaries because he penned more than 1,200 plays and peopled Spanish life with dozens of characters, many of which are still alive and well in Andalusia and Asturias but who never traveled abroad. The appellation "monster of nature" used in this respect should with justice be reserved for Shakespeare, who certainly produced more exportable archetypes than any other author in the history of letters. There are not many countries on earth where the names of Hamlet, Macbeth, Romeo and Juliet, Falstaff, Ariel and Caliban, Prospero, Othello, and Shylock are entirely without significance. Frankenstein, Sherlock Holmes, and Hercule Poirot are among the more successful lesser creatures of this kind. The great Victorian detective, especially, generated many imitators who stalk the darker side of human society in every latitude and have now been joined by an abundant harvest of spies and counterspies from the same *écurie*.

54. The unchallenged English dominance of the world's art market was established publicly with the 1954 sale of the enormous collection of the deposed King Farouk, cataloged jointly by Sotheby's and Rheims, and by Sotheby's Goldschmidt sale of 1958, when seven important impressionist paintings sent from the United States realized the then-unheard-of sum of 781,000 pounds sterling. The position was consolidated in 1964, with Sotheby's acquisition of Parke-Bernet of New York, until that time the premier auction house in the United States.

55. Lionel Robbins, *The Theory of Economic Policy in English Classical Political Economy* (London, 1953): 4.

how to emulate the economic prowess of the Western nations by freeing
their economies largely in the manner prescribed by the English classical
economists. Against this contemporary background, it is all the more
interesting to observe that Robbins restricted his analysis to the work
of those he described as the "English Classical Economists," by which
of course he meant "the two great Scotch philosophers, David Hume
and Adam Smith, and their followers, most of whom belonged to the
first two generations of the London Political Economy Club—conspic-
uously, Ricardo, Malthus, Torrens, Senior, McCulloch and the two Mills
. . . and Jeremy Bentham." He then noted that he had deliberately ex-
cluded any economists other than "inhabitants of this island" and explained that he had no desire to be insular in outlook but that it seemed
clear to him that the theories he was about to examine "originated predominantly in this country, [and] that beyond a vague derivation from
the *Wealth of Nations*, the continental writers have little or no organic
relation with the movement over here, and that indeed it is the differences, in this connexion, between English and continental theories rather
than the similarities, which are significant for the history of thought."[56]
There can be some argument about this, but there is little doubt that the
mainstream of classical economic thought associated with modern industrialism and its consequent prosperity and continuing expansion is
the one identified with an English intellectual tradition that rests principally on the works of the economists listed by Lord Robbins; indeed,
England nurtured the Industrial Revolution as well as its most plausible
and lasting theoretical interpretation and, in Karl Marx, then laboring
away in the Reading Room of the British Museum, one of its earliest
and most troublesome adversaries.

This working hypothesis about the quasi-Hellenistic aftermath of empire does not require exhaustive listings; the examples already mentioned more than suffice to illustrate the range and popularity of some
of the traits and artifacts created by the English. Their ubiquity should
be as well established as the fact that their acceptability need not be
related to positive intrinsic qualities. That the Mediterranean world of
the second century B.C. preferred Greek to Aramaic was the consequence
of factors other than grammatical excellence. There are those who are
prepared to believe that soccer is a better game than rugby because it is
more popular, or that Conan Doyle is superior to George Eliot for the
same reason, but this is to stride vigorously in a very odd direction in-

56. Ibid., 2–3n.

deed. Far better and simpler, it would seem, is to assume that widespread acceptance is in good part an adequate reflection of an earthy capacity to respond to contemporary human needs, worthy or otherwise, and if the proposition is not to be discarded altogether that meaning rests on usage and that what people do, matters, then weight must be accorded to the overwhelming acceptance by millions upon millions of our contemporaries of the cultural artifacts generated during the English Industrial Revolution. As the parallel process of unforced adoption of the cultural traits of the Athenians has fittingly been labeled "Hellenistic," it does not appear to be injudicious, and it may prove illuminating, to think of our time as a distant but comparable aftermath of the demise of the empire of the English.

A World Made in English

To call our times a Hellenistic aftermath is an option initially as fetching and illuminating as it is ultimately unsatisfactory. The main difficulty is that the striking parallelism and its dependent working hypothesis can only be sustained by minimizing unacceptably the role of the United States or, as I have done here, by overlooking it intentionally to emphasize the initial comparison. The problem is not resolved by adopting the popular alternative course of casting the English-speaking Americans in the role of a latter-day Rome. The Latini used a language entirely different from that of the Athenians; the United States uses English, ingeniously modified, but English nonetheless. The United States is a creature of the English moment; Rome had origins distinct and distant from those of Hellas. England, the United States, and the other English-speaking nations are encompassed by a seamless and familiar cultural continuity, but in antiquity, even if the rise of the Latini is classed as a Hellenistic phenomenon, as Toynbee has done, the differences remain almost absolute between the Athenian and the Roman construction of their respective worlds.

Another possibility is to think of the United States as the Macedonia of our time, busily taking the culture of England and her successors into every corner of the globe, but this is even less appropriate, because the Americans are obviously much more than just efficient distributors of English artifacts. Regardless of the merits or otherwise of the resulting

traits, signifiers, habits, and fads, the American cultural moment is pro-
digiously creative, and most of its products are evidently as popular
within as they are without its boundaries.[1] Moreover, the process
whereby they have been so readily adopted elsewhere echoes the English
and the Hellenistic experience in owing nothing to duress and much to
the simplest of all incentives: very many people find them attractive. No
one could seriously believe that Yankee bayonets offer the ultimate explanation of why there are well-patronized McDonald's hamburger restaurants in St. Petersburg, Rome, Paris, and Moscow or why basketball
and volleyball are preferred sports of the Chinese people,[2] or better, why
it is that the Japanese, who are so disinclined to accept foreign immigrants, are none the less enthusiastic about celebrating a festival as alien
to their culture as *Kurisumasu*, as well as St. Valentine's Day, Father's
Day, Mother's Day, and Easter.[3] Would anyone suggest that the popularity among the inhabitants of the former Soviet Union, before as well
as after glasnost and perestroika, of chewing gum, VCRs, toilet paper,
blue jeans, Dixieland jazz, and Coca-Cola owes something to the activities of the U.S. Marines? Or that it represents, as it has been proposed
of the Hellenistic period, the palatable aspect of "large-scale economic
and imperial exploitation" by the metropolitan power?[4]

No plausible attempt to understand the extraordinary diffusion of
these and of so many other creations of the English-speaking Americans
can ignore the fact that during the past two and a half centuries, the
metropolitan center of industrial modernity has remained well within
the ambit of Archilochus's foxes who, as the Greek poet indicated, know

---

1. Not invariably. Some very visible cultural artifacts of the American moment have
proved remarkably sluggish and homebound. Frisbees, for example, are seldom seen outside the United States; the Soapbox Derby has not had a legion of imitators abroad; nor
has the semantic coyness characteristic of "gender-free" speech and "political correctness"
elicited more than dismissive good humor in other countries.

2. Basketball and volleyball, with Ping-Pong, are reputed to be by far the most popular
sports in China. It can be affirmed with confidence and without benefit of detailed surveys,
that the number of Chinese who play volleyball and basketball today is greater than the
total population of the United States in the early 1890s, when both sports were invented,
respectively, in the Springvale and Holyoke branches of the Massachusetts YMCA, itself
an offspring of the first Young Men's Christian Association, founded in London in 1844,
with impeccable credentials as a stronghold of Victorian England's muscular Christianity
at its exemplary best.

3. Gregory Clark comments, plausibly, "It's not as though the Japanese lack their own
holidays and festivals. But if we Westerners have something called Christmas then Japan
wants it too." This disposition is not reciprocated. As far as is commonly known, there is
not one single major Japanese or Chinese festival that has acquired a universal acceptance
even remotely comparable to the one enjoyed by Kurisumasu in Japan. "Have a Happy
and Humble *Kurisumasu*," *The Australian*, December 20, 1989, 11.

4. Green, *Alexander*, xv.

many things and have now also shown an uncanny ability to thrive on the kind of latitudinarian diversity that elsewhere, under different cultural auspices, would be regarded as an ominous portent of confusion, perhaps even of moral dissolution and chaos. The Hellenistic analogy becomes intriguingly paradoxical when considered against the background of this continuing and intimate association of the English-speaking peoples with industrial modernity, because while its defining parallelism is strengthened, the original meaning is negated; the former, because the "Hellenistic" cultural inheritance of the English has continued to expand vigorously, assisted by the unprecedented prosperity and creativity of the English-speaking Americans, and the latter, because instead of signaling the end of our soi-disant Hellenistic Age, as the emergence of Rome marked the twilight of post-Alexandrine Hellenism, this very visible rise of the United States promises to retain the overwhelming cultural influence of the English-speaking peoples well into the twenty-first century and perhaps beyond. For the Hellenistic analogy usefully to survive, it should have been possible to compare the dominant focus of cultural creativity after the dissolution of the British Empire to that of the Latini, but what we are witnessing, to continue using our comparison with the Hellenistic Age, is equivalent to an unchallenged preponderance by one of the Hellenistic kingdoms. Had the Attalids, Ptolemaics, or Seleucids, or even the Carthaginians, succeeded, after Cannae, in imposing their culture over the ancient world, then this analogy would have applied most rewardingly. This has not occurred. The Industrial Revolution that was born in England now resides in the United States, and the possibility of its metropolitan center emigrating elsewhere in the foreseeable future is virtually insignificant.

The suggestion that this metropolitan center of modernity may cross the Pacific, to the neighborhood of Osaka or Singapore, is based on a misunderstanding of the nature of modern industrialism, which is emphatically not simply a capacity to produce great quantities of goods at lower prices but principally an ability to create as well as to produce, copiously and continuously, new cultural traits, artifacts, and signifiers useful, acceptable, or attractive to the great multitudes of the modern world. Looked at from this vantage point, Japan and the other enormously successful industrial economies of the western Pacific have proved beyond question that they must be counted among the most diligent disciples that the English-speaking peoples have ever had. They have succeeded not only in adopting but also in improving the ways to produce the goods of the industrial age, but they have proved indifferent apprentices of the manner of consumption of their English-speaking mentors. Big and smaller dragons are immensely convincing producers but unimpressive both as creators of new cultural artifacts and as consumers of the goods that they have learned so efficiently to produce.[5] During the past half century, the people of Japan have embraced the cultural signifiers of their mentors with truly remarkable enthusiasm and have made them their own.[6] They have dismantled, studied, and perfected motorcycles, automobiles, jukeboxes, photographic cameras, electric toothbrushes, television receivers, wristwatches, washing machines, electric toasters, and computers, but with very few exceptions indeed, they have not strayed so far that their original models cannot be recognized. The best Japanese camera—and their cameras are very good indeed—remains an apparatus that can claim direct descent from Fox Talbot's ingenious invention.[7]

The specific intent of the original act of creation has not been dissipated; rather, it has often been reinforced by vastly improved designs and production techniques. This generalization applies also to cultural artifacts very distant from the factory floor. For example, both the form and the content of the most popular Japanese television offerings, including quiz shows, interviews, advertisements, documentaries, and soap opera series, have been successfully patterned after well-known

5. Protests notwithstanding, as exemplified in Sheridan M. Tatsuno's *Created in Japan: From Imitators to World-Class Innovators* (New York, 1990), in which the argument is reinforced that the Japanese excel in adapting and refining Western ideas generally. Citing Henry E. Riggs, of Stanford University, Tatsuno notes that Japan performs best in the area of process technology, while the United States remains a leader in product development. "In almost all fields," he adds, "the Japanese excel when research targets are clearly defined and fixed, whereas Americans do better when targets are vague. . . . Japanese companies analyze the limitations of existing processes and make small improvements. They are incrementalists." This is precisely why the metropolis of industrialism is unlikely either to acquire a new lingua franca or to move across the Pacific (16–17).

6. Including advances as readily associated with the Japanese electronic prowess as, say, the "computer-on-a-chip," or microprocessor, at the heart of virtually every electronic product, from videocassette recorders to automobile engines, but which few know as the invention of an American, Gilbert P. Hyatt, who was finally granted a patent in 1990 for an invention that he had registered twenty years earlier but failed to exploit commercially. Once the patent was granted, the major Japanese electronic companies promptly agreed to pay royalties to Hyatt, whose rights will expire in the year 2007. It has been estimated that the first payments made to Hyatt will be in the neighborhood of $100 million. *The New York Times*, February 1, 1992, 35–36.

7. William Henry Fox Talbot, not Jacques Louis Mande Daguerre. It is Talbot's invention that is at the heart of modern photography because he could produce multiple prints from a negative, while each daguerrotype was, and is, in a very real sense, unique. Fox Talbot did for visual imagery what Gutenberg had done for the written word. In 1844, Fox Talbot published the first book illustrated with photographs, memorably entitled *The Pencil of Nature*.

models in the United States, and their popularity appears to depend on this identification, regardless of artistic flaws or merits.

This is also illustrated by the alacrity with which literally millions of people in every one of these prosperous Asian countries has welcomed the unpretentious culinary offerings of the characteristically American fast-food chains. Perhaps one should pause to consider that Japan and China, and their neighbors, are heirs to some of the oldest continuing cultural traditions of mankind; more, that in gastronomy, these traditions have achieved unsurpassed heights of subtlety and elegance that are not the exclusive domain of an elite but a very visible part of contemporary everyday life at all levels of society. These are not, therefore, cultural deserts where the inhabitants are so deprived that any edible alms will be gratefully received. And yet, there are at present almost one thousand thriving Kentucky Fried Chicken outlets in Japan, with an annual volume of sales of just over $900 million, which is considerably less than the $1.09 billion taken in by the 677 McDonald's outlets; Hong Kong has the largest Pizza Hut in the world (400 seats); in Peking, very near to Tiananmen Square, is the largest (510 seats) and busiest Kentucky Fried Chicken outlet on earth.[8]

The popular reception accorded to these particularly unheroic, almost humble, latter-day products of the English Industrial Revolution is paralleled by the more demanding acceptance of sports such as baseball, volleyball, golf, and tennis, any one of which has a much greater following than, say, sumo wrestling or any other Japanese, Chinese, or Korean alternative. And after so many travelers' tales and learned reports have regaled us with accurate and vivid descriptions of the legendary ritual and etiquette that accompany the drinking of sake, what are we to make of the intriguing intelligence that Japan is the second largest consumer of whisky in the world?

It is also erroneous to regard the impressive performance of the economies of the Pacific Rim as a portent of the imminent decline of the twice-centenary Industrial Revolution of the English-speaking peoples. This is not so. The earnestness with which Japan, China, and the "Little Dragons" are embracing the cultural traits and artifacts that continue to issue forth from the English-speaking world suggests, on the contrary, that they are responding positively and rather flatteringly to the creative

8. The largest McDonald's outlet in the world (700 seats) is, of course, in Pushkin Square, only a couple of blocks away from the Kremlin. *Time*, December 25, 1989, 66; February 5, 1990, 43.

vitality of an Industrial Revolution that continues to shape our modern world. The very least that can be observed, without falling into the trap of making invidious and unhelpful comparisons, is that the zeal with which, for example, the Japanese try to master the fine points of contract bridge or baseball, or the Chinese the production of large quantities of blue jeans, Band-Aids, and transistor radios, is not reciprocated in the English-speaking world. Here and there a few clubs encourage the practice of yoga, sumo, or tai chi; elsewhere oriental restaurants have become part of the urban landscape, and there is a fair sprinkling of dedicated *Mah-Jongg* players in the better suburbs[9] and black-belted athletes in gymnasiums everywhere, but even if all these people were taken together, including the clientele of the restaurants, they would be fewer than those among their Japanese and Chinese counterparts who are diligently trying to master volleyball, memorize Shakespeare, or imitate the antics of Elvis Presley, the Beatles, or the Rolling Stones.

The widespread misunderstanding about the import of the economic success of some Asian countries is partly the consequence of a previous error about the nature of industrial production and its significance within the complex process of modernization. This conceptual error can be illustrated by noting the difference in kind, not of degree, that exists between using a photographic camera, making it, and, rarest of all, inventing one. That there should be any confusion about this is in large measure precisely a result of the great changes in the nature of production brought about by the Industrial Revolution. Those momentous technological transformations, and their social consequences, towered so impressively over the nineteenth century that they induced an almost reverential attitude toward what then appeared clearly to be the single driving force responsible for the coming of industrialism and modernity.

Marx was convinced that the mode of production determined "the general character of the social, political and spiritual processes of life," and although not completely blind to the complexities of human society, he nevertheless believed he had seen, with devastating clarity, that above all else, "production predominates."[10] Those early decades of the Industrial Revolution overwhelmed us with a vision of our capacity to pro-

9. Mah-Jongg is the trade name of a variation on one of many similar Chinese games designed and introduced into the English-speaking world in 1919 by Joseph Babcock, who also invented the name.

10. Karl Marx, "The Material Forces and the Relations of Production," excerpts from *A Contribution to the Critique of Political Economy*, trans. N. I. Stone, from the 2d German ed. (New York, 1904), in Talcott Parsons et al., *Theories of Society* (New York, 1965): 136–138.

duce, and the fateful "relations of production" became the critical historical dimension, the prophetic entrails of modern society for
soothsayers to scrutinize. Marx was certainly not the only one prepared
to attribute to the changes in the manner in which goods were produced
the decisive responsibility for the advent of the modern world and for
everything else before and after. His seminal concept of the "relations
of production" retained for well over a century a hypnotic hold over the
modern imagination; it became almost impossible, without risking dismissal for obscurantism, even to suggest that a more complex approach
to the problem was appropriate.

In our time, however, we have rid ourselves of this quasi-idolatrous
myth and have advanced far above and beyond the relatively simple
processes whereby things are produced. Even excluding the use of robots
and the like, we know that almost any human grouping can be taught
to master sequential techniques that will result in the production of extremely complex products; scarcely literate Taiwanese and South Kore-
ans work efficiently and safely and are paid very good wages to manufacture computers that they would be quite incapable of using, let alone
understanding. In Australia, Malaysia, and Brazil, automobile components of extraordinary electronic complexity are produced by workers
otherwise incapable of explaining why an internal combustion engine
functions at all. In a subtle, almost elegant sense, we have emancipated
ourselves from the tyranny of production; now we know very well how
to produce anything, anywhere, and virtually under any physical condition imaginable. That the little dragons can produce word processors,
food processors, and washing machines quickly and inexpensively
should not surprise. Well-trained managers ought to be able to bring
forth a comparable performance from any group of well-fed Patagonian
fishermen, Anatolian peasants, Paraguayan fruit growers, or Pakistani
carpet weavers.

The crucial problem of industrialism is not solely, as Marx and Lenin
thought, how to produce but mainly what to produce; it is not simply
about plumbing but principally about architecture, not only about making things but about inventing them. What truly distinguishes the Industrial Revolution of the English-speaking peoples is not so much the
expediency of their manufacturing arrangements as the immense variety
of goods and services that they have proved increasingly able to create
as their industrialization continues to grow in size and complexity. The
Japanese have manufactured more pianos in the last two or three decades than the whole of Europe since Beethoven, as well as a consider-

able number of trombones, trumpets, flutes, guitars, violins, bassoons, saxophones, and other musical instruments of European origin, but the average music critic would be hard-pressed to think of half a dozen Japanese compositions incorporated into the repertoire. Albanians can press records as easily and quickly as the English can, but they cannot put together a Beatles foursome that anyone outside Tirana wishes to hear. The printers of Hong Kong and Singapore are infinitely more efficient at publishing the collected works of Mark Twain than, say, the printers of Milwaukee or Cincinnati; their problem, however, is not one of printing quickly and inexpensively but of writing something worth printing. Is there a Singaporean Mark Twain? Where is the Henry Ford of Taiwan? How can we discover the name of the Josiah Wedgwood of South Korea? The problem, ultimately, is not simply one of mastering the production of Frankfurt sausages but of inventing the hot dog;[11] not simply one of knowing how to manufacture film equipment and produce films but how to create an important proportion of the major myths of our time and present them in understandable, attractive, and exportable images; not simply one of excelling in draftsmanship and the production of pencils but of begetting Donald Duck and Mickey Mouse.

Some very unusual sociologists have argued that behind Donald Duck there lurks a quasi-conspiratorial intent to sap the forces that may otherwise resist the inroads of American capitalism.[12] Although unintended,

11. Sausages were well known in antiquity; Homer devoted a few lines of the *Odyssey* to praise of a well-roasted sausage, but the type used to make the modern hot dog was first produced in Frankfurt, of course, around 1852. The legendary version is that its curved shape was suggested by a butcher who wanted the sausage to resemble his pet Dachshund. The sausage became very popular and was marketed alternatively as the Frankfurt sausage or the Dachshund sausage. In summer 1906, Tad Dorgan, a cartoonist for the Hearst newspapers, heard the sausage vendors in the Polo Grounds, home of the New York Giants, promote their product with the shout, "Get your red-hot Dachshund sausages!" Dorgan drew a cartoon of a Dachshund, adorned with mustard and wedged inside a bun. The legendary sequel is that unable to spell Dachshund, Dorgan settled for the simplest solution and captioned his cartoon, "Get your hot dogs!" Charles Panati, *Extraordinary Origins of Everyday Things* (New York, 1987): 396–399. There is an alternative version of the origins of the ubiquitous sandwich that traces it to the North German *Halberstadter* sausage, which is said to be the "same sausage that most other Germans call a *Wiener*." The proponent of this equally entertaining theory ends by suggesting, "If our American hot dog could talk, or even bark a few syllables, I am convinced it would proudly proclaim: *Ich bin ein Halberstadter!*" This may well be so, but it does not affect the clear North American paternity of the popular, albeit pedestrian, sandwich. James P. O'Donnell, "Casing the Sausage," *Bostonia* (January–February 1991): 40–42.

12. Commenting on the very great popularity of the Disney characters, Dorfman and Mattelart complain—and one wonders whether there is a touch of unintended humor here—because "in more countries than one it has been observed that the popularity of Mickey Mouse exceeds that of the national hero." And further on they signal their displeasure with the intelligence that in 1972, a woman's magazine in Chile had proposed that Walt Disney should be honored with the Nobel Peace Prize. Ariel Dorfman and Armand Mattelart, *Para leer al Pato Donald* (Valparaíso, 1973): 12.

this is telling homage to a dimension of the culture of the United States that is clearly incompatible with the working hypothesis of the Hellenistic aftermath. In a handful of generations, the English-speaking Americans, especially those working in Hollywood and the surrounding territory, generated an unprecedented number of characters, myths, and legends that continue to prove enjoyable, acceptable, and even credible to children and adults almost everywhere. Donald Duck is certainly one of them, together with the members of his family; and so are Dick Tracy, Bugs Bunny, Goofy, and Betty Boop, the Marx Brothers, Greta Garbo, the Muppets, and the Teenage Mutant Ninja Turtles, King Kong, Marilyn Monroe, Popeye, and Charlie Chaplin, Shirley Temple, Buster Keaton, Tom and Jerry, Tarzan, Humphrey Bogart, Laurel and Hardy, and many others, some of whom have proved as persistent and ubiquitous on the cultural horizon as have the exploits of cowboys and Indians and the dastardly deeds of Chicago gangsters, New York shrinks, and Californian divorcées. No other country in modern times has been as prolific; none has succeeded so convincingly in simultaneously capturing the interest, often the affection as well, of so many people for such a diverse array of creatures of the imagination.[13] To attribute this feat principally to the quasi-monopoly exercised by Hollywood misses the point and reinforces the original argument.

The popularity of these myths and legends and their colorful protagonists need not be a reflection of good taste, impeccable direction, intelligent scripts, or strikingly original plots. From time to time, a few of these amiable virtues emerge, but more often than otherwise, the chasm that separates what is basically an ephemeral and unpretentious species of entertainment from the realm of significant literature and drama remains unbridged. It would be an error, however, to be dismissive about the quality of human energy and imagination that produces a film, say, like *Rambo III*, which earns a paltry $55 million in the United States but makes amends abroad with sales of $105 million; or *Indiana Jones and the Last Crusade*, which pleases enough reasonably able-minded human beings to achieve sales of $197 million within the United States and $250 million in foreign cinemas. These figures reflect a trend that

13. This dominance is now also reflected in the commercial arrangements for the marketing and distribution of films. Until recently, the principal film market was the Cannes International Film Festival, which in 1990 had sales of $345 million, compared with $362 million transacted in the American Film Market in Santa Monica by over 2,000 independent movie and video producers and distributors from over sixty countries. Founded scarcely ten years ago, the AFM is today the busiest single motion picture industry trade fair in the world. Larry Rohter, "World's Film Dealers Converge on Santa Monica," *The New York Times*, March 5, 1991, C11.

displeases filmmakers elsewhere because although they are accustomed to Hollywood being in the vanguard of the film market, "its dominance is now so great that it is crushing filmmakers in other countries." Further, "the world's demand for American entertainment seems insatiable, and Hollywood is ever ready to please, titillate and excite for the price of a movie ticket."[14] The financial returns are eloquent: in 1989, revenues from cinemas in the United States and Canada amounted to something over $5 billion, but the revenues from overseas markets were over the $3 billion mark and still growing, and foreign customers are already purchasing well over 40 percent of all film videos.

The torrent does not flow unimpeded. South Korean nationalists have occasionally released snakes in cinemas where Hollywood films are shown, while characteristically humorless French governments have for long endeavored to erect the highest possible legal fences "to protect their people against their own bad taste."[15] Hollywood has afforded some grounds for disquiet among nationalists and purists everywhere with its undeniable influence over the contemporary view of things. Its film companies, directors, and producers have been filling the screens of the world with scenes of a way of life that may or may not be that of every American family but that do portray their aspirations in a plausible manner, well founded, moreover, on a reality that overflows from the shelves of supermarkets, department stores, and suburban shopping centers and that, though abhorred as "consumerism" by the intelligentsia of the more prosperous regions of the English-speaking world, is not without admiring friends overseas. Prime Minister Nikolai Ryzhkov was the highest-ranking Soviet political figure ever to visit Australia. When preparations were under way, in February 1990, Australian protocol inquired about the minister's preferred use of his one free morning in what was, by necessity, a crowded schedule. It was suggested that the minister would possibly enjoy a couple of hours at the National Gallery of Victoria, or perhaps the Melbourne Zoo or the world-famous Botanical Gardens, but the minister was unhesitant in his decision; unmoved by the fashionable rejection of consumerism, he announced that he wished to visit Safeway, which he did, and in the course of the morning inspected every aspect of the operation, declaring himself especially im-

---

14. Howard G. Chua-Eoan, "Movie Muscle," *Time*, May 28, 1990, 56.
15. M. Jack Lang, the French minister of culture, explained the policy of imposing special taxes on videos and severe quotas on the foreign content of local television programs by affirming that the destiny of the French people "is not to become the vassals of an immense empire of profit." Chua-Eoan, "Movie," 58.

pressed by the way in which the computerized electronic scanners, first introduced by IBM in 1980, expedited a checking-out process that controlled sales and inventories simultaneously and with the greatest of ease.

The "form of life" of the people who created the cornucopia is made visible and given actuality by the magic of cinema and television, and in a sequence reminiscent of "cargo cult" expectations, people all over the world have tended to adopt the cultural trappings of the Promethean creators of wealth and happiness. Millions of television viewers and moviegoers unable otherwise to move away from their localities have had the American way of life placed before them on their cinema screens or inside their own homes. Chairman Mao and the Ayatollah Khomeini were probably right when they protested that this intrusion threatened the stability of the way of life of their people, but theirs was a hopeless struggle against the irresistible tide of brightly colored images.[16]

In the absence of a latter-day Homeric mythology, our world has settled down to watch *Dallas*, a soap opera that during the past twelve years has been broadcast in ninety-nine countries to such huge audiences that it has become, by far, the most popular drama in the history of mankind. The quantity of television programs produced in the United States and viewed by foreign eyes is substantial. In 1988, according to the Motion Picture Association of America, the United States exported $2.5 billion more in television programs and films than it imported. Except for the manufacture of aircraft, this trade surplus is higher than that generated by any other industry in the country. Some, understandably, have been moved to hyperbole by this undoubted success. In the opinion of M. Dornemann, president of the Bertelsmann Music Group, an entity not unaffected by this trend, "America is the cultural heart of the world."[17] Others have simply jumped onto the speeding bandwagon. Matsushita Electric Industrial Company paid $7.4 billion for MCA, Inc., scarcely a few weeks after Sony Corporation had agreed to pay $3.5 billion for Columbia Pictures Entertainment, Inc. Neither trans-

16. The argument for resistance against the intrusion has formidable classical antecedents. Tacitus observed that when the Romans invaded Britain, Claudius enlisted "the delights of luxury" to consolidate the conquest and render "a race of rude and primitive men . . . peaceful and tranquil." The local chieftains were encouraged and helped to build temples and houses, and their sons were instructed in the liberal arts, thus enabling them to confront earthy wit with learning and erudition and ensuring that those unfamiliar with Latin would be regarded as lacking in eloquence. They were also encouraged to adopt the Roman style of dress, and the toga became common. "Little by little they were lured to the blandishments of vice, to porticoes and baths, and to luxurious feasts. In this way, an unsophisticated people learnt to mistake the path of servitude for the highroad to culture." Tacitus, *Agricola*, 21.

17. *The Age*, Melbourne, December 2, 1989, Extra, 4.

action, one supposes, was concluded to satisfy the new proprietors' wish to use the huge American studio facilities to produce Japanese-content films and soap operas.[18]

The plausible dreams that gush forth from television and cinema screens influence and help to shape the cultural ambit of millions who are otherwise earthbound and static, but those other millions who actually travel for one reason or another are borne aloft by a cultural artifact and begetter of concrete human actions as quintessentially American as the world engendered by Hollywood. The modern airliner is an unalloyed cultural creation of the English-speaking Americans. From the momentous 1903 flight at Kitty Hawk through the endless mechanical refinements, experiments, accidents, and disappointments of the following years in Dayton, Ohio, to the swift advances dictated by the war, the accelerated pace of air travel after 1920, the circling of the globe by passenger aircraft in 1935, and on to our time of frequent and effortless tourism for the millions, the United States has remained among the small group of two or three countries that have never relinquished the technological, scientific, and commercial vanguard of an activity that is well on the way to becoming a principal symbol of the twentieth century.

The modern airliner is an American cultural artifact. Most long-range passenger airplanes are produced by only two manufacturing companies in the United States. In addition, the elaborate ritual of attending to the sale of tickets, the reception of passengers, scrutiny of credentials, embarkation, seating arrangements, service personnel, rules and regulations imposed on passengers during flight, entertainment, cuisine and beverages, duty-free sales, paliatives for jet lag, disembarkation procedures, frequent-flyer incentive schemes, arrangements administrative

18. Although American and English recording artists are invariably at the very top of the world's sales charts, four of the five principal record companies in the United States and in the world are owned by foreign entities: CBS, by Sony; RCA, by Bertelsmann; PolyGram, by NV Philips; and Capitol-EMI, by EMI. These acquisitions have generated some public debate, but it is now clear that what these foreign competitors are doing is to buy what they cannot make in their own countries. Many reasons have been advanced to explain why these producers have been unable to imitate the American products elsewhere, but one of the most interesting, suggested by Richard Schickel, film critic for *Time* and historian of Hollywood, is that the studios in the United States established a cinematic "language" and series of genres—westerns, gangster pictures, musicals, and horror films— that have become familiar to audiences everywhere. "For better or worse . . . the American style of film-making is the established standard around the world." *The Age*, Melbourne, December 2, 1989, Extra, 4. This view received formidable support when early in 1991, three months after having been acquired by Sony Corporation, Columbia Pictures Entertainment, announced its intention to establish a number of "Sonyland" amusement parks in the United States to compete with a chain of Disneylands that now includes parks in Tokyo and Paris. One wonders whether it is possible to dismiss as without significance the fact that 300,000 paying Japanese visit the Tokyo Disneyland every week of the year.

and mechanical for the retrieval of baggage, and virtually every other detail that helps to shape the form of life of the millions of people who travel by air every year was devised in the United States and subsequently adopted with minor variations by airlines everywhere, together, it must be added, with the use of the English language as the official lingua franca of aircrews and traffic controllers in almost every airport on earth.

This kind of unmistakable stylistic "Americanism" is as evident in the standard passenger airliner as it is in the skyscraper, without doubt the characteristic edifice of industrial modernity. Even today, when there is strong and widespread opposition to the construction of sunlight-blocking towers as well as to the basic principles of modern architecture, more skyscrapers are being built in cities around the world than ever before. Each of these tall structures, whether constructed in Nairobi or Hong Kong, Beirut, Naples, or Buenos Aires, is a less or more distant relation of the first skyscrapers of Chicago and New York, themselves the consequence, largely intended, of the invention of the "safe hoist" by the master mechanic Elisha Graves Otis, of Yonkers, which made possible the effortless and periodic occupation of the man-made heights of the modern era, and of the subsequent development of a method of construction based on the use of a steel frame instead of masonry walls to carry the vertical load of the building. Thus was born the skyscraper, which is simply a tall building, the higher levels of which are made accessible by Otis's ingenious lifting device, and which has impressed its practicalities on the growth of modern cities under a variety of fashionable adornments that have never quite obscured its decisive origin in the heartland of the United States. Ambitious or modest, elegant or absurd, ugly or beautiful, small or large, the skyscraper precedes by generations the stylistic and conceptual claims to preeminence in modern architecture that issued forth from Germany's Bauhaus and from France's Le Corbusier.[19]

19. Otis's invention dates from 1852. In 1885, the ten-story Home Insurance Building was completed in Chicago; the first building designed so that its frame and not its walls should bear the vertical weight. Strictly speaking, this was the first "skyscraper." During the following twenty years, Chicago retained the primacy in the building of skyscrapers with the Tacoma Building, completed in 1889 and rising to 165 feet; followed by Adler and Sullivan's Auditorium of 1890 which rose to 270 feet. Only in 1903, with the "Flat Iron" Building, rising to 286 feet, did New York take the lead. In 1919, the Woolworth Building rose 792 feet with the help of the first automatic system of passenger lifts; it remained the world's tallest structure until 1930 when it was overtaken by the Chrysler Building, 1,046 feet high, and the Empire State Building, 1,250 feet high. More recently, these impressive heights have been surpassed by gigantic structures such as the New York World Trade Center, rising 1,386 feet and Skidmore, Owens & Merrill's Sears Tower in Chicago, at 1,454 feet, the world's tallest building.

The skyline of the modern city does not resemble that of Siena or Salamanca but decisively the skylines of Atlanta, Houston, and Milwaukee. Among the reasons that help us to understand why this is so must be included the economic and demographic circumstances that accompanied their planning and construction. Nonetheless, it would be an error to think that the very high buildings that give the modern urban centers their characteristic profile are simply a by-product of real estate economics and that their universality is an uncomplicated consequence of urban agglomeration. If it was only a matter of space, relative or absolute, then skyscrapers would be rare in Melbourne, Buenos Aires, Lusaka, São Paulo, and Lagos. This is not the case. Not even on the island of Manhattan, where circumstances are indeed unique, can scarcity of land be advanced as the sole explanation for the prodigious increase in the height and mass of office buildings. If all the buildings of Manhattan were reduced to an average height, they would not exceed the legendary ten stories of the first Chicago skyscraper. To insist that the loftiness of the Chrysler Building is directly a consequence of economic necessity, or of some recondite neo-Ricardian application of the theory of rent, has all the marks of a misunderstanding as gross as to explain banana splits and popcorn in terms of the need to assuage the people's hunger. It would appear that the architectural feats achieved in the great American cities demand, and deserve, less mercenary and more plausible interpretations.

A recent visitor to Chicago observed that "the skyscrapers, like the towers of San Gimignano, seem to be there as much for reassurance as for self-aggrandisement."[20] This is possible and certainly not incompatible with a cultural moment characterized by constant mobility. In a society in which, by definition, everybody either moves or could move all the time, up and down as well as sideways, the need eventually arises to discover a very visible means of marking the satisfaction of ambition, a tranquil permanence, a reassuring continuity of purpose that explains, praises, and justifies. The architect John Burgee, who has created many of these lofty structures, noted, "A skyscraper is an emotional term; it talks about ambition."[21] Skyscrapers are the ultimate monuments of mo-

20. Chicago is "still one of the beautiful cities of the world, more beautiful perhaps than it used to be, beautiful not because it has acquired the patina of age but because it retains . . . its Modernist enthusiasm. It's the kind of city, glass stumps by the dozen, that would make Prince Charles commit suicide. . . . Civic pride in Chicago starts with the architecture. . . . In no other city in the world is the built environment such an object of popular interest and enthusiasm." Richard Gott, "Crumbs and the Capitalists," *The Guardian*, January 20, 1989, 21.

21. William S. Ellis, "Skyscrapers: Above the Crowd," *National Geographic* (February 1989): 165.

dernity. Their proliferation in the metropolis of power is not a function of land scarcity but of a sense of achievement. With great churches and equestrian statues out of fashion, these are the monuments of our time, rising higher than anything ever made by the hand of man to proclaim the permanence of a mode of action whose raison d'être is to be impermanent and that appears neither to be waning nor to be losing credibility as the century draws to an end, its vociferous band of detractors notwithstanding.

More interesting, these undeniably American cultural artifacts, which owe as much to inspired engineering as to the mood of the time, have become accepted models for the rest of the world.[22] With few exceptions, the buildings that give modern architecture its dominant public face and largely determine the form of the cities of the industrial era are patterned after American designs. It would be very difficult to find a commercial urban center built during the past two generations that cannot be confused with parts of downtown Jacksonville or Detroit. This has very little to do with the quality of the designs or the skill with which the edifices are constructed but everything to do with their public appearance; no one could possibly imagine that the office buildings constructed during the past twenty or thirty years in, say, Lyon, Santiago, or Singapore would be absolutely out of place in Minneapolis, New Orleans, or downtown Los Angeles. The weighty horizontality proposed by Le Corbusier and, before him, by Frank Lloyd Wright as well as the myriad distinguished alternative solutions to the design problems posed by large shopping centers, housing estates, and commercial buildings of all kinds have proved insufficient to stem the tide. Different though they are in many other ways, the buildings constructed during the past few decades in Melbourne, Bogotá, Singapore, and Bordeaux resemble each other and those in Boston and Indianapolis as much and as convincingly as the buildings erected in Pergamum, Alexandria, Antioch, and Halicarnassus resembled each other and their Athenian models.

Firmly rooted in the culture that cradled it, the skyscraper has nonetheless proved to be as good a traveler as plastic credit cards, pinball

---

22. Even when relegated to the outskirts of the existing city, as in Florence or Paris. Municipal authorities are rightly concerned with the preservation of the inner city, partly for aesthetic reasons and partly also in the interests of a healthy tourist trade. New constructions in the outer suburbs, however, tend to follow the Chicago lead, albeit in a minor scale; the center of Florence is very unlike the heart of Milwaukee, but the outer suburbs bear an amusing resemblance. Less anxious about the transformation of tiny fishing villages into museums, Spain has allowed seasonal tourism to flourish unimpeded, and the demand for hotel accommodation has resulted in the swift transformation of much of its southern coast and the Balearic Islands into serviceable local versions of Miami or Atlantic City, rather, one may add, than of Biarritz, Bournemouth, or Portofino.

machines, jumbo jets, laundromats, potato chips, vacuum cleaners, and rock and roll. Even terrorists prepared to lose their lives attacking American installations go about their disquieting business chewing gum and clad in T-shirts, blue jeans, and jogging shoes.[23] The sartorial preferences of the young all over the world run almost parallel to their liking for rock and roll, hard rock, jazz, heavy metal, acid, rap, or whatever current variety of very loud syncopated music happens to be in fashion. This immensely popular kind of music originated in the cultural hinterland of the United States, and its principal variant, also dominant in the popularity charts, is Liverpudlian in origin and remained for many years directly identified with English ensembles, principally those of the Beatles and the Rolling Stones.[24] Whether rock music is or is not, as some authors have suggested, "the music of triumphant vulgarity," is not at issue.[25] What is important here is to observe that in the past few decades this kind of music has achieved a universality that is truly without precedent. This preponderance owes much to the parallel development of electronic means of reproducing sound, but lest someone propose that herein lies the hidden hand of imperialism, it must be noted that these technological advancements are also readily accessible for the reproduction of folk music from China, Iran, Argentina, or Lithuania.

Of the many distinguished folkloric musical traditions made accessible to millions of listeners by the new electronic techniques, it is only rock music, in one or another of its modes, proximate or distant, that

23. The fiercest denunciations against the cultural influence of the United States and Britain are not infrequently broadcast over radio and television by politicians who then drive back to their homes to be comforted by refrigerators, electric toasters, freezers, microwave ovens, washing machines, and VCRs, with the same aplomb with which the satrap Mausollus must have enjoyed the architecture of his new Hellenistic capital city of Halicarnassus during the intervals of his wars and conspiracies against the hated Athenians. In this respect, it is not unimportant that the neo-Nazi songs banned by the German government in 1992, when trying to stem the violence that swept that country in the aftermath of reunification, were without exception rendered by nationalist rock groups producing sounds indistinguishable from those generated by their counterparts on the other side of the Atlantic.

24. It is not out of place to note that as the world entered the last decade of the millennium, a survey by Broadcast Music International indicated that Paul McCartney's song "Yesterday" was "the most played song in the world"; that is, played over radio or television and computed for copyright purposes. Errol Simper, "Songs of Yesterday Top the Airwaves," *Weekend Australian*, December 22, 1990, 7. There is no doubt that the most often performed song on earth will remain for a very long time Mildred Hill and Patty Smith Hill's "Happy Birthday to You," for details of which see n. 31, below.

25. "Rock is the music of triumphant vulgarity. Rock begins in America, and its roots are deep in the same soil that gives birth to the great experiment of vulgar democracy. In the egalitarian spirit of vulgarity, rock recognizes no class boundaries." Robert Pattison, *The Triumph of Vulgarity: Rock Music in the Mirror of Romanticism* (New York, 1987): 9.

can convincingly claim to have achieved virtually universal popular acceptance. Radio Zet, Poland's first independent station since the ousting of the Communist regime, plays music twenty-four hours a day for an insatiable audience that is very happy with a menu that each hour ranges "from Elvis Presley to Madonna to M. C. Hammer, the popular American rap singer." Brazil, hardly a country suffering from a dearth of folk music, has been host to what are described as the two greatest rock music festivals in history. The first took place in 1985 and attracted 1.3 million paying customers; the second one, Rock in Rio II, held in 1991, attracted a complaint in *The New York Times* that

> programs handed out at the door contained the lyrics of English-speaking performers to promote English-language courses. Lazzo, a singer from Bahia who joined Jimmy Cliff for one song, said afterward, "Backstage, I felt like a stranger in my own country, because everybody was speaking English." . . . On the FM band in Rio de Janeiro, it is easier to hear James Taylor than to find *pagode* music. The American, British and Australian bands at Rock in Rio II seemed confident that they were the world, hardly considering language and culture gaps. . . . Rock seemed to be the advance guard of American-style consumption. Loving the kind of rock that's popular in the English-speaking world may symbolize hope for affluence.[26]

At least as visible from every corner of the earth was Berlin's outburst of popular enthusiasm when the infamous wall was finally brought down in 1990. And few must have failed to note that the celebrations did not culminate with a Te Deum or a military parade but with a very loud rock music concert to which thronged hundreds of thousands of young people proudly adorned with buttons and stickers proclaiming their loyalty to Led Zeppelin, Bob Dylan, Elvis Presley, Black Sabbath, and the Rolling Stones.[27]

The apparel, ritual, and paraphernalia normally associated with these performing groups, as well as the deportment of many of their members and loyal fans, appear to run counter to one of the most extraordinarily pervasive contributions to everyday life made by the English-speaking American heirs of the Industrial Revolution. Personal cleanliness has preoccupied civilized human societies since the dawn of history, but

26. Jon Pareles, "Samba Takes a Back Seat to Spectacle," *The New York Times*, January 27, 1991, H27.

27. The growing acceptance of rock music in the countries of Central and Eastern Europe is abundantly documented; less well known is the very great popularity that jazz enjoys in Berlin as well as in Prague, Budapest, and Warsaw. Quasimodo, the famous Berlin nightclub, is now generally regarded as one of Europe's principal jazz performing centers.

never before did it become so securely established as a key social grace, accessible to everyone through the use of a handful of cosmetic preparations and devices invented scarcely a few generations ago but found today in bathroom cabinets all over the world. King Gillette, for example, came upon the idea of the safety razor that bears his name in Brookline, Massachusetts, in 1895. After several years of working together with William Nickerson, of the Massachusetts Institute of Technology, he succeeded in producing the modern safety blade in 1903. A few months later, 300,000 razors and half a million blades had already been sold, and the product remained unchallenged until 1931, when the electric shaver, also invented in the United States, by Jacob Schick, made its diffident first appearance.[28] A few decades earlier, in 1888, the first compound designed specifically to stop underarm perspiration was sold under the trade name Mum. During the next thirty years, the product sold briskly, although no one dared to state in print what it was that it was supposed to prevent, until in 1919, *Odo-Ro-No* published for the first time an advertisement in which the socially offensive condition was described as B. O. The appalling coyness did not impede the rapid adoption of the product throughout the advanced countries of the world until its use became de rigueur not only in polite society but among civilized peoples everywhere.[29] To body deodorants and shaving equipment soon were added a great variety of cosmetics, cleansers, scrubbing liquids, dishwashing fluids, window cleaners, antiseptic mouth rinses, and a vast number of soaps, especially made to address this, that, or the other variety of dirt, muck, or grime. To this formidable array was added the virtual invention of suntanning as a socially desirable emblem of health and vigor, swiftly followed by the introduction of suntanning lotions and dark glasses.

No list can possibly do justice to the richness and complexity of a creative moment that has given us the ice-cream cone, roller skates, salted peanuts, tap dancing, candy bars, suitcases with wheels attached, beatniks, hackers, hippies, ski bums, supermarkets, dry martinis, whiskey sours, washable underclothes, hotdogging, Broadway musicals, Mormons, Pentecostals, Christian Scientists, drive-in movie theaters, banks, churches, microwave ovens, vacuum cleaners, dishwashers, cel-

28. It is interesting to note that among the first American industrial ventures of considerable importance in the immediate post–Cold War period is the agreement by the Gillette Corporation to produce razor blades in new manufacturing facilities in the former Soviet Union.
29. Panati, *Origins*, 255–256.

luloid, cellophane, nylon, brown paper bags, Santa Claus,[30] and the only immediately recognizable tune for celebrating birthdays.[31] The fact must be considered to be firmly established that the people of the United States have shared with the rest of the English-speaking world a prodigious ability to create a veritable avalanche of artifacts that have proved universally attractive.

They have also demonstrated exceptional skill in adopting cultural signifiers from elsewhere and stamping them with an unmistakable American character, showing as much originality when inventing basketball and volleyball, for example, as when they redefined running, which the human species has been doing since the dawn of history, into a sartorially formalized and immensely popular activity called jogging,[32] when they institutionalized crossword puzzles,[33] or when they took the

30. St. Nicholas was the bishop of Myra, in the third century, but the modern Santa Claus was first brought to life in 1863 by an American cartoonist named Thomas Nast, who depicted the amiable visitor attired in the now-familiar red and white garments and driving a sled pulled by a team of reindeer.

31. "Happy Birthday to You" is thought to be the most frequently sung music in the history of the world. It was first published in 1893 by the sisters Mildred Hill and Patty Smith Hill, of Louisville, Kentucky. The book was entitled *Song Stories of the Kindergarten*, and the "Happy Birthday" song appeared under the title "Good Morning to All." Mildred Hill, who composed the tune, was a church organist and a concert pianist who died before her tune donned its "Happy Birthday" garb. Her sister, Patty Smith Hill, wrote the original lyrics of the song while she served as principal of the Louisville Experimental Kindergarten School. Later she became head of the Department of Kindergarten Education at Columbia University's Teachers College and was honored as professor emeritus on her retirement. The Misses Hill published their book in 1893. Thirty years later, the same song under the same name appeared in a pirated edition published by Robert H. Coleman. The only difference was that the opening of the second stanza read "Happy Birthday to you" instead of "Good morning dear children." Ten years later, the song had become an international hit under the name "Happy Birthday to You." A third sister, incensed at the blatant theft and the lack of royalties, took the case to court and won, and an astonished world learned that the by now familiar tune belonged to the Hill family and royalties were payable every time it was sung. Panati, *Origins*, 34–35.

32. In the past quarter of a century jogging has taken the world by storm; the traditional marathon has been endlessly multiplied in every conceivable form, while a considerable manufacturing sector has evolved around the design and production of what is now regarded as the indispensable and increasingly refined attire necessary to jog down parks, highways, and especially constructed paths, and a large number of weekly and monthly journals provide enthusiasts with detailed information about the latter-day complexities of this form of exercise. Jogging even acquired a sacred text of sorts, in the form of the then-astonishing best-seller entitled *The Complete Book of Running*, by J. F. Fixx, first published in 1977, which literally transformed elemental running into ritualized jogging.

33. The earliest word puzzles were published in England in the nineteenth century, but it was in the United States that the first modern crossword puzzle appeared in the pages of the *New York World*'s Sunday supplement *Fun*, on December 21, 1913. Ten years later there was scarcely a newspaper in the country that did not offer its readers a crossword at least once a week. It was then, at the height of the Roaring Twenties, that the American crossword puzzle sailed across the Atlantic and conquered its land of origin. C. H. R. Thorn, *Complete Crossword Reference Book* (New York, 1956).

ancient children's game of rounders and transformed it into the country's national sport. While the correctness of this latter claim is a subject of legitimate argument (what about poker?), in its vivid, brash, noisy, and colorful American version, baseball has proved irresistibly appealing to people who possibly would have remained unresponsive to rounders and who, moreover, given the political circumstances, were presumably disinclined to welcome anything with American antecedents. As it happened, baseball is not only the most popular sporting activity in Cuba and Japan but has succeeded in collecting followers in countries as unlikely as Spain, host to the 1991 world baseball championship, and the former Soviet Union, which scarcely a few months before its dissolution applied successfully to join the International Baseball Association.[34]

The transformation of rounders into a summer ritual that can fairly be described as typically American is not unique; the modern luxury hotels, for instance, spawned by the early development of railways in the English cradle of the Industrial Revolution, remained in their native land the exclusive haunt of the rich, and it was left to the United States to impress on them their equally luxurious and at least as pretentious and expensive contemporary egalitarian trappings. There is only one Savoy and only three hotels on earth that can credibly carry the name of Cesar Ritz, but there must be hundreds, possibly thousands, of architecturally indistinguishable and predictably comfortable, hygienic, and efficiently managed hotels strewn throughout the tourist routes of the globe that bear the uncontestable imprint of their American genesis. The reason this is so is more banal than mysterious, but the result is that with minor differences in the embellishments, all rooms in modern hotels on earth, from Tripoli to Kiev and from Managua to Kuala Lumpur, have approximately the same overall dimensions, the same items of furniture similarly placed (including a television set and a well-stocked refrigerator bar), the same procedures for arrivals, departures, payment (credit cards?), laundry, and dry cleaning, the same sanitary facilities and ice-dispensing machines, even the same menu available for a breakfast that can be ordered on roughly the same kind of printed forms the world over.

Of the many examples of this robust capacity to assimilate and then re-create exotic cultural artifacts by impressing on them a novel and

34. It is worthwhile to note that when the Soviet Union joined CEBA, the European Confederation of Baseball Associations, the official world champion of the sport was Cuba, and Barcelona was chosen by acclamation to be the host for the Intercontinental Cup of 1991, for which event the Olympic city promised to build a special stadium. All this in a country that has not built a bullring for more than a generation. *El País*, Madrid, October 14, 1987, 52.

typically American form, the automobile must surely rank among the most dramatic and far-reaching in its influence. The social and economic effects of improved automobiles and roads and the profound cultural transformations elicited by these technological changes bear a principal responsibility for the shape of modern society everywhere, but their origin can easily be traced to the United States. The first internal combustion engines and the earliest practical automobiles were designed and produced in Germany and France,[35] but the culture of the automobile is distinctly, almost uniquely, a creature of the United States, particularly of the Midwest and California. In both cases, this is the consequence less of deliberate policy than of the popular use of the automobile as an instrument to address the problems of midwestern rural isolation and the Californian demand for suburban, quasi-rural privacy.

When the legendary Model T Ford made its appearance, the market for expensive automobiles in the large cities had already been saturated, and it was the fortuitous combination of rising farm incomes and the falling price of the new cars that made the midwestern farmers "yearning to get out of the mud the mainstay of the developing automobile market. By the mid-1920s, the Model T had become a rural necessity. Few farmers by then remained autoless [sic]."[36] This was not the only factor that impressed on the American automobile its distinctive character, but it probably contributed more than anything else to the irreversible transformation of what had arrived from Europe as a luxury vehicle into a people's car, de facto if not de jure. In 1902, it was possible to suggest that by acquiring automobiles, "the millions of our rural population will be brought into closer relations with the towns and with neighbors, and the loneliness of farm life . . . will no longer . . . prevent a proper distribution of population."[37] This use of the automobile as an expeditious means of getting into cities was paradoxically reversed in California, where it enabled urban dwellers to indulge in the luxury of getting out of the city and build one-family homes surrounded by greenery from

35. "It is unequivocal that continental automobile manufacturers were at least a decade ahead of their British and American counterparts in the technological development of the gasoline automobile. Like the automobile itself, the internal-combustion engine had no single inventor. Two-cycle versions were patented by Stuart Perry, a New York inventor, in the United States in 1844 and 1846, and by Etienne Lenoir, a Belgian mechanic, in France, in 1860. There were others. Credit for being 'first' is generally given to Lenoir, because his engine was commercially successful." James J. Flink, *The Automobile Age* (Cambridge, 1988): 11.

36. Car ownership in the farming districts was almost universal. In 1926 in Iowa, for example, 89 percent of tenants and 93 percent of farmers owned cars. By contrast, car ownership in urban areas was rare. Flink, *Automobile*, 131–132.

37. William J. Lampton, "The Meaning of the Automobile," *Outing Magazine* (September 1902): 699.

which it became possible to drive every day to work in the city. Henry Ford described the process succintly: "We shall solve the city problem by leaving the city."[38] This did occur, overwhelmingly, in southern California. "Nowhere in the world has mass motorization been more pervasive in its impact."

The prevalent American conception of "the good life" became epitomized by spacious residential suburbs, where homes could be built separate the one from the other, comfortable, predictable, and private. This idea combined perfectly with the automobile to form the basis for the unprecedented dispersal of Los Angeles. Between 1919 and 1929, the population of this city doubled, but the number of automobiles increased by 550 percent; from 141,000 to 777,000 registrations. A survey conducted in 1931 of the number of automobiles entering the central business district of the larger cities in the country indicated that during an identical twelve-hour period, well over a quarter of a million vehicles entered Los Angeles, compared with 113,000 in Chicago and 66,000 in Boston.[39]

The preponderance of the automobile in everyday life in southern California seventy-five years ago was a portent of what was to come elsewhere in the wake of industrial modernity. In this last decade of the century, 88 percent of the world's motor vehicles are owned by the 17 percent of the population that lives in the most advanced countries. Scarcely 7 percent of the world's population owns automobiles, and only a very small proportion of this minority lives in the poorer countries. By 1980, in the United States, 87.2 percent of households owned one or more motor vehicles; 51.5 percent owned more than one; and 95 percent of domestic sales were for replacement. "Automobile ownership in the United States . . . has spread to all except the hard-core poor, people too infirm or too handicapped to drive, and those who prefer alternatives to individualized automotive transportation." More important, while in the metropolis there are doubts about the desirability of this trend to continue unchecked, in the less prosperous countries, the desire to own a car remains unabated.[40]

38. Henry Ford, in collaboration with Samuel Crowther, *My Life and Work* (New York, 1922): 80, 115.
39. The skyscraper made a very late appearance in the heart of Los Angeles, partly because of the dispersal of the economic activities that provided employment and partly because of the fear of earthquakes, which after 1906 led to a height limitation of 150 feet that was not lifted until the mid-1950s. Flink, *Automobile*, 140–141, 143.
40. For example, it would appear that if the 1975 Western European rate of automobile ownership were to be achieved in Japan, roads, streets, and cities would become

The overwhelming presence of the automobile in the everyday life of so many people has left an imprint that in one way or another has spread to every country where automobiles are not a rarity. The pervasive influence of the American experience with the automobile can everywhere be detected, from the design of gas stations and the vast array of structures and mechanisms necessary to maintain modern roads in good order, including the ancillary landscape of traffic lights, parking meters, motels, road signs, police patrols, speed regulations, and roadside fast-food outlets, to vintage car rallies, hot-rod clubs, truck racing, drag racing, the hallowed Soapbox Derby, and the Indianapolis 500. The automobile has also been largely responsible for the genesis and continued prosperity of some of the most visible cultural entities of the English-speaking Americans.

Enterprises such as McDonald's, Kentucky Fried Chicken, Howard Johnson's, and Burger King could not have been established, nor would they have thrived as they have, in the absence of the automobile. When the legendary Ship's coffee shop in the Westwood Village neighborhood of Los Angeles was closed down in 1984 to make way for a new building, Alan Hess wrote that it

> had been finely tuned to the car culture of Southern California. . . . A pavilion in a parking lot, its bold shapes and colorful spaces beckoned to drivers far down the street by offering a protected oasis in the midst of the noise and hustle of the traffic. It provided a convenient and fitting stage for a rest and a meal along the arteries of the car city. It had been a people's palace, one of the hundreds of coffee shops and drive-ins built nationwide during the fifties and sixties.[41]

The golden arches of McDonald's that now grace the skies of Moscow, Rome, Peking, and Budapest are only the best known of myriad emblems and signifiers that spilled over the world astride artifacts and habits shaped by the culture of the automobile and the expansion of the suburban latter-day version of the advancing American cultural frontier:[42]

---

completely saturated, bringing the island to a virtual standstill. Additionally, in the absence of major technological improvements, the level of pollution would become intolerable. Flink, *Automobile*, 359.

41. Alan Hess, *Googie, Fifties Coffee Shop Architecture* (San Francisco, 1985): 15–16.

42. "The first McDonald's hamburger stands were distinctive products of Southern California related to Coffee Shop Modern. Their designs' origins were obscured by their proliferation nationwide, but they were designed by a Southern California architect in the region's tradition of fanciful and ultramodern roadside buildings. Like the coffee shops, they were scaled to the commotion and expanses of western roadside strips. The out-of-

"the promised land where the middle class could realize the American dream—buying a new single-family house and a capacious new car and leading a well-rounded family life in a relaxed, wholesome non-urban environment. The evolution of the suburbs rapidly reformed the visual and physical character of the American landscape and radically revised middle America's lifestyle."[43] This reassessment was vividly reflected in the arts of the time, especially as they depicted American food, household brand names, and the boxed, packaged, canned, and wrapped consumer goods necessitated by the swift proliferation of self-service stores throughout the expanding suburban hinterland.

Packages ceased to be simple functional containers and became bright, cleverly designed, and persuasive inducements to consume; their imaginative intimations of predictable, effortless domesticity, the raw material for a characteristically vigorous and influential moment in American art. Andy Warhol was not the first artist to depict brand-name products in his works; earlier in the century French cubists had included passing references to alcoholic beverages and cigarettes, but they did it diffidently, almost inadvertently. Not so in the case of Warhol, whose 1961 fanfare of 32 Campbell's soup cans followed only a few weeks later by his canvas depicting 210 Coca-Cola bottles changed irreversibly the perception of the cultural moment.[44] Warhol's painting could not even be dismissed as propaganda; in 1961, Coca-Cola was being purchased at the rate of 65 million servings per day and was by far the single most popular beverage in world history.

Warhol's immensely original and confident incursion could be interpreted as a glorification of consumer goods, consumers, and consumption. The elevation of canned soups to the status of suitable subject for artistic depiction led to the discovery of the neighborhood supermarket and the corner drugstore as sources of inspiration. The pioneering paintings of Coca-Cola bottles and Campbell's soups were soon joined on the walls of art galleries by canvases devoted to individual slices of cherry

---

doors self-service suited the benign, semiarid climate and the mobility of Southern California's post–World War II generation." Hess, *Googie*, 97.

43. Sidra Stich, *Made in USA, an Americanization in Modern Art, the 50s and 60s* (Berkeley, Los Angeles, and London, 1987): 58.

44. "Campbell's was a telling choice. A pioneer in the convenience food industry, Campbell's condensed soup ('just add water') exemplified the theory of product expansion. Within the company's first seven years, the original tomato soup of 1897 was augmented by nineteen other varieties. Even with the postwar competition of freeze-dried and frozen soups, Campbell's held its command of the market, developing new products and, in 1958, extending its operations overseas." Stich, *USA*, 90.

pie, rows of hot dogs, bottles of salad dressing, canned asparagus, Hawaiian pineapples, and corn on the cob and on the floor, by disconcertingly large boxes of Brillo pads, gigantic sailcloth hamburgers, and carefully stitched vinyl and kapok sculptures of french fries with tomato ketchup. The artists, of whom possibly the best known are Wayne Thiebaud, Claes Oldenburg, Roy Lichtenstein, Richard Estes, Tom Wesselman, and Jasper Johns, joined Warhol in the Valhallah of pop culture while their unorthodox models went forth to be embraced and enjoyed by millions upon millions who obviously found them attractive as well as inexpensive.

A century and a half and many millions of corpses later, the world of Karl Marx, in which "above all else . . . production predominates," is in ruins. The proximate cause has been the tenacious resistance and protests of millions of determined human beings throughout Eastern Europe, very few of whom have ever read or studied the ideas of Adam Smith, Edmund Burke, or John Stuart Mill but who have found their motivation in an elemental desire for a better, more interesting life, in which freedom from drudgery, monotony, and discomfort can be facilitated by a ready access to the consumer goods characteristic of a world in which, despite Marxist strictures, the dog of production is wagged lustily by the tail of consumption.

The cutting edge of this truly new world heralded by the Industrial Revolution has not been a stirring pamphlet or a learned philosophical treatise but an immensely democratic capacity to please very large numbers of people mainly by conceiving, and also by producing, an infinite number of goods, not all of which are acceptable to everyone but all created in the expectation that they will satisfy someone's wishes, real or imagined, legitimate or contrived, elegant or tasteless.[45] There is no good reason to suppose that this cannot in the fullness of time be done over and over again, by different groups of human beings belonging to diverse cultural traditions, acting under a variety of auspices and with similar or even greater success; it is also clear that this has not yet occurred.

The capacity to generate large numbers of these unpretentious and

45. In defiance of regiments of sociologists, theologians, social anthropologists, and political scientists, so-called, who have been marching up and down the groves of academe intoning chants against the sins of "consumerism." This is a dimension of the problem brilliantly addressed in a book that appeared just as this one was going to press and that will forever change the basis of the continuing argument about the nature and function of consumption in the modern world. See Colin Campbell, *The Romantic Ethic and the Spirit of Modern Consumerism* (Oxford, 1992).

universally attractive cultural forms, artifacts, traits, habits, and signifiers appears thus far to have been exercised more rewardingly within
the tradition that cradled the Industrial Revolution. It would seem that
the English-speaking peoples have made the most of the opportunities
created by their own Industrial Revolution and that they have done this
in ways comparable to the manner in which the Spanish-speaking
peoples responded to the challenging opportunities created by their own
Counter-Reformation, except that unlike the Spanish experience, the
results of their enterprise are now moving effortlessly across the frontiers
of the world and are adopted willingly by millions upon millions of ordinary people. This process shows no signs of abating. On the contrary,
the events of the past few years, especially in Eastern Europe, should
justly be interpreted as an invitation to include the prevalent modern
concept and practice of political and economic freedom and social mobility among the principal cultural artifacts of English provenance that
have proved acceptable to people elsewhere.

It is not entirely bereft of antecedents, for it is perfectly possible
to describe even the hallowed French Revolution as a bungled attempt
to transform France into the island polity of the English, as it was then
perceived and experienced by those zealous philosophes who, as Leopold von Ranke observed, even when they were attacking England, "it
was the independence of an English peer, the dignified position of a
member of the House of Commons, which they particularly wished to
achieve."[46] Further, if language is to be accorded importance, what are
we to make of the persistent habit among despots everywhere to adopt
the Westminster nomenclature to disguise their political indecencies?

It is always risky to predict anything, but only the unusually foolhardy
would venture to propose dates for the eventual attenuation of the ascendancy of the English-speaking peoples. Nothing has yet appeared on
the horizon of modernity to indicate that once their power is spent their
cultural preponderance will also vanish. The opposite prognosis would
appear to have better credentials, leading to what must perforce be a
very tentative suggestion that we may be moving, very slowly, toward a
time, well after the demise of the political and military power of the
metropolis, when their myriad cultural artifacts will continue to command the affection, the allegiance, or the rapacity of millions upon millions of human beings. The temptation, therefore, to establish a direct

46. Leopold von Ranke, *The Theory and Practice of History*, ed. Georg G. Iggers and
Konrad von Moltke (New York, 1973): 91–92.

comparison between that distant Hellenistic aftermath and the vigorous process of cultural diffusion that is occurring before our eyes is almost irresistible; almost but not quite, for to acquiesce, the creative prowess of the English-speaking Americans must either be overlooked or its importance diminished unacceptably. This is not possible, but the change of emphasis suggested above should suffice to retain the crucial thrust of the Hellenistic reference, while simultaneously underlining the definitive role of the English-speaking peoples in continuing to shape the world of their Industrial Revolution. Our time probably does not qualify strictly as a Hellenistic aftermath, but it would be difficult to object to its being described as not entirely made in England but most certainly made in English.

The Culture of the Latin American Economy

An unusually large number of special commissions, financial institutions, national and international committees, academic centers, institutes, think tanks, and seminars emerged during the latter half of the twentieth century in the United States and elsewhere in the hemisphere, as well as in Europe, in response to the economic and political tribulations of the countries of Latin America.[1] Their number, their initiatives, and their consequences have all been out of the ordinary, and considered as a group, it has certainly earned a niche in the history of our times as the most vocal and least effective undertaking ever engendered by public concern about the troubled circumstances of any major region of the world.

Some of these novel entities—notably the United Nations Economic Commission for Latin America, founded in 1948, the Interamerican Development Bank, the Central American Common Market, and the Latin American Free Trade Area, all launched in 1960, and the Andean Pact, brought into being with the signing of the Cartagena Agreement of

---

1. In the United States, the proliferation of academic initiatives of this kind was sufficiently important to justify coordinating arrangements that led in 1966 to the creation of the nationwide Latin American Studies Association, which soon became the largest such organization devoted to area studies in the country, probably in the world, with well over twenty major centers and four thousand members. The contrast is stark between this extraordinary abundance of interest and the dearth of centers of any importance, academic or otherwise, in Latin America and the Iberian countries devoted to the study of the English-speaking peoples of the New World.

1969—were created specifically to address the economic difficulties of the region. However, possibly because of the implied urgencies frequently assigned to these problems, and also in part reflecting the fashionable ideological acceptance of the primacy of the "relations of production," virtually all the other centers, institutes, and seminars succumbed, sooner rather than later, to the temptation of trying to find convincing remedies for the economic ills of the region.[2] Most of these prescriptions were carefully sown on fertile bureaucratic soil where they thrived and matured, transforming the already existing forest of rules and regulations into a luxuriant and impenetrable jungle of controls, laws, decrees, quasi-autonomous entities, subsidies, permanent committees, and state corporations. Further, given contemporary academic conventions and expectations, those recommendations that failed to beget controls or institutions were seldom denied the minor consolation of appearing in print, and today there are library shelves groaning everywhere in the New World under the weight of quantities of less or more readable tomes and voluminous reports written with the deliberate purpose of describing, analyzing, and explaining why the American heirs of the Spanish imperial moment proved unequal to the challenge posed by the economic dimension of modernity, what it is that they ought to do, or cease doing, and how, if they are to overcome this problem.

Although seldom devoid of erudition and invariably enriched by good intentions, it is now obvious that the passage of time has not been kind to the results of most of these researches. Some were of small moment even when first penned and published; others were overtaken by grim events that neither experts nor specialized institutions could have anticipated; and excepting a half dozen or so that may possibly survive as scholarly sources for historical inquiries, the rest do not bear rereading today, having been additionally pushed into obsolescence by a stubborn cultural circumstance that proved beyond the capacity of the authors and their seminars and committees to comprehend.[3] It is certainly not

2. This is not a latter-day fashion. In 1932, an author experienced in Latin American affairs stated firmly that while economics "may not be wholly determinative of the national life to the exclusion of less material forces . . . its influence is so great that it easily takes first place in any analysis of the conditions or trends in any one of [the countries of Latin America]." Henry Kittredge Norton, *The Coming of South America: El Resurgimiento de Sud América* (New York, 1932): 22.

3. No such list could possibly be compiled today, but it is difficult to imagine that future historians of the period will proceed with their investigations without first glancing at the UN Economic and Social Council's *Informe Preliminar de la Comisión Especial encargada de estudiar el proyecto de creación de una Comisión Económica para América Latina*, E/AC.21/15, December 10, 1947; Raúl Prebisch, *The Economic Development of*

deficient scholarship or dearth of information that doomed them; far from it. Whether in relation to area, population, or productive capacity, the economy of the countries of Latin America is probably the most exhaustively documented, measured, and accounted for in detailed statistical compilations prepared and kept impeccably up to date with the help of the most advanced electronic equipment, but rarely has the purposeful assiduity of such a large number of experts been graced with so little theoretical illumination and such unrewarding practical results. The contrast between this and the descriptive and analytical frugality that preceded and accompanied the economic surge of the Little Dragons of Southeast Asia is sobering. It is even possible to conjecture that the torrents of data, theoretical speculations, and doctrinal clarifications that smother economic reflection in Latin America are better understood as a distant echo of the legalism and bureaucratic prolixity of Counter-Reformation casuistry than as a portent of modern industrial growth. Not even the most sympathetic perusal of the present state of the economies of Latin America can fail to perceive that those massive and immensely well-intentioned researches and the resulting recommendations, as well as an alarming proportion of the vast amount of legislation and most of the private and public initiatives based on them, have produced little but a disappointing harvest.[4]

Occasionally overoptimistic and institutionally committed, the annual scrutinies conducted by the UN Economic Commission for Latin America have nonetheless seldom failed to confirm these discouraging impressions. One of the latest among such reports, for the year 1990, opened with a sobering paragraph:

> In the midst of great difficulties, Latin America and the Caribbean are still trying to put a definitive end to the crisis that has been overwhelming them

---

Latin America (New York, 1950); Celso Furtado, The Economic Growth of Brazil (Berkeley and Los Angeles, 1963); Victor Urquidi, The Challenge of Development in Latin America (London, 1964); Osvaldo Sunkel, "La inflación chilena: Un enfoque heterodojo," El Trimestre Económico 25, no. 4 (1958) (English translation in International Economic Papers, no. 10 [London, 1960]); A. O. Hirschman, Journeys Towards Progress (New York, 1968).
    4. Which is not to say that some authors were not prepared to express firm views on the subject. In the opening sentence of his study of the economic difficulties of Latin America (based on special studies of Chile and Brazil), Frank stated, "I believe, with Paul Baran, that it is capitalism, both world and national, which produced underdevelopment in the past and which still generates underdevelopment in the present." With the problem thus clearly outlined, Dr. Frank devoted the rest of his popular book to filling in the details. A. G. Frank, Capitalism and Underdevelopment in Latin America (New York, 1967): vii.

for nearly a decade now. They base their hopes on the results of the profound irreversible structural changes taking place in the countries of the region. However, the region's recovery of the path to development still remains an elusive goal: the burden of the debt overhang and the transfer of resources abroad is still excessive; investment processes are taking a long time to renew themselves; the purchasing power of broad segments of the population is depressed; fiscal structures remain fragile and the degrees of freedom for economic policy are limited. Stagnation, inflation and the severe cumulative deterioration in living conditions bear witness to the difficulty with which the processes of structural change are advancing, the time they will require in order to crystallize and the enormous magnitude of the obstacles they face. These problems are exacerbated by an insuffiency of foreign capital, a weakness in the markets for major exports, and trade restrictions.[5]

This gloomy offering deserves to be cited not so much because of the information it conveys but because its spirit and intent, even its style, recur so insistently among the vast number of official and less official economic reports, exhortations, accords, declarations, charters, treatises, and manifestos that have appeared during the past half century that they have by now become part of the folkloric credo of the regional economy. Its key assertions can be applied to almost every country in the region, several times over, at least once every decade since the Second World War. For example, few would quarrel, yesterday or two generations ago, with the assertion that "the region's recovery of the path to development still remains an elusive goal." Nor would there be much heated opposition to the affirmation that an insufficiency of investment capital is causally related to these difficulties or that their ultimate solution, the one on which hopes are riding, is for these

5. United Nations Economic Commission for Latin America and the Caribbean, LC/ G.1646, *Preliminary Overview of the Economy of Latin America and the Caribbean 1990*, December 19,1990, 1. This is worth comparing with the opening paragraphs of the 1989 report. "As in 1988, the poor performance of most of the economies of the region was due mainly to problems deriving from the speeding up of inflation or from the policies applied to control it, rather than to a shortage of foreign exchange for purchasing critical imports. Indeed, exports continued to expand thanks to increases in their volume and the recovery in the prices of a number of primary commodities, thus enabling the region to increase its trade surplus. This has not been reflected in a higher level of activity, however, while even more countries which have fallen into arrears on their debt service, and now includes three of the main debtor countries for the first time together. Thus, after eight years of struggling to achieve adjustment, stabilization, growth and the restructuring of production, beset by external debt servicing problems and with little access to new external financing, most countries of the region continue to display the same complex syndrome of structural imbalances accompanied by fiscal deficits, low levels of investment, stagnation and inflation." UN Economic Commission for Latin America and the Caribbean, LC/ G.1574, September 1989, *Economic Panorama of Latin America, 1989*, Santiago, 5.

countries and regions to sustain such "profound, irreversible structural changes" that, in effect, they will become different societies altogether, made up of people and entities innocent of indebtedness, austere, industrious, living tranquil and prosperous lives under just, incorruptible, and compassionate governments. Even earlier, in 1886, Félix Vicuña believed that the relative backwardness of the regional manufacturing industries had three causes: dearth of capital; the unwillingness of governments to grant protection to infant industries; and the absence of habits of work and austerity further exacerbated by inadequate technical educational facilities.[6] Only minimal modifications are required to make these two arguments, otherwise separated by a century, coalesce into a familiar diagnosis that rests on capital remaining scarce, governments continuing to be unhelpful, and bad habits stubbornly refusing to vanish.[7]

Persistent problems such as these are rendered more interesting by notorious anomalies and discontinuities. For example, during the same postwar half century when many of these countries had more than a fair share of afflictions, the regional economy grew fivefold.[8] Previously healthy economies are now crushed under the weight of inflation, political corruption, stagnation, and debt, but there are some that have achieved exceptionally high rates of growth over several years, while still others have notched spectacular performances in the stock market that appear to negate the otherwise all too visible penury endured by the population. This is certainly true. It must also be noted, however, that not a few of these recent episodes of prosperity have been the consequence of the profitable incorporation of hitherto untapped natural resources, or sudden changes in the price of commodities, or the result of quite unexpected and short-lived floods of speculative investments, or

6. Félix Vicuña, "Situación económica," *Revista Económica* I, no. 1 (November 1886): 9–20.

7. It would be unfair to leave this aspect of the matter without mentioning, even if in passing, the one original contribution in an otherwise undifferentiated chorus of predictable complaints. The Chilean historian Francisco Encina published in 1911 a seminal essay entitled *Nuestra inferioridad económica*, which, though flawed by outmoded concepts, is one of the most courageous and incisive ever written about the economy of a Latin American country. The manifestations of the economic inferiority of Chile are neither ephemeral nor susceptible to being resolved by fiscal or monetary solutions, wrote Encina. On the contrary, "They reveal a chronic condition of the social organism, a permanent prostration, an economic weakness that is ancient and persistent." Francisco A. Encina, *Nuestra inferioridad económica* (Santiago, 1972): 27.

8. Enrique V. Iglesias, "Perspectivas del desarrollo de América Latina," *Estudios Internacionales* 14 (July–September 1981): 312.

some comparable external factor brought about by circumstances distant and unpredictable. This explains in part why they have been as surprising and welcome as they have proved ephemeral, rarely spreading their beneficial effects much beyond the immediate vicinity of the exceptional factors that brought them about and seldom, if ever, surviving their disappearance.

The rapid and vastly overpublicized rise experienced in 1991 and 1992 by some principal Latin American stock exchanges in the wake of the conversion to free-market economics of previously staunchly interventionist regimes would certainly fall under this category. From the vantage point of foreign investors, for example, the Brazilian market rose most encouragingly by 140 percent; Chile's, by 100 percent in the same period; and Mexico's, by 70 percent; but the best performance was that of the Argentine stock exchange, which topped 400 percent, largely encouraged by a determined attempt by the government of President Carlos Saúl Menem to bring order and stability to the economy.[9] However, less than a year later, the market plunged well over 60 percent in less than four months and it was possible for experienced analysts of the local economy to affirm that "the biggest challenge for Argentine companies is streamlining operations to cope with international competition. Business here has been noted for its bloated payrolls, antiquated equipment and management strategies that focused on paying bribes to government officials in exchange for lucrative contracts."[10]

Such outbursts notwithstanding, it is by now disturbingly clear that the general economic health of the countries of Latin America has not been good for a considerable time. The confidence that the Economic Commission for Latin America has shown in the past in the salutary results of a program of centrally determined reforms may or may not

9. The implied parallelism with the contemporary changes in Russia and Eastern Europe may have contributed to this euphoria. However, *The Economist* points out that these markets are relatively small and illiquid, and their narrow base makes these gains less impressive than it appears at first sight. What investors have done, and this is certainly not a break with tradition, is to bet that under free market policies, the economy of the region will prosper. A closer look indicates that while this may well be possible, it remains basically a speculative prospect. Even in the Chilean stock market, in 1992, in a country that has already outperformed the region during many years, about 200 companies had a market capitalization of only $20 billion; a fourth of the stocks represented accounted for three-fourths of the volume; and, on the average, stocks were selling at more than twice their book value. *The Economist*, August 31, 1991, 63.

10. Nathaniel C. Nash, "On the Rebound in Argentina," *New York Times*, December 6, 1992, sect. 3, 15.

have been widely shared, but it is embarrassingly obvious that few, if any, of the other equally ambitious and widely supported economic initiatives of recent decades have survived as credible prospects for the closing years of this century. The attempts to establish regional or local common markets are either dead, or moribund, or owe their resurrection to dire necessity and political expediency rather than to economic practicalities as is the case with the "Southern Cone" initiative or Cuba's latter-day rapprochement with the rest of the continent. Even more disquieting is the likelihood that the initial welcome accorded to the North American Free Trade Area, especially in Mexico, the only Latin American country to have gained admittance, could simply be founded on a tacit acceptance of its relative inability to resolve its economic problems and the encouraging prospect that this may be facilitated by entering into an amiable partnership with Canada and the United States. As for the violent revolutionary onslaught so frequently foreshadowed by the academic admirers of the Sino-Soviet prowess, it has obviously failed to attract the requisite support except among the terrorists and common criminals of Sendero Luminoso, the MIR, the Frente Manuel Rodríguez, and other such groupings, a fact that strengthens the general statement.

The import-substitution panacea remains as illusory as the expectation that a resurrected centralist state encumbered with a refurbished Thomist and "communitarian" Christian Democratic conscience could bring about the desired leap to industrial modernity, while the endeavor to "integrate" the countries of the region to resolve their economic problems has so far proved fruitless.[11] It would be unjust to be dismissive about the current attempts to follow the example of Chile, and bring about the desired transformations by embracing the tenets of economic liberalism, but it should be observed that at least part of the enthusiasm generated by these prescriptions is founded on the expectation that the

11. This is not idle rhetoric. In the preamble for a formal statement published in 1973, the Secretaría Permanente del Tratado General de Integración Económica Centroamericana affirmed truthfully that its long-term strategy was the formation of "a true economic union in Central America, the principal object of which is the creation of the conditions that will ensure the increased well-being of the people of Central America." Instituto para la Integración de América Latina (INTAL), Interamerican Development Bank, *El desarrollo integrado de Centroamérica en la presente década* (Buenos Aires, 1973): vii–viii. It should be unnecessary to draw attention to the melancholy course of events in Central America during the ensuing two decades and to the obvious fact that the desired integration and consequent development appear to be as distant today as they were in 1973.

required changes that earlier could not be brought about by decree or by persuasion will now occur automatically, swiftly, and without cost. This is an unlikely possibility even in the best of cases.

Such difficulties and setbacks answer to many causes of varying significance, some of which have been accorded less attention than they deserve, and although to assign priorities in matters of this kind is next to impossible, it would also be difficult to exaggerate the importance that the misuse of the postrevolutionary concepts of "economic growth" and "development"—and, of course, the related terms "developed" and "underdeveloped"—have had in hindering the comprehension of the economic problem. Economic growth is appropriately described as a postrevolutionary concept precisely because it is the creature and not the progenitor of the English Industrial Revolution and, by implication, also of the French Revolution. Even at its most undemanding level, the expectation that things will progress, or that the material condition of human beings generally will improve, is a late product of modern Western thought, certainly not much earlier than the eighteenth century. Among the factors that help to explain its delayed arrival must be counted the absence of progress itself and of the expectation of progress. As Arndt has indicated, "Even utopia must be conceivable. People did not begin to think of material progress until events proved that it was possible."

The reasons for the virtual absence of economic growth, or progress, over the millennia that preceded the Industrial Revolution are deceptively uncomplicated. Keynes described them, succinctly and memorably: "Lack of progress was due to two reasons—to the remarkable absence of important technical improvements and to the failure of capital to accumulate."[12] The modern concept of development had to wait even longer, until the momentous fruition of the technological and social changes associated with the Industrial Revolution made possible the widespread acceptance of the notion that material progress is a desirable and attainable condition of human society. Before this had occurred, a country or region could certainly be rich, prosperous, powerful, prestigious, possibly even happy, but none of these desirable circumstances included constraints and qualifications about a fair distribution of income, freedom of association, social mobility, welfare arrangements, or

12. H. W. Arndt, *The Rise and Fall of Economic Growth: A Study in Contemporary Thought* (Melbourne, 1978): 5–6. J. M. Keynes, *Essays in Persuasion* (London, 1933): 360.

equality of opportunity.[13] These were added much later, in the aftermath of the Second World War, as distant consequences of the maturation of British industrialism and the pervasive political influence of the French Revolution. The former derived its exemplary authority from a characteristically practical and unadorned description of what in fact occurred in England and what the English did about it; the latter was mostly based on a sui generis French Enlightenment interpretation of life in eighteenth-century England, cast in the form of a stirring revolutionary slogan that legitimized political freedom and social equality as necessary concomitants of economic advancement. Once yoked together, it became politically inexpedient and morally suspect even to try to separate these mutually reinforcing but practically unrelated sets of expectations, especially in regions far removed both from the industrial Midlands and from Paris. It was far easier to respond generously and efficiently to Shaftesbury's philanthropic appeals in Manchester or Leeds or to support Napoleon III's Saint-Simonian interpretation of the revolutionary aftermath in the imperial capital than to do it today in Melipilla, Piura, or Zacatecas.

It is hardly astonishing to discover that in the latter years of our century, Latin Americans have found themselves the inheritors of an appealing, confused, and unrealistic concept that has proved extraordinarily unhelpful in the current endeavor to understand and address the economic problems of the region. In its most popular incarnation, the use of the term "development" carries with it the implication that it refers to something that is both good and desirable and that in the absence of accidental or intentional impediments, ought naturally, normally, inevitably, to occur, that is, to unravel, to grow, until it attains its appropriate stature.[14] Thus to describe tadpoles as "developing" or banana saplings as "underdeveloped" is reasonable because all tadpoles, if left unhindered, are doomed to develop into their true selves, that is, to attain the shape and particular features normally associated with fully grown toads. From this vantage point, it is possible to regard all tadpoles

13. The United Nations declared the 1960s the decade of development, the basic thesis being that "the problem of the underdeveloped countries is not just growth, but development. Development is growth *plus* change; change, in turn, is social and cultural as well as economic, and qualitative as well as quantitative. . . . The key concept must be improved quality of people's lives." *The UN Development Decade: Proposals for Action,* 1962, cited in Arndt, *Rise and Fall,* 96.

14. Nor is this bizarre concept of "development" a function of age; China and India are both very ancient and presumably "underdeveloped," while Australia and Singapore are certainly young and new in many respects, but they are clearly "developed." Mariano Grondona, *Bajo el imperio de las ideas morales* (Buenos Aires, 1987): 166.

as being equally enabled to become toads and all banana saplings similarly and equally endowed with the inalienable right to develop into large green things that bear bananas. The problem arises when we observe that nothing has occurred in history that should induce us to believe that countries will, if left unhindered, "develop" into, say, fully fledged variants of Switzerland, Australia, or Massachusetts or, for that matter, of Bulgaria, Borneo, or Transylvania. Nothing, moreover, has ever happened in history that could be interpreted as evidence that all human groupings, like all tadpoles and all banana trees, are essentially the same and that, consequently, in the fullness of time they will all become as like each other as a mob of toads. Not so.

If, as we have been invited to accept, the only thing we know about the future is our past, then we can assert with some force that there are no historical foundations for the belief that the different nations and countries of our world, if left free to blossom forth, will attain comparable levels of anything at all. On the contrary, the little we can glean from our common recorded experience suggests, certainly to me, that "development," like prosperity, power, influence, glory, well-being, happiness, peace, and tranquillity, is not something apportioned equally among the children of God but is a glittering prize, normally secured with great effort or very good luck, or both, in small doses and in a manner that many would be content to describe as fundamentally mysterious and unpredictable.

This gently skeptical view of the elusive "development" distances me greatly from the one held by my Araucanian ancestors who, at the time of the arrival of the Spaniards, peopled much of the Central Valley and the southern forests of what is now the Republic of Chile. The Araucanians knew that when unimpeded by malefice, all men enjoy perfect health and live forever, but as the incontrovertible evidence of their senses indicated that malefice was indeed hindering things, they judiciously invested time and energy, under the guidance of expert witch doctors, in ritual exercises designed specifically to discover the sources of the evil. These procedures were astonishingly effective and seldom failed to identify the culprits, almost invariably hostile strangers from neighboring tribes, against which the Araucanians were then obliged to launch fully justified attacks so as to apprehend and punish the malefactors to ensure the safety of innocent Araucanians who could thus return forthwith to the full enjoyment of their unblemished health and immortality.

Reflection on the concept of "development" in general, or about the particular Latin American variant, leads effortlessly in the direction of the Araucanian working hypothesis, and the zest is consistent with this linkage, with which so many specialists who should have known better have devoted their researches to the identification and punishment of those responsible for obstructing the natural and felicitous unraveling of the prosperity and equality of the inhabitants of the former Spanish Indies. The culprits, as was the case with the Araucanians, have almost without exception turned out to be strangers, often from the more prosperous countries of the world, whose well-being, when scientifically scrutinized, has been found to be directly the consequence of the reduced circumstance of the countries of the former Spanish Indies. In other words, "Latin America was conquered and its people colonized by the European metropolis so as to expropriate the economic surplus of the satellite's labour and to appropriate it for the capital accumulation of the metropolis—initiating thereby the present underdevelopment of the satellite and the economic development of the metropolis."[15]

The "dependent" mode of the countries of Latin America is not, therefore, the consequence of domestic shortcomings but has been imposed from abroad, with the complicity of the national bourgeoisie, by foreigners able to control investment capital and advanced technology who are committed to a regime of international competition in which Latin America will always be disadvantaged and doomed to backwardness and misery. This being so, "everything indicates that what awaits [these countries] in the future is a long process of profound political and military confrontations and profound social radicalization leading to a dilemma between strong-armed governments tending towards fascism, and popular revolutionary governments tending towards socialism. All intermediate solutions are vacuous and utopian."[16] Having exposed the complicity of the bourgeoisie and their unwillingness to resolve these problems, and given the stark clarity of the ensuing confrontation, some theorists of *dependencia* conclude that it is intolerable to decline to take sides in such a struggle and that "to applaud and in the name of the

15. Frank, *Capitalism and Underdevelopment*, 20–21. Or as another author explains, "While progress might have materially improved the lot of some elites, whetted the appetites of the emerging middle classes, and won the approval of the European mentors, it plunged Latin America into deeper dependency. . . . It impoverished the majority of the Latin Americans, who were not better off at the end of the [nineteenth] century than they had been at the beginning. In fact, the argument can be put forth that they were worse off." Burns, *Poverty of Progress*, 10–11.

16. Theotonio Dos Santos, *Dependencia y cambio social* (Santiago, 1970): 67–68.

people even to support the bourgeoisie in its already played-out role on the stage of history is treacherous or treachery."[17]

Reread two decades later, the pronouncements of the dependencia theorists do not impress except as a melancholy modern variant of the Araucanian hypothesis, with which they share an infinite capacity to expose miscreants with an incapacity at least as vast to do away with ill health or ensure immortality. Had there been early doubts about these traits and their consequential actions, by this time—after the tired populism of Juan Perón's second coming and the revolutionary simplicities that spearheaded the Peruvian adventures of Velasco Alvarado and Alan García; following the well-engineered disorder that visited Chile under Salvador Allende's Unidad Popular and the pathetic reliance on Soviet financial largesse to which both Cubans and Nicaraguans owed the survival of their melancholy regimes; after the noisy, tragic, and altogether dismal experience in government of every Latin American strongman attuned to the tenets of the dependencia theorists—such doubts surely should have dissipated.

The acceptance of this concept of "development" has also nourished the somewhat contradictory assumption, especially popular among more worldly political and academic circles, that the economic predicament of the countries of Latin America is essentially a consequence of structural inflexibilities that, by hindering the mobility of the factors of production, effectively impede the dynamic processes whereby the economy can respond to changes in demand. As the mobility of the factors of production is a condition sine qua non of successful modern industrialism, the prompt elimination of these structural obstacles should necessarily become a principal object of policy, which being obviously beyond the reach of any entity other than the central government, also justifies, or even makes it mandatory, that the state should assume responsibility not only over investment decisions but over the whole economy so that the required changes are implemented which will ensure fair, orderly, and uninterrupted prosperity.

Other difficulties notwithstanding,[18] this approach must by necessity be founded on the view that industrial modernity and economic development are discrete cultural artifacts of irrelevant parentage that can be transferred with ease from one locality to another once local obstacles

---

17. Frank, *Capitalism and Underdevelopment*, xiii.
18. Such as are tellingly described by Arndt in an article, "The Origins of Structuralism," *World Development* 13, no. 2 (February 1985).

to their transplantation have been safely removed, such as the rigidities, cultural or otherwise, capable of hindering the desirable mobility of the factors that must sustain the processes of production. Those who hold this view may have been unnecessarily quick to dismiss the likelihood that the Industrial Revolution, in common with lesser artifacts of English provenance, is rooted in the cultural traditions of its progenitors and that many elements that we recognize as decisive in its subsequent emergence, such as the sui generis individualism of the English, the rule of the Common Law within a reasonably unified political entity, and the generalized antibureaucratic disposition to volunteer, were present in England long before the earliest intimation of the coming of industry.[19] This need not, indeed should not, be considered to be an assertion of absolute cultural specificity, but it seems to me that to ignore this aspect of the matter distorts the evidence most unhelpfully and, among other important errors, lends comfort to those who believe that modern industrialism, like bubble gum, champagne, hula hoops, antibiotics, or supermarket bar code readers, can be successfully adopted by people anywhere who are given access to the correct formula, the book of rules, the necessary instructions, or the appropriate policies. The magnitude of the problem has been well expressed by Mario Vargas Llosa in a recent essay in which he states that the reforms that are required in Latin America in the economy, the system of education, and the administration of justice are virtually impossible to effect and if possible, are doomed to be ephemeral,

> unless they are preceded or accompanied by a reform of our customs and ideas, of the whole complex system of habits, knowledge, images and forms that we understand by "culture." The culture within which we live and act today in Latin America is neither liberal nor is it altogether democratic. We have democratic governments, but our institutions, our reflexes and our *mentalidades* are very far from being democratic. They remain populist and oligarchic, or absolutist, collectivist or dogmatic, flawed by social and racial

19. According to Macfarlane, "It is no longer possible to 'explain' the origins of English individualism in terms of either Protestantism, population change, the development of a market economy at the end of the middle ages, or . . . other factors." Further on he notes that he has taken back the search for the origins (of English individualism) for nearly eight hundred years from the present, to the start of the thirteenth century, without finding the roots. Unable to proceed further because of the lack of sources, he expresses approval of Montesquieu's suggestion that those roots are possibly to be found in "borrowings" from Germanic tribes so early that they are described by Tacitus in his *On the Manners of the Germans*. Alan Macfarlane, *The Origins of English Individualism* (London, 1978): 170, 196, 206.

prejudices, immensely intolerant with respect to political adversaries, and devoted to the worst monopoly of all, that of the truth.[20]

The exaggerated trust in universally valid formulas and prescriptions for good economic health can be readily recognized as a not too distant echo of that characteristic Enlightenment faith in reason, knowledge, and technique that is as much in evidence in Schikaneder's *Magic Flute* as in the reformism of Pombal and Campomanes or the authoritarian benevolence of O'Higgins, Bolívar, and San Martín. Like most well-intentioned faiths, it was not long before this elemental virtue invited dogmatic embellishment, and it was thus adorned that it crossed the Atlantic to be embraced eagerly by the founding fathers of the Ibero-American republics, who surrendered enthusiastically to the uncompromising belief that good constitutions were all that was required to bridge the distance between a despised, obscurantist colonial past and a republican future brilliantly illuminated by reason.

The indifferent success of the large number of good and better constitutions frequently and noisily promulgated by every one of the fledgling republics has not deterred latter-day bureaucrats and politicians, it is now all too clear, from attributing similar virtues to good economic policies. If a good constitution can transform cunning Brazilians into incorruptible Swiss Calvinists, why should it not be possible for a good economic policy to conjure lasting prosperity from the mysterious depths of the Peruvian or the Nicaraguan abyss? Of course, this species of faith in the application of good policies cannot alone be held responsible for the continuing economic malaise of the southern half of the New World and the perplexing failure to comprehend its causes, but its ubiquity and persistence are consistent precisely with a mode of thought that has played a protagonistic role, both practical and theoretical, in the somber saga of sterility, silliness, and irresponsibility that has for so many decades shaped a considerable proportion of the economic arrangements of Latin America. It must be seriously taken into account if the attempt is to succeed to use cautious comparison to cast light on the causes of the differing performance of the two great transplanted cultures of the New World during the past half millennium.

Comparison and emulation must be prudently employed if they are

20. Mario Vargas Llosa, "América Latina y la Opción Liberal," in Barry Levine, ed., *El desafío neoliberal: El fin del tercermundismo en América Latina* (Bogotá, 1992): 17–36.

to survive undamaged in the proximity of an overpowering dogmatic trust in the efficacy of technical solutions, whether these are good political constitutions or correct economic policies. There is no dearth of cautionary episodes about the discouraging consequences of policies based on imprudent comparisons that at the time were considered to be technically, even scientifically, correct. Many such policies were adopted precisely, often forcefully, because they appeared to be supported by empirical evidence of earlier successes, and their subsequent application was directly inspired by a sincere wish to emulate those good results. Few examples are as apposite, and sobering, as that offered by the fate of the impeccably prepared, efficiently carried out, and immensely well-intentioned Alliance for Progress launched by President John F. Kennedy in March 1961.

Although the Alliance was ultimately the result of political decisions adopted by government officials, it was shaped decisively by the work on development economics carried out by a group of Boston academics (including Max Millikan, P. N. Rosenstein-Rodan, John Kenneth Galbraith, Lincoln Gordon, David Bell, and, most important, W. W. Rostow), later dubbed the "Charles River economists," who argued that the correct role of foreign aid was not simply to extend technological and military help but to assist the organized promotion of national development in the recipient countries.[21] The problem implicit in this affirmation—about how best to proceed to achieve the worthy objective—was furnished with a historical and theoretical rationale by Rostow's writings on the stages of economic growth, from which it was generally deduced that countries that wished to achieve the elusive "takeoff into sustained growth" were unlikely to succeed unless they transformed themselves from within in a manner and with consequences comparable to those experienced by the advanced industrial countries that had gone before them, albeit in less time and possibly in a more amiable fashion.[22]

Rostow explained that his theory was a "way of generalizing the

21. The earliest statement of this approach was offered by Millikan and Rostow in 1957, in a book entitled *A Proposal—Key to a More Effective Foreign Policy.* "The goal, the Charles River economists said, was to enable underdeveloped nations, in Rostow's phrase, to 'take off' into self-sustaining growth. . . . When it was reached, the need for special external assistance would end." Arthur M. Schlesinger, Jr., *A Thousand Days: John F. Kennedy in the White House* (London, 1967): 467–468.

22. W. W. Rostow, "The Stages of Economic Growth," *The Economic History Review,* 2d ser., Vol. XII, no. 1 (1959): 1–16. See also, W. W. Rostow, *The Process of Economic Growth* (Oxford, 1953); and W. W. Rostow, ed., *The Economics of Take-Off into Sustained Growth,* Proceedings of a Conference held by the International Economic Association, London, 1963.

sweep of modern economic history," arranging it in accordance with a sequence of stages of growth, starting with the one corresponding to traditional nonindustrial society, moving on to the preconditions for takeoff, followed by the takeoff, a drive toward maturity, and ending with the stage of high mass consumption. This sequence was based on detailed researches on the experience of the first industrial nation and led to the conclusion that for sustained growth to occur, radical transformations were required in three nonindustrial sectors: first, an important buildup of social overhead capital; second, a technological revolution in agriculture; and third, an expansion in imports financed by more efficient production and marketing of natural resources.[23] When translated into policy, these changes necessitated far-reaching transformations of the preindustrial fiscal system, agriculture, and the administration of the state. There was certainly no shortage then, or now, of sound arguments why this should be judged a practical course of action.[24] The opening paragraph of a recent important book on English economic history maintains that "since England was the first country to industrialize, it is considered to be a good guide to those Third World countries also wishing to do so. . . . This motive is widely acknowledged; if we could understand why the 'industrial revolution' occurred first in England and what *caused* it we might be able to encourage economic growth elsewhere."[25] This cannot be dismissed as an excessive claim. Nor does it strain the bounds of reason to imagine that properly con-

23. Rostow notes that "Britain was the first of the European nations to move from the stage of preconditions into take-off" and adds that "the existence of the British take-off from, say, 1783, set in motion a series of positive and negative demonstration effects which progressively unhinged other traditional societies or accelerated the creation of the preconditions for take-off, where the precondition process was already under way." He explains, nonetheless, that he will not examine the preconditions process in the nations that "in Louis Hartz's phrase were 'born free' of traditional societies, mainly deriving from a British society already well advanced in the preconditions process or in regular growth. I refer to the United States, Canada, New Zealand, Australia, etc." Rostow, "Economic Growth," 4–5.
24. Rostow's interpretation has important antecedents in Latin America, including many of the more articulate and influential responses to the early evidence, in the nineteenth century, of the growth and prosperity associated with the Industrial Revolution, which at that time translated readily into a policy of meticulous imitation of the vanguard, in the seemingly plausible expectation that if Colombians and Argentinians conducted themselves like Englishmen or Frenchmen, they would in good time be visited by the prosperity enjoyed by those enviable Europeans. These expectations sustained the "liberal pause" that from approximately the middle of the last century interrupted the centralist economic continuities characteristic of the Spanish Indies and helped to bring about the prolonged prosperity purchased with the sale of agricultural and mineral exports in the growing markets of the northern hemisphere, which did not end until the Great Depression of 1929. See C. Véliz, *Centralist Tradition*, 163–188.
25. Alan Macfarlane, *Origins*, 7.

ducted and addressed to modest ends, such an approach could be beneficial, if not for bringing about economic growth effortlessly and
swiftly, at least for gaining a better understanding of the complexities of
the process.

The Alliance for Progress was ultimately founded on a most scholarly
interpretation of the causes of the English Industrial Revolution. It was
launched with unparalleled enthusiasm and administered at least as efficiently as any comparable enterprise in the New World, but thirty years
and a dozen or so agrarian, fiscal, and administrative reforms and many
thousands of casualties later, not much is left of the young president's
stirring call, when he inaugurated the new policy, to "transform the
American continent into a vast crucible of revolutionary ideas and efforts—a tribute to the power of the creative energies of free men and
women—an example to all the world that liberty and progress walk
hand in hand."[26] It would be an error, nevertheless, to think that there
is little about that moment other than what has been conjured by the
rhetoric of some sympathetic historians. Arthur Schlesinger, Jr., saw
"the future everywhere . . . bright with hope," and so it was, especially
when viewed from Washington or Havana, where the Communist revolution, scarcely a few months old, was also enjoying its fleeting moment
of glory. The circumstances in both cases appeared to be exceptionally
encouraging; it was certainly not a time for caution and reflection.

Not everyone, however, was swept away by the wave of enthusiasm.
A group of Latin American economists, including Felipe Herrera, Raúl
Prebisch, Antonio Mayobre, Jorge Sol, and José A. Mora, considered
that the almost diffident interventionist proposals of the Alliance were
flawed by an excessive reliance on market forces. And only five days
before the formal announcement, on March 8, 1961, they presented a
document to President Kennedy in which they stated their disagreement
with the suggestion that the free play of economic forces could be assigned a role in bringing about the required structural changes, asserting
instead that "vigorous state action" was required and that it would not
be easy to overcome the resistance of private groups. In their conclusion,
cautious and rather cryptic, they stated that "Latin America cannot go
through the same stages which capitalist development passed in the
course of its historic evolution. We are likewise disturbed at the thought
of imitating methods which pursue their economic objectives at the cost

26. Schlesinger, *Thousand Days*, 176.

of fundamental human freedoms. Latin America still has time to avoid this, but not much time."[27]

This attempt to retain the central state as the decisive arbiter of economic life was ignored in favor of the more moderate and presumably technically correct prescriptions sponsored by the Alliance for Progress, which, as we now know, proved disappointing everywhere. As for the pseudoscientific precepts espoused contemporaneously by the Cuban leader at the instigation of his Marxist-Leninist friends in the Soviet Union, they were zealously and expensively implemented and also failed, but noisily, disastrously, and at leisure, demonstrating not only that time was not in short supply, as the dissenting Latin American economists had indicated, but also that the heirs of the imperial Indies were then, and continue to be today, quite capable of augmenting substantially the repertory of economic calamities with or without assistance from well-intentioned friends abroad.[28]

It is against this background of error, inconsistency, and disillusionment, perhaps still understood imperfectly, that the dogged endurance of the Latin American economic predicament clamors for an explanation other than oversimple and unsustainable accusations of obscurantism, incompetence, or political chicanery. An explanation, moreover, that need not be put forward in the guise of coy preamble to yet another technically impeccable formula for securing economic prosperity but simply as an attempt—and it cannot be more than that—to understand why it is that during the first half-millennium of the New World, the Gothic foxes and the Baroque hedgehogs went about their affairs in the manner they did and with such strikingly differing results. Such an explanation should address the economy and its problems not as one would discrete bits of plumbing, easy to replace or substitute, or as immutable determinants of everything else, but as important elements of the architecture of society, modified constantly by the changing aspirations, the fears and beliefs, of its members, in a manner comparable to that described by Ruskin when he wrote about the ancient buildings of

27. Ibid., 175.
28. There is no dearth of explanations for these failures, but possibly not the least important is that economic policies, unlike analgesics or penicillin, do not necessarily have universal application and predictable effects. The same fiscal reform that will spur the inhabitants of Flanders, Yorkshire, or Massachusetts into feverish activity may leave *porteños* and *serranos* unmoved; the same agrarian transformation that will make the Israeli desert blossom or squeeze huge harvests from Taiwanese terraces may cause distress and confusion among those who till the land in Arequipa, Temuco, or Popayán.

Venice, that there was not one "which has not sustained essential change in one or more of its most important features; . . . in many instances, the restorations or additions have gradually replaced the entire structure of the ancient fabric, of which nothing but the name remains, together with a kind of identity, exhibited in the anomalous association of the modernised portions: the Will of the old building asserted through them all, stubbornly."[29] As stubbornly, it is fair to indicate, as the Industrial Revolution has maintained its own kind of identity through the many successive and profound transformations experienced during the last two centuries. Being well and deeply rooted in the history of those who brought it into the world, like language, cuisine, or religion, or like the venerable old palaces brought to life in Ruskin's prose, its style persists and its character stubbornly asserts its will.

The key to the understanding of the unquestionable centrality of the economy in our modern industrial world is not to be found in the writings of Marx or his disciples but in the creative vitality of each successive stage in the evolution of the economic culture of the English-speaking peoples. Indeed, the fact merits reiteration that the islanders have never surpassed the overwhelming cultural prowess of their Industrial Revolution, and if doubts about this remain, nothing is required to dissipate them other than to recall Wren's glorious epitaph, *Lector, si monumentum requiris, Circumspice*, noting that while originally the field to be surveyed was the heart of a city, now it is the whole world.

The dominance of the economic dimension of our time of modernity is as incontrovertible, as manifest, as generally accepted, as that of religion and its categories during the centuries of the Spanish ascendancy. In the aftermath of Wittenberg and Trent, we classified, judged, castigated, acquiesced, damned, or absolved in accordance with the tenets of the faith, in any one of its conflictive manifestations. Outside religion, a civilized existence was then as unthinkable and as impractical as life outside the national economy would be today, life, that is, deprived of a passport and of documents enabling the holder legally to work and earn a living. Religion filled the cultural horizon of the Spanish centuries as convincingly as the economy dominates the centuries of the English Industrial Revolution. God can be pronounced dead in this, our time of

29. And he concludes with a most convincing example: "The church of St. Mark itself, harmonious as its structure may at first sight appear, is an epitome of the changes of Venetian architecture from the tenth to the nineteenth century." Cited by Wolfgang Kemp, *The Desire of My Eyes: The Life and Work of John Ruskin*, trans. Jan van Heurck (London, 1991): 169–170. The original quotation is from the first preface to *The Stones of Venice*.

triumphant industrialism but certainly not the economy. Marx was only one among a throng of artists, writers, and scholars, some of whom are justly revered as the founding fathers of virtually every one of the social sciences, who perceived the crucial significance of industrialism and its concomitant technological advances in shaping modern society, a perception rendered literally impossible in the absence of a thriving Industrial Revolution. From Ruskin's earliest childhood poem, an ode to the steam engine, to Turner's splendid paintings of steamboats in stormy seas, from the relatively trivial to the sublime, such responses were only possible against the background of a robust industrializing process. Modernity is nothing if not an immensely diverse and uneven fusion of such responses, and it would be exceptionally foolish even to attempt to minimize the crucial contributions of authors and artists such as, say, Durkheim, Nietzsche, Freud, Dilthey, Ortega y Gasset, Weber, and certainly Byron, Blake, Pugin, Whitman, Wagner, Disraeli, Zola, Joyce, Yeats, Spengler, Picasso, Eliot, and many others who helped to fashion it and coaxed us into diverse modes of engaging its complexities; as unacceptable as to ignore that these are crucial, occasionally definitive, responses to an awesome process of industrialization without which there would have been no dissolution of traditional community, no tortured transition from *Gemeinschaft* to *Gesellschaft*, no isolation in the midst of the metropolis, no anomie, no alienation, no repression, angst, or ennui. A hypothesis contrary to a fact? Certainly, but one that sheds additional light on the indisputable verity that without an Industrial Revolution, there could not have been responses, intelligent and otherwise, to its consequences; in the absence of smoke-belching satanic mills, it is unlikely to find poets calling for new Jerusalems surrounded by greenery.

Not immune to the raptures characteristic of the romantic century, Marx did succumb to the temptation of upgrading his (not so original) insight into a universal principle and projecting it backward and forward until it encompassed the whole of history. Others demurred and addressed the immediate problem more cautiously, without thinking it necessary to insist that the relations of production had always been and would continue forever to be the foundation of all things human. Marx, now we know, was wrong and the others, almost without exception, right. The economy is indeed the prevalent circumstance of our own time but not necessarily of all time. There is an awful lot of history during which those hallowed relations of production were distant indeed from being the alpha and omega of human action. This was undoubtedly the case during the millennia that preceded the coming of modern industry, and there is no good reason to believe that our present situation will remain forever unchanged in this respect. During the sixteenth and seventeenth centuries, before the inception of industrialism and regardless of assurances by Marx, Engels, and their followers, it was not the economy, the factory, or the stock exchange that stood at the crossroads of history but the church militant; Paris was purchased with a mass, not with a favorable merger or a dubious equity float.

In the five modern centuries since the fall of Constantinople, the Western cultural tradition has engendered a large variety of imperial ventures, some more significant than others, but only three that have either claimed or attained plausibility as universal entities: the English, the Castilian, and in our time, the Russian.[30] Now that the pathetic failure and the barrenness of the brief Marxist-Leninist interlude has been well and truly confirmed, the Castilian and the English imperial experiences tower even more impressively over the modern epoch; the former consummated her imperial progress with the Counter-Reformation; the latter reshaped the world with its Industrial Revolution; the former established religion so firmly as the ultimate dimension of human affairs that it remained thus for almost two centuries, until the latter (in a fit of absentmindedness?) ushered in the economy and placed it at the center of things.

There is an abundance of well-known reasons to explain why the Spanish world, the Indies in particular, did not find it astonishingly easy to come to terms with this change. Certainly not the least important is that everything that sustained the imperial enterprise and the crowning achievement of the Counter-Reformation, every conceivable feature that favored their eventual outcome, every personal trait and every social circumstance, every prejudice and every social virtue that nurtured the style of life that flourished in that sheltered world, was inimical to the establishment and growth of a modern economy. It has even been argued that the prosperity of the Indies proved to be a hindrance, because their unprecedented capacity to ship large amounts of gold and silver to Spain, as well as to satisfy their own demand for foodstuffs and for most essential manufactures, was so soundly established that it may have

30. The Napoleonic enterprises—both of them—cannot be ignored, but it is worth noting that when Paris dazzled the world with her brilliance and aplomb and metrication and champagne were marching forth, the claim to universality was already dead and buried and no one would have pretended otherwise, especially in the aftermath of Sedan. As for the nationalist-socialist German venture, it was as implausible as it was tragic and short-lived.

played a role not in delaying but in hastening the economic decline of the imperial metropolis.[31]

Salvador de Madariaga observed that "the very delights [of life in the Indies] and its continued peace worked against that progress of the sciences and the crafts without which the Empire was bound to fall."[32]

The prosperity and the manner of life that blossomed in the Indies, he explained,

> owed its shape, colour and aroma to the fact that Spain had kept her Empire, if not altogether closed and isolated, at least screened from the world. It was like a water-garden which developed in a slow-flowing canal shunted off from the main stream of history. This main stream was leading men away from the Christian fold . . . towards the era of the Machine which is now swallowing us. The Spanish world was, and to a great extent, still is, on the margin of that evolution of western man. Its aversion to technique had a positive as well as a negative aspect. It was . . . an instinctive spring whereby the individual soul defends its integrity and its autonomy against that huge mechanized master—the modern community. Hence the strange attitude which even now, now perhaps more than ever, the Spanish world maintains towards events: as the spectator of a drama in which it plays no part. This is today, as it was for the Indies, a grievous loss. The Spanish world did not accompany the rest of men in their glorious and terrible experiences through the hell of the machine age.[33]

Instead, Madariaga argued, echoing Rodó's *Ariel,* "unmoved by this evolution which enslaves man to his future, the Indies blossomed in a

31. In *Restauración de España,* published at the close of the sixteenth century, Sancho de Moncada attributes the economic decline of Spain directly to the lure of the Indies that attracted the commerce of the kingdom away from its traditional European destinations. Beneyto, *Historia social,* 255. Philip IV concurred in 1638, when he responded to protests against increased taxation in the Indies, affirming that "most of our present need comes . . . from the discovery of the Indies, because their possession has provoked such powerful enmities and attracted so many people that Spain is now exhausted and depopulated." Domínguez Ortiz, *El antiguo régimen,* 418; see also David E. Vassberg, *Land and Society in Golden Age Castile* (Cambridge, 1967): 185. It is now a commonplace that the gold and silver of the Indies enabled Spain to stop working and thus to ease the path to her eventual decline. The American treasure allowed her to indulge and purchase anywhere she pleased the manufactured products she required, dispensing with the irksome necessity of producing them herself.

32. Salvador de Madariaga, *The Rise of the Spanish American Empire* (London, 1947): 332.

33. Thomas Gage visited the Indies in the first half of the seventeenth century and reported that in New Spain, "the chief delight of the Inhabitants consisteth in their houses, and in the pleasure of the Country adjoyning, and in the abundance of all things for the life of man. . . . They are contented with fine gardens, with variety of singing birds and parrots, with plenty of fish and flesh, which is cheap, and with gay houses, and so lead a delicious, lazy and idle life, not aspiring much to trade and traffique." Madariaga, *Rise of the Spanish American Empire,* 331–333.

luminous present like the lilies of the field which toil not. And their life seemed beautiful and desirable to the best of men."[34] So beautiful and so desirable, one may add, that those best of men were, understandably perhaps, immensely uninterested in changing it; given the choice, they vastly preferred to leave things as they were.

There is much to distinguish the realm of the hedgehog from that of the fox but nothing as striking as the chasm that separates the titanic endeavor of the Spanish Counter-Reformation to arrest change from the unleashing by the English Industrial Revolution of the greatest process of transformation in human history. The former sought to bring alteration forever to a halt; the latter engendered, perhaps inadvertently, a society that was essentially the result of endless alteration—"the only society ever to live by and rely on sustained and perpetual growth; . . . the first society to invent the concept and idea of progress, of continuous improvement."[35] The demands made by the resulting transformations sharpened the polarity between the two monumental cultural revolutions, emphasizing the incompatibility between all manner of stable, predictable, traditional arrangements, however advantageous or morally justified, and the requirements of a rapidly changing industrial society dependent on continuous innovation, which can only mean "doing new things, the boundaries of which cannot be the same as those of the activities they replace."[36] Industrialists and romantics found themselves in agreement, worshiping the same gods of incessant mobility and change.[37] Byron's *Childe Harold* sought change at any price, even at the risk of death; but at the marketplace and in the manufactories, the only certainty was that things would change and that technological innovation would not cease and would continue therefore to push and pull the rest of society into a world of its own making. Industrial capitalism

---

34. Madariaga, *Rise of the Spanish Empire*, 333.
35. Ernest Gellner, *Nations and Nationalism* (Oxford, 1983): 22.
36. Ibid., 24.
37. Here again the important work of Colin Campbell must be mentioned, even if in passing. Challenging the view that the sole function of advertising is to advance the pecuniary interests of the producers at the expense of the gullibility of the public, he argues that the reverse relationship must be taken seriously, "with the 'romantic' ingredient in culture regarded as having had a crucial part to play in the development of modern consumerism itself; indeed, since consumption may determine demand and demand supply, it could be argued that Romanticism itself played a critical role in facilitating the Industrial Revolution and therefore the character of the modern economy." Campbell, *Romantic Ethic*, 2. See also Neil McKendrick, John Brewer, and J. H. Plumb, *The Birth of Consumer Society: The Commercialization of Eighteenth-Century England* (London, 1982); Neil McKendrick, "Home Demand and Economic Growth: A New View of the Role of Women and Children in the Industrial Revolution," in Neil McKendrick, ed., *Historical Perspectives: Studies in English Thought and Society in Honour of J. H. Plumb* (London, 1974).

became the economic face of romanticism; it was a romantic disposition that enabled engineers, bankers, scientists, speculators, and technologists to become risk-bearing entrepreneurs by investing present time, effort, and capital in ventures that they hoped would come to fruition in a future that they could imagine transformed convincingly and efficiently by their own actions. This is vastly different from the demands for cash over the counter characteristic of pirates, gangsters, brigands, and mafiosi invariably ready to endanger their lives for immediate rewards but unlikely to endorse projects that necessitate sustained efforts over extended periods for the sake of results that are, almost without exception, risky constructions of intelligent imaginations.

Occasionally, when endeavoring to understand a historical moment, it is as useful to note the absence of principal features as to confirm the presence of others. This would appear to be the case with the romantic blind spot in the historical experience of the Spanish-speaking world. Popular perceptions and prejudices notwithstanding, what generally passes for romanticism in the southern latitudes is little more than sentimentalism in one or other of its various manifestations, be these amorous, patriotic, or self-pitying. This can fairly be described as a species of truncated, incomplete romanticism, usually found in the company of much rebellious fury, excessive ardor, and even more self-indulgence, but none of the pensive, somber moods, the brooding, nostalgic evocation of ancient roots, the intense sense of the past, and the feeling for the sublime in nature that are definitive characteristics of the romantic moment. These absences were particularly important during the formative decades of the republics spawned in the distant Indies by the Napoleonic onslaught. The newly constituted entities were unlikely to find inspiration or solace in a past dominated by the hated Spanish oppressor but even less inclined to bring about a profound cultural transformation of society that would result in entirely different patterns of behavior. Not untypically, the response to these constraints was pragmatic; they rejected their own roots in favor of a "black legend" of Spanish barbarism that survives to this day, and by also retaining their vast reserves of indifference to the natural world, they ensured the incompleteness of a romantic experience that would never quite overcome the enervation of derivative sentimentality and bathos.

That the cultural tradition of the Spanish-speaking peoples should have proved unresponsive both to romanticism and to industrial capitalism is vastly more than an interesting coincidence and goes some way toward explaining why it is that compared with the transplanted world of the Gothic foxes, the domed ambit of the Iberians nurtured a society encumbered with a pervasive aversion to risk.[38] This does not mean that in Latin America, or in Spain, there has ever been a dearth of people prepared to gamble everything they own on the turn of a card, or to imperil their lives for serious or frivolous causes, or generally to behave in ways that do not accord with what is normally understood as an abhorrence of risk. These occasionally heroic or foolish activities, however, are sustained by a network of attachments and allegiances to family, social class, region, and traditional community that is as morally resilient and socially predictable as fighting bulls, seducing married women, bombing police stations, and other such antics are unsafe. The aversion to risk characteristic of the Baroque hedgehogs refers to acts considerably more uncertain and perilous than these, acts that may endanger not the life of one Don Juan, or the fortune of another, but the customary assumptions, the predictable enmities, reliable loyalties, symmetries, and proportions of stable social arrangements. All this could be roughly interpreted as reflecting an overriding affection for persons rather than a respect for things; a reluctance to sever the cords of the safety net; an inclination to rely on the monarch anointed and enthroned in the center of things; a distrust of novelty and, generally, a sturdy disinclination to step outside the dependable protection of the dome, even in this, our own century of modernity.

From this vantage point, the Spanish-speaking peoples appear to be sheltered (imprisoned?) by a magnificent past, unable to come to terms with a disappointing present, and yet incapable of moving on toward an uncertain future because of their fear of forfeiting much of what justifies and nourishes their unusual pride. This has not passed unobserved by thoughtful authors who believe such a disposition to be the enduring consequence of many generations of strife, a kind of fatigue of a whole people, *un gran cansancio*, a grand national resignation; a withdrawal to a form of *sensatez* (which translates imperfectly as sensibleness, or perhaps prudence) that shuns shallow innovations and distrusts risky undertakings, so that when the vanguard of the modern world embarked on the magnificent adventure of revolutionary industrialism,

38. Among the many unwanted legacies of decades of Communist dominance in Eastern Europe, the aversion to take risks may well prove to be one of the most insidious and damaging and could become a principal obstacle in the process of economic reconstruction, even in regions such as Bohemia, with an ancient and distinguished tradition of entrepreneurial activity. Roger Scruton, "Reflections of the Revolutions in Eastern Europe," *The Boston Conversazioni* (Boston, 1991): 14–17.

Spain and her Indies abstained proudly, with a disdain not untouched by nobility.[39]

Industrial modernity in one shape or another has now been at work in the former Indies of Castile for several generations, but the dissolution of the established community has proceeded sluggishly, and traditional modes have proved unexpectedly resilient. Far from attenuating the power of the hallowed central state, the battering ram of industrialism has, initially at least, tended to bolster the bureaucratic apparatus.[40] Even the process of secularization took an unexpected direction, when the overwhelming and sanguinary anticlerical victories of the late nineteenth and early twentieth century bequeathed Catholic majorities at least as great as those that existed before the onslaught.[41] Evidently, the constraints that hindered industrial expansion explain in part the limited effects of the coming of industry to the region, but at least as important has been the disposition of the local protagonists of industrialism, who

39. After filling the pages of history with his mad adventures, Don Quixote, on his deathbed, returns to sensatez. According to López Ibor, Spain paralleled the transit of Don Quixote, and after the Invencible armada and the undoing of the emperor's European project, she became immensely uninterested in tinkering with technical and scientific trinkets. "The Spaniard remained loyal to his old ways because of inertia." Juan José López Ibor, El español y su complejo de inferioridad (Madrid, 1958): 62–64n. A recent study of the origins of Spain's economic backwardness concludes that if there are many Spains, it is that of Philip II and the Inquisition that predominates. "This is the Spain that dominates the centuries, and it is fundamentally anti-modern." Joseph Perez, "España y la modernidad," in Bartolomé Bennassar y otros, Orígenes del atraso económico español (Barcelona, 1985): 201.

40. The strategic position of the central state, as main controller of the flow of resources generated by the export sector, enabled it to play a decisive role in directing these funds into industrial promotion. Within one generation, in the aftermath of the Great Depression, national governments consolidated their key position with respect to three of the principal aspects of modern economic policy; they became the main financial entity able to supply capital to private industrial ventures; they assumed the function of arbiter in the process of income redistribution through the implementation of a variety of social policies and purposefully assigned a dynamic role to the public sector by channeling toward it the financial resources required for the development of an adequate industrial infrastructure. See Osvaldo Sunkel and Pedro Paz, El subdesarrollo latinoamericano y la teoría del desarrollo (México, 1970): 377. It is clear that a major difference between the Industrial Revolution in Britain and the process of industrialization in Latin America is that while the former had a peripheral origin and eventually resulted in a relative attenuation of traditional central power, which henceforth had to be shared with industrialists, trade unionists, and other groups that owed their existence to the coming of industry, in the latter case, the main impetus came from the center and, far from weakening it, strengthened it considerably. See Véliz, Centralist Tradition, 260–261.

41. As for religion, by the middle of our century the political and juridical objectives of the anticlerical movements in the major countries of the region had all been successfully accomplished, and yet in each of these countries, the Catholic church remained without a shadow of doubt the central and dominant religious institution, the only de facto national religion. Véliz, Centralist Tradition, 189–217.

have delighted in prosperity but not at the price of relinquishing *Gemeinschaft*. Their preference has invariably been to eat the cake and to keep it, to sacrifice little and to change even less.

As it frequently occurred in Spain during the liberal hegemony, the would-be merchant adventurers and industrialists of Latin America have never ceased casting wistful glances in the direction of the dome. Even when loudly committed to the rigors of the free market, they have seldom declined to show their preference for the tranquillity that comes with stable government contracts and judicious tariff protection, rather than risk the perils of unregulated and hazardous competition. "Rather than trust to the processes of development," wrote Raymond Carr of the situation at the turn of the century, "Spaniards hankered after a Messiah: a reputable economist could represent British prosperity as the unaided achievement of Adam Smith. They constantly appealed to the state and when the state could do nothing to induce prosperity they talked of 'the absence of the state.' "[42] A comparable attitude has most certainly played a role in the initial failure of some of the liberal experiments undertaken recently in Latin America. These have almost invariably been launched under the name of one or another prestigious academic economist of liberal tendencies, enticed into shouldering the awesome responsibility of satisfying the Messianic expectations of constituencies that would probably prefer to remain forever under the familiar shelter of the dome.

This decisive predilection for stability negates the mobility of factors without which the entrepreneurial activities of industrial capitalism cannot prosper.[43] At its crudest and simplest, this aversion to risk can be interpreted as a consequence of an unspoken acceptance that ours is basically a well-ordered world, spiritually imperfect, of course, but not desperately in need of material improvement; at its most subtle and obstructive, it impedes and generally denies scope to the entrepreneurial activities that sustain the pace of industrial innovation and progress. It should be unnecessary to rehearse the well-known Schumpeterian arguments to justify the importance of the entrepreneur as the usher of the changes normally associated with the prosperities of industrial capital-

42. Raymond Carr, *Spain, 1808–1939* (Oxford, 1966): 398.
43. It may also help to explain the alacrity with which Spanish-speaking societies have responded to periods of affluence based on the exploitation of abundant natural resources, conveniently distant from the major urban centers and carried on by a relatively small labor force. Under these conditions, maximum returns and a correspondingly increased capacity to consume are coupled with minimum disruption to established arrangements.

ism.[44] It suffices to note that according to Joseph Schumpeter's seminal work, first published in 1911, the entrepreneur is much more than a manager or the organizer of routine business activities. "He is the innovator, the practical introducer of something new. The innovation might be a new product or process, new markets opened, new sources or types of supplies developed, or a new form of organisation. . . . The entrepreneur, in other words, moved things forward by creating change. He was the disturber of the peace, the destroyer of existing values." It is therefore abundantly clear that "not every society would form an equally favourable breeding ground and field of action for the Schumpeterian entrepreneur."[45] Not, indeed, and if the society of English Gothic foxes offered, as it certainly did, the most favorable environment for the development of industrial capitalist entrepreneurship, there can be little doubt that the conditions proffered by the Baroque hedgehogs of the Spanish-speaking world during the past century cannot be classed as equally attractive.

This is consistent entirely with the observation that among the qualities valued highly in the realm of the Gothic fox, there are very few that rank above the capacity to adapt expeditiously to changing circumstances and to thrive on the uncertainties and diversities that accompany the maturation of a robust individualism. The contrast with the domed ambit of the Baroque hedgehog, within which it is a cardinal virtue to place consuetudinary affection above expediency, and honor and a sense of shame above the efficiencies of rationality, cannot be more telling.

Earlier it was argued that the continuing phenomenon of the Industrial Revolution derives its dynamic style and character as much from the manner in which things are produced as from the apparently inexhaustible ability of the English-speaking peoples to invent and to design

44. Later, he modified his original, more dynamic interpretation, although he continued to assert that in the early stages of the process "the function of entrepreneurs is to reform or revolutionize the pattern of production by exploiting an invention or, more generally, an untried technological possibility for producing a new commodity or producing an old one in a new way, by opening up a new source of supply of materials or a new outlet for products." However, as the economy prospers and matures, Schumpeter believed that this entrepreneurial function would lose importance "at an accelerating rate . . . even if the economic process itself of which entrepreneurship was the prime mover went on unabated." This opinion was offered in 1942; half a century later, it is fair to say that while Schumpeter's descriptive analysis has fared well, his predictions have not. Joseph A. Schumpeter, *Capitalism, Socialism, and Democracy* (New York, 1950): 132.

45. Sydney Pollard, "Reflections on Entrepreneurship and Culture in European Societies," *Transactions of the Royal Historical Society*, 5th ser., vol. 40 (London, 1990): 159–160.

attractive and inexpensive consumer goods. The foundation of industrial modernity is not simply an advanced mode of production but also a radically different manner of consumption, a "commodification of culture," sustained by the creation of a multitude of goods, important and unimportant, useful and trivial, judged to be worth producing principally because they have been thought likely to prove acceptable to large numbers of independent consumers able to exercise a reasonably free choice in the marketplace. This controversial but very real aspect of industrial modernity has proved particularly unyielding for an Iberian tradition unable, thus far, to emulate its own distinguished creative ancestry by generating modern cultural artifacts attractive to significant numbers of consumers within as well as beyond its boundaries. This has clearly not been regarded as an especially important facet of the economic life of the Spanish-speaking peoples, and when the issue has been raised, the tendency has been for the ambit of the hedgehog to echo Miguel de Unamuno's resounding phrase, "*Que inventen ellos!*" which the sage immortalized as a fitting reply to those who chided Spaniards for their failure to contribute to the repertoire of modern inventions. Unamuno pointed out that electric lights illuminated the Spanish nights and locomotives puffed through the Castilian countryside with the greatest of ease, although neither had been invented locally. Let them invent their trinkets; Spaniards will choose those that are worth using. The Romans knew little about art and less about mathematics, but this did not prevent them from playing a crucial and noble role in human affairs. Unamuno was not alone in thinking in this fashion.

Other weighty voices contributed to a climate of opinion that regarded the technological concomitants of modern economic advancement as little more than a superficial ornament. Well into our century, when automobiles were already wreaking a social and economic revolution in the United States, José Ortega y Gasset opined that although unimportant as a means of transportation, automobiles were useful symbols, to be kept highly polished by underpaid chauffeurs.[46] This species of arrogant sterility was correlated with other complex factors also bound up with a mistrust of innovation, such as a strong affection for the native soil, a tenderness for family ties and old friendships, an inclination to nurture unassailable loyalties, and a respect for status, all of which are consistent with the survival of *Gemeinschaft*. In addition to providing daunting obstacles to the unimpeded mobility of the factors

46. López Ibor, *Complejo de inferioridad*, 55. Carr, *Spain*, 398.

of production, these qualities are also distinctly appealing and can be relied on to maintain a decisively unfavorable environment for what would no doubt be regarded as the brazen, destructive, and invariably unscrupulous schemes of Schumpeterian social-climbing entrepreneurs.

From the vantage point of the inhabitants of the Spanish Indies, the two centuries that bridged the conquest and the advent of the English Industrial Revolution were experienced mainly as a period of imperial preeminence, tranquillity, and ease.[47] This attitude found ample justification in the sixteenth century, under the reigns of the emperor Charles and Philip II, and also during a seventeenth century that, other symptoms of decline notwithstanding, vindicated abundantly the title of "Golden Age" bestowed on it by contemporaries and ratified by succeeding generations. These perceptions were strengthened considerably when both that early military and political preeminence and the artistic achievements that followed were pressed into the service of the prospering Catholic crusade that appeared ultimately to place the Spanish world firmly on the vanguard of Christendom. Even later, when the deterioration of the domestic economic and other arrangements of the Iberian metropolis became embarrassingly obvious, the Indies continued to enjoy a level of material well-being that measured by the standards of the time was strikingly higher than that found in the English-speaking settlements of the north and was probably among the highest achieved anywhere before the advent of modern industry. To qualify this by adding that such prosperity was not readily accessible to the whole population obfuscates the issue unhelpfully, for the same can be said of the austere comforts available to the settlers of Massachusetts and Virginia and, for that matter, of those enjoyed at that time by the inhabitants of any European country. The charming anachronism of those who would have the indigenous Quechua and Aymará heirs of Tahuantinsuyo adopt at that time the standards and the style of living of their European conquerors owes more to kindness and to modern sensibilities and ideological zeal than to knowledge of life in the sixteenth and seventeenth centuries.[48]

47. There were exceptions, notably associated with the Araucanian War in southern Chile and the Chichimec incursions in northern Mexico and, toward the end of the colonial period, the attacks by English, Dutch, and French pirates. The secular situation of the colonies, however, is best reflected in the fact that with the exception of the Chilean frontier, there was no need until the eighteenth century, and then only to deal with the attacks by pirates, to make provision for standing armies.

48. Among the more popular distortions is that arising from the unjustified depiction of the pre-Columbian empires as exemplars of responsible economic organization, welfare, and communal arrangements morally superior as well as much in advance of equivalent developments in Western Europe. Occasionally, this latter-day resurrection of the mythical

The waning of the economic prosperity of Latin America during these closing decades of the century has been additionally disappointing because it contrasts so starkly with its earlier promise. Until only a few generations ago, it appeared that although the Iberian world had seldom moved anywhere except downward since the days of the imperial ascendancy, the economic performance of the new republics afforded some grounds for optimism. Argentina, Uruguay, Colombia, Cuba, Brazil, and Chile had achieved respectable levels of economic well-being sustained principally by the exportation of primary commodities to the industrial markets of the Northern Hemisphere.[49] Whether freak departures or not, that elemental stage of the export-based prosperity would seem to be exhausted. In the absence of major novelties, it is not inconceivable that the Iberian half of the New World could find itself settling, reluctantly, into a middling social and political existence, harried intermittently by the infirmities that have become characteristic of the economic life of the region but also brightened from time to time by generous foreign loans, euphoric bouts of stock market speculation, invitations to join affluent free trade areas, or the arrival of large numbers of rich and affable visitors in search of sunny beaches, quaint villages, photogenic ruins, exotic ski runs, and unspoiled tropical forests.

---

noble savage in the guise of collectivistic bureaucrat has been embraced with special zeal by those seeking antecedents for modern socialist policies in a time-hallowed, idyllic "folk" regime unpolluted by Europeans. For the development of some of these themes, see José Carlos Mariátegui, *Siete ensayos de interpretación de la realidad peruana* (Santiago, 1955); Louis Baudin, *A Socialist Empire: The Incas of Peru* (New York, 1961); Darcy Ribeiro, *The Americas and Civilization* (New York, 1971); and more recently, E. Bradford Burns, *Poverty of Progress.* Not all students of the pre-Columbian era share these views. A recently published history of Tahuantinsuyo alludes to the problem, stating that "for many years the organization of the Inca [empire] was praised and admired by European authors as the realization of utopia. It was then thought that the massive storage of produce by the Incas had humanitarian objectives, such as the succor of the population in case of natural disaster, but this interpretation only demonstrates the lack of understanding of the economic arrangements of the [Inca] state." María Rostworowski de Diez Canseco, *Historia del Tanhuantinsuyo* (Lima, 1988): 262.

49. It is simplistic to suggest that the prosperity of the second half of the nineteenth century which resulted from the massive exportation of primary commodities was dissipated as soon as those exports languished, without major beneficial long-term effects for the economic life of the region. Cortés Conde has argued that "the expansion of the economy based on its exporting sector was not only a consequence of [the] exploitation of an abundant resource, but was made possible, primarily and fundamentally . . . through the incorporation of resources that were scarce . . . and which had to be combined . . . with existing ones in order to allow the production of these resources to enter the market," thus making an enduring contribution that has not been generally acknowledged. See Roberto Cortés Conde, *The First Stages of Modernization in Spanish America* (New York, 1974): 5, 156–157.

CHAPTER IX

The Crumbling Dome

The persistent decline of Spain and her empire over the past three centuries has frequently been attributed to the abandonment of the robust loyalties and virtues judged to be responsible for their earlier and notable achievements.[1] Vastly more plausible, however, is to regard the protracted deterioration not as the consequence of capricious changefulness but of cultural tenacity.[2] What the Spanish-speaking peoples have demonstrated abundantly and over a long period of time is precisely

---

1. Seldom with greater eloquence than Prescott's. In the 1837 preface to his first work on Spanish history, he wrote,

> I cannot quit the subject, which has so long occupied me, without one glance at the present unhappy condition of Spain; who, shorn of her ancient splendour, humbled by the loss of empire abroad and credit at home, is abandoned to all the evils of anarchy. Yet, deplorable as this condition is, it is not so bad as the lethargy in which she has been sunk for ages. Better be hurried forward for a season on the wings of the tempest than stagnate in a deathlike calm, fatal alike to intellectual and moral progress. The crisis of a revolution, when old things are passing away and new ones are not yet established, is indeed fearful. Even the immediate consequences of its achievement are scarcely less so to a people who have yet to learn by experiment the precise form of institutions best suited to their wants, and to accommodate their character to these institutions. Such results must come with time, however, if the nation be but true to itself. And that they will come, sooner or later, to the Spaniards, surely no one can distrust who is at all conversant with their earlier history, and has witnessed the examples it affords of heroic virtue, devoted patriotism, and generous love of freedom; "*Che l'antico valore—non e ancor morto.*"   (*Ferdinand and Isabella*, xi)

2. Octavio Paz proposed an interesting variation on this theme by attributing "the paralysis of colonial society" to what he describes as a circumstance rarely examined, this being that "the decadence of European Catholicism as the source of Western culture coincided with its expansion and apogee [in the New World]. The religious life—a source

an admirable attachment to those modes of thought and action, dispositions and arrangements, to which can be attributed the glory of a Counter-Reformation that presides mightily over everything else that they ever achieved and that, far from having been an unquestioning reiteration of antique customs and beliefs, was originally conceived as an early version of modernity, imaginative, severe, and consistent entirely with the character of the contemporary challenge to which it was addressed.

Gothic foxes and Baroque hedgehogs do not symbolize a polarity between tradition and modernity but one between alternative responses to the challenge posed by modernity. When put to the test, Baroque Spain was already in the vanguard of the modern monarchies and responded to the novel problems of social and economic disruption in a modern way, aptly represented as a "culture of containment" or, in Maravall's own descriptive phrase, as a "guided culture"—but in either case, "a response designed to reintegrate and bind together a society living under the shadow of social and intellectual disruption."[3] Regarded from this vantage point, the wresting of the Iberian peninsula from the Arabs after seven centuries of intermittent war can be justly interpreted as an unintended preparation, a portent of the devout enterprise; the conquest of the Indies, as the closing chapter of the longest and most victorious crusade in Christendom; the Golden Age and the flowering

---

of great creativity in an earlier epoch—became mere inert participation for the vast majority. For the minority, wavering between faith and curiosity, it became a sort of ingenious game and, finally, silence and sleep." Paz, *Labyrinth*, 167. This interpretation does not appear to be quite fair to a Church that did not, and could not, even begin to discover how to bring about a process of industrialization. No amount of contemporary creativity on the part of Catholicism, in Europe or in the Indies, could possibly have initiated a process of economic and social change parallel to that inaugurated in Europe by the English Industrial Revolution. Post-Tridentine Catholicism was neither interested nor equipped to respond effectively to issues that were then and still are subordinate to the paramount task of ensuring the salvation of the immortal soul. Current trends notwithstanding, it is still useful to remember that Christianity is neither an economic doctrine nor an instrument for commercial advancement, and it would be as unrealistic to expect guidance in economic matters from the Church of Rome, flourishing or decadent, as it would be to look for spiritual enlightenment from chambers of manufacturers or banking associations.

3. According to Elliott, Maravall "sought to identify and trace through the premodern age the characteristic features of the world as we know it today. At first sight it might be thought that Spain, so long a byword for everything *anti*modern, was a peculiar choice of terrain for this particular enterprise. But it is all too easily forgotten that sixteenth-century Spain, the imperial Spain of Charles V and Philip II, was the first great bureaucratic state of the modern world. Indeed, much of Spain's subsequent history may be read as an object lesson in the price of pioneering, in this instance, bureaucratic pioneering." J. H. Elliott, "Concerto Barocco," *The New York Review of Books* XXXIV, no. 6 (April 9, 1987).

of the Baroque, as rewarding, integrating, and auspicious consequences of the championship of the truth.

Alarmed by the Lutheran challenge, the Spain that produced more audacious rogues and adventurers in a generation than other European countries in a thousand years turned military, political, and bureaucratic skills that had been hardened in the crucible of conquest to the crowning task of building an all-encompassing conceptual structure: an inspiring dome, majestic and flawless, its superb symmetry designed to soar loftily above human society, well and stoutly constructed to resist the inroads of heretical dissidence. More, because it was intended to be invulnerable to change, the great dome was also the fitting symbol for a triumphant empire and a confident Church that having reformed itself from within could dismiss with aplomb the need for additional improvement. But even more than a political, ecclesiastical, or religious statement, the Baroque dome of the Counter-Reformation was the secular *Summae* of the hedgehog, fashioned as much by soldierly strife and bureaucratic zeal as it was by the sublime ecstasies of inspired mystics. Tempered severally by the grief of virtuous power and the quiet inducements of political expediency, it became a worthy home for the collective consciousness of the Iberians, its existence and resilience an additional and weighty argument for the morality of acquiescence. With their works as well as with their lives, saints, heroes, artists, inquisitors, and scholars raised that dome high above the pedestrian immediacies of partisan canonical skirmishes until it became the impregnable and enduring symbol of a harmonious polity and a universal faith. It should not astonish, therefore, that its architecture should have continued to captivate across the centuries, especially the intellects and feelings of the heirs of the Indies of Castile among whom the longing persisted for the vanished greatness and the mute hope that glorious achievements would once again reward the single-minded commitment, the unifying quest, the passionate obstinacy that once had so strikingly served to halt the tide of heresy and confirm the unquestionable validity of the one true Church.

This consolidating centralist tenor of the imperial Indies has not passed unobserved in our time. Paz, for example, described it in a way that would fit helpfully in a manifesto penned for Baroque hedgehogs, explaining that it was because of this all-encompassing character of Catholicism that

> colonial society managed to become a true order. . . . Form and substance were one. There was no barrier between reality and institutions, the people and the law, art and life, the individual and society; on the contrary, everything harmonized and everyone was guided by the same concepts and the

same will. No man was alone, regardless of his situation, and neither was society; this world and the next, life and death, action and contemplation were experienced as totalities, not as isolated acts or ideas. Every fragment participated in the whole, which was alive in each one of its parts.[4]

Time passes very slowly for such a considerable feat. The Counter-Reformation occurred the day before yesterday; its echoes are clearly audible; its relics still work miracles; its heirs continue to savor the glory of their triumphant ancestry and to draw comfort even from trifling intimations that a centrally determined solution to the problem—any problem—will finally prevail which accords with the way things ought to be, that is, symmetrical, concentric, well integrated, readily perceived and defined, and, above all, when considered from the vantage point of the dominant center, unified, harmonious, and predictable. For a people fired with such an expectant faith, it has not been hard to persevere and continue to oppose anything that suggests a retrogression away from authority and certainty and toward the menacing outer realm of diversity, libertinage, precariousness, and chaos.

These feelings and expectations have found expression in the most unlikely contexts. Consider, for example, Darcy Ribeiro's approving description of pre-Columbian Andean society.

> There being no private ownership of land, no coin . . . and no slavery, no conditions existed for the rise of a seigneurial caste and another of slaves, or of mercantile and latifundian sectors. Within this community *the peasant was a free worker because he was governed only by an overall order embracing the whole society, personified by the Inca and represented locally by the imperial bureaucracy.* The Inca civilization was characterized by the development of a state collective system—as opposed to the slavistic [*sic*] mercantile and capitalistic structures.[5]

---

4. Paz, *Labyrinth*, 166. Others have found more suggestive names for this feature of the Iberian political tradition. Wiarda, for example, calls it "corporatism" and explains that "corporatism, once thought to be synonymous with fascism and reaction, is now viewed as a national organizational form that may take liberal, Christian-democratic, and syndicalist directions as well as bureaucratic-authoritarian ones. . . . If we are to comprehend Iberian and Latin American political society and development on their own terms rather than through the ethnocentric notions of North American social science, we must come to grips with corporatism. Corporatism may well be to Iberia and Latin America what liberalism has been to the United States: the dominant political-cultural and institutional framework within which political and social life is organized." Howard J. Wiarda, *Corporatism and National Development in Latin America* (Boulder, 1981): xi–xii.

5. Darcy Ribeiro, *The Americas and Civilization* (New York, 1971): 140–141 (my emphasis). Such well-meaning but anachronic descriptions are not restricted to mythical pre-Columbian societies. Burns has written with unusual warmth about folk societies in mid-nineteenth-century Latin America. "Folk culture was based on a common language, heritage, beliefs, and means of facing daily life. It instilled a feeling of unity, loyalty, and

The abundance in the Iberian world of incisive and topical versions of a disposition, such as the one illustrated here, that is content to regard freedom as a consequence of governance by a single all-embracing power derives intellectual and moral sustenance from the successful experience of a Counter-Reformation that was the harbinger of many of the enlightened modernities to which we have grown inured during the past four centuries, which range from the enlistment of the visual arts in the service of single truths and the exposure of multiple errors to the marshaling of architecture and rhetoric to the tasks of sacred persuasion and propaganda and the efficient use of the higher levels of education, especially that of the powerful, in the secular crusade for the defense of Christendom. Not surprisingly, such sentiments and inclinations have not lacked a hospitable reception within the Catholic Church itself, none more enthusiastic than that proffered by the upholders of the so-called Liberation Theology, that late Christian Democratic flowering of the seedlings nursed by the neo-Thomist philosopher Jacques Maritain, whose holistic interpretations had earlier nourished the *integriste* doctrines of Action Française. The views of the Colombian priest, Father Camilo Torres, who studied Maritain's works at Louvain, offer a telling illustration of the direction the French philosophers' "integral humanism" did take once released from the doctrinal discipline of the Catholic establishment. It is true that the militant beliefs of Father Torres and his friends were extreme, but they were not immensely distant from those of at least a plurality of their less vehement brethren and in each crucial point reflected a concurrence that does not always disappear as one moves across the spectrum of political opinion within the Church. For example, when addressing the problem, otherwise unusual for an ordained priest and university chaplain, of whether "uncommitted persons" ought to be permitted to shoulder revolutionary responsibilities, Father Torres stated,

---

tradition within the folk. . . . A unity of feeling and action accompanied a sense of harmony with the environment to satisfy inner needs. The combination of unity, harmony and satisfaction comprised the soul of the people." These astoundingly well-integrated communities "expected their leader to represent and strengthen their unity, express their soul, personify their values, and increase their harmony; in short, to be as one with the people he led." To lead such people was no mean feat, and those charged with the awesome responsibility "exuded a natural, a charismatic, leadership of the majority, who found in him an adviser, a guide, a leader, a protector. . . . They surrendered power to him; he exercised it for their benefit. He embodied the collective will; he encarnated authority." Not every reader will fail to notice the compatibility, obviously unintended by the author, between this description and the notorious Central European slogans of the 1920s and 1930s. Burns, *Poverty of Progress*, 89–91.

The revolutionary struggle cannot be carried out unless there is a complete and integrated *Weltanschauung*. That is why it is difficult in the contemporary Western world for this struggle to be undertaken apart from Christian and Marxist ideologies which, for all practical purposes, are the only ideologies that possess an integral *Weltanschauung*. And for this reason it is difficult for uncommitted persons who do not belong to one of these ideological camps to assume revolutionary leadership.[6]

A year later, after his formal laicization, he published his "Message to Communists," in which he stated, "I have said that as a Colombian, as a sociologist, as a Christian, and as a priest I am a revolutionary. I believe that the Communist Party consists of truly revolutionary elements, and hence I cannot be an anti-Communist either as a Colombian, a sociologist, a Christian, or a priest."[7]

The republics of Latin America have never suffered from a shortage of attempts, mostly well intentioned and frequently disastrous, to place order and truth—one truth—in the center of the stage and to bundle every error out of sight. These ameliorating initiatives have been so numerous that it is even possible to conjecture that had it not been for the unscheduled eighteenth-century irruption of English industrialism and

6. Camilo Torres was born a Colombian aristocrat. After spending part of his youth in Switzerland and Spain, he began studies in law, but an unhappy love affair drove him to the priesthood against the opposition of his family. Immediately following his ordination, he went to Louvain where he obtained a master's degree in sociology. On his return to Colombia, he was appointed lecturer and chaplain at the National University. In June 1965, he was ordered laicized because of his open advocacy of violent revolutionary action. He then joined a self-styled "Army of National Liberation" group. In February 1966, his detachment ambushed a military patrol, and he was killed in the ensuing fighting. The text cited here is taken from a paper presented in French by Father Torres at the Second International Congress of Pro Mundi Vita in Louvain, in September 1964, and published by this organization in 1965 under the title *Programmation Economique at Exigences Apostoliques*. An English version entitled "Revolution: Christian Imperative" was published in John Gerassi, ed., *Revolutionary Priest: The Complete Writings of Camilo Torres* (London, 1973): 298.

7. Gerassi, *Camilo Torres*, 376. Although possibly the best-known exponent of this approach to communism, Father Torres was not being immensely novel. In 1960, when Fidel Castro declared himself a convert to Marxism-Leninism, Father Moisés Arrechea, a Havana priest, declared on television that in his opinion, the "humanism" espoused by Castro "is the work of God himself." *Time*, May 30, 1960, 18. Even earlier, in 1948, Eduardo Frei, the leader of the Chilean Falange, which in 1957 became the organizing nucleus of the Christian Democratic party, affirmed that "worse than communism, is anticommunism." His attitude reflected accurately the disposition of the Falange, at the time not averse to reaching understandings with Marxist parties, explained as an "opening" to like-minded popular forces committed to widespread reforms. See Jaime Guzmán, "El miedo: Síntoma de la realidad político-social chilena," *Estudios Públicos*, no. 42 (Otoño 1991): 272. This disposition explains, for example, why it was that in the mid-1950s the Santiago daily *El Espectador*, owned by Socialists, secretly ceded the control of its political pages to the Christian Democratic party without such an arrangement being made public or resulting in problems with the tabloid's editorial policy.

a romantic movement obsessed with the sublimity of disorder and diversity, the post-Tridentine edifice would probably have continued to offer comfortable shelter to many generations of less or more enlightened Latin American centralists who would have felt safe in the enjoyment of the presiding notion "that One is good, Many—diversity—is bad, since the truth is one, and only error is multiple."[8]

It is only of late, in these closing years of our century, especially after the Eastern European revolutions of 1989, the dissolution of the Soviet Union in 1991, and the pitiful decrepitude of Cuba's revolutionary regime, that the domed view of things appears finally to have lost respectability in the world at large and possibly to have exhausted the patience even of its more loyal Spanish- and Portuguese-speaking supporters in the New World. This, however, is a latter-day circumstance in a region that has offered hospitality to a surfeit of political initiatives that, with or without justification, have kept alive the hope that human affairs, most certainly including economic arrangements, can be conducted in a scientifically and technologically correct fashion, enlightened, reliable, and predictable. The list of such movements and parties is very long and ranges widely from socialists, communists, national socialists, Sandinistas, and Falangistas to those espoused by the Catholic Left, anticlerical radicals, Peronists, Christian Democrats, Castroist revolutionaries, the latter-day zealots of Peru's dismal Maoist Shining Path, and other lesser but equally clamorous creeds that have shared little other than the profound conviction that while errors abound, they and their comrades are tied to the mast of the ship of truth. Once that single, shining, and incontestably enlightened verity is discovered or revealed, it becomes sinful, criminal, and a betrayal to tolerate deviations that will assuredly impede the development of the economy, the feeding and care of the poor and destitute, the defense of the nation, or the salvation of our immortal souls. Torres's view of the merits of Soviet planning, which he prefaced with an appeal to "abide by the facts and analyze them as they [occur] historically," was simply that "the Soviet Union, largely because of its system of economic planning, with state control of the means of

8. Only one hypothesis contrary to a fact should be allowed per book; but until this regulation is proclaimed officially, perhaps one can be forgiven for indulging. Kant was understandably impressed with the progress made by the natural sciences, and one of his objectives was to offer a rational explanation of why this was so; a feasible and worthy project with or without an Industrial Revolution, but one wonders whether the mixture of Kantian moral autonomy, romanticism, and nationalism would have proved as explosive and influential in the absence of those dark satanic mills in the English Midlands. Isaiah Berlin, "The Apotheosis of the Romantic Will," in *The Crooked Timber of Humanity* (New York, 1991): 208, 216–217.

production, has now become at least the second greatest economic power in the world, although it began as an underdeveloped country in the year 1917. To what can we primarily attribute this development? . . . [To the fact] that the Soviet Union has utilised in a progressive manner and almost in its totality the profits of national production for common purposes and projects that were technically planned." The reason for this is presented as yet another matter of fact: "If we compare Marxist analyses strictly pertaining to the socioeconomic structures of these countries, with capitalist analyses, we will find that the Marxist analyses are better adapted to reality [because] in economic planning Marxists [hold] the first place." And we know that "to seek authoritative economic planning [is] an obligation for the Christian [because] planning is essential to efficacy in the authentic service of the majorities and . . . a condition of charity. . . . It is most probable that the Marxists will take over the leadership of this planning." When this occurs, Torres concluded encouragingly, "the Christian must collaborate [so that] in the underdeveloped countries there will be no recurrence of the struggles among groups seeking structural reforms. Without factionalism . . . Christians will be able to participate in the building of a better world."[9]

The Spanish Civil War loomed very large on the Latin American horizon for obvious and weighty reasons, but also because the fratricidal struggle between the Popular Front and the Nationalists was, in Hugh Thomas's sentence, a "War of Two Counter Revolutions," each side defending a credible and forceful alternative proposal to restore the hedgehog's dome to its former glory.[10] If the republic survived, the Communists would dominate it with the help of their scientifically minded Russian comrades; if Franco emerged victorious, the Falange was poised to take control with the help of its German and Italian supporters. In either case, one or another latter-day version of the domed view of things would be vindicated, and a strong central government, firm in the hedgehog's knowledge of the "one big thing," would ensure that the economy was managed efficiently, without dissention or abrupt and disconcerting

9. Gerassi, *Camilo Torres*, 278.
10. An expectation not devoid of poignancy when considered against the country's unimpressive economic situation, which circumstance was accorded special significance in the book's concluding sentences: "The civil war had moments of glory. But it was essentially a terrible tragedy and interruption in the life of a European people—the one major European people, it might be gloomily remembered, that before 1936 was too poor to have a modern armament industry." Hugh Thomas, *The Spanish Civil War* (London, 1977): Bk. 4, "The War of Two Counter Revolutions," 946.

changes. Social and economic disorder would cease; there would be an end to uncertainty.

There have been some memorable cultural revolutions in the past century and a half, the purpose of which was to put a stop to many of the changes associated with industrial modernity. Some were intended specifically to preserve political orthodoxies; others, as was the case in Iran, to comply with particular interpretations of ancient religious requirements. None has succeeded, and some, notably those in Russia, China, Iran, and Cuba, have been unmitigated disasters.[11] Compared with these costly failures, the Spanish Counter-Reformation must be counted among the more successful and enduring cultural revolutions in history, although even when judged in this light, it should be placed immediately on the same shelf with the better-known attempts by Doctor Faustus, Peter Pan, and Dorian Gray to negate change, arrest the passage of time, and bring irksome uncertainty to an end.

The young Ruskin defined man as a being who repeats himself, especially when compared with the infinite variety of the natural world that surrounds him.[12] In this he was evidently wrong, because it is nature that repeats itself; the changes and innovations it sustains being mostly of the geologic or evolutionary variety, which from our vantage point can be described fairly as a species of stability, founded on endless and virtually identical repetition. Every flowering seed repeats the process whereby it blossoms in the spring; every young gosling goes about its business in ways that are in essence the same favored by its progenitors over thousands of generations; every chrysalis is transformed in a manner that is a predictable repetition of the transformations undergone by its ancestors since the time of Erasmus. Only the human species is doomed to change because it is the only one graced with history.[13] The

11. There have also been "cultural revolutions" unleashed precisely with the opposite objective, that is, to help bring about the rapid modernization of traditional societies. Among the most notable of these must be counted those led by Kemal Ataturk in Turkey, Sun Yat-Sen in China, and the Shah Reza Pahlevi in Iran, none of which had especially encouraging results. Of those seeking to arrest unwanted change and innovation, one of the most successful was that of Tokugawa Japan, which kept the distant island realm isolated from the rest of the world for well over a century, a considerable feat but one that still falls short of the Spanish achievement.

12. Kemp, *The Desire of Mine Eyes*, 89.

13. Peter Berger's comments notwithstanding. He notes, correctly, that although history impresses immediately because of its variety, "at the same time . . . there is a remarkable continuity of forms of life, especially on the lower levels of society and in the area of material life. No matter what king was ruling . . . or what empire supposedly held sway . . . the great mass of human beings eked out their existence in a very similar manner."

elder Ruskin should have reconsidered his definition and turned it on its head: man is the only being who cannot repeat himself; even when he tries to do so, the vaguest intimation that he knows what he is about will ensure that intent, context, and consequences will differ. No creature of man is immune from history, and although the Spanish Counter-Reformation was addressed principally to the things of God, the means whereby the pious task was to be fulfilled took the form of a secular revolution managed by human beings which, like all other things of the world, was flawed, imperfect, and ultimately vulnerable.

Four centuries intervened, however, between inception and eventual outcome, during which this cultural revolution proved more resistant to change than any comparable enterprise in modern history. That this was partly due to the lateness of the industrial challenge is evident; but it was also in part a reflection of the plausibility of the domed conception of things as a tenable centralist response to the challenge of modernity. Mainly, though, it could be argued, it was a consequence of its being founded on the passionate acceptance of a stability that mirrored the fixity of divine things, and it was from this stance that it eschewed novelty, sanctioned repetition, and was not always disinclined to link inner peace with quietude and haughty resignation.

Unamuno's scornful "Que inventen ellos!" reflected a deeply rooted anxiety that for the Spanish world to become an efficient producer of industrial goods, a transformation of such magnitude would be required that everything that was noble and admirable in the character of the people would be threatened. Once the production of goods is accorded the protagonic role, to transform its modalities necessarily alters everything else. No such fears were entertained with respect to the acquisition for use (consumption?) of industrial goods and services generated elsewhere. Unamuno and his contemporaries delighted in the way in which electric lights illuminated their joyful zarzuelas and swift locomotives carried admirable bullfighters to their destiny, without negating the essential Spanish mode of conceiving the world and going about things. So they believed, together with most of their venerable colleagues in

---

This is true, but unlike the blanket continuities that affect all birds and all bees at all times, some human beings, at the very least most kings, emperors, and their courtiers, artists, and scholars, were precisely and efficiently conscious of many of the diversities, changes, deteriorations, and improvements uncovered, perhaps even illuminated, by the passage of time and were in a position to respond to this intelligence in a purposeful manner. Peter Berger, *The Capitalist Revolution: Fifty Propositions About Prosperity, Equality, and Liberty* (London, 1987): 33.

Latin America. Now we know that they were wrong, understandably, but wrong nonetheless. They could hardly have been expected to notice at that time, in the earlier decades of our century, when all around them production appeared indeed to predominate, especially in the totalitarian states of Europe, that our world was crossing the threshold into our own time, when consumption would become dominant. Unamuno could not anticipate that the same electricity that illuminated the music halls of old Madrid would bring radio and television in its wake and would alter the habits, tastes, and timetables of millions, burying the zarzuelas under a thousand soap operas and mini-series, as convincingly—and perhaps as unjustly—as soccer, tennis, basketball, and golf have relegated bullfighting to the category of quaint tourist attraction. Had Unamuno survived into these closing years of the century, he would have been pained and disheartened to see the magnificent dome finally reconciled with history and the passage of time by showing alarming signs of deterioration. The edifice is still there, but its elaborately decorated interior surfaces are peeling off, the rain pours through gaping cracks in the masonry, and the foundations are suspect.

After four centuries of steadfast resistance to dangerous doctrinal innovations—bristling with pikes and swords, walled by stone and girdled with steel, armored stoutly against canonical deviations, steadfast against the progress of latitudinarian diversity, with battlements manned by sentries alert to the danger of excessive zeal and unquiet curiosity—the lofty dome of the Spanish cultural revolution has in the end proved defenseless against blue jeans, computer graphics, jogging shoes, and electric toasters. It is now crumbling, not because it has been bested by rival doctrines or pulled asunder and brought down by ideological deviations but because it has been overwhelmed by the tidal heaving and pulling of an immense multitude of inexpensive, pedestrian, readily accessible, and unpretentious products of industrial capitalism. No canonical reconsideration is required to play volleyball; nor is it necessary to abjure the faith to use a credit card, wear T-shirts, buy dishwashing machines, or enjoy heavy metal. The tail of consumption is wagging the dog of production so vigorously that the kennel is disintegrating. It was far less complicated to discourage Lutheran proclivities in the relaxed Italian city-states than to persuade the faithful of Buenos Aires, Coquimbo, or Guayaquil to abstain from watching television sitcoms; immensely easier to organize workers to march in favor of higher wages than to stop them from eating hamburgers, enjoying rock music, drinking Coca-Cola, or accepting the electronic precisions of supermarket bar code readers. It has proved virtually impossible to stop sizable numbers of consumers from responding to the entreaties of the charming, articulate, helpful, understanding, and impeccably packaged ambassadors from the world beyond the dome, a fact that has not been overlooked by a number of Catholic writers who have tried, without much success, to alert the faithful.[14] The ramparts, however, have now been breached, not by outsiders fighting to get in, but by very large numbers of insiders trekking out in the direction of supermarkets and shopping centers. It took one bite at the apple to open the gates of the Garden of Eden, but today the road that leads from the crumbling dome is lined with hot dog stands and pizza parlors.

Ultimately, the earthy truism has been vindicated; nothing fails like failure, and it is a surfeit of failures that is responsible for the decrepit condition of the dome. The military and diplomatic setbacks of the past are now virtually meaningless, and only professional historians ponder over the consequences or the causes of Rocroi, the Armada, the Alamo, or the *Maine*,[15] but very few Latin Americans are unaware of the parlous circumstance of most of the republics. Not many are conversant with the details of the protracted imperial decline, but fewer have failed to notice that the horizon of the former Indies is filled with cultural artifacts and *res gestae* bearing the imprint of the Gothic fox; not too many Spanish- and Portuguese-speaking inhabitants of the New World are particularly enamored of the United States or Britain, but even fewer decline to learn English if the opportunity offers; a miniscule number of Latin American intellectuals have been swept off their feet by a rereading of Adam Smith or John Stuart Mill, but none are unaware of the melancholy fate of the centralist economic prescriptions espoused by almost every local political grouping during the postwar decades.

Taken separately, each of these symptoms of retreat could possibly have been neutralized, diverted, or even ignored, but their visitation has

14. A representative recent essay tellingly enlists the authority of Aristotle, St. Augustine, Aquinas, and Leo XIII in an effort to warn the faithful against the spiritual dangers posed by "consumerism," noting that it is not material possessions that are objectionable per se but the corrupting tendency to excessive and disorderly accumulation. Fernando Moreno, *Consumo y "Sociedad de consumo": Estudios Públicos*, no. 47 (Invierno 1992). This concern is echoed in the recent encyclical *Centesimus annus* in which Pope John Paul reiterates the warning against consumerism (par. 33), George Pell, "Rerum Novarum: One Hundred Years Later," *The Boston Conversazioni* (Boston, 1992): 16.

15. Although it is difficult to ignore the melancholy symmetry of Cuba's role in the closing stages of two crumbling empires. At the close of the nineteenth century, the island was at the center of the confrontation that marked the end of the Spanish empire in the Indies. Today, Cuba is once more courting notoriety, but this time as the pathetic detritus left behind after the dissolution of the Soviet empire.

been in battalions, within the span of a few decades, and taken together they provide a sobering preamble, perhaps even some of the determinants, of what eventually may be judged to have been the most profound social transformation this century in the Iberian half of the New World, of vastly greater moment than the Mexican, Bolivian, Cuban, Peruvian, and Nicaraguan revolutions put together. In less than a generation, more Latin American Catholics have converted to Protestantism than ever before in the history of the Indies. Never before since the Reformation have so many Catholics converted to Protestantism in such a brief period of time.

Thirty years ago, Chile had the largest non-Catholic minority in Latin America, and it amounted to less than 7 percent of the population—a figure that included members of all other churches, sects, and denominations as well as atheists, agnostics, and assorted nonbelievers. In 1920, there were 54,800 evangelical Protestants in Chile, or 1.4 percent of the population; today, they number 549,900, or 16 percent of the population. Such absolute figures are indeed important, but the trend they reflect merits special attention, for the annual rate of growth of evangelical Protestantism between 1920 and 1940 was only 2.5 percent; from 1940 to 1970, it increased to 3.2 percent, and last year it reached 4.8 percent. As conversions among the upper middle and upper classes are virtually nonexistent, the inroads made among the working class are proportionately greater.[16] Twenty percent of the 150 million people who inhabit Brazil are now Protestant; six years ago, there were 15,000 full-time Protestant pastors in that country, compared with only 13,000 priests, and there are many more today. Guatemala is now over 30 percent Protestant; Nicaragua, 20 percent; Costa Rica, 16 percent. In 1916, Protestants constituted a very small minority, possibly less than 1 percent throughout Latin America, made up mainly of immigrants from Germany, Britain, Scandinavia, and the United States. During the following decades, there was limited growth as a result of missionary activity, but, as David Martin indicates in his recent study of the phenomenon,

> The take-off came in the sixties. At the beginning of this period evangelical Protestants counted some 5 million members, excluding children, and their

---

16. David Martin, *Tongues of Fire: The Explosion of Protestantism in Latin America* (Oxford, 1990): 50–52. For a meticulous and exhaustive analysis of the available data for Chile, see Arturo Fontaine Talavera and Harald Beyer, "Retrato del movimiento evangélico a la luz de las encuestas de opinión pública," *Estudios Públicos*, no. 44 (Primavera 1991): 91, 123–124.

wide constituency extended to some 15 million. Two decades later that constituency extended to at least 40 million, which is remarkable even allowing for rapid growth in total population. It may even be the case that in parts of Latin America the number of Protestants regularly involved in worship and fellowship exceeds the number of Catholics.[17]

To regard these admittedly unprecedented numbers of conversions as the ultimate consequence of a thoughtful doctrinal renunciation of the Catholic faith would be to misunderstand the problem. It is not that the people are turning their backs on Catholicism in particular but rather that they are abandoning the domed shelter of the hedgehog and everything associated with it, including Catholicism. The manner in which this is occurring may even suggest a "cargo cult" response to the perceived new circumstances that attributes the capacity to sustain a prosperous good life as well as to generate attractive consumer goods and cultural artifacts directly to a culture of industrial capitalism that, even without benefit of Weberian insights, appears closely bound up with the tenets of evangelical Protestantism.[18]

Against this, it could be argued, plausibly, that there are large regions of Europe where forms of modern industrial capitalism flourish among peoples that are Catholic almost without exception. The case of Spain complicates things further because, while sharing many of the conditions that have contributed to the Latin American situation, it has not been affected by others that may well be decisive. For example, the Castilian metropolis could hardly have experienced the distance from Europe and, more important, the effective isolation from the source of the policies, institutions, and cultural artifacts with which the imperial Crown so consciously shaped the political and religious circumstance of the seaborne empire. Distance was of the essence in preserving many of these features in the Indies far beyond the reach and continuing influence of the conditions, often abrasive and conflictive, that helped first to bring them about and later to modify, attenuate, or render them ineffectual. Spain, moreover, is now a member of the European Community and has been attracting 40 or 50 million tourists every year for the past decade. This is the equivalent of a multitude of mineral discoveries and at least comparable to the flow of bullion from the imperial Indies. This massive

17. Martin, *Tongues of Fire*, 50.
18. Among the more important conclusions of the Fontaine-Beyer study cited above is that Chilean evangelical Protestants tend to explain poverty as a consequence of moral failures and associate economic prosperity to moral virtue and "faith in God." A significant related observation points to the strong rejection of alcoholism among Protestants and, to a considerable extent and precisely because of this, to a growing popularity of the new faith among working-class women. Fontaine and Beyer, "Retrato," 123.

and benign invasion of paying customers has influenced the national economy most decisively and may help to explain why the general disposition of the Spanish people appears to be diverging intriguingly from that prevailing among the inhabitants of the former Indies. Evidently this involves other factors as well, and taken together they may help to explain why it is that the large-scale conversions that are taking place in Latin America have not been replicated in the Iberian peninsula. Put simply, Macaulay's assumption that Catholicism was uniquely responsible for the indifferent economic performance of the Iberian world is probably oversimple. The most that can be said at present is that Catholicism is a principal and most visible circumstance affecting the life of the heirs of the imperial Indies and that for a number of complex reasons, some unnecessary, others possibly unjust, the Catholic Church has become symbolically associated with social and political arrangements that, regardless of other considerations, have sustained repeated and catastrophic economic failures and are now widely regarded as inimical to the advancement of industrial capitalism and modernity.

Although the ample shelter of the Baroque hedgehogs was originally founded on the *summae* of the experience and rationality of its day, well over two centuries before the Industrial Revolution, its intriguing compatibility with some of the more influential modern interpretations of the opportunities and threats posed by industrial society kept that promise alive until our time, when it otherwise should have been decisively negated by the rise of modern industry. It would be unfair to forget that even Comte made much of this compatibility and proposed his own Religion of Humanity, well characterized as "Catholicism minus Christianity," which he modeled after the ecclesiastical structure of the Catholic Church, but motivated by scientific, "positive" principles and instruments of social action.

The attempts to improve on this Comtian initiative, or to perfect it, have not vanished with the advance of industrialism. Quite the contrary; examples appear to be more abundant in our century than in that of the father of sociology. It would be difficult, however, to find a more poignant and pathetic illustration of this paradoxical relationship than the one offered by Torres's already cited explanation that, as he saw it, "Christian and Marxist ideologies . . . are the only ideologies that possess an integral *Weltanschauung*."[19] Torres's assertions must al-

---

19. Gerassi, *Camilo Torres*, 298. The acceptance of a special relationship between the Catholic Church and some left-wing revolutionary movements in Latin America was not as exceptional as it may seem. In an influential text published originally in English in 1977 and in Spanish in 1980, Father Jeffrey Klaiber maintained that "the Catholic church,

ways be considered with much caution, but in this instance, he was neither alone nor entirely mistaken in perceiving a degree of harmony and commonality, almost a correspondence, between these two principal views of the world, otherwise so immensely dissimilar in intent and moral commitment. A learned Jesuit, writing in *Mensaje*, the quasi-official Chilean journal of the Society, proposed that if Marxism is to be understood as "a willingness to construct a new society in which all can participate equally, without the intrusion of private property as a source of privilege or power; if by Marxism we mean the conscious acceptance of the necessary struggle to make possible such a new society, Christians cannot reject it, but must accept it in the name of their faith. . . . There are no difficulties in the collaboration between Communists and Christians."[20] This article was written in response to Pope Paul VI's apostolic letter marking the eightieth anniversary of *Rerum novarum*, in which reference was made to the attraction that socialist ideas had for many Christians but noting that under the word "socialism" can be found many political forms, some of which are irreconcilable with the Catholic faith. A lengthy editorial article published in *Mensaje* interpreted this in a most unusual fashion, by lamenting that the pope had not been more precise about relations with socialism and concluding that from his text, "it can be deduced that the road to socialism is now open to Christians."[21] Fidel Castro agreed warmly, declaring,

> It is not possible to love humanity and be anti-Communist. . . . [Communism and Christianity] need not be antagonistic. We are in agreement 90 percent of the time; let us then agree on this and work together. . . . We can work together in social, economic, and human affairs. . . . There is the problem of the faith, but the strictly philosophical aspects do not present a fundamental problem, because what is understood by Marxism [refers] only to the economy. Therefore one can be a Christian and a Marxist in economic, political, and other such things, without ever straying into philosophical questions.[22]

---

which had always enjoyed a vital contact with the lower classes from colonial times, became the new forum in which the lower classes sought to integrate their popular traditions with their new expectations of radical social change. . . . Religion and revolution could be viewed as harmonious and complementary realities." Jeffrey L. Klaiber, S. J., *Religion and Revolution in Peru, 1824–1976* (South Bend, 1977): 198–199.

20. Pierre Bigo, S. J., "El materialismo marxista: Ensayo de discernimiento," *Mensaje*, no. 204 (November 1971): 537.

21. "*Rerum novarum*: Ochenta años después," 201.

22. Hubert Daubechies, S. J., "Fidel Castro habla a Los 80," *Mensaje*, no. 206 (January–February 1972): 60.

It is not difficult to imagine that the importance attributed to this controversial relationship by the better-known and more widely publicized theologians of liberation, as well as by the more zealous among their followers, may have encouraged, perhaps even helped to trigger, the massive exodus from a civic and ecclesiastical refuge so emphatically associated with catastrophic past failures, present disillusionment, and the promise of a dangerous future as the spiritual partner, albeit naive, of the more ruthless contemporary apostles of revolutionary violence.[23]

This disquieting dimension of the social and spiritual transformation is reflected both in the forthright manner and the essential content of Pope John Paul's opening address to the Fourth General Conference of the Latin American Bishops on October 12, 1992. The pope called on the clergy to follow the example of the Good Shepherd and defend the flock entrusted to them against what he described as the "attack of wolves." Having thus dealt with the external challengers, he turned within to find the reasons for the apparent vulnerability of the body of the Church, explaining that "the alarming phenomenon . . . of the growth of the sects and pseudospiritual movements . . . reveals the existence of a pastoral lacuna whose cause can frequently be found in a lack of formation, which threatens Christian identity and results in a situation in which large numbers of Catholics who do not receive adequate religious care—because of the lack of priests, among other reasons—are at the mercy of the sects' very active campaigns of proselytism." With this rather perfunctory statement out of the way, the Holy Father then turned with unusual vigor to the heart of the matter, stating that "the faithful do not find in pastoral workers that strong sense of God which they must show in their lives. Situations like that can be the reason why many poor and simple people . . . become easy prey to the sects in which they try to find life's religious meaning, a meaning which perhaps they did not find in those who should have been able to offer it

---

23. The disinclination of the evangelical sects to encourage or even to accept any kind of political involvement appears to be an important attraction from the vantage point of working-class families that are tired, disconcerted, and fearful after decades of political violence. This has proved of special value in the conversion of women, who would much rather have their husbands and sons praying at home than dodging grenades at the barricades. In more tranquil times, the classical correlation between sobriety, hard work, austerity, family prayers, and economic prosperity has not escaped the attention of women who appear to have discovered that "evangelical religion . . . preaches an ideology which can be used by women to domesticate men." Elizabeth Brusco, "The Household Basis of Evangelical Religion and the Reformation of Machismo in Colombia" (Ph.D. dissertation, City University of New York, 1986), cited in Martin, Tongues of Fire, 181.

to them."[24] It would be difficult to discover a franker, clearer, and more authoritative description of what seems to be a principal consequence of the policies and attitudes advanced by the upholders of a theology that has indeed led to a species of liberation—but possibly not the one intended by its well-intentioned progenitors.

That the reasons behind these mass conversions to various Protestant evangelical denominations are unusually complicated does not require reiteration, nor can it be doubted that their elucidation will engage the attention of scholars for a long time to come, but it is unlikely that future investigations will set aside as totally without significance the enthusiasm with which so many have been prepared to greet the alleged secular compatibility of the established Church of the Indies with the great Counter-Reformation structure that it helped originally to design, erect, and keep in good repair for almost four hundred years. Although it would appear implausible to explain the decrepitude of the dome of the Counter-Reformation simply as the result of an unsuccessful theological confrontation with the disciples of Luther and Calvin, or even as the delayed consequence of the triumph of nineteenth-century liberal anti-clericalism, the fact cannot be ignored that among the principal reasons it is now possible to think that the edifice is crumbling is that for the first time in the history of the Iberian New World such very large numbers of the faithful are relinquishing its shelter. Their departure need not have been a main determinant of the contemporary crisis but is probably the most visible occurrence of the penultimate stages of a lengthy process of disillusionment.

What we are witnessing today in Latin America is consistent with the crepuscular phase of an immense disenchantment shared by a whole culture, brought about not, as Weber would have proposed, by the obliteration of "the spontaneous affections of the heart, the hatreds of the moment, the comely and honourable ways of tradition,"[25] but by a resigned and melancholy acceptance that the promise of national greatness and economic resurrection that for so long was thought, or felt, to be

24. "Address to Bishops of Latin America," *L'Osservatore Romano*, Weekly Edition (in English), no. 42 (October 21, 1992): 7.

25. The famous phrase that Weber borrowed from Schiller is usually translated as "the disenchantment of the world," but its meaning in German is much more precise and could even be paraphrased as "the driving out of magic from things" in a world peopled by bureaucrats, officeholders in big government, big business, or big political parties. Weber thought that a dictatorship was indeed in the offing, not of the proletariat but of officials. Donald G. MacRae, *Weber* (London, 1974): 86–87.

embodied in the "communitarian" credos that blossomed under the glittering dome is unlikely ever to be fulfilled. The crucial importance and the complex demands posed by matters religious, political, and economic ought not to obscure the fact that regardless of doctrinal inspiration, spiritual sources, or intellectual rigor, ultimately these are constructions of the human mind and must be regarded as cultural artifacts, even as human exploits, achievements, eloquent cultural statements, no doubt vastly more involved and demanding than, say, roller skates, safety razor blades, or cordless telephones, but creatures of man nonetheless and therefore eventually subject, like all others, to the modifying processes of history. The ease with which many children take to the ghastly habit of chewing gum, or young men to wearing absurd T-shirts, or older ones to jogging, avoiding fatty foods, or holding breakfast "brainstorming" business sessions may well be a function of the elemental gratification or readily perceived functionality of these rather undemanding, occasionally inane, cultural artifacts of foreign provenance. It is far easier and immediately satisfying to understand the usefulness of a vacuum cleaner than to agree that an uncritical commitment to Marxism-Leninism may not be the most efficient way of obtaining one. The sequential pattern of the diffusion of the practices, habits, and expectations generally associated with modern industrialism, whether regarded as desirable or otherwise, suggests strongly that there could be an as yet undefined correlation between the rate of dispersion of its products, in other words, of its cultural artifacts, and their intrinsic complexity.

If this were even partly true, then it should be possible to suggest that what we have witnessed of late in the former Indies of Castile can usefully be described as a process of assimilation that has progressed from the simple to the more complex; from the introduction of sporting activities, sartorial fashions, gastronomic innovations, and a huge array of immediately appealing labor-saving devices to the immensely demanding incorporation of modes of thought, political concepts, dispositions of the spirit, and economic arrangements deemed to be related to, or perhaps even to determine, the ability to generate the endlessly useful and attractive cultural artifacts whose gradual and uncomplicated admission into the countries of Latin America has so visibly signaled the coming of the industrial modernity of the Gothic foxes. The latest cultural artifacts, therefore, embraced by a very considerable proportion of the population of Latin America are those associated with spiritual and economic matters. Religion and economic policy are now traveling the same road that earlier brought volleyball, color television, hot dogs, and jogging to Antofagasta, Quito, and Popayán.

It is now also clear that the changes in the economic arrangements have been rapid and widespread. Reporting on the state of the region during 1991, the Economic Commission for Latin America indicated that "most of the economies of the region are now functioning on new foundations."[26] They are indeed, and a principal feature of this approach that departs radically from five centuries of virtually uninterrupted central control is "a greater reluctance to engage in public regulation of economic activity." This pragmatic disinclination has been accompanied by a marked improvement in the confidence with which economic agents face the challenge of the marketplace. This is attributed to "the generalized acceptance of the new foundations for the functioning of the economies, both with regard to the possible benefits and the undoubted costs involved."[27]

Whether the reception and efficient utilization by the Baroque hedgehogs of the economic policies, devices, strategies, or modes of thought that proved so clearly rewarding in the ambit of the fox can be achieved with the swiftness and good results that its upholders expect is at best a matter of informed conjecture. What is evident today is that in the aftermath of the demise of socialism, economic policies other than those bearing the imprimatur of the Gothic foxes appear to be generally unpromising. This is so even though—with the exception of Chile, the country that led the exodus to the promised prosperities of the free market—the early experience of those countries that have already embraced economic liberalism has not proved an immediate and undiluted success. This leaves open the intriguing possibility that the explanation of the Chilean economic prowess, and much else, may have more to do with the country's sui generis insularity with respect to the mainland of Latin America, a feature that is immediately comparable to Britain's insularity with respect to Europe or Japan's with respect to Asia, than with the application of this or that fashionable economic prescription.

Perhaps it should also be noted that peremptory exigencies of perfection are singularly inappropriate in matters such as these, and it could well be that what are now regarded as gross economic inadequacies in the management of Peru, Brazil, or Colombia are merely the difficulties

26. United Nations, Economic Commission for Latin America, *Economic Panorama of Latin America 1991*, LC/G. 1680 (Santiago, 1991): 5.
27. ECLA, *Economic Panorama 1991*, 9.

that would normally attend a very demanding and lengthy transformation. Those who would lament the imperfect fashion in which Attalids and Ptolemaics went about the business of Hellenizing their respective realms ought to bear in mind that at the time the options other than Hellenization were mostly implausible or unattractive. With the benefit of hindsight, the least that can be affirmed with confidence about the Hellenistic enterprise is that considering the circumstances of its inception, even at its worst, it turned out to be memorable and could perhaps be fairly described as having been reasonably successful.

Although the extraordinary Latin American reception both of free market economics and evangelical Protestantism during the closing years of our century clamors for decisive explanations, these concluding reflections need not be accorded more than the status of a working hypothesis. It ought not to be forgotten that until fairly recently, it was still thought possible that with judicious adjustments and modifications, the dilapidated Baroque structure could somehow be repaired and adapted to respond to the demands posed by modern industrial society. Although the memorable witticism that human beings retain at all times a robust capacity to astonish each other has not yet been negated, it does now appear extremely unlikely that the *diadochi* and the *epigoni* of the Iberian achievement will insist in trying to reconstruct the traditional domed shelter and make it serve the needs of a modern society, or that if they are able to complete the rebuilding, their efforts will prove rewarding.

It is not easy to forget that until recently the discussion was about the manner in which this reconstruction ought best to proceed, not about whether it was desirable or even possible. Every government in the region, and every department of economics, had available a generous repertoire of prescriptive combinations of state intervention and free enterprise, each believed by its advocates to be the condition sine qua non for bringing about economic prosperity without the need to relinquish the traditional centralism of the national bureaucratic establishments. Today the consensus of opinion overwhelmingly regards the constraints of the centralist order as a chief impediment to the creative processes that are at the heart of industrial modernity.

There appears to be general agreement that the best strategy is diversity and that creativity is most likely to thrive in a climate of civilized chaos, possibly akin to Gibbon's legendary "tumultuous freedom" that attended the noblest moments of the Roman state. The task at hand, therefore, is not to discover ways of restoring a crumbling dome to its former glory but to clear the rubble as expeditiously as possible. This is, of course, oversimple. It is as difficult, if not impossible, completely to obliterate the relics and remnants of our past as it is to reproduce it. It cannot be assumed that unwelcome surprises are not in store for those who believe firmly that the application of the same correct policies will necessarily bring about the same good results obtained elsewhere, under different auspices and circumstances.[28] Ultimately, there are no options other than to make do with what is at hand, which in this case must include some stones from the old dome, many of them elaborately carved. How best to use these, and any other materials found strewn about, is impossible to predict, apart from noting that there is no reason to suppose that the countries of Latin America will be spared the travail that elsewhere has attended the full blossoming of the privileges and responsibilities that invariably attend the coming of modernity.

What ought by now to be abundantly clear, unless obfuscated by doctrinal zeal or misplaced loyalties, is that regardless of the means employed—and there is indeed a very great diversity of available means—the ends will remain for a long time immediately recognizable as those defined, not strictly but in a manner characteristically latitudinarian, by the habits, the skills, the artifacts, usages, and aspirations of the English-speaking originators of the Industrial Revolution. It should also be very clear that just as the surfeit of shrill anticelebratory rhetoric unleashed before and during 1992 failed to conceal the imprint left by the Baroque conception of things on the early centuries of the realm discovered by Columbus, it also failed signally to obscure the fact that when the former Indies of Castile crossed the threshold into the latter half of their first millennium, the new world about them was unmistakably that of the Gothic fox.

---

28. Heinz Arndt addresses both the obduracy of the traditionalists and the iconoclasm of latter-day converts with characteristic moderation and common sense when he indicates that "what above all, distinguishes [preconditions, including culture, etc.] from economic policies is that in their nature they are largely given, possibly slowly emulated, but not easily adopted by an effort of political will. . . . It is the policies that may have lessons for other developing countries, [for] policies are at least in principle open to choice. Even if the preconditions are unfavourable, it is useful to know which are better and which are the worse policies." H. W. Arndt, *Industry and Development*, no. 22 (Vienna, 1987): 18, 26.

Selected Bibliography

Abraham, George D. *The Complete Mountaineer*. London: Methuen, 1907.
"Address to Bishops of Latin America," Pope John Paul II. *L'Osservatore Romano*, weekly ed. (in English), no. 42, October 21, 1992, 7.
Alberti, Leone Battista. *Ten Books on Architecture*. Edited by J. Rykwert, English translation by James Leoni. New York: Transatlantic Arts, 1966.
Aquinas, St. Thomas. *Summa Theologiae*. Vol. 1. Edited by Thomas Gilby O.P. Cambridge: Blackfriars, 1964.
Arce de Vásquez, Margot. *Gabriela Mistral: The Poet and Her Work*. New York: New York University Press, 1964.
Ariosto, Ludovico. *Orlando furioso*. Translated and with an introduction by Barbara Anderson. Harmondsworth, England: Penguin Books, 1975.
Arndt, H. W. *Industry and Development*, no. 22. Vienna: United Nations Industrial Development Organization, 1987.
———. "The Origins of Structuralism." *World Development* 13, no. 2 (February 1985).
———. *The Rise and Fall of Economic Growth: A Study in Contemporary Thought*. Melbourne: Longman Cheshire, 1978.
Aveling, J. C. H. *The Jesuits*. London: Blond and Briggs, 1981.
Bailey, N. *Universal Etymological English Dictionary*. London: E. Bell, 1721.
Baker, William J. *Sports in the Western World*. Rev. ed. Chicago: University of Chicago Press, 1988.
Balmes, Jaime. *Protestantism and Catholicity Compared in their Effects on the Civilisation of Europe*. Translated by C. J. Hanford & R. Kershaw. London: John Murphy Co., 1849.
Bannan, John F. *The Philosophy of Merleau-Ponty*. New York: Harcourt, Brace & World, 1967.
Barros Arana, Diego. *Proceso de Pedro de Valdivia*. Santiago: Librería Central de A. Raymond, 1873.

Baudin, Louis. *A Socialist Empire: The Incas of Peru.* Princeton: Van Nostrand, 1961.

Beckett, J. V. *The Aristocracy in England 1660–1914.* Oxford: Blackwell, 1988.

Bell, Daniel. *The Cultural Contradictions of Capitalism.* New York: Basic Books, 1976.

Bellah, Robert N., Richard Madsen, William M. Sullivan, Ann Swidler, and Steven M. Tipton. *Habits of the Heart, Individualism and Commitment in American Life.* New York: Harper & Row, 1985.

Bembo, Pietro. *Prose della volgar lingua.* Venice: Giouan Tacuino, 1525.

Benavides Rodríguez, Alfredo. *La arquitectura en el Virreinato del Perú y en la Capitanía General de Chile.* Santiago: Ediciones Ercilla, 1941.

Beneyto, Juan. *Historia social de España y de Hispanoamérica: Repertorio manual para una historia de los españoles.* Madrid: Aguilar, 1973.

Berger, Peter. *The Capitalist Revolution: Fifty Propositions About Prosperity, Equality, and Liberty.* London: Gower, 1987.

Berger, Peter L., and Thomas Luckmann. *The Social Construction of Reality: A Treatise in the Sociology of Knowledge.* New York: Doubleday, 1966.

Berlin, Isaiah. *The Crooked Timber of Humanity.* New York: Knopf, 1991.

———. *The Hedgehog and the Fox.* London: Weidenfeld & Nicolson, 1953.

———. *Russian Thinkers.* London: Hogarth Press, 1978.

———. *Vico and Herder, Two Studies in the History of Ideas.* London: Hogarth, 1976.

Bernales Ballesteros, Jorge. "La pintura en Lima durante el Virreinato." In *Pintura en el Virreinato del Perú.* Lima: Banco de Crédito de Peru, 1989.

Berners, Dame Juliana. *Treatyse of Fysshinge With an Angle.* London: E. Stock, 1880.

Bigo, Pierre. "El materialismo marxista: Ensayo de discernimiento." *Mensaje,* no. 204 (November 1971): 537.

Blainey, Geoffrey. *A Game of Our Own, the Origins of Australian Football.* Melbourne: Victoria, 1990.

———. *The Tyranny of Distance: How Distance Shaped Australia's History.* Melbourne: Macmillan, 1966.

Bloch, Marc. *Feudal Society.* 2 vols. London: Routledge & Kegan Paul, 1967.

Blunt, Anthony, ed. *Baroque and Rococo: Architecture and Decoration.* New York: Harper & Row, 1978.

Boase, T. S. R. *Giorgio Vasari: The Man and the Book.* Princeton: Princeton University Press, 1979.

Botsford, G. W., and C. A. Robinson. *Hellenic History.* New York: Macmillan, 1948.

Bottineau, Yves. *Living Architecture: Iberian-American Baroque.* English translation by Yvan Butler. London: McDonald & Co., 1971.

Braham, Helen. *Rubens, Paintings, Drawings, Prints, in the Princes Gate Collection.* London: Courtauld Institute Galleries, University of London, 1988.

Braudel, Fernand. *The Mediterranean and the Mediterranean World in the Age of Philip II.* 2 vols. London: Collins, 1973.

Brooke, Rupert. *Letters from America.* New York: Scribner's Sons, 1916.

Brown, Jonathan, and J. H. Elliott. *A Palace for a King, the Buen Retiro and the Court of Philip IV.* New Haven: Yale University Press, 1980.

Brusco, Elizabeth. "The Household Basis of Evangelical Religion and the Reformation of Machismo in Colombia." Ph.D. dissertation, City University of New York, 1986.

Burckhardt, Jacob. *Der Cicerone.* Basel: Schweighauserische Verlagsbuchhandlung, 1855.

Burns, E. Bradford. *The Poverty of Progress.* Berkeley, Los Angeles, and London: University of California Press, 1980.

Butler, Philip. *Classicisme et Baroque dans l'oeuvre de Racine.* Paris: Nizet, 1959.

Butterfield, Herbert. *The Statecraft of Machiavelli.* London: G. Bell, 1955.

Cabral de Mello, Evaldo. *Imagens do Brasil Holandes 1630–1654.* Rio de Janeiro: Ministerio da Cultura, 1987.

Campbell, Colin. *The Romantic Ethic and the Spirit of Modern Consumerism.* Oxford: Blackwell, 1992.

Campofiorito, Quirino. *A Proteção do Imperador e os Pintores do Segundo Reinado, 1850–1890.* Rio de Janeiro: Edições Pinakotheke, 1983.

Cannon, John. *Aristocratic Century: The Peerage of Eighteenth-Century England.* Cambridge: Cambridge University Press, 1984.

Carlyle, Thomas. *Sartor Resartus: Heroes and Hero Worship, Past and Present.* London: Ward, Lock & Co. Ltd., Minerva Library, 1888.

Carr, Raymond. *Spain 1808–1939.* Oxford: Clarendon, 1966.

Cartwright, W. C. *The Jesuits: Their Constitution and Teaching.* London: J. Murray, 1876.

Castedo, Leopoldo. *A History of Latin American Art and Architecture.* New York: Praeger, 1969.

Castellanos, Juan de. *Elegias de varones ilustres de Indias.* Madrid: Imp. de los Sucesores de Hermano, 1914.

Centesimus Annus. Encyclical letter, Pope John Paul II. Vatican City: Libreria Editrice Vaticana, 1991.

Céspedes del Castillo, Guillermo. *América Hispana, 1492–1898.* Barcelona: Editorial Labor, 1983.

Clark, Gregory. "Have a Happy and Humble *Kurisumasu.*" *The Australian,* December 20, 1989, 11.

Clissold, Stephen. *Latin America: A Cultural Outline.* London: Hutchinson University Library, 1965.

Comellas, José Luis. *Historia de España moderna y contemporánea.* Madrid: Ediciones Rialp, 1983.

Copplestone, F. C. *Aquinas.* Harmondsworth, England: Penguin Books, 1975.

Corrigan, Philip, and Derek Sayer. *The Great Arch: English State Formation as Cultural Revolution.* London: Blackwell, 1985.

Cortés Conde, Roberto. *The First Stages of Modernization in Spanish America.* New York: Harper & Row, 1974.

Coubertin, Pierre de. *Une campagne de 21 ans.* Paris: Libraire de L'Education Physique, 1908.

———. "Les Jeux Olympiques de Much Wenlock." *Sports Athletiques* (December 25, 1890).

———. "Olympia." In *The Olympic Idea: Discourses and Essays*, ed. Carl-Diem-Institut and the Deutschen Sportshochschule, 113–114. Koln, Rev. Liselot Diem and O. Anderson, trans. J. G. Dixon. Stuttgart: Hoffman, 1967.

———. "A Typical Englishman: Dr. W. P. Brookes of Wenlock." *American Monthly Review of Reviews* 15 (1897): 63.

Cruz de Amenábar, Isabel. *Arte y sociedad en Chile, 1550–1650*. Santiago: Universidad Católica de Chile, 1986.

D'Ailly, Pierre. *Imago mundi*. With annotations by Christopher Columbus. Boston: Massachusetts Historical Society, 1927.

Daubechies, S. J. Hubert. "Fidel Castro habla a Los 80." *Mensaje*, no. 206 (January–February, 1972): 60.

Dealy, Glen Caudill. *The Public Man, an Interpretation of Latin American and Other Catholic Countries*. Amherst: University of Massachusetts Press, 1977.

Díaz-Plaja, Fernando. *Otra historia de España*. Madrid: Espasa Calpe, 1987.

Dilthey, Wilhelm. *Gesammelte Schriften. VII. Der Aufbau der geschichtlichen Welt in den Geisteswissenschaften*. 2d ed. Edited by B. Groethoysen. Stuttgart: Teubner, 1958.

Domínguez Ortíz, Antonio. *El antiguo régimen: Los Reyes Católicos y los Austrias*. Madrid: Alianza Editorial Alfaguara, 1983.

Dorfman, Ariel, and Armand Mattelart. *Para leer al Pato Donald*. Valparaíso: Ediciones Universitarias de Valparaíso, 1973.

Dos Santos, Theotonio. *Dependencia y cambio social*. Santiago: Centro de Estudios Socio-Económicos, Universidad de Chile, 1970.

Durkheim, Emile. *The Division of Labour in Society*. New York: Free Press, 1964.

Eco, Umberto. *The Aesthetics of Thomas Aquinas*. Translated by Hugh Bredin. Cambridge: Harvard University Press, 1988.

Economic Panorama of Latin America, 1989. Santiago: United Nations Economic Commission for Latin America and the Caribbean, September 1989.

Economic Panorama of Latin America, 1991. Santiago: United Nations Economic Commission for Latin America, 1991.

El desarrollo integrado de Centroamérica en la presente década. Buenos Aires: Instituto para la Integración de América Latina (INTAL), Interamerican Development Bank, 1973.

Elias, Norbert. "The Genesis of Sport as a Sociological Problem." In *The Sociology of Sport*, ed. Eric Dunning. London: Cass, 1971.

Eliot, T. S. *Notes Towards the Definition of Culture*. London: Faber and Faber, 1948.

Elliott, J. H. "Concerto Barocco." *The New York Review of Books* XXXIV, no. 6 (April 9, 1987).

———. *Imperial Spain 1469–1716*. New York: New American Library, 1966.

Ellis, J. R. *Philip II and Macedonian Imperialism*. London: Thames and Hudson, 1976.

Encina, Francisco A. *Nuestra inferioridad económica*. Santiago: Editorial Universitaria, 1972.

English: A World Commodity. London: The Economist Intelligence Unit, 1988.

Eyquem, Marie-Thérese. *Pierre de Coubertin, L'Epopée Olympique.* Paris: Calmann-Lévy, 1966.

Fixx, J. F. *The Complete Book of Running.* New York: Random House, 1977.

Flink, James J. *The Automobile Age.* Cambridge: MIT Press, 1988.

Fontaine Talavera, Arturo, and Harald Beyer. "Retrato del movimiento evangélico a la luz de las encuestas de opinión pública." *Estudios Públicos,* no. 44 (Primavera 1991): 91, 123–124.

Fontana, Vincenzo, and Paolo Morachiello, eds. *Vitruvio e Rafaello: Il "De Architectura" di Vitruvio nella traduzione inedita di Fabio Calvo Ravennate.* Roma: Officina, 1975.

Ford, Henry. *My Life and Work.* In collaboration with Samuel Crowther. Garden City, N.Y.: Doubleday, Page & Company, 1922.

Frank, A. G. *Capitalism and Underdevelopment in Latin America.* New York: Monthly Review Press, 1967.

Frankl, Paul. *The Gothic: Literary Sources and Interpretations Through Eight Centuries.* Princeton: Princeton University Press, 1960.

Friedlander, Paul. *Plato.* Princeton: Princeton University Press, 1969.

Froude, James Anthony. *Lectures on the Council of Trent, delivered at Oxford 1892–93.* New York: Scribner's Sons, 1896.

Fuentes, Carlos. Prologue to José Enrique Rodó, *Ariel.* Edited by Margaret Sayers Pedén. Austin: University of Texas Press, 1988.

Furtado, Celso. *The Economic Growth of Brazil.* Berkeley and Los Angeles: University of California Press, 1963.

García Icazbalceta, Joaquín. *Don Fray Juan de Zumárraga.* México: Andrade y Morales, 1881.

García Morente, Manuel. *Ideas para una filosofía de la historia de España.* Madrid: Ediciones Rialp, 1957.

Gellner, Ernest. *Nations and Nationalism.* Oxford: Blackwell, 1983.

Germann, George. *Gothic Revival in Europe and Britain: Sources, Influences and Ideas.* London: Lund Humphries [for] the Architectural Association, 1972.

Giménez Fernández, Manuel. "Las bulas alejandrinas de 1493 referentes a las Indias." *AEA* I (1944): 243.

Golding, John. "The Expansive Imagination." *The Times Literary Supplement,* March 27, 1987, 311.

Gott, Richard. "Crumbs and the Capitalists." *The Guardian,* January 20, 1989, 21.

Grant, Robert. *Oakeshott.* London: Claridge Press, 1990.

Green, Peter. *Armada from Athens.* Garden City, N.Y.: Doubleday, 1970.

———. *Alexander to Actium: The Historical Evolution of the Hellenistic Age.* Berkeley, Los Angeles, and Oxford: University of California Press, 1990.

Grodecky, Louis. *Gothic Architecture.* New York: H. N. Abrams, 1976.

Grondona, Mariano. *Bajo el imperio de las ideas morales.* Buenos Aires: Editorial Sudamerica, 1987.

Grote, George. *A History of Greece; From the Earliest Period to the Close of the Generation Contemporary with Alexander the Great.* New York: AMS Press, 1971.

Gutman, Allen. *From Ritual to Record: The Nature of Modern Sports.* New York: Columbia University Press, 1978.

Guzmán, Jaime. "El miedo: Síntoma de la realidad político-social chilena." *Estudios Públicos,* no. 42 (Otoño 1991): 272.

Haya de la Torre, Victor Raúl. *Aprismo: The Ideas and Doctrines of Victor Raúl Haya de la Torre.* Edited and translated by R. J. Alexander. Kent, Ohio: Kent State University Press, 1973.

Harvey, John. *The Perpendicular Style, 1330–1484.* London: Batsford, 1978.

Hess, Alan. *Googie, Fifties Coffee Shop Architecture.* San Francisco: Chronicle Books, 1985.

Hester, Marcus B. *The Meaning of Poetic Metaphor, an Analysis in the Light of Wittgenstein's Claim that Meaning is Use.* The Hague and Paris: Mouton, 1967.

Hibbert, Christopher. *The Grand Tour.* London: Thames Methuen, 1987.

Hill, Mildred, and Patty Smith Hill. *Song Stories for the Kindergarten.* Chicago: C. F. Summy, 1893.

Hirschman, A. O. *Journeys Towards Progress: Studies of Economic Policy-Making in Latin America.* New York: Greenwood Press, 1968.

Hollier, Denis. *Against Architecture: The Writings of Georges Bataille.* Cambridge: MIT Press, 1989.

Homer. *Odyssey.* Translated by S. H. Butcher and A. Lang. New York: Macmillan, 1974.

Honour, Hugh. *Romanticism.* London: Pelican, 1981.

Hughes, Thomas. *Tom Brown's Schooldays.* New York: Oxford University Press, 1989.

Hyman, Anthony. *Charles Babbage, Pioneer of the Computer.* Princeton: Princeton University Press, 1982.

Iglesias, Enrique V. "Perspectivas del desarrollo de América Latina," *Estudios Internacionales* 14 (Julio–Septiembre 1981): 312.

Il Maccabees. Translated by Jonathan A. Goldstein. Garden City, N.Y.: Doubleday, 1983.

Janelle, Pierre. *The Catholic Reformation.* Milwaukee: Bruce Publishing Company, 1963.

Johnson, Paul. *A History of Christianity.* London: Weidenfeld & Nicolson, 1976.

Johnson, Samuel. *Dictionary of the English Language.* London: W. Strahan, 1755.

Jones, J. R. *The Revolution of 1688 in England.* London: Weidenfeld & Nicolson, 1988.

Jordan, Robert Welsh. "Vico and the Phenomenology of the Moral Sphere." In *Vico and Contemporary Thought,* ed. Giorgio Tagliacozzo et al. Atlantic Highland, N.J.: Humanities Press, 1976. Papers presented at the conference on Vico and Contemporary Thought at the New School for Social Research, New York City, 1976.

Jouguet, Pierre. *Macedonian Imperialism and the Hellenization of the East.* London: Kegan Paul, Trench, Trubner & Co., 1928.

Junquera, Paulina, and María Teresa Ruiz Alcón. *Real Sitio de Aranjuéz*. Madrid: Editorial Patrimonio, 1985.

Kamen, Henry. *The Iron Century, Social Change in Europe, 1550–1660*. London: Weidenfeld & Nicolson, 1971.

Karst, K. L., and K. S. Rosen. *Law and Development in Latin America*. Berkeley, Los Angeles, and London: University of California Press, 1975.

Kelemen, Pal. *Baroque and Rococo in Latin America*. New York: Dover Publications, 1967.

Kemp, Wolfgang. *The Desire of Mine Eyes: The Life and Work of John Ruskin*. Translated by Jan van Heurck. London: Harper Collins, 1991.

Kennedy, Paul. *The Rise and Fall of the Great Powers*. New York: Vintage Books, 1989.

Keynes, J. M. *Essays in Persuasion*. London: Macmillan, 1933.

Kidd, B. J. *The Counter-Reformation, 1550–1600*. London: S.P.C.K., 1963.

Klaiber, S. J., Jeffrey L. *Religion and Revolution in Peru, 1824–1976*. South Bend: University of Notre Dame Press, 1977.

Lane Fox, Robin. "Hellenistic Culture and Literature." In *Greece and the Hellenistic World*, ed. John Boardman, Jasper Griffin, Oswyn Murray. The Oxford History of the Classical World. Oxford: Oxford University Press, 1988.

Lever, Janet. "Soccer in Brazil." In *Sport and Society*, ed. J. T. Talamini and C. H. Page, 141–142. Boston: Little, Brown, 1973.

Levillier, Roberto. *América la bien llamada*. Buenos Aires: G. Kraft, 1948.

Lewy, Guenter. *Constitutionalism and Statecraft during the Golden Age of Spain: A Study of the Political Philosophy of Juan de Mariana, S.J.* Geneva: E. Droz, 1960.

López Ibor, Juan José. *El español y su complejo de inferioridad*. Madrid: Ediciones Rialp, 1958.

Lübcke, Wilhelm. *Geschichte der Architektur von den Altesten bis auf die Gegenwart*. Leipzig: Seeman, 1865.

McAdam, E. L., and George Milne, eds. *Johnson's Dictionary*. London: Gollancz, 1982.

MacAloon, John. *This Great Symbol: Pierre de Coubertin and the Origins of the Modern Olympic Games*. Chicago: University of Chicago Press, 1981.

Macaulay, Thomas Babington. *Critical and Historical Essays Contributed to the Edinburgh Review*. London: Longman's, Green & Co., 1874.

Macaulay, Thomas Babington. "Von Ranke." Review essay on Leopold Von Ranke's *The Ecclesiastical and Political History of the Popes of Rome, During the Sixteenth and Seventeenth Centuries*, in *Critical and Historical Essays Contributed to the Edinburgh Review*. London: Longman's, Green, & Co., 1874.

McCrum, Robert, William Cran, and Robert MacNeil. *The Story of English*. London: Faber, 1986.

McGrade, Arthur Stephen. *The Political Thought of William of Ockham, Personal and Institutional Principles*. Cambridge: Cambridge University Press, 1974.

Macfarlane, Alan. *The Origins of English Individualism: The Family, Property and Social Transition*. Oxford: Blackwell, 1978.

Machiavelli, Niccolò. *Il Principe*, in *Opere*, vol. VI. Genova, 1798.

McKendrick, Neil. "Home Demand and Economic Growth: A New View of the Role of Women and Children in the Industrial Revolution." In *Historical Perspectives: Studies in English Thought and Society in Honour of J. H. Plumb*, ed. Neil McKendrick. London: Europa, 1974.

McKendrick, Neil, John Brewer, and J. H. Plumb. *The Birth of a Consumer Society: The Commercialization of Eighteenth-Century England.* London: Europa, 1982.

MacRae, Donald G. *Weber.* London: Fontana Collins, 1974.

Madariaga, Salvador de. *The Rise of the Spanish American Empire.* London: Hollis & Carter, 1947.

Mafra de Souza, Alcídio. *A Era do Barroco.* Rio de Janeiro: Museu Nacional de Belas Artes, 1982.

Magnani, Alberto. *Amerigo Vespucci.* Roma: Fratelli Treves, 1926.

Makkreel, Rudolf A. *Dilthey: Philosopher of the Human Studies.* Princeton: Princeton University Press, 1975.

Male, Emile. *L'Art religieux du XIIIe siècle en France.* Paris: A. Colin, 1919.

———. *The Gothic Image: Religious Art in France in the Thirteenth Century.* Translated by Dora Hussey. New York: Harper & Row, 1958.

Mander, John. *Static Society: The Paradox of Latin America.* London: Gollancz, 1969.

Manuel, Frank E., and Fritzie P. Manuel. *Utopian Thought in the Western World.* Cambridge: Belknap Press of Harvard University Press, 1979.

Maravall, José Antonio. *La cultura del barroco: Análisis de una estructura histórica.* Barcelona: Ariel, 1983.

———. *Estado moderno y mentalidad social.* Madrid: Revista de Occidente, 1972.

Marías, Julián. *España inteligible: Razón histórica de las Españas.* Madrid: Alianza Universidad, 1985.

Mariátegui, José Carlos. *Siete ensayos de interpretación de la realidad peruana.* Santiago: Editorial Universitaria, 1955.

Martin, David. *Tongues of Fire: The Explosion of Protestantism in Latin America.* Oxford: Blackwell, 1990.

Marx, Karl. *A Contribution to the Critique of Political Economy.* Translated by N. I. Stone, from the 2d German ed. New York: International Library Publishing Co., 1904.

Matthew, Christopher. *A Different World: Stories of Great Hotels.* New York: Paddington Press, 1976.

Merriman, R. B. *The Rise of the Spanish Empire in the Old World and the New.* 4 vols. New York: Macmillan, 1918.

Millikan, Max F., and W. W. Rostow. *A Proposal—Key to a More Effective Foreign Policy.* New York: Harper, 1957.

Moncada, Sancho de. *Restauración Política de España.* Madrid: Sánchez, 1619.

Moreno, Fernando. "Consumo y 'Sociedad de consumo,'" *Estudios Públicos,* no. 47 (Invierno 1992).

Morse, Richard M. "The Heritage of Latin America," in *The Founding of New Societies*, ed. Louis Hartz. New York: Harcourt, Brace & World, 1964.

Nash, Nathaniel C. "On The Rebound in Argentina." *The New York Times,* December 6, 1992, sec. 3, 15.

Nebrija, Antonio de. *Gramática Castellana.* Edited by Pascual Galindo Romeo and Luis Ortíz Munoz. Madrid, 1946.

Norton, Henry Kittredge. *The Coming of South America: El Resurgimiento de Sud América.* New York: John Day Company, 1932.

Oakeshott, Michael. *On History, and Other Essays.* London: Blackwell, 1983.

Ockham, William of. *Ockham: Studies and Selections,* by Stephen Clark Tornay. La Salle, Ill.: Open Court Publishing Company, 1938.

Oliveira, Fernão de. *Gramática da linguagem portuguesa.* Lisboa: Biblioteca Nacional, 1981. Facsimile of 1536 edition published in Lisbon by G. Galharde.

Orrego Vicuña, Eugenio. *Don Andrés Bello.* Santiago: Leblanc, 1940.

Panati, Charles. *Extraordinary Origins of Everyday Things.* New York: Perennial Library, 1987.

Panofsky, Erwin. *Gothic Architecture and Scholasticism.* New York: Meridian Books, 1957.

Pareles, Jon. "Samba Takes a Back Seat to Spectacle." *The New York Times,* January 27, 1991, H27.

Parry, J. H. *The Discovery of South America.* New York: Taplinger Publishing Co., 1979.

———. *The Spanish Seaborne Empire.* London: Hutchinson & Co., 1966.

Parsons, Talcott, et al. *Theories of Society: Foundations of Modern Sociological Theory.* New York: Free Press of Glencoe, 1965.

Pattison, Robert. *The Triumph of Vulgarity: Rock Music in the Mirror of Romanticism.* New York: Oxford University Press, 1987.

Paz, Octavio. *The Labyrinth of Solitude, and The Other Mexico, Return to the Labyrinth of Solitude, Mexico and the United States, The Philosophic Ogre.* Translated by Lysander Kemp, Yara Milos, and Rachel Phillips Belash. New York: Grove Press, 1985.

Pell, George. "Rerum Novarum: One Hundred Years Later." *The Boston Conversazioni.* Boston: Boston University, University Professors, 1992.

Pérez de Oliva, Fernán. *Historia de la Invención de las Indias,* ed. José Juan Arrom. Bogotá: Instituto Caro y Cuervo, 1965.

Pérez Embid, Florentino. *Los descubrimientos en el Atlántico y la rivalidad castellano-portuguesa hasta el Tratado de Tordesillas.* Sevilla: Publicaciones de la Escuela de Estudios Hispanoamericanos de Sevilla, 1948.

Pérez, Joseph. "España y la modernidad." In Bartolomé Bennassar y otros, *Orígenes del atraso económico español.* Barcelona: Ariel, 1985.

Peters, F. E. *The Harvest of Hellenism.* New York: Simon and Schuster, 1970.

Pevsner, Nikolaus. *An Outline of European Architecture.* London: John Murray, 1951.

———. *The Englishness of English Art.* London: Architectural Press, 1956.

Pike, Fredrick B. *Spanish-America, 1900–1970, Tradition and Social Innovation.* London: Thames and Hudson, 1973.

Plato. *The Republic.* Translated by Benjamin Jowett. New York: Quality Paperback Club, 1992.

Pollard, Alfred F. "The 'New Monarchy' Thesis: Towards Absolutism." In *The "New Monarchies" and Representative Assemblies*, ed. A. J. Slavin. Boston: Heath, 1964.

Pollard, Sydney. "Reflections on Entrepreneurship and Culture in European Societies." *Transactions of the Royal Historical Society*, 5th ser., vol. 40. London: Printed for the Society, 1990, 159–160.

Pollitt, J. J. *Art and Experience in Classical Greece*. Cambridge: Cambridge University Press, 1972.

Prebisch, Raúl. *The Economic Development of Latin America*. New York: United Nations Publications, 1950.

Prescott, William H. *History of the Conquest of Peru*. London: George Routledge, 1847.

———. *History of the Reign of Ferdinand and Isabella the Catholic*. London: Bickers & Son, 1885.

Pugin, A. Welby. *Contrasts; or, A Parallel Between the Noble Edifices of the Middle Ages and Corresponding Buildings of the Present Day: Shewing the Present Decay of Taste*. New York: Humanities Press, Victorian Library Edition, 1969.

Ranke, Leopold von. *The Ecclesiastical and Political History of the Popes of Rome, During the Sixteenth and Seventeenth Centuries*. Translated from the German by Sarah Austin. 3 vols. London: J. Murray, 1840.

———. *The Theory and Practice of History*, ed. Georg G. Iggers and Konrad von Moltke. New York: Irvinton Publishers, 1973.

Regla, Juan. "La época de los tres primeros Austrias." Vol. III of *Historia de España y América, social y económica*. Edited by J. Vicens-Vives. Madrid: Vicens-Vives, 1982.

"*Rerum novarum*: ochenta años después." *Mensaje*, no. 199 (June 1971): 201.

Ribeiro, Darcy. *The Americas and Civilization*. New York: Dutton, 1971.

Riegl, Alois. *Die Entstehung der Barockkunst in Rom*. Vienna: A. Schroll & Co., 1908.

Riesman, David, and Reuel Denney. "Football in America: A Study in Culture Diffusion." In *The Sociology of Sport*, ed. Eric Dunning. London: Cass, 1971.

Ritz, Marie Louise. *Cesar Ritz, Host to the World*. London: G. G. Harrap, 1938.

Rodó, José Enrique. "Ariel." In *Obras Selectas*. Buenos Aires: El Ateneo, 1964.

———. *Ariel*. Edited and with introduction and notes by Gordon Brotherston. Cambridge: Cambridge University Press, 1967.

Robbins, Lionel. *The Theory of Economic Policy in English Classical Political Economy*. London: Macmillan, 1953.

Rostovtzeff, M. *Greece*. New York: Oxford University Press, 1970.

Rostow, W. W. *The Process of Economic Growth*. Oxford: Clarendon Press, 1953.

———. "The Stages of Economic Growth." *Economic History Review*, 2d ser., XII, no. 1 (1959): 1–16.

Rostow, W. W., ed. *The Economics of Take-Off into Sustained Growth*. Proceedings of a Conference held by the International Economic Association, London: Macmillan, 1963.

Rostworowski de Diez Canseco, María. *Historia del Tanhuantinsuyo*. Lima: Instituto de Estudios Peruanos, 1988.

Ruskin, John. *The Stones of Venice*. London: Smith, Elder & Co., 1874.

Saavedra Fajardo, D. *Idea de un príncipe político y cristiano, representada en cien empresas*. Madrid: Aguilar, 1946.

Sánchez, Luis Alberto. *Haya de la Torre y el APRA*. Lima: Editorial Universo, 1980.

Sánchez Agesta, Luis. *El concepto del estado en el pensamiento español del siglo XVI*. Madrid: Instituto de Estudios Políticos, 1959.

San Cristóbal, Antonio. *Arquitectura virreynal religiosa de Lima*. Lima: Librería Studium, 1988.

Sanger, David E. "Japanese Giants Ask, Gilbert Who?" *The New York Times*, February 1, 1992, 35–36.

Schlesinger Jr., Arthur M. *A Thousand Days: John F. Kennedy in the White House*. London: Mayflower-Dell, 1967.

Schumpeter, Joseph A. *Capitalism, Socialism, and Democracy*. New York: Harper, 1950.

Scott, James Brown. *The Spanish Origin of International Law*. 1. *Francisco de Vitoria and His Law of Nations*. Oxford: Clarendon Press, 1934.

Scruton, Roger. "Reflections of the Revolutions in Eastern Europe." *The Boston Conversazioni*. Boston: Boston University, The University Professors, 1991.

Sebastian, Santiago. *Contrarreforma y barroco; Lecturas iconográficas e iconológicas*. Madrid: Alianza, 1985.

Segel, Harold B. *The Baroque Poem, a Comparative Survey*. New York: Dutton, 1974.

Shiels, S. J., W. Eugene. *King and Church: The Rise and Fall of the Patronato Real*. Chicago: Loyola University Press, 1961.

Simper, Errol. "Songs of Yesterday Top the Airwaves." *Weekend Australian*, December 22, 1990, 7.

Sitwell, Sacheverell. *Southern Baroque Art*. London: Duckworth, 1924.

———. *Spanish Baroque Art*. London: Duckworth, 1931.

Spargo, Demelza, ed. *This Land Is Our Land; Aspects of Agriculture in English Art*. Royal Agricultural Society of England. London: Mall Galleries, 1989.

Spitz, Lewis W. *The Protestant Reformation, 1517–1559*. New York: Harper & Row, 1985.

Stanton, Phoebe B. *The Gothic Revival and American Church Architecture, 1840–1856*. Baltimore: Johns Hopkins University Press, 1968.

Stein, Stanley J., and Barbara Stein. *The Colonial Heritage of Latin America*. New York: Oxford University Press, 1970.

Stich, Sidra. *Made in USA, an Americanization in Modern Art, the 50s and 60s*. Berkeley, Los Angeles, and London: University of California Press, 1987.

Stiven, Agnes Bain. *Englands Einfluss auf den deutschen Wortschatz*. Marburg: B. Sporn, 1936.

Stothert, James. *French and Spanish Painters*. London: Bickers, 1877.

Strachey, Lytton. *Eminent Victorians.* London: Chatto and Windus, 1948.

Sunkel, Osvaldo. "La inflación chilena: Un enfoque heterodojo." *El Trimestre Económico* 25, no. 4, (1958). English translation in *International Economic Papers*, no. 10, London, 1960.

Sunkel, Osvaldo, and Pedro Paz. *El subdesarrollo latinoamericano y la teoría del desarrollo.* Mexico: Siglo Veintiuno Editores, 1970.

Swaan, W. *The Gothic Cathedral.* London: Ferndale Editions, 1981.

Tacitus, Cornelius. *Tacitus on Britain and Germany.* A translation of the Agricola and the Germania by H. Mattingly. Harmondsworth, England: Penguin Books, 1964.

Talbot, William Henry Fox. *The Pencil of Nature.* London: Longman, Brown, Green & Longmans, 1844.

Tapié, V. L., and F. Chueca, *Baroque et Classicisme.* Paris: Plon, 1957.

Tasso, Torquato. *Gerusalemne liberata.* Torino: Società Editrice Internazionale, 1933.

Tatsuno, Sheridan M. *Created in Japan: From Imitators to World-Class Innovators.* New York: Harper & Row, 1990.

Tawney, R. H. *Religion and the Rise of Capitalism: A Historical Study.* London: Penguin Books, 1975.

Terry, Quinlan. "Classical Architecture and the Christian Faith." Unpublished paper read at the Department of Philosophy, King's College, London, February 22, 1990.

Thomas, Hugh (Lord Thomas of Swynnerton). *The Spanish Civil War.* London: Hamish Hamilton, 1977.

Thucydides. *History of the Peloponnesian War.* Translated by Rex Warner. New York: Penguin, 1986.

Tocqueville, Alexis de. *Democracy in America.* Translated by G. Lawrence and edited by J. P. Mayer. New York: Harper & Row, 1988.

Torres Restrepo, Camilo. "Programmation Economique et Exigences Apostoliques." Paper given at the Second International Congress of Pro Mundi Vita, Louvain, September 1964, and published by this organization in 1965. An English version entitled "Revolution: Christian Imperative" was published in *Revolutionary Priest: The Complete Writings of Camilo Torres,* ed. John Gerassi, 298. Harmondsworth, England: Penguin, 1973.

Toynbee, Arnold. *Hellenism: The History of a Civilization.* London: Oxford University Press, 1959.

———. *A Study of History.* 12 vols. London: Oxford University Press, 1954.

Trevelyan, G. M. *English Social History.* London: Longmans, Green & Co., 1947.

Trevor-Roper, Hugh (Lord Dacre of Glanton). *From Counter-Reformation to Glorious Revolution.* London: Secker & Warburg, 1992.

———. *Princes and Artists; Patronage and Ideology at Four Hapsburg Courts, 1517–1633.* New York: Harper & Row, 1976.

———. *Renaissance Essays.* London: Fontana Press, 1986.

Troeltsch, Ernst. *The Social Teachings of the Christian Churches.* 2 vols. New York: Harper, 1960.

Uribe Rueda, Alvaro. "Sor Juana Inés de la Cruz o la culminación del siglo barroco en las Indias." *Thesaurus*. Boletín del Instituto Caro y Cuervo, Bogotá, Tomo XLIV, Enero–Abril de 1989, 112–148.

Urquídi, Victor. *The Challenge of Development in Latin America*. London: Pall Mall, 1964.

Vargas Llosa, Mario. "América Latina y la Opción Liberal." In *El desafío neoliberal; El fin del tercermundismo en América Latina*, ed. Barry Levine. Bogotá: Editorial Norma, 1992.

Vasconcelos, José. *A Mexican Ulysses, An Autobiography*. Translated and abridged by W. Rex Crawford. Bloomington: Indiana University Press, 1963.

Vassberg, David E. *Land and Society in Golden Age Castile*. Cambridge: Cambridge University Press, 1984.

Véliz, Claudio. *The Centralist Tradition of Latin America*. Princeton: Princeton University Press, 1980.

Véliz, Claudio, ed. *Obstacles to Change in Latin America*. Royal Institute of International Affairs. London: Oxford University Press, 1965.

Véliz, Zahira, ed. and trans. *Artists' Techniques in Golden Age Spain*. Cambridge: Cambridge University Press, 1986.

Vicens-Vives, Jaime. *Approaches to the History of Spain*. Translated and edited by Joan Connelly Ullman. Berkeley and Los Angeles: University of California Press, 1970.

Vico, Giambattista. *The New Science of Giambattista Vico*. Translated by T. G. Bergin and M. H. Fisch. Ithaca: Cornell University Press, 1970.

Vicuña, Félix. "Situación económica." *Revista Económica* I, no. 1 (November 1886): 9–20.

Vitoria, Francisco de. *Relecciones del estado, de los indios, y del derecho de la guerra*. Edited and with an introduction by Antonio Gómez Robledo. México: Editorial Porrua, 1974.

Voltaire, François Marie Arouet. *Letters on England*. Translated by L. Tancock. Harmondsworth, England: Penguin, 1980.

Walbank, F. W. *The Hellenistic World*. London: Fontana Paperbacks, 1981.

Walton, Izaak. *The Compleat Angler*. London: T. Maxey for R. Marriot, 1653.

Weber, Max. *The Protestant Ethic and the Spirit of Capitalism*. Translated by Talcott Parsons. New York: Charles Scribner's Sons, 1958.

Weisbach, Werner. *Der Barock als Kunst der Gegenreformation*. Berlin: P. Cassirer, 1921.

———. *Spanish Baroque Art*. Cambridge: Cambridge University Press, 1941.

Wiarda, Howard J. *Corporatism and National Development in Latin America*. Boulder, Col.: Westview Press, 1981.

Wölfflin, Heinrich. "Das Erklaren von Kunstwerken." In *Bibliothek der Kunstgeschichte*, ed. Han Tietze. Leipzig: Band Eins, 1921.

———. *Renaissance and Baroque*. Translated by Kathrin Simon. Ithaca: Cornell University Press, 1984.

Young, George. *Tourism, Blessing or Blight?* Harmondsworth, England: Penguin, 1973.

Zeldin, Theodore. *France 1848–1945*. II. *Intellect, Taste, Anxiety*. Oxford: Clarendon Press, 1977.

Index

Rocroi, Battle of, 41, 220
Rodó, José Enrique (1872–1917), 4, 6–10, 69, 199
Rodríguez de Fonseca, Juan, 30
Rolling Stones, 126, 156
Roman Law. *See* Civil Law
Romanticism, 13, 96–97, 102, 118, 197, 200–202, 215
Rosenstein-Rodan, Paul N. (1902–1985), 192
Rostovtzeff, M., 123
Rostow, W. W., 192–193
Rostworowski de Diez Canseco, María, 208n
Rubens, Peter Paul (1577–1640), 63–65
Rugby School, 134, 140–141, 143
Ruskin, John (1819–1900), 13, 97, 195–196; nature of Gothic, 99–107, 217–218

Sack of Rome, 56n, 88, 97
St. Quentin, Battle of, 41, 88
Salamanca, University of, 48–49n; *clerecía*, 80; *Plaza mayor*, 83n, 85
Salvation Army, 147
Sánchez Agesta, Luis, 26n
San Cristóbal, Antonio, 73n
San Martín, José de (1778–1850), 191
Santa Claus, 169n
Sarmiento, Domingo Faustino (1811–1888), 7; orthographic reform, 36n
Saussure, Ferdinand de (1857–1913), 128
Schick, Jacob, 168
Schikaneder, Emanuel Johann (1751–1812), 191
Schlesinger, Jr., Arthur M., 192n, 194
Scholasticism, 13, 51–52, 92–95
Schumpeter, Joseph A. (1883–1950), 204–207
Scott, James Brown, 48n
Scruton, Roger, 202n
Sebastian, Santiago, 66n
Sendero luminoso, 184, 215
Septuagint, 122, 122n
Seymour, James (1702–1752), 108n
Shakespeare, William (1564–1616), 12–13, 126, 148n, 156
Sharawaggi. *See* Walpole, Horace
Shaw, George Bernard (1856–1950), 36n
Shiels, W. Eugene, S. J., 39n
Shining Path guerrillas. *See Sendero luminoso*
Siqueiros, David Alfaro (1898–1974), 6
Sitwell, Sir Sacheverell (1897–1988), 66n, 79
Skyscrapers, 163–166
Soccer. *See* Sports

Society, 16–17; as an organism, 50–51
Society for the Prevention of Cruelty to Animals, 148
Society of Jesus, 46, 130; and the Counter-Reformation, 56–65; and education, 57, 75; and final breach with Protestantism, 61; Peter Paul Rubens and church of the Jesuit college at Antwerp, 63; and the culture of the Baroque, 67–68, 70; and art, 77; and central bureaucracy, 78; relations between Christians and Marxists, 223–226
Socrates (470–399 B.C.), 119
Sol, Jorge, 194
Sotheby's, 148
Southey, Robert (1774–1843), 130n
"Spanglish," 125n
Spanish-American cultural modes, 13, 130–131; attachment to traditional community, 14–15; monarchical disposition, 110; and single-party systems in Mexico and Cuba, 111
Spanish-American War, 5n, 220
Spitz, Lewis W., 48n
Sports: basketball, 20; rugby, 115; in Japan, 132, 155; and sartorial usage, 132n; and the Industrial Revolution, 131–133; football, including soccer, 132–134, 149, 219; tennis, 134; croquet, 134–135; baseball, badminton, field hockey, swimming, 135; track and field, 135–136; mountaineering and alpine skiing, 137; angling, 137n; boxing, horse-racing, fox-hunting, golf, 137–139; the concept of sport, 139; basketball and volleyball, preferred in China, 152, 155; jogging, 169n. *See also* Baseball; Football; Gymnastics; Tennis
Stein, Stanley J., and Barbara, 25n
Stich, Sidra, 174n
Stubbs, George (1724–1806), 108n
Suárez, Francisco (1548–1617), 2n, 48
Sunkel, Osvaldo, 180n, 203n
Swaan, W., 92n

Tacitus, Cornelius (55–120), 161n, 190n
Tagliacozzo, Giorgio, 20n
Tahuantinsuyo, 81, 207
Talavera, Hernando de, Bishop of Avila, 22n, 37
Talbot, William Henry Fox (1800–1877), 154
Tasso, Torquato (1544–1595), 68n, 81n
Tawney, Richard H. (1880–1962), 2, 50, 52
Television, 115, 145–146, 161, 219

Designer: U.C. Press Staff
Compositor: Wilsted & Taylor
Text: 10/13 Sabon
Display: Sabon
Printer: BookCrafters
Binder: BookCrafters